MUST KNOW

HIGH SCHOOL ESL

Danielle Pelletier DePinna

Mc
Graw
Hill

New York   Chicago   San Francisco   Athens   London   Madrid
Mexico City   Milan   New Delhi   Singapore   Sydney   Toronto

1 2 3 4 5 6 7 8 9   LCR   27 26 25 24 23 22

ISBN   978-1-264-25865-9
MHID   1-264-25865-8

e-ISBN   978-1-264-25866-6
e-MHID   1-264-25866-6

Interior design by Steve Straus of Think Book Works.
Cover and letter art by Kate Rutter.

McGraw Hill books are available at special quantity discounts to use as premiums and sales promotions or for use in corporate training programs. To contact a representative, please visit the Contact Us pages at www.mhprofessional.com.

McGraw Hill is committed to making our products accessible to all learners. To learn more about the available support and accommodations we offer, please contact us at accessibility@mheducation.com. We also participate in the Access Text Network (www.accesstext.org), and ATN members may submit requests through ATN.

Contents

4 Nouns and Pronouns   125

5   Talking About Ongoing Activities   173

6 Talking About Past Activities   **211**

9 Connecting the Past and the Present   327

10 Compound, Complex, and Compound-Complex Sentences   389

11 Writing Paragraphs and Essays 457

Introduction

Welcome to your new English as a Second Language book! Let us explain why we believe you've made the right choice. You may have found that a lot of books make a lot of promises about all the things you'll be able to accomplish by the time you reach the end of a given chapter. In the process, those books can make you feel as though you missed out on the building blocks that you actually need to master those goals.

With *Must Know High School ESL,* we've taken a different approach. When you start a new chapter, you will immediately see the **must know** ideas. These are the essential concepts behind what you are going to study, and they will form the foundation of what you will learn throughout the chapter. These **must know** ideas will be your guide as you make your way through each chapter.

To build on this foundation you will find easy-to-follow discussions of the topic at hand, accompanied by comprehensive examples and lots of useful charts that will increase your ability to communicate in English. And because we know ESL is special kind of learning, we've even deviated from our normal Must Know books in this case. We give you thoughtful Success Strategies, exercises and more practice throughout the chapters (with answers in the Answer Key), and occasional Pop Quizzes to make sure you understand the material as you move through the book. That repetition and learning support will come in handy as you get to the more challenging chapters. Each chapter ends with review questions—more than 800 combined throughout the book—designed to instill confidence as you practice your new skills. Whether you are a beginner or more advanced, we've got you covered. With this book, you not only get what you **must know**, you get all you need to know!

This book has other features that will help you on your ESL journey. It has a number of sidebars that will provide helpful information or just serve as a quick break from your studies. The **BTW** sidebars ("by the way") point out important information as well as tell you what to be careful about English-wise. Other times, an **IRL** sidebar ("in real life") will tell you what the material you're studying has to do with the real world; other IRLs may just be interesting factoids.

In addition, this book is accompanied by a flashcard app that will give you the ability to test yourself at any time. The app includes 100-plus "flashcards" with a review question on one "side" and the answer on the other. You can either work through the flashcards by themselves or use them alongside the book. To find out where to get the app and how to use it, go to the next section, "The Flashcard App."

Before you get started, however, let us introduce you to your guide throughout this book. In addition to over 20 years' experience as an ESL educator, Danielle Pelletier DePinna has written *Easy English Step-by-Step for ESL Learners*. Having had the opportunity to work together before, we know that Danielle is unmatched in her enthusiasm for and knowledge of English language training and culture education. She understands what you should get out of an ESL course and has developed strategies to help you get there. Danielle has also seen the kinds of trouble that students run into, and she can show you how to overcome these difficulties. In this book, she applies her teaching experience to show you the most effective way to learn a given concept. We are confident that we are leaving you in good hands (Danielle knows her stuff!) as you develop new English skills.

Good luck with your studies!

The Editors at McGraw Hill

The Flashcard App—with Audio!

This book features a bonus flashcard app to help you test yourself on what you have learned as you work through the book. The app includes 100-plus "flashcards," both "front" and "back," featuring exercises covering topics in the book. The book gives you two options on how to use it. You can jump right into the app and start from any point that you want. Or you can take advantage of the handy QR Codes near the end of each chapter in the book; they will take you directly to the flashcards related to what you're studying in that part of the book.

To access the flashcard feature, follow these simple steps:

Search for the *McGraw Hill Must Know* App from
either Google Play or the App Store.

↓

Download the app to your smartphone or tablet.

↓

Once you've got the app,
you can use it in either of two ways.

↙ ↘

Just open the app and you're ready to go.	Use your phone's QR code reader to scan any of the book's QR codes.
You can start at the beginning, or select any of the chapters listed.	You'll be taken directly to the flashcards that match your chapter of choice.

↘ ↙

Be ready to test your English knowledge!

ESL Audio

The app also includes a ton (to use the technical term) of ESL audio. It has been designed to help with both your pronunciation and listening skills. On the app, you'll find extensive English dialogues and helpful mini lectures, along with the text so you can read along.

Look for the audio icon, 🔊, at the end of each applicable chapter. Use the QR code, also at the end of the chapter, to get to that chapter's app content. Or you can look at the app's easy-to-follow Contents and choose the section that interests you the most. Listen closely, and we're confident your English skills will improve fast!

Author's Note

Welcome to *Must Know High School ESL*! I'm so glad you have this book. If you're a high school student, this is the perfect book for you. It gives you the language you need to speak English confidently, and it has cultural notes so you can understand Americans better. If you're an instructor, this book will guide your students toward skillful use of English. You can go through the book sequentially or jump around to customize your lessons. Each chapter contains a variety of expressions we use in daily life in the United States as well as grammar lessons, cultural guidelines, useful vocabulary, and success strategies for effective listening, speaking, pronunciation, reading, and writing. You've made a great choice with this book. Enjoy learning this wild and crazy English language!

For English Language Learners: Tips to Help You Learn English Quickly

Learning and using a language to communicate is a very creative process. Although you learn many English grammar rules in this book, I recommend you "play" with the language. Take what you learn and try it out in the real world as if the world is your laboratory and you are a scientist experimenting with the language. See what works and what doesn't. Take what works and expand on it. Tweak what doesn't work to improve your communication skills. This will help improve your confidence.

Ways to Improve Your Listening Skills

■ Watch shows or movies in English with English subtitles (also known as closed captions, or cc) for 15 to 60 minutes every day. You can watch shows on TV, the internet, or social media. Find a favorite show and watch the whole series!

■ Listen to podcasts, talk shows, news shows, and advertisements for 15 minutes every day in your car, at home, or anywhere.

■ Listen to an audio book and read the book at the same time. This is one of my favorite strategies because you can follow along in the book while listening to someone speak the words you're reading. This not only improves your listening skills, but it also improves your vocabulary, spelling, pronunciation, and reading skills. If you have to read a book for a class, do this!

■ Listen to local people chatting at school, in line at cafés, at the bus stop, and anywhere there are people. It's okay if you do not understand much at the beginning. The more you listen, the more you will learn and the faster your English will improve.

Ways to Improve Your Speaking and Pronunciation

■ Create reasons to speak English: ask questions in class, at the market, at a restaurant—everywhere you go.

■ Make a goal to ask two questions every day. As you build your confidence, ask more questions.

■ Practice speaking English aloud in the shower, while driving, and when you are alone at home, at work, or at school.

■ Challenge yourself by calling a store or company to ask for the price of a product or service. This is a good way to measure your listening and speaking skills. As you increase your fluency, this task will become easier. Use the "elephant-in-the-room" strategy to help you. Learn more about this *Success Strategy* in Chapters 1 and 3.

■ Practice the pronunciation tips in the book silently anytime in public: while walking down the street, riding on the bus, or waiting in line. Even singing in your mind is an effective strategy for practicing pronunciation.

Ways to Improve Your Reading and Vocabulary

- Read something every day. Choose a topic you enjoy such as sports, food, or fashion and read for 10 to 20 minutes at a time.
- Read aloud every street sign you see.
- Read menus at restaurants to learn food vocabulary.
- Read one children's book every day. If you have children, read with them!
- Keep a notebook or make flash cards of new vocabulary. Review these words and expressions every day. Use each new vocabulary term five times to learn it well.

If you'd like to see how a vocabulary word, verb tense, phrase, or expression is used in everyday English, check out a linguistic corpus. It will show you how your search term is used in regular American dialogue. An example of one of these free search databases is Corpus of Contemporary American English (COCA), and there are multiple others.

Ways to Improve Your Writing and Grammar

- Practice writing the alphabet (both capital and lowercase letters) in your notebook.
- Write five sentences in your notebook every day. Use a period at the end of each sentence.
- Write five questions in your notebook every day. Use a question mark at the end of every question.
- In your written sentences, use the grammar and verb tenses you are learning in this book.
- Check the subject-verb agreement in every sentence.

For Instructors

This book works systematically through verb tenses, sentence structures, and cultural conventions so your students can optimize their use of English in the classroom and in life. A large percentage of the vocabulary from the Academic Word List (AWL) is used throughout the book, which can help your students acquire understanding of common academic vocabulary.

Expansion Activities

Speaking expansion activity suggestions:
When introducing a new topic, ask students to share with each other (pair share or small groups) what they already know about the topic. This activates their schema. Some students may know more than others, and they can learn from each other. It also gives the students an opportunity to use English in an informal way with peers.

Verb tense expansion activity suggestions:
- Get the students involved by having them find images of people in action (from magazines, advertisements, photos on their phone gallery, or the internet). Then they can formulate, write, and speak one or more sentences to describe the image.
- Alternatively, invite students to write yes/no and WH questions on the board. Then elicit descriptive answers from the class about an image. For example, for the present progressive verb tense, a student might write the question "What is the girl doing?" and answer with "She is playing tennis."
- For the simple present, images of routines, habits, traditions, customs, and bus schedules can be used.
- Use a **linguistic corpus** to show students how a vocabulary word, verb tense, phrase, or expression is used in American conversation or written material. An example of one of these free search databases is COCA (Corpus of Contemporary American English), and there are multiple others.

Writing expansion activity suggestions:

- Have students create dialogues based on the specific skill and/or topic they're learning. See the example dialogues in the chapter for guidance.
- Students can create conversations based on their personal experience. If it's more comfortable for them, students can create characters for their dialogue. For instance, students can create avatars and write a short biography about their avatar using vocabulary, verb tenses, expressions, and any other language item from the chapter. As a teacher, you could prepare avatars beforehand on index cards with images of the avatar and let the students choose their own. Images can be of real people or they can be animated characters.
- Students can engage in discussions through pair, small group, or even large group conversations. Scenarios can be given to students or they can come up with their own. Students can also script their conversation before performing them, or they can converse spontaneously.
- Students could write a classic academic paragraph on a topic and employ the vocabulary, phrases, verb tenses, expressions, and other grammar and language lessons learned in the chapter.

Reading expansion activity suggestions:

Employ the three strategies for reading effectively:

1. **Pre-read:** The purpose of pre-reading activities is to prepare the mind for the reading. Activating schema helps students understand the reading passage more easily. There are myriad ways to do this, some of which are to:
   - Predict what the reading will be about based on the passage title and images.
   - Read subtitles and the first and last sentence (or paragraph) of the passage and predict what it's about.
   - Skim and scan the reading for repeated words, phrases, and ideas.
   - Ask and answer questions about the images, title, charts, and so on.
   - Let the students discuss what they already know about the topic.

2. **Actively read:** When we actively read, we stay more focused and engage with the material, which helps students better understand the subject matter. Here are some ways to read actively:
   - Highlight key words.
   - Underline important ideas.
   - Circle new vocabulary.
   - Write definitions, questions, and notes in the margins.

3. **Understand the reading:** There are a variety of ways students can check their understanding of a passage. Have your students:
   - Summarize the reading—in speaking and/or by writing a paragraph.
   - Write and ask yes/no and WH questions about the content of the passage and discuss the answers.
   - Give their opinions and discuss by agreeing or disagreeing politely.
   - Act out the passage. They can get creative by playing charades or writing the skit and acting out the dialogue.
   - Read about a current event and check comprehension with yes/no questions. They can discuss it in small groups, forming and asking opinion questions.
   - Use newspaper articles to formulate, ask and answer WH questions in pairs, triads, or small groups.

1 Meeting People

I n this first chapter, you will learn common expressions for greeting and meeting people and using *small talk* to get to know someone in the United States. You will also learn body language and facial expressions typically used by Americans. By the end of this chapter, you will understand how to meet people, and you will have the language you need to speak confidently even if you are just starting out.

Greetings

We always greet people we know, and we sometimes greet people we don't know. To greet someone is to say "hello." There are different ways to greet others. Neutral greetings can be used in any situation, so learn those first. Use informal greetings with people in your peer group (they are your age or in your grade). Very informal greetings are usually used with good friends and others you know really well. Formal greetings can be used with teachers, parents, and others who are older than you to show respect and to be polite. Common greetings we use are shown in the following table.

Neutral	Informal	Very Informal	Formal
• Hello	• Hi	• Yo!	• Good morning
• Hello there	• Hi there	• What's up?	• Good afternoon
• How are you?*	• Hey		• Good evening
• How are you doing?*	• Hey there		
	• Howdy		
	• What's happening?		
	• Long time no see!		

*****Note:** Americans often use questions as greetings, and they don't always expect an answer..

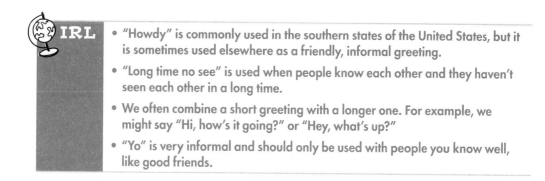

IRL

- "Howdy" is commonly used in the southern states of the United States, but it is sometimes used elsewhere as a friendly, informal greeting.
- "Long time no see" is used when people know each other and they haven't seen each other in a long time.
- We often combine a short greeting with a longer one. For example, we might say "Hi, how's it going?" or "Hey, what's up?"
- "Yo" is very informal and should only be used with people you know well, like good friends.

To understand when to use "good morning," "good afternoon," and "good evening," use these time tips:

- Morning: before 12:00 p.m. (noon)

- Afternoon: 12:01 p.m. to approximately 5:00 p.m. or 6:00 p.m.

- Evening: Approximately 5:00 p.m. or 6:00 p.m. to 12:00 a.m. (midnight)

- "Good night" is *not* a greeting. It means "good-bye" or "I'm going to sleep."

Responding to Greetings

How do you respond to someone that greets you? A **rule of thumb, or a generally accepted rule,** is to respond with the same or similar greeting if you're not sure what to do. For example, if someone greets you by saying, "Hello," you can respond with "Hello." In most situations, it depends on your relationship with that person. If you know the person and he or she is from your peer group, then you can respond informally. If you know the person really well, you can respond very informally. With your friends, you can mix the informal and very informal expressions. For someone you don't know or someone you want to show respect to, use neutral or formal responses. See a variety of common responses and examples in the following table.

Neutral Questions	Responses	Examples
	Note: The adjectives in the responses below are in order of best (you are happy) to worst (you are not happy).	
	It's common and polite to say "thank you" and then ask the question back.	
How are you?	I'm . . .	I'm great! You?
	excellent! / great! / very good! / really good! / good. / pretty good. / fine. / okay.	Pretty good.
		Good, thanks. And you?
	Note: Sometimes, we use *fine* when things are *not* fine. Listen for the tone of voice to give you a hint whether *fine* means good or not.	
How are you doing?	I'm doing . . .	I'm doing okay.
	well. / good. / fine. / okay.	Fine. And you?
How are things?	Things are . . .	Things are pretty good.
	pretty good. / fine. / okay. / all right. / not bad.	All right. How are you things with you?
	Note: The expression *not bad* can mean "good!"	
How's it going?	It's going . . .	It's going well.
	very well! / well.	Very well! What about you?
		Good, thanks.
		Note: To answer this question, you should use an adverb; however, most people incorrectly use an adjective.
		It's common to hear these responses, too:
		Excellent! / Great! / Very good! / Really good! / Good. / Pretty Good. / Fine. / Okay.

Informal Questions	Responses	Examples
What's happening? What's been happening? What's new? What's going on? What's been going on?	Not much. / Nothing. / Nothing much.	Not much. What about you? Nothing. You?

Very Informal Questions	Responses	Examples
What's up? **Note:** This question is often pronounced /Wassup / or even reduced to the single syllable /sup / like this: 'Sup?	Nothing. / Nothing much. / Not much. **Note:** *Nothing* is usually pronounced without the final /g/ sound like this: /nuthin/.	Nothing much. You? Not much.

Formal Questions	Responses	Examples
How are you today / this morning / this afternoon / this evening?	I'm doing well. / very well.	I'm doing very well, thank you. Well, thank you.

Additional Responses:

Add these two responses to be polite and continue the conversation:

1. Thank you. / Thanks!
2. What about you? / And you? / You?

Eye Contact and Facial Expressions

Now that you know different ways to greet people, let's learn about eye contact and the best facial expression to use, too. The two most important things to learn are these:

1. Make eye contact.

2. Smile.

Making Eye Contact

When you see or meet someone, look that person directly in the eyes. Eye-to-eye contact is called *making eye contact*. This is very important because it builds trust. See the DOs and DON'Ts below for making eye contact.

Tips for Making Eye Contact

DOs	DON'Ts
• Look this person directly in the eyes • Hold a steady gaze	• Do not look away • Do not look at someone's forehead • Do not look down

Smiling

When you meet someone for the first time or you see someone you already know, smile! It's an easy facial expression to make and it helps to build relationships. Smile often. =) There are times, however, when smiling isn't appropriate. These include:

- When you hear bad news
- When you have to tell someone bad news
- When you apologize

Introducing Yourself

Now that you know how to greet people and what body language and facial expression to use, it's time to learn how to introduce yourself. There are many ways to do this. Let's talk about the most common ways to introduce yourself, specifically expressions and body language. The rule of thumb is to smile whenever you meet someone.

IRL In the United States, it's customary to introduce yourself to people you do not know when you are in a shared situation, such as sitting next to someone in class or being on the same sports team. It's not common to introduce yourself to strangers in public.

Expressions to Use When Introducing Yourself

What are the things we say when we introduce ourselves? In the following table, see the expressions we often use.

Common	Less Common
I'm _____ (say name).	My name is _____ (say name).
(Say name.) **Note:** If it's an informal situation, your first name is all you need to say. If it's a more formal situation, say your first and last name.	

Usually, if you introduce yourself first, the other person will voluntarily reciprocate with their name. It's generally not necessary to ask someone what their name is.

Tips on Names

In the United States, there are many people from all over the world. Everyone's name is unique and important to them, so be sure you hear and understand another person's name clearly. If you don't understand the name they said, ask for clarification. You can do this politely by smiling and:

- Repeating back the name you heard with a rising intonation to check if you heard it correctly

- Asking for repetition if you're uncertain with rising intonation, using expressions like these:

  - Could you repeat your name, please?
  - I'm sorry, what was your name?
  - Did you say (repeat what you heard) . . . ?

A good practice is to repeat back the name you heard so you remember it. People like to hear their names, so it's perfectly acceptable to do this.

Saying Your Name Clearly

Here are some tips for saying your name clearly. These are tips for saying your first and last names:

- Say your first and last names **slowly**. Slow down a lot! Say it slower than you're used to.

- **Pause for a moment** between your first (given) and last (sur or family) name, so people can hear each name clearly.

- Use **rising pitch** on your first name and **falling pitch** on your last name.

- **Pronounce each syllable** of your name. Don't skip syllables or say them too quickly.

- **Smile** and **give a helpful tip** for pronouncing your name correctly.

 **IRL** One of my friends knows her name is not common, so when I met her she gave me a tip to help me remember her name and I've never forgotten it. She said, "Hi! I'm Jana. Like *banana*." She *broke the ice**, we both laughed, and I've pronounced her name correctly since that moment. You can do this, too. If you have a unique name, you can create a quick way for people to remember it with a rhyme or other tip to make it easy to remember.

***Note:** To "break the ice" means to break the silence by speaking to make people feel more comfortable in a new situation.

Body Language to Use When Introducing Yourself

The most common body language to use is the handshake. We use it for people of any age and any sex. Anyone can initiate a handshake. It is neutral and it can be used in most situations. Informal alternatives to the handshake are a fist bump, a high five, the elbow bump, and the "air hug" if you are practicing physical distancing. See the BTW sidebar for some tips on how to give "air" versions of these.

How to Shake Hands

- Shake with your **right hand**.

- Extend your arm out so that you are **one arm's length away** from the other person.

- Your elbow should be close to your body.

- Put the palm of your hand firmly in the other person's hand and **shake once or twice.**

- Shake **firmly**. Do not shake too quickly.

- Hold his/her hand firmly—**not too strongly and not too lightly**.

- **Then, let go** of the person's hand.

- **Look the person in the eye and smile** when shaking hands.

In a time when many people are physically distancing themselves from others, "air" fist bumps, high fives, and elbow bumps are appropriate and acceptable. The "air" part means that you never make physical contact with another person. Rather, you show the gesture of a fist bump, for example, without actually bumping your fists together.

Note: In general, it is **impolite to *not* shake hands** if someone extends a hand for a handshake. However, if you don't want to shake hands, you can smile and nod with your hands behind your back, or you can offer an "air" handshake, a fist bump, an elbow bump, or a high five. You may also offer a short explanation such as "I'm not feeling well today."

How to Fist-Bump or Elbow-Bump

To fist-bump someone, you extend your right arm out at full arm's length with the knuckles of your fist pointing forward. The other person will do the same and your fists will "bump." For an elbow bump, extend your right elbow forward instead of your fist. If you have a cold or you're physically distancing, you can also offer an "air" fist bump or elbow bump. In this case, offer a smile and a fist or elbow at a distance.

Saying Goodbye

When we leave or when others leave, we say goodbye. In the following table are some common expressions we use.

Neutral	Informal	Very Informal	Formal
Bye.	Bye-bye.	Later.	Goodbye.
See you later / soon.	See you. / See you around / See ya. / See ya 'round.	Later, _____ (expression of friendship) Example: Later, dude.	Take care.
	Talk to you later.		See you (day / time).

If you are saying goodbye to someone you just met, you can also add these expressions:

Neutral	Informal	Very Informal	Formal
Good / Great to meet you. Good / Great meeting you.			It was nice / great / good / a pleasure meeting / to meet you. / Pleasure meeting you. / A / My pleasure.

Small Talk

Small talk is the brief conversation we have when we first meet someone. It's usually light in tone, and it's focused on simple, relevant, nonpersonal, and noncontroversial topics such as the weather, shared situations, and physical surroundings. It can start as a statement or a question directed at someone near you. Small talk is helpful when you want to acknowledge another person's presence or to break the ice.

Topics for Small Talk

The expressions we use for small talk usually depend on the situation, but there are some common topics that we use. See some of these types of situations and examples of small talk on the following page.

Examples of Places/Situations in the Same Physical or Virtual Location	Common Topics	Examples of Small Talk
	• Your physical / virtual surroundings • Topic relevant to why you are in this place • Technology or devices • Weather	
In a face-to-face class	Topic: Homework	Student 1: Did you finish the homework? Student 2: Yeah, but it was hard.
At lunch (in the cafeteria or at a café)	Topic: Food	Student 1: This pizza is hot! Student 2: Yeah, and good.
Outside school gymnasium	Topic: Sports game after school	Student 1: Are you going to the game? Student 2: Nah, I have homework.

We say "no" in many different ways. Here are some **informal ways we say "no"**: *nope*, *no way*, *nah*, *nuh-uh*, *negative*, and *yeah, right* (which is sarcastic). Here are some ways that high schoolers say **"no" to invitations**: *I'll let you know*; *probably not*, *maybe*, and *possibly*.

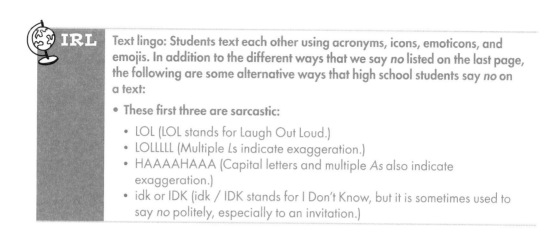

IRL Text lingo: Students text each other using acronyms, icons, emoticons, and emojis. In addition to the different ways that we say *no* listed on the last page, the following are some alternative ways that high school students say *no* on a text:

- These first three are sarcastic:
  - LOL (LOL stands for Laugh Out Loud.)
  - LOLLLLL (Multiple *L*s indicate exaggeration.)
  - HAAAAHAAA (Capital letters and multiple *A*s also indicate exaggeration.)
  - idk or IDK (idk / IDK stands for I Don't Know, but it is sometimes used to say *no* politely, especially to an invitation.)

Success Strategy: Naming the Elephant

One strategy you can use to create successful communication is to "**name the elephant in the room.**" This is an expression that means you are stating something obvious that no one wants to talk about. To take control of your communication and build your confidence, **tell people you are learning and practicing English.** When you do this, you are taking responsibility for your communication and you are helping to create effective communication. Ultimately, you are showing people you care about understanding them and being understood by them. This is a great way to achieve successful communication. Here are some ways you can do that. Use one that is appropriate for your situation. Smile when you say these sentences!

- I'm practicing my English, so if I'm not clear, please let me know.

- I'm working on my English pronunciation. Am I saying that correctly?

- I'm working on my English. Is that the right word?

- English is my second/third/fourth language. Did I say that right?

You can use any combination of these sentences. By using this name-the-elephant-in-the-room success strategy, you can become an effective communicator, and it makes a great impression!

Simple Present Tense: Asking and Answering Questions

Being able to ask clear questions is a skill that every English learner needs. There are two main types of questions: the ***yes/no question***, which requires a yes or no answer, and the ***information question***, which usually begins with a WH-word or phrase, such as *when* or *where*, and asks for specific information about a topic, such as location, time, and manner. Note that when we meet people, we often use the **simple present verb tense** in questions. You will learn more about this verb tense in Chapter 2. Let's take a closer look at these two types of questions and how to form them.

Forming Yes/No Questions

Yes/no questions with the verb BE are formed differently than yes/no questions with all other verbs. See how to form them and read examples of each on the following page.

Yes/No Questions in the Simple Present Verb Tense

	With the BE Verb	With All Other Verbs
Example sentences:	**1.** Are you a student here?	**2.** Do you go here?*
Forming yes/no questions—use this formula:	BE verb + subject + rest of question + ?	Auxiliary verb DO / DOES + subject + base form of the main verb + rest of question + ?
Example sentence illustrated: **BE and main verb bolded and underlined;** [DO auxiliary bracketed;] (Subject circled)	<u>**Are**</u> (you) a student here? Notice that the BE verb—in this case *are*—goes before the subject, *you*. Inverting the subject and verb is required to form a yes/no question with the *BE* verb.	[Do] (you) **go** here? * Notice that the DO auxiliary verb goes before the subject, *you*. Then the main verb comes after the subject. To form a yes/no question with every other verb, you must use the DO auxiliary at the beginning, then use statement word order so that the subject comes before the main verb.

*Note: Do you go here? is an expression we use to ask, Do you attend this school?

PRONUNCIATION

▶ **Note:** When we ask yes/no questions, we usually say it with rising pitch. This means that our voice uses a higher pitch at the end of the question. When people hear a rising pitch, they know that you are looking for an answer and they will respond. See the Appendix for more about end-of-sentence pitches.

Notice that yes/no questions with the BE verb are simple to form: you invert the order of the subject and BE verb to form a question. However, with all other verbs, yes/no questions require the DO auxiliary verb and the statement word order for the subject and main verb. See examples of both kinds of questions.

Yes/No Questions in the Simple Present Verb Tense

	With the BE Verb	With All Other Verbs
Examples **Note that the verb in each question is underlined.** **Notice the subject-verb agreement of BE or Do with the subject of the sentence.**	• <u>Are</u> you a student here? • <u>Is</u> she your teacher? • <u>Are</u> they your friends? • <u>Is</u> it a fun class? • <u>Are</u> we late? • <u>Are</u> the tests hard?	• <u>Do</u> you <u>go</u> here? • <u>Does</u> she <u>give</u> a lot of homework? • <u>Do</u> they <u>complete</u> the homework every day? • <u>Does</u> the lecture <u>help</u> you? • <u>Do</u> we <u>sit</u> in the front of the class? • <u>Do</u> they <u>require</u> essay answers?

Notice that the BE verb and the DO auxiliary verb must agree with the subject in the sentence. This is called **subject-verb agreement**. This is often indicated with the acronym SVA. For sentences that use the DO auxiliary, the **main verb is always in its base form**, which means there are no verb endings. The only subjects that use *does* are *she*, *he*, and *it*. *She*, *he*, and *it* do *not* agree with *do*. The following table shows how this works.

	DO Auxiliary Verb	Subject	Main Verb
Singular subject	Do	I	study every night?
	Do	you	study every night?
	Does	she	study every night?
	Does	he	study every night?
	Does	it	matter?
Plural subject	Do	we	study every night?
	Do	you	study every night?
	Do	they	study every night?

Now that you know how to form yes/no questions in the simple present verb tense, let's consider typical short answer replies to these questions.

Forming Contractions

In natural speech, we use contractions. A contraction is two or more words combined to make one word. We use apostrophes to indicate where letters are omitted. For example, to make a contraction with *do + not*, we omit the *o* in *not* and replace it with an apostrophe like this: *don't*. Similarly, to contract *does + not*, we omit the *o* in *not* and replace it with an apostrophe like this: *doesn't*. **To make contractions with the BE verb**, there are a couple of different options. With the subject pronouns *he, she, it, you, we,* and *they*, we can contract them in two ways:

1. Combine the subject pronoun with the BE verb in affirmative and negative forms (they are = they're / they are not = they're not).

2. Combine the BE verb with the negative *not* (they are not = they aren't).

There is only one way to contract *I am not*, and that is to make a contraction with the subject pronoun *I* and the BE verb *am* whether it's affirmative or negative (I am = I'm / I am not = I'm not). See examples of contractions with the BE verb.

Using Contractions with the BE Verb

Subject Pronoun	BE Verb	Negative	Contraction
I	am	-	I'm
I	am	not	I'm not
You	are	-	You're
You	are	not	You're not / You aren't
She	is	-	She's
She	is	not	She's not / She isn't

(continued)

Subject Pronoun	BE Verb	Negative	Contraction
He	is	-	He's
He	is	not	He's not / He isn't
It	is	-	It's
It	is	not	It's not / It isn't
We	are	-	We're
We	are	not	We're not / We aren't
They	are	-	They're
They	are	not	They're not / They aren't

Answering Yes/No Questions

In conversations with teachers, parents, and other adults, we may answer yes/no questions with complete answers or short answers. With classmates and friends, short answers are more common.

Yes/No Question with the <u>BE Verb</u>	Complete Yes Answer Short Answer	Complete No Answer Short Answer
Are you in class right now?	Yes, I **am** in class right now. Yes, I **am**.	No, I**'m not** in class right now. No, I**'m not**.
Is she on the soccer team?	Yes, she **is** on the soccer team. Yes, she **is**.	No, she **isn't** on the soccer team. / No, she**'s not** on the soccer team. No, she **isn't**. / No, she**'s not**.
Are they tired?	Yes, they **are** tired. Yes, they **are**.	No, they **aren't** tired. / No they**'re not** tired. No, they **aren't**. / No, they**'re not**.

Yes/No Question with <u>DO Auxiliary</u>	Complete Yes Answer Short Answer	Complete No Answer Short Answer
Do you study every night?	Yes, I **do** study every night. Yes, I **do**.	No, I **don't** study every night. No, I **don't**.
Does it work?	Yes, it **does** work. Yes, it **does**.	No, it **doesn't** work. No, it **doesn't**.
Do they enjoy their classes?	Yes, they **do** enjoy their classes. Yes, they **do**.	No, they **don't** enjoy their classes. No, they **don't**.

When answering yes/no questions with the BE verb or the DO auxiliary in complete sentences, we usually do not contract the BE verb or the DO auxiliary **in affirmative answers**. This is because we **stress the BE verb and the DO auxiliary in affirmative answers when speaking**. When the answer is negative, **we stress the negative** whether it's contracted or not (*not* or *n't*).

Short Answers for Yes/No Questions

We often answer yes/no questions with *short* **yes or no answers**. See these example questions and short answers.

Yes/No Question with the <u>BE Verb</u>	Yes Short Answer (Not Contracted)	No Short Answer
Are you in the gym?	Yes, I am.*	No, I'm not.
Is he serious?	Yes, he is.	No, he isn't. / No, he's not.
Are they there?	Yes, they are.	No, they aren't. / No, they're not.

Note: *I am* is not contracted in an affirmative short answer. We don't answer *Yes, I'm* because it's incorrect. We must say *Yes, I am.*

Yes/No Question with <u>DO Auxiliary</u>	Yes Short Answer (Not Contracted)	No Short Answer
Do you study every night?	Yes, I do.	No, I don't.
Does he eat hamburgers for lunch every day?	Yes, he does.	No, he doesn't.
Do they like sports?	Yes, they do.	No, they don't.

Quick Answers for Yes/No Questions

To answer someone we know very well, such as a friend or classmate, quick answers are appropriate. These answers are as simple as saying *yes*, *no*, or *I don't know*. Young adults, however, often give these answers in a variety of ways. Review some common ways to say *yes*, *no*, or *I don't know* in very informal situations.

Ways to Say *Yes*	Ways to Say *No*	Ways to Say *I Don't Know*
Yes	No	I don't know.
Yeah / Yah	Naw / Nah	I dunno.
Yep	Nope	Dunno.
No yeah	Uh-unh	No clue. (Short for *I have no clue.*)
Yeah no for sure	Yeah no	No idea. (Short for *I have no idea.*)
Sure	Yeah, right (said sarcastically) = No	Beats me.
Yeah no yeah = I'm willing to do it.	No yeah no = There's no way I'm doing it.	Who knows. (This is not a question.)

Let's review yes/no questions and answers in short conversations on the next page. The answers are <u>underlined</u>.

Seamus and Joe don't know each other. It's the first day of school and they are sitting next to each other in math class.

Joe: Hi. I'm Joe.

Seamus: Seamus. Does the teacher give a lot of homework?

Joe: <u>I dunno</u>, but my friend said the tests are hard.

Seamus: <u>Yeah</u>.

Madison and Sari don't know each other. They are in line at a fundraiser in the park near the school.

Sari: Hi! Do you go here?

Madison: <u>Yeah</u>.

Sari: Me, too. I heard the teachers are hard.

Madison: <u>Yeah no for sure</u>.

Mike and Ethan are friends.

Mike: Hey, Ethan. What's up?

Ethan: Nothing much. You?

Mike: Gotta study for the math test. You ready?

Ethan: <u>No yeah</u>. I studied.

Audrey and Arianna are friends at school.

Audrey: Are you ready for lunch?

Arianna: <u>Yeah no</u>.

Audrey: Whaaa?

Arianna: I have homework.

Audrey: Okay. See you later.

 IRL Per the conversations:

gotta = I have got to

Whaaa? = What? Expressing surprise

Forming Information Questions

Information questions (also known as WH questions) are formed using WH question words, such as *what*, *where*, *when*, *why*, and *how*. We ask these questions when we want specific information about someone or something. Information questions with the BE verb are formed differently than information questions with other verbs. See how to form information questions and read examples of each on the following page.

Information Questions with the Simple Present Verb Tense

	With the BE Verb	With All Other Verbs
Example sentences	<u>Where</u> is your class?	<u>Where</u> do you go to school?
Forming information questions—use this formula	WH question word + BE verb + subject + rest of question + ?	WH question word + auxiliary verb DO + subject + base form of the main verb + rest of question + ?
Example sentence illustrated *WH question word in italics* **BE verb and main verb bolded and underlined;** [DO auxiliary bracketed] (Subject circled)	*Where* **is** (your class?) Notice that the WH question word starts the sentence. *Your class* is the subject. You can see this more clearly in the statement form: My class is on the second floor. (My class) **is** on the second floor.	*Where* [do] (you) **go** to school? Notice that the WH question word starts the sentence. The DO auxiliary verb goes before the subject, *you*. Then the main verb (*go*) comes after the subject. To form an information question with every other verb in the simple present verb tense, you must use the DO auxiliary, then use statement word order so that the subject comes before the main verb.

See more examples of information questions in the simple present verb tense using BE and other verbs in the following table.

Information Questions in the Simple Present Verb Tense

	With the BE Verb	With All Other Verbs
Examples: Note that the *WH question word* or phrase is in italics and the <u>verb</u> in each question is underlined.	• *How* <u>are</u> you? • *What's* up? • *When* <u>is</u> the test? • *Who* <u>is</u> your teacher? • *How long* <u>is</u> football practice? • *Why* <u>is</u> the class fun? • *How old* <u>are</u> you? • *Which* class <u>is</u> better?	• *Where* <u>do</u> you <u>live</u>? • *How much* homework <u>do</u> we <u>have</u>? • *What* sport <u>do</u> you <u>play</u>? • *When* <u>does</u> the quiz <u>begin</u>? • *How* <u>does</u> she <u>calculate</u> this problem? • *Which* one <u>do</u> you <u>like</u> better? • *How far* <u>does</u> he <u>run</u> in track? • *Why* <u>do</u> they <u>do</u> it?

WH Question Words

See common WH question words, the information we seek when we use them, and examples in this table.

WH Question Word	Information You Seek	Example
Where	Place / Position	Where is the gymnasium? Where do I buy the textbook?
When / What time	Time	When is the homework due? What time is it? When does class start?
Who	Person	Who is he? Who do you know here?
What	Thing / Object / Idea	What is that? What do you mean?
Why	Reason / Explanation	Why is he late? Why do we multiply this number?
How	Way / Manner / Form	How are they? How do I start the car?
Which one	Choice	Which one is better? Which one does she like?
How much	Amount (Used with noncount nouns)	How much is that? How much juice do you want?
How many	Quantity (Used with count / countable nouns)	How many are in the class? How many does she have?
How far	Distance	How far is the bookstore? How far does he drive to school?
How often	Frequency	How often are they absent? How often does the bus run?

Dialogues: Greeting and Meeting People

Now that you know how we greet and meet people, see how it all comes together in these sample dialogues. Can you identify all the expressions you have learned?

Dialogue 1: Griffin just moved to a new town. He is a tenth-grade student in high school. This is his first day of class, and he is walking into his history class. Ms. Sato is his history teacher.

> **Ms. Sato (smiling):** Good morning. What's your name?
>
> **Griffin (smiling):** Hello. My name is Griffin Schumacher.
>
> **Ms. Sato:** I'm Ms. Sato. How are you today, Griffin?
>
> **Griffin:** I'm good, thank you. Did you say Ms. Sato?
>
> **Ms. Sato:** Yes, that's right. Are you ready for history class?
>
> **Griffin:** Yes, I am.
>
> **Ms. Sato (smiling):** Good! Let me know if you have any questions about class or the homework.
>
> **Griffin (smiling):** Okay, thank you.

Dialogue 2: Henry and Khalid are sophomores in high school. They don't know each other. They are eating lunch at the same table in the cafeteria.

> **Henry:** Hey. I'm Henry.
>
> **Khalid:** Hi, Henry. Khalid.
>
> **Henry:** Are you new here?
>
> **Khalid:** Yeah, I just moved here last month.
>
> **Henry:** Do you like it here?
>
> **Khalid:** Yeah no for sure.
>
> **Henry:** Nice. The food here isn't bad, but I usually go to the café and get a sandwich.

Khalid: Is it better?

Henry: No yeah. Way better.

Khalid: Okay.

Henry: Nice to meet you, Khalid. I gotta finish my homework for math.

Khalid: You, too. See ya 'round.

Henry: See ya!

Lecture: Time Zones in the United States

You may already know about the four time zones in the continental United States, so use this lecture as an exercise in pronunciation. Read the lecture aloud and practice pronouncing numbers and acronyms. An acronym is when we abbreviate a phrase using the first letter of each word. One example is EST. When you pronounce this, you stress the name of each letter, stressing the last one a bit more. For example, EST is pronounced "ee-ess-TEE." Try it out for yourself.

Time Zones in the United States

The continental United States has four time zones: Eastern Standard Time (EST), Central Standard Time (CST), Mountain Standard Time (MST), and Pacific Standard Time (PST). There is a three-hour time difference from one end of the country to the other. Massachusetts, New York, Washington, DC, and Florida are all in the Eastern time zone. States such as Illinois, Minnesota, and Texas are in the Central time zone. In the Mountain time zone are states like Colorado, Montana, and Arizona. Finally, in the Pacific time zone, you can find Nevada, Oregon, Washington, and California. Each time zone is a one-hour difference from its neighboring time zone. For example, if it's 6:00 p.m. in Boston, Massachusetts, then it's 5:00 p.m. in Chicago, Illinois. Simultaneously, the time in Denver, Colorado, is 4:00 p.m. and in Los Angeles, California, it's 3:00 p.m. The farther west you go, the earlier the time is. If you live in San Francisco, California, and call your friend in New York City at 10:00 a.m. PST, you would say "Good afternoon" because it would actually be the afternoon in the Eastern time zone.

Success Strategy: Strengthen Your Listening, Speaking, and Pronunciation

In the Introduction to this book, you read ways to quickly improve your listening, speaking, and pronunciation. Here is another strategy you can use. Read along as you listen to the audio files that correspond to this book. Follow these five steps:

1. Listen and read along with the text two to three times.

2. Close the book and close your eyes and listen (do not read) as many times as you like (one to three times). The more you do this, the better results you will have.

3. Open the book, and listen and read along again. Try to figure out what you could and could not "hear" with your eyes closed.

4. Repeat step 2 and try to "hear" what you could not understand before. Did you hear it this time?

5. Repeat steps 1–4 frequently. I recommend you do this for at least 15 minutes every day.

EXERCISES

EXERCISE 1-1

Now that you know the time zones in the continental United States, read the situations and answer the questions that follow.

Situation 1: John lives in Washington, DC, where it's 5:00 p.m. EST. He calls his friend, Jeremy, who lives in Texas. What time is it in Texas when John calls? _____

How would John greet Jeremy? *Good* _____

Situation 2: Monique lives in Chicago, Illinois, and she wants to FaceTime her cousin who lives in San Diego, California. It's 12:00 p.m. in Chicago. What time is it in San Diego when Monique calls? _____

How should she greet her cousin? *Good* _____

Situation 3: The Butrago family lives in Seattle, Washington. They want to videoconference with their children's grandparents, who live in Fort Lauderdale, Florida. It's 8:00 a.m. in Seattle. What time is it in Fort Lauderdale? _____

How might they greet the grandparents? *Good* _____.

EXERCISE 1-2

List two ways we say "hello" to someone using different levels of formality. Then, write two appropriate responses to these greetings.

1. Neutral expressions for *hello*:

    a. _____ Response: _____

    b. _____ Response: _____

2. Formal expressions for *hello*:

    a. _____ Response: _____

    b. _____ Response: _____

3. Informal expressions for *hello*:

    a. _____ Response: _____

    b. _____ Response: _____

4. Very informal expressions for *hello:*

    a. _____ Response: _____

    b. _____ Response: _____

EXERCISE 1-3

Write* T *for True or* F *for False on the line next to each statement.

1. _____ It is okay to ask someone to repeat their name if I'm not sure I heard it correctly.

2. _____ I should look down when I speak with someone.

3. _____ I should make eye contact with someone when I speak to them.

4. _____ It's acceptable to say my name very quickly when I introduce myself.

5. _____ I should pause between my first and last names when I introduce myself.

6. _____ It's good to smile when I meet someone.

7. _____ When I shake hands, I should use my left hand.

8. _____ It's appropriate to shake hands with someone from the opposite sex.

9. _____ A fist bump is when you punch your fist toward the sky.

10. _____ An "air" elbow bump is appropriate if you are physically distancing.

EXERCISE 1-4

Choose the best answer for each question. A question may have more than one correct answer.

1. You and one other student are in the classroom before class begins. You want to acknowledge this person because you two are the only ones in the room. Choose appropriate ways to do this.
   a. Hi, how's it going?
   b. Homework was hard, wasn't it?
   c. Later, dude.
   d. Nice to meet you!

2. Your first class of the day is Physical Education (PE). It's 7:00 a.m. and it's cold out. Your teacher tells you to run five laps around the field. You are running with a classmate you haven't met yet. What are appropriate ways to make small talk?
   a. Good evening.
   b. Yo!
   c. Wow, it's cold!
   d. Do you like rap music?

EXERCISE 1-5

Form correct yes/no and information questions with the words given. Put the words in the correct order and remember to put a question mark at the end of the question.

1. BE / she / smart   _____

2. Go / she / to the same school   _____

3. When / class / start   _____

4. Where / BE / the cafeteria   _____

5. How / BE / you   _____

6. Study / they / every night   _____

7. How / I / get / an A in this class   _____

8. What / BE / his name   _____

9. BE / you / okay   _____

10. Why / BE / she / late   _____

AUDIO 🔊

Flashcard App

 **2**

Talking About Habits, Routines, Customs, and Schedules

MUST ⚡ KNOW

⚡ We use the simple present verb tense to talk about habits, routines, customs, and schedules.

⚡ Use *do* or *does* in negative statements for verbs other than BE.

⚡ Adverbs of frequency explain how often you do something.

⚡ Prepositional phrases of time can help describe when something happens.

hat are some things you do regularly? Do you wake up at 7:00 a.m. every day? Do you play sports after school? Do you usually do homework in the evening? Do you go to the movies on the weekends? When we talk about our habits, customs, routines, and schedules, we use the simple present verb tense. Adverbs of frequency and prepositions of time are helpful, too. You already learned yes/no and information questions with the simple present in Chapter 1. Now, you're ready to learn affirmative and negative statements, tag questions, and more. Let's take a look at how we form and use the simple present tense.

Simple Present Verb Tense

We use this verb tense to talk about things we do regularly. Look at some example sentences below about habits, routines, customs, and schedules. Notice that we use time words and expressions to indicate how often we do things. These time words and expressions are underlined:

EXAMPLES

▶ Greg walks five miles <u>every morning</u>.

▶ They have tennis lessons <u>every Wednesday and Friday afternoon</u>.

▶ She checks the oil in her car <u>about every two weeks</u> because her car is old.

▶ <u>On the first of every month</u>, I review my class assignments for due dates.

▶ Do you go to the dentist <u>twice a year</u>?

▶ Kristin and Sue throw a birthday party for Jim <u>every year</u>.

▶ Where does your family celebrate the <u>Fourth of July</u>?

▶ The school bus comes <u>every 20 minutes</u> until 8:00 a.m.

▶ <u>Every fall and spring</u>, the drama club at school puts on a musical production.

▶ Dad goes to his high school reunion <u>every five years</u>.

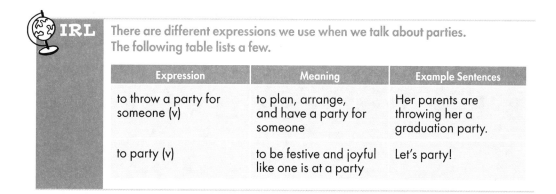

IRL   There are different expressions we use when we talk about parties. The following table lists a few.

Expression	Meaning	Example Sentences
to throw a party for someone (v)	to plan, arrange, and have a party for someone	Her parents are throwing her a graduation party.
to party (v)	to be festive and joyful like one is at a party	Let's party!

The preposition *about* has several meanings. When we refer to frequency, it means **approximately**. Another preposition used is *around,* and an expression we use is *–ish*. It's a suffix put at the end of a word to indicate approximately. The word *approximately* is more formal. Here are some examples of these expressions:

EXAMPLES

▶ She arrives every day <u>about 2 p.m.</u>

▶ She arrives every day <u>around 2 p.m.</u>

▶ She arrives <u>at 2ish</u> every day.

▶ She arrives <u>at approximately 2 p.m.</u> every day.

Simple Present Tense: Forming the Affirmative

How do we form the simple present in affirmative statements? Let's look at the structure we use for this verb tense with the **BE verb, irregular verbs,** and **regular verbs**. Regular verbs generally follow the grammar rules; however, irregular verbs do not follow these rules. The most common irregular verbs in English are *be*, *do*, *have*, and *go*. Let's see how we form the **BE verb** in the simple present affirmative.

Forming the Affirmative with a BE Verb

Subject Pronoun	Verb in Simple Present Form	Example Sentences
I	am	I **am** fine. I **am** 16 years old.
You / We / They	are	You **are** hungry. We **are** tired. They **are** brothers.
He / She / It	is	He **is** funny. She **is** happy. It **is** sunny today.

Forming Contractions with Affirmative BE (Subject Pronoun + BE Verb)

Subject Pronoun	BE Verb Form	Contraction of Subject Pronoun + BE	Example Sentences
I +	am =	I'm	I'm glad.
You / We / They +	are =	You're / We're / They're	You're curious. We're fine. They're angry.
He / She / It +	is =	He's / She's / It's	He's here. She's happy. It's okay.

Here's how we form **irregular verbs** in the simple present affirmative.

Forming the Affirmative with Common Irregular Verbs: Do, Have, Go

Subject Pronoun	Verb in Simple Present Form—Do	Example Sentences
I / You / We / They	**do**	I **do** my homework every evening. You **do** your homework every evening, too. We **do** yoga every Sunday morning. They **do** the dishes after dinner every evening.
He / She / It	**does**	She **does** her homework in the afternoon. He **does** yoga three times a week.

Subject Pronoun	Verb in Simple Present Form—Have	Example Sentences
I / You / We / They	**have**	I **have** soccer practice every day after school. You **have** a track meet every weekend. We **have** fun every day after school. They **have** play rehearsal every Saturday.
He / She / It	**has**	She **has** water polo practice three days a week. He **has** a baseball tournament every weekend this spring.

Subject Pronoun	Verb in Simple Present Form—Go	Example Sentences
I / You / We / They	**go**	I **go** to my friend's house to study every afternoon. You **go** to the café for coffee every morning. We **go** to the library every week. They **go** to the movies every Friday night.
He / She / It	**goes**	She **goes** to her brother's baseball game on Saturdays. He **goes** to his sister's golf tournament every weekend.

Here's how we form **regular verbs** in the simple present affirmative.

Forming the Affirmative with Regular Verbs

Subject or Subject Pronoun	Verb in Simple Present Form	Example Sentences
I / You / We / They	**listen**	I **listen** to rock music on the weekends.
	Note: We listen *to* someone or something.	My sister Sophia and I **listen** to musicals every morning before school.
		My parents frequently **listen** to classical music.
He / She / It	**listens**	Nacho usually **listens** to punk rock in the morning.
		Maggie rarely **listens** to pop music.

Pronunciation: Three –s Ending Sounds

In English, **we have three different sounds for the final –s.** You can find these sounds in the **third person singular verb form with regular verbs** and **in plural count nouns** such as toy**s** and pet**s**. It is also found in **possessive nouns and pronouns** such as it**s** and Jane'**s**.

How Do You Know Which –s Ending to Use?

The sound of the –s ending is determined by the **last consonant sound in the word**. Let's look at some examples.

EXAMPLES

> The last consonant sound in the verb **take** is /k/. The /k/ sound is **voiceless**. This means that we use **only air** to make this sound. Our vocal cords are not engaged. Rather, they are open to allow air to pass through them. Because the final consonant sound /k/ is voiceless, the sound of the –s ending will also be voiceless. It will sound like /s/ as in **s**uper.

▶ The last consonant sound in the verb *give* is /v/. The /v/ sound is **voiced** because we engage our vocal cords, which vibrate, to make this sound. We can feel this vibration when we touch our throat as we pronounce the word. Because /v/ is voiced, the sound of the –s ending should also be voiced. It will sound like /z/ as in **z**ebra.

▶ The third –s ending sound **adds a syllable to the word.** This syllable is pronounced just like the BE verb *is.* We illustrate it like this: /iz/.

See the table for a list of sounds, rules, and examples.

Final –s Sound	/s/	/z/	/ɪz/
Final consonant sounds	/f/ /k/ /p/ /t/ /θ/ (voiceless /th/)	/b/ /d/ /g/ /l/ /m/ /n/ /ŋ/ (/ng/) /r/ /ð/ (voiced /th/) /v/ /w/ /y/ and all vowel sounds	/dʒ/ /s/ /ʃ/ (/sh/) /tʃ/ (/ch/) /ʒ/ (/zh/) /z/
Rules and notes	This final –s sounds like a snake—*sssss*. It is a **voiceless sound** because it does not engage the vocal cords. We use **only air** to make this sound. Put your hand on your throat when you make this sound. There is **no vibration**.	This final –s sounds like a bee—*zzzzzzz*. It is a **voiced sound** because it **engages the vocal cords**, which means they vibrate. Put your hand on your throat and **feel the vibration** when you make the sound *zzzzz*.	This –s ending **adds a syllable** to the word. It is **pronounced like the BE verb** *is*. It is a voiced sound.
Examples **Note:** The final consonant sound is underlined.	takes, stops, puts, makes, starts, its, Pat's, Jeff's, tips, socks	drives, gives, does, says, shows, loves, problems, friends, schools, rings, Rob's, Joan's, Mom's, hers	wishes, misses, watches, chooses, judges, houses, Mitch's, Josh's

Simple Present Tense: Forming the Negative

How do we form the simple present in negative statements? Let's learn the structure we use for this verb tense in the negative with the **BE verb** and **all other verbs**. First, look at how we structure the BE verb.

Forming the Negative with the BE Verb

Subject Pronoun	BE Verb Form	Negative	Example Sentences
I	am	not	I **am not** worried.
You / We / They	are	not	You **are not** hungry. We **are not** there. They **are not** envious.
He / She / It	is	not	He **is not** here. She **is not** on time. It **is not** too late.

Simple Present Tense: Forming Contractions with the Negative BE Verb

Most people use contractions when they talk because it's faster and feels more natural. There are two ways to form contractions with the negative BE verb. Check out both ways:

1. Contractions with the Negative BE Verb (BE + Negative)

Subject Pronoun	BE Verb Form	Negative	Contraction Verb BE + Negative	Example Sentences
I	**am**	**not**	-	I am not at school.
You / We / They	**are** +	**not** =	aren't	You **aren't** sick. We **aren't** healthy. They **aren't** at home.
He / She / It	**is** +	**not** =	isn't	He **isn't** in gym class. She **isn't** at the beach. It **isn't** a good day.

2. Contractions with the Negative BE Verb (Subject Pronoun + BE)

We sometimes use this type of contraction to emphasize the negative meaning.

Subject Pronoun	BE Verb Form	Contraction of Subject + BE Verb	Negative	Example Sentences
I	+ am =	I'm	not	I'm **not** late.
You	+ are =	You're	not	You're **not** with her.
We	+ are =	We're	not	We're **not** in study hall.
They	+ are =	They're	not	They're **not** in the cafeteria.
He	+ is =	He's	not	He's **not** at the party.
She	+ is =	She's	not	She's **not** in town.
It	+ is =	It's	not	It's **not** a problem.

Forming the Negative with All Other Verbs

In Chapter 1, you learned that we use *do* or *does* with verbs that are not the BE verb to form yes/no and information questions. In this section of Chapter 2, you'll learn that with non-BE verbs, **we need *do* or *does* to form negative statements**, too. Check out how we do this and read the example sentences.

Subject or Subject Pronoun	DO or DOES	Negative	Main Verb (Base Form)	Example Sentences
I / You / We / They	do	not	take	I **do not take** the bus to school.
			get	You **do not get** a ride to school.
			walk	We **do not walk** to school.
			ride	They **do not ride** their bikes to school.
He / She / It	does	not	take	He **does not take** the bus to school.
			walk	She **does not walk** to school.
			make	It **does not make** a difference.

Simple Present Tense: Forming Negative Contractions with All Other Verbs

Remember, we usually use contractions whenever we speak because it's less formal. We also use contractions in informal writing like in emails, text messages, and social media posts.

Subject Pronoun	DO or DOES	Negative	Contraction of DO/DOES + Negative	Main Verb (Base Form)	Example Sentences
I / You / We / They	do +	not	= don't	like	I **don't like** math.
				study	We **don't study** on Saturdays.
				go	They **don't go** to this school.
He / She / It	does +	not	= doesn't	care	He **doesn't care** about that.
				want	She **doesn't want** ice cream.
				matter	It **doesn't** matter.

Important: Do not add an **–s** to the main verb when it's negative. Study this in these two example sentences:

EXAMPLES

> **Incorrect:** He <u>does not ~~takes~~</u> the train to work.

> **Correct:** He <u>does not take</u> the train to work.

Indicating Frequency

When we talk about our habits, routines, customs, and schedules, we usually use adverbs of frequency. These words and phrases describe **how often** we do something. The most common ones we use are listed below.

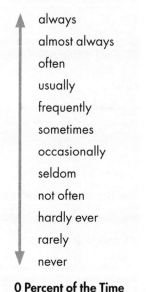

100 Percent of the Time

always

almost always

often

usually

frequently

sometimes

occasionally

seldom

not often

hardly ever

rarely

never

0 Percent of the Time

Adverbs of frequency go **after the BE verb if it's the main verb.** However, they go **before all other verbs.** See the example sentences for each adverb of frequency. Notice the placement of the adverb:

EXAMPLES

▶ Owen <u>always</u> **does** his homework after dinner.

▶ Dani <u>almost always</u> **shares** her lunch with me.

▶ It **is** <u>often</u> chilly in this classroom. (BE verb)

▶ We **are** <u>usually</u> finished with homework before bedtime. (BE verb)

▶ The teacher in leadership <u>frequently</u> **ends** class late.

▶ We <u>sometimes</u> **bring** our lunch to school.

▶ Mr. Sampson <u>occasionally</u> **gives** pop quizzes.

▶ She <u>seldom</u> **makes** it to class on time.

▶ We don't <u>often</u> **eat** out.

▶ The Ferguson family <u>hardly ever</u> **goes** on vacation.

▶ Carrie <u>never</u> **takes** the bus to school.

POP QUIZ!

Which verb tense do we use to talk about habits, routines, customs, and schedules?

If you said the simple present verb tense, you are correct!

Expressions of Time

Regarding habits, I regularly exercise in the morning. What do you do **in the morning**? What do you do **on the weekends**? What do you do **for the holidays**? To describe when we do things, **prepositions of time** really help. We use them in **prepositional phrases**. Prepositional phrases start with a preposition and end with a noun or noun phrase. An example of a prepositional phrase <u>ending with a noun</u> is **on Saturday**, in which the noun is *Saturday*. An example of a prepositional phrase <u>ending with a noun phrase</u> is **in the afternoon**. The noun phrase is *in the afternoon*. Let's learn about the most common prepositions of time that we use to talk about habits, routines, customs, and schedules.

Prepositional Phrase of Time	Examples	Prepositional Phrase of Time	Examples
in + amount of time	in two hours in 10 days	*on* + day	on Monday on Thanksgiving day
for + amount of time (duration)	for one week for three months	*in* + month / year / decade / century	in June in 2050 in the 2100s
at + specific time	at 8:40 a.m. at midnight	*in* + period of day	in the morning in the afternoon in the evening
at + night	at night	*on* + the weekend / a weekday	on the weekend on a weekday
during + length of time	during the holidays during the semester	*over* + period of time (usually longer)	over the summer over the academic year

Practice 2-A

Now, review the following example sentences that describe habits, routines, customs, and schedules using prepositional phrases of time. There are two things to notice in these sentences:

1. Notice that you can begin the sentence with a prepositional phrase of time. When we do this, we put a comma after it. There are four sentences with this writing technique. Can you find them?

2. Notice that you can use more than one prepositional phrase of time in a sentence. There are three sentences with two prepositional phrases of time and one sentence with three. Which ones are they?

▶ The science teacher holds optional lab workshops <u>during first and second periods</u>.

▶ <u>Over the winter break</u>, we visit my grandparents in Sacramento, California.

▶ Marjorie drinks black tea <u>in the morning</u> and green tea <u>in the afternoon</u>.

▶ <u>For one week</u> every semester, Chenyu's brother comes home from the university.

▶ My friends and I eat lunch <u>at noon</u> every school day.

▶ <u>In the evening</u>, I sit on the couch and do my homework before I watch TV <u>for one hour</u>.

▶ Parent-teacher conferences take place <u>for two weeks</u> <u>in the fall</u> and <u>in the spring</u>.

▶ Midterm exams are scheduled <u>for one week</u> <u>in the middle of the fall term</u>.

▶ My Spanish class starts <u>at 7:40</u> every Monday, Wednesday, and Friday.

▶ <u>On Monday afternoons</u>, the Leadership Team works on the student body election.

See Practice 2-A in the Answer Key to check your answers to the questions above on prepositional phrases of time.

Simple Present Tense: Using Tag Questions

Tag questions are short questions we put at the end of statements to verify information. These are common in conversations. The important thing to know is that **we use negative tag questions with affirmative statements and affirmative tag questions with negative statements**. See the examples with BE verbs and other verbs. Notice how DO/DOES is used:

EXAMPLES

▶ She goes here, <u>doesn't she</u>?

▶ Hee Jeong and Robert are students at Brown High School, <u>aren't they</u>?

▶ Rafael is an A student, <u>isn't he</u>?

▶ She isn't late, <u>is she</u>?

▶ The Hendersons aren't on vacation yet, <u>are they</u>?

▶ The spring musical isn't on the schedule yet, <u>is it</u>?

▶ The fall dance happens this weekend, <u>doesn't it</u>?

▶ You're not here yet, <u>are you</u>?

▶ The homework is due tomorrow, <u>isn't it</u>?

▶ The monitors don't visit classes every week, <u>do they</u>?

Using Intonation with Tag Questions

We use tag questions in two ways: **to verify information and to seek agreement**. If we want to verify information, which means to be sure we understand something, then we use **rising intonation**. If we seek agreement, we use **falling intonation**. Check out the example sentences with pitch patterns. Also, see the Appendix for more information on the pitches we use in American English.

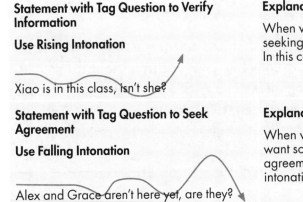

Statement with Tag Question to Verify Information

Use Rising Intonation

Xiao is in this class, isn't she?

Explanation:

When we don't know the answer and we are seeking information, we verify information. In this case, we use rising intonation.

Statement with Tag Question to Seek Agreement

Use Falling Intonation

Alex and Grace aren't here yet, are they?

Explanation:

When we know the answer and we want someone to agree with us, we seek agreement. In this case, we use falling intonation.

Note: Pitch patterns are shown above, below, and through the words of sentences to illustrate that our pitches change as we speak.

Using Affirmative or Negative with Tag Questions

It seems counterintuitive, but with an affirmative statement, the tag question is negative, and with a negative statement, the tag question is affirmative. Here are some things to remember:

- Regarding affirmative and negative, the tag question is opposite that of the statement.

- With affirmative statements (negative tags), we usually expect an affirmative answer.

- With negative statements (affirmative tags), we usually expect a negative answer.

- We can answer any tag question affirmatively or negatively.

Some students find tag questions tricky, but let's keep it simple. See the table to clarify how we use them. Notice that we need a comma before the tag question every time.

Affirmative Statement	Negative Tag Question	Expect Affirmative Answer
Sue has your book,	**doesn't** she?	Yes, she **does**.
They play in the game today,	**don't** they?	Yes, they **do**.
We have softball practice tomorrow,	**don't** we?	Yes, we **do**.
She is here now,	**isn't** she?	Yes, she **is**.
They are on vacation,	**aren't** they?	Yes, they **are**.

Negative Statement	Affirmative Tag Question	Expect Negative Answer
She doesn't have your book,	**does** she?	No, she **doesn't**.
They don't play the game today,	**do** they?	No, they **don't**.
We don't have softball practice tomorrow,	**do** we?	No, we **don't**.
She isn't here now,	**is** she?	No, she **isn't**.
They aren't on vacation,	**are** they?	No, they **aren't**.

Remember that you can verify information or seek agreement for any kind of tag question with your intonation. Pay attention to the intonation of a speaker—rising or falling—to determine whether they are verifying information or looking for agreement.

Forming Tag Questions with a BE Verb

See the table below to learn how to form a tag question using a BE verb. Notice that the tag question is affirmative if the BE verb is negative, and it's negative if the BE verb is affirmative.

Subject or Subject Pronoun	BE Verb	Negative	Rest of the Sentence + Comma	Tag Question BE Verb (Affirmative or Negative—Opposite of Main BE Verb)	Tag Question Subject Pronoun + Question Mark
He	is	-	in class now,	isn't	he?
He	is	n't	in class now,	is	he?
They	are	-	here,	aren't	they?
They	are	n't	here,	are	they?

The exception to these rules is with the pronoun *I* in negative tag questions. When we use tag questions with the BE verb and the subject pronoun I, we seldom use the tag question, *am I not*? It's formal, so we don't normally use it in everyday conversation. Instead, we use *aren't I*? See the examples below.

I	am	-	on time,	aren't	I?
I	am	-	on time,	am	I **not**? (Formal)

Forming Tag Questions with All Other Verbs

Subject or Subject Pronoun	Negative	Main Verb	Rest of the Sentence + Comma	Tag Question DO/DOES (Affirmative or Negative—Opposite of Main Verb)	Tag Question Subject Pronoun + Question Mark
They	-	have	a game this weekend,	don't	they?
They	don't	have	a game this weekend,	do	they?
She	-	attends	private school,	doesn't	she?
She	doesn't	attend	private school,	does	she?

Answering Tag Questions

Answering tag questions can be tricky for students of English, but this is important to learn because we use them often in classroom conversations. Practice using these every day so you become skillful. In the previous section on affirmative or negative tag questions, you learned expected answers. When you use the wrong type of answer, it is confusing. Remember it this way: whatever the statement is—affirmative or negative—is what the expected answer is. For example, if the statement is affirmative, then an affirmative answer is expected. If the statement is negative, then a negative answer is expected. Recognize and learn the expected answers so you are clear and easy to understand. Carefully review and study the following example sentences and expected answers.

Affirmative Statement	Negative Tag Question	Expect Affirmative Answer
Tyler **is** with the teacher,	**isn't** he?	Yes, he **is**.
Aleen **attends** a university,	**doesn't** she?	Yes, she **does**.
You **like** poke,	**don't** you?	Yes, I **do**.

Negative Statement	Affirmative Tag Question	Expect Negative Answer
Max **isn't** a senior,	**is** he?	No, he **isn't**.
Audrey **doesn't walk** to school every day,	**does** she?	No, she **doesn't**.
They **don't want** ice cream,	**do** they?	No, they **don't**.

More on Tag Questions

To clarify how we use tag questions a bit more, check out the five points outlined on the following pages. I recommend you practice one of these per week, so you get comfortable using all types of tag questions.

1. Remember that even though there is an expected answer, the opposite answer is possible. **Provide whatever answer is true.** See the examples.

Affirmative Statement	Negative Tag Question	Answer
Sheridan **teaches** music,	**doesn't** she?	Yes, she **does**. (Expected) No, she doesn't.

Negative Statement	Affirmative Tag Question	Answer
Lina **doesn't coach** tennis,	**does** she?	No, she doesn't. (Expected) Yes, she **does**.

2. When using negative words, such as *never* and *nothing*, we use affirmative tags. See the following examples.

Statement with Negative Word	Affirmative Tag Question
She's **never** visited you,	**has** she?
Nothing is wrong,	**is** it?

3. When we use *everyone, everybody, someone, somebody, no one,* and *nobody,* we use the pronoun **they** in the tag. Check out these examples.

Statement with Indefinite Pronoun	Tag Question with *they*
Everyone does it,	don't **they**?
No one knows the answer to this test question,	do **they**?
Somebody in this class understands this math problem,	don't **they**?
Nobody goes there,	**do** they?

4. When using *this* or *that*, the tag is **it**. *These* and *those* become **they**.

Statement with Demonstrative Pronoun	Tag Question with *it* or *they*
This is correct,	isn't **it**?
That isn't fair,	is **it**?
These shoes aren't comfortable,	are **they**?
Those are the ones to buy,	aren't **they**?

5. For *there is* or *there are*, we must use **there** in the tag.

Statement with *There is/There are*	Tag Question with *there*
There is an answer key,	isn't **there**?
There aren't any essay questions on the test,	are **there**?

Note that the tag questions in #1, #4 and #5 follow the rule that the tag is the opposite of the statement: If the verb in the statement is affirmative, the tag question verb is negative and vice versa.

Using the Simple Present Tense for Schedules

We have discussed how the simple present verb tense is used to talk about habits, routines, customs, and schedules. In this section, we'll take a closer look at how the simple present is used for schedules. To refer to **set schedules, such as a bus schedule, store hours,** and **a movie schedule,** use the simple present. Even though the schedule may refer to future times, we use the simple present rather than the future verb tense. Let's see how we talk about schedules using the simple present verb tense. As a quick reminder, see how to form the simple present with non-**BE** verbs in the following tables.

Simple Present: Forming the Affirmative

Subject or Subject Pronoun	Verb in Simple Present Form	Example Sentences
I / You / We / They	take	They <u>take</u> the train to work every day.
He / She / It	come**s**	The bus <u>comes</u> every twenty minutes until noon.

Simple Present: Forming the Negative

Subject or Subject Pronoun	Do or Does	Negative	Main Verb (Base Form)	Example Sentences
I / You / We / They	do	not (don't)	arrive	We usually <u>don't arrive</u> to work until 9 a.m.
He / She / It	doe**s**	not (doesn't)	run	This bus <u>doesn't run</u> on Sundays.

In the following table are verbs we often use to talk about schedules.

to come	to arrive	to open	to start
to begin	to leave	to depart	to close
to end	to finish	to run (to operate)	

Now, look at some example sentences with the simple present that talk about schedules using these verbs.

▶ On Monday through Friday, this train <u>comes</u> every 30 minutes.

▶ The last #52 bus <u>leaves</u> at 4:20 p.m.

▶ The train to downtown usually <u>arrives</u> on time, but the bus <u>doesn't arrive</u> on time.

▶ On the weekend, the train <u>departs</u> every hour on the hour until 8 p.m.

▶ The department store <u>opens</u> at 8 a.m. and <u>closes</u> at 8 p.m.

▶ The train on the red line <u>doesn't run</u> on weekends.

▶ On holidays, most of the commuter trains <u>don't run</u>.

▶ The express bus <u>doesn't start</u> until 8 a.m. on Saturdays.

▶ On Sundays, the produce stand <u>opens</u> at 7 a.m. and <u>closes</u> at 3 p.m.

▶ The feature film <u>starts</u> at 7 p.m. in the big cinema.

Vocabulary: Public Transportation and Schedules

Here are some vocabulary words and phrases used for public transportation. Do you know any of these vocabulary words? Put a star * next to the terms you know. Do you know any other vocabulary words or phrases related to public transportation? Add them to this list.

a bus station	a bus stop	a bus route	a bus driver
a bus/train line	to catch a bus/train	to get on a bus/train	to get off a bus/train
to miss a bus/train	a ticket	a ticket counter	a kiosk
a conductor	a train station	a terminal	a customer service agent
to embark	to disembark		

Vocabulary: Expressions of Time Used for Schedules

We often use specific expressions of time when we talk about schedules. See common expressions below. Again, put a star * next to the time expressions you know. Add others!

to <u>be</u> on time	every hour	on the hour	every hour on the hour
to <u>not be</u> on time			
Note: Be sure to use the correct form of the BE verb.			
to <u>be</u> early	every 15 minutes	every half hour	every 2 / 5 / 10 / 20 minutes / hours
to <u>be</u> late			
Note: Be sure to use the correct form of the BE verb.			
at _____ (specific time such as 8:15 a.m.)	until / till _____ (a specific time such as 12:00 p.m.)	the first / last bus / train	

Let's look at some example sentences that describe schedules using the simple present verb tense and time expressions.

EXAMPLES

▶ The bus <u>is</u> never late.

▶ The train always <u>arrives</u> on time.

▶ The train <u>departs</u> every hour on the hour.

▶ The #29 bus <u>runs</u> every half hour.

▶ The bus <u>leaves</u> the station at 6:30 a.m.

Dialogue: Clubs in School

Marly and Eva are friends in their junior year of high school. They are talking about the different clubs to join. Notice the use of the simple present verb tense, adverbs of frequency, prepositional phrases of time, and tag questions.

Marly: What about clubs? Are you interested?

Eva: Well, I was thinking about the Philosophy Club again.

Marly: Really? That's so . . . impressive! When does the club meet?

Eva: It meets every week on Monday and Thursday at 4:00 p.m.

Marly: There are snacks at the meeting, aren't there?

Eva: Yeah no yeah. We bring them ourselves. We take turns.

Marly: What happens in the meetings?

Eva: We almost always talk about different philosophies and philosophers, and we sometimes argue about them.

Marly: That doesn't sound like fun to me.

Eva: I like debates! It's really fun. What about you?

Marly: I was considering the Math Club because I need the practice.

Eva: When does it meet?

Marly: It usually meets every Tuesday and Friday after school at 3:30 p.m., but sometimes they cancel Fridays.

Eva: What happens in the Math Club?

Marly: We work on math problems, equations, and formulas and all that kind of stuff. It's pretty cool. I enjoy it.

Eva: Nice!

Marly: Yeah.

Lecture: Holiday Customs in the United States

When you read this lecture, notice the use of the simple present verb tense with the BE verb and other verbs, the prepositional phrases of time, and the adverbs of frequency.

Holiday Customs in the United States

The United States boasts a great diversity of people, cultures, and ethnicities, which means we have a variety of holidays to celebrate all year long. Residents are from all over the world, and they bring their heritage with them to the United States. As a result, we enjoy a variety of food, events, and customs. Over the past 240ish years, the United States has adopted many different holiday customs from its inhabitants. There are too many celebrations to list them all, but let's look at some of the primary holidays that we celebrate each month.

We celebrate the start of the New Year on January 1 every year. Many people celebrate the night before by staying up to toast and cheer at the stroke of midnight. When the clock turns to 12:00 a.m., people rejoice and shout, "Happy New Year!" Many pop champagne bottles, throw streamers, and hug and kiss the people in their lives to celebrate the New Year and a new beginning. It's also popular to make resolutions, which are intentions to create new habits and accomplish goals.

A popular holiday in February is Valentine's Day. On February 14 every year, love is celebrated. Historically, this was a holiday for romantic partners. Today, however, we celebrate all kinds of love: romantic love, familial love, friendship, and even the love we have for our pets! It's common for people to give others Valentine's Day cards with expressions of love and appreciation on this day. Common gifts include chocolate, flowers, and meals at restaurants.

In March, the day to party is the 17th. On this day, many celebrate St. Patrick's Day. Originally, it was a Christian holiday in Ireland, but Irish immigrants who came to the United States made it into a secular holiday to celebrate all things Irish. The leprechaun is this holiday's mascot and the four-leaf clover is a symbol of luck. It's customary on this day to go to a pub or bar and drink green-colored beer, wear green clothes, and sing Irish songs. It's a festive celebration.

In April, Easter is a holiday that many celebrate. It's a Christian holiday that many people celebrate by being with family and close friends and oftentimes attending a church service. Children enjoy this holiday because of the Easter egg hunt, which is primarily a hunt for hidden candy that children find and eat. An Easter egg is a colorful plastic egg filled with candy, which the Easter Bunny brings to all children. Pastel colors are popular and the Easter Bunny is the mascot for this holiday.

In the month of May, we celebrate Mother's Day. It is traditional for a family to eat a meal at a restaurant or to cook breakfast, lunch, or dinner at home for their mother. Mothers receive appreciation, flowers, greeting cards, and other gifts on this day. People express gratitude on this day for all that mothers do every day.

In June, we celebrate Father's Day. This is similar to Mother's Day, but it celebrates fathers and all they do for the family. Family gatherings and gifts are traditional for this holiday.

The Fourth of July, also called Independence Day, is the big holiday in July. On this day, we celebrate the independence that Americans won from the British in 1781. This day is typically celebrated with family and friends at a cookout, also known as a barbecue. A cookout is an outdoor meal cooked on an outdoor grill and usually consists of hot dogs and hamburgers. People drink beer and soda and enjoy the company of family and friends. It's a national holiday, which means many businesses are

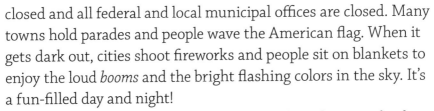

closed and all federal and local municipal offices are closed. Many towns hold parades and people wave the American flag. When it gets dark out, cities shoot fireworks and people sit on blankets to enjoy the loud *booms* and the bright flashing colors in the sky. It's a fun-filled day and night!

August doesn't have any major holidays, but it's a month when many people take vacation from work or go on summer trips, such as camping and traveling to visit family.

In September, we celebrate Labor Day on the first Monday of the month. This holiday acknowledges the contributions and achievements of American workers. This is also a federal holiday, and many people take a long weekend to celebrate this day.

The most popular holiday in October is Halloween, which is on the 31st of the month. It began as a Celtic festival to ward off evil, and the Christian faith made November 1 All Saint's Day, which incorporates some of the Celtic traditions. Most children only know this holiday as a time to dress up in fun costumes and go from house to house to say "Trick or Treat!" and collect candy. Many adults join children in celebrating this holiday by hosting or attending costume parties. Jack-o'-lanterns are carved pumpkins with candles inside that light up the doorsteps of houses. The mascots for this holiday are witches, black cats, and ghosts.

On the third Thursday of November, we celebrate Thanksgiving, which represents gratitude for the abundance we have in our lives. This holiday dates back to the time of the Pilgrims, who first arrived in New England in the 1600s. On this Thursday, families get together and cook a large meal together. The entrée is usually a turkey or ham. Potatoes, squash, and cranberry sauce are popular, too. Most people eat a lot of food and then take a nap and watch a football game or a movie on TV.

Finally, in December, the big holiday is Christmas, which occurs on the 25th of the month. It's origins are Christian, but it's now a large commercial holiday. It's traditional to buy gifts for the people in your life to show appreciation and love. People wrap their Christmas gifts and put them under a Christmas tree decorated with lights, ornaments, and garlands. Children love this holiday because they get to unwrap gifts! The mascot for this holiday is Santa Claus. The tale is that Santa Claus flies all over the world and delivers Christmas gifts to children who behaved well all year. Santa's elves make these gifts in their workshop at the North Pole. It's a story that many children believe until they grow up and realize they are the ones who must buy Christmas gifts for their loved ones.

These are just a few of the holidays that we celebrate in the United States. You can see that there are many opportunities to be with loved ones, celebrate, and have fun. I hope you enjoy some of these holidays and more!

Success Strategy: Shadowing—a Listening Technique

One simple way to improve your listening skills is to "shadow." When you shadow, you follow closely behind someone or something. **In this listening strategy, you repeat what you hear immediately after you hear it.** Although this technique is simple, the results are great. All my students employ this strategy, and it expands their pitch range, builds their vocabulary, improves their pronunciation, and strengthens their listening skills. I recommend you use this strategy daily. Here is how to use it with this book.

How to Shadow

As you read through the example sentences, dialogues, and lectures in this book, listen to the audio files that come with the book. Follow these simple steps:

1. Listen as you read.

2. Pause the audio file after a sentence or two.

3. Repeat what you heard.

4. Repeat steps 2 and 3 as necessary to become familiar with the sound of American English.

Helpful Tips

When you repeat what you heard, try to imitate the voice you hear exactly. Pretend you are an actor and you are playing an American speaking English for a movie. To be successful, you need to learn your lines and sound like an American. Play the actor and have some fun! Do this consistently throughout the book. Listen, pause, and repeat. It's simple and effective and it will build your confidence, too. Go back to the beginning of this chapter and try this strategy.

You can use this same strategy with any video that comes with a transcript, an audio book with the written version of the book, and music lyrics. Anything that has both a written and spoken version works well. Have fun shadowing!

EXERCISES

EXERCISE 2-1

Choose the correct verb form for each sentence describing habits, routines, customs, and schedules.

1. Kenny and Ian _____ at 7:00 a.m. every day for school.

   wake up / wakes up

2. Charlene _____ a shower before school every day.

   take / takes

3. Danielle _____ a peppermint mocha coffee in the morning.

   drink / drinks

4. I _____ bagels for breakfast.

   enjoy / enjoys

5. You _____ to school with your sister every day, don't you?

   drive / drives

6. We often _____ to the café for lunch.

   go / goes

7. Mr. Yu _____ a pop quiz once a week.

   give / gives

8. The school _____ a dance every fall and spring.

   have / has

9. She _____ with the team every day after school.

   swim / swims

10. At the end of every month, Ms. Zelenko _____ snacks for us.

    bring / brings

EXERCISE 2-2

Choose the correct BE verb form for each sentence.

1. Where _____ you going?   are / am / is

2. She _____ a student at the community   are / am / is
   college, isn't she?

3. They _____ so happy to pass the test!   are / am / is

4. Wednesday _____ a half day of school.   are / am / is

5. Mike and Steve _____ best friends.   are / am / is

6. Michelle _____ my sister.   are / am / is

7. My classes _____ difficult this year.   are / am / is

8. His study habits _____ really good.   are / am / is
   He has an A in every class.

9. I _____ tired today.   are / am / is

10. There's no school today, so I _____ still   are / am / is
    in bed.

EXERCISE 2-3

Choose the correct form of the auxiliary DO for each question using the simple present verb tense.

1. _____ Harry go here?   Do / Does

2. When _____ the class begin?   do / does

3. _____ you know what time it is?   Do / Does

4. Where _____ you live?   do / does

5. How many students _____ the teacher   **do / does**
   know?

6. What time _____ they leave for the   **do / does**
   game?

7. Which one _____ she like?   **do / does**

8. What kind of food _____ you want?   **do / does**

9. _____ the teacher give tests every week?   **Do / Does**

10. How _____ they know her?   **do / does**

EXERCISE 2-4

Write a sentence in the simple present verb tense. Be sure to write the correct form of the auxiliary DO for each negative statement.

1. Perry / NEGATIVE / play / hockey.

   _____

2. Jack / NEGATIVE / take / the bus to school.

   _____

3. My parents / NEGATIVE / drive / to work.

   _____

4. Grace / NEGATIVE / work / after school.

   _____

5. Sandi and Jana / NEGATIVE / study / a lot.

   _____

6. Vivek / NEGATIVE / worry / about tests.

   _____

7. Sheena and Takako / NEGATIVE / like / pizza.

   _____

8. I / NEGATIVE / drink / coffee in the afternoon.

   _____

9. We / NEGATIVE / want / any more pop quizzes.

   _____

10. You / NEGATIVE / arrive / on time.

    _____

EXERCISE 2-5

Write a sentence in the simple present verb tense using adverbs of frequency. Be sure to put the adverb of frequency in the correct position and use the correct form of the BE verb or other verb.

1. Jane / BE / late / for school.   (hardly ever)

   _____

2. The owner / open / the café / by 5:30 a.m.   (usually)

   _____

3. My aunt and uncle / BE / happy.   (always)

   _____

4. Jonah and his brother / attend / temple services / **(sometimes)** with their parents.

   _____

5. The Smiths / BE / home over the summer.   **(rarely)**

   _____

6. He / miss / history class in the morning.   **(frequently)**

   _____

EXERCISE 2-6

Write the correct tag question for each statement. Be sure to check the rules.

1. He's happy at this school, _____?

2. There are some seniors here, _____?

3. Paul isn't with you, _____?

4. Sammy and Jen like it, _____?

5. No one believes it, _____?

6. Maria doesn't want it, _____?

7. There is only one winner, _____?

8. Aidan and Finn eat sushi, _____?

9. They don't feel sick, _____?

10. You understand it, _____?

EXERCISE 2-7

Look at the bus schedule below, and then write sentences from the words provided. Use the simple present verb tense. Note that when there is only one of something, we use the article the. Don't forget a period for each statement! Follow the example.

Bus/Routes to Mendocino	Arrival Times						
	Monday–Friday Morning						
Mendocino 23	6:00	6:30	7:00	7:30	8:00	8:30	9:00
Fort Bragg 34	5:30	6:00	6:30	7:00	7:30	8:00	8:30
Fort Bragg 91	7:00	8:00	9:00	10:00	11:00		
Little River 14	6:00	6:10	6:20	6:30	6:40	6:50	7:00
Albion 9	4:00	5:00	6:00	7:00	8:00		
Ukiah 11	5:30	5:40	5:50	6:00	6:10	6:20	6:30
Ukiah 26	7:00	7:30	8:00	8:30	9:00	9:30	
Willits 15	5:00	5:15	5:30	5:45	6:00	6:15	6:30

Example: Ukiah 11 / come / every _____ minutes / from _____ to _____

The Ukiah 11 comes every 10 minutes from 5:30 a.m. to 6:30 a.m. _____

1. last bus to Mendocino / arrive / at the station / at _____

2. _____ bus / run / until 8:30 a.m.

3. _____ bus / come / every 15 minutes / from _____ to _____

4. The Albion 9 / run / every _____ / from _____ to _____

5. _____ and _____ / run / for only one hour in the morning

EXERCISE 2-8

Look at the bus schedule to Mendocino again, and write sentences about the bus routes. Use the simple present verb tense, vocabulary, and relevant expressions of time. Follow the example.

Example: The Ukiah 11 <u>*runs every 10 minutes until 6:30 a.m.*</u>

1. The Mendocino 23 _____

2. The Fort Bragg 91 _____

3. The Little River 14 _____

4. The Ukiah 26 _____

EXERCISE 2-9

Cristian needs to get to Mendocino. He's new in town, so he goes to the bus station to ask for help. Write a dialog between Cristian and the customer service agent at the bus station. Use the bus schedule to Mendocino provided in Exercise 2-7. Refer back to relevant sections in this chapter to guide you.

Cristian: (Politely get the customer service agent's attention and use a WH question to ask about which bus goes to Mendocino.)

_____

Customer Service Agent: (Ask a clarification question to get more information.)

_____

Cristian: (Answer the question.)

_____

Customer Service Agent: (Give information about which buses go to Mendocino. Provide a few different options.)

_____

Cristian: (Ask for more information about one of the buses using a clarification question.)

_____

Customer Service Agent: (Answer the question. Use the simple present.)

_____

Cristian: (Ask for additional information, for example, where the bus stops in Mendocino.)

_____

Customer Service Agent: (Answer the question with relevant information.)

_____

Cristian: (Paraphrase the information you get to check understanding.)

_____

Customer Service Agent: (Give confirmation or correction.)

_____

Cristian: (Express gratitude.)

_____

Customer Service Agent: (Respond to the gratitude.)

_____

AUDIO

3 Describing People, Places, and Things

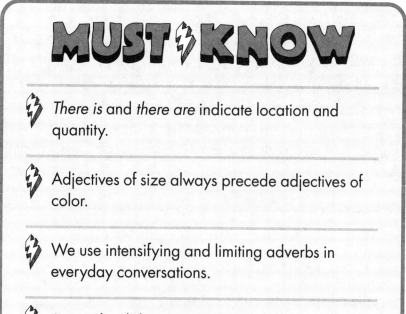

MUST KNOW

- *There is* and *there are* indicate location and quantity.

- Adjectives of size always precede adjectives of color.

- We use intensifying and limiting adverbs in everyday conversations.

- *Just* and *only* have several meanings.

- You can ask for repetition or paraphrase someone's statement to check for understanding.

sing a language successfully means effectively communicating ideas about people, places, and things. Some grammar constructions and parts of speech in English can help us do this. For example, to tell your friend about a new park in town, it's helpful to describe it with adjectives and explain its location with prepositions and directions. Let's learn how to talk about specific people, places, and things! We will begin with the grammar construction *there is/there are*.

Describing Location and Quantity with *There Is / There Are*

We use *there is* and *there are* to talk about the <u>location</u> of people, places, and things and how to find them. We also use *there is* and *there are* to talk about the <u>quantity</u> of people and things. When we talk about **one thing**, we use *there is*. When we describe **two or more things**, we use *there are*. Be sure to follow these subject-verb agreement rules. Here are some example sentences:

EXAMPLES

▸ <u>There is</u> a beach at the end of town.

▸ On the counter, <u>there is</u> a pitcher of lemonade.

▸ <u>There is</u> only one patient in the doctor's waiting room.

▸ In the musical, <u>there is</u> one female lead singer.

▸ <u>There are</u> two houses on that dead-end street.

▸ Down the stairs, <u>there are</u> some more offices.

▸ <u>There are</u> 35 students in the classroom.

▸ In the Philosophy Club, <u>there are</u> 16 members.

Forming the Affirmative

In sentences using ***there is/there are***, the subject comes after the verb. The verb is a form of BE (is or are). We normally contract ***there is***, but we don't contract ***there are***. Look at the chart below to see how to form the affirmative ***there is*** and ***there are***.

SVA (Subject-Verb Agreement)	*There*	BE Verb	Contraction	Subject	Location
Singular subject + singular BE verb	There	**is**	There's	a beach	at the end of town.
Plural subject + plural BE verb	There	**are**	-	two houses	on that dead-end street.

 IRL It is common these days to hear the grammatically incorrect "*There's* + plural noun." We know that a plural noun requires *there are*; however, many native speakers of American English use *there's* with a plural noun. I recommend you use the grammatically correct form!

Sometimes, we form the sentences with the location first. Notice that we use a comma after the location. See the examples below.

SVA (Subject-Verb Agreement)	Location	*there*	BE Verb	Contraction	Subject
Singular subject + singular BE verb	On the counter,	there	**is**	there's	a pitcher of lemonade.
Plural subject + plural BE verb	Down the stairs,	there	**are**	-	some more offices.

BTW

Let's look at some more examples of sentences with *there is* and *there are*:

EXAMPLES

▶ In the fridge, there is a homemade dessert for you.

▶ There are some very heavy textbooks on the table. Are they yours?

▶ On the door, there's a small sign. What does it say?

▶ In the glove compartment, there are two state maps. Please hand them to me.

▶ There are some wonderfully fragrant flowers on the table.

▶ In my class, there are 20 diligent students.

▶ There's a new teacher at the front of the classroom.

▶ Along the dusty road, there are beautiful wild flowers.

▶ There's something black in your hair!

▶ There are dozens of colorful Koi fish in that little pond outside the restaurant.

Practice 3-A

Notice which sentences in the last example box begin with the location or position and which sentences begin with **There is/There's** and **There are**. Put a star next to the ones that begin with **There is/There's** and **There are**. See Practice 3-A in the Answer Key to check your work.

Practice 3-B

Look around you right now. What people or things can you describe using **there is/there's** and **there are**? Find three single items and three plural items and write sentences using *there is/there's* and *there are* to describe their location. Start some sentences with **There is/There's** and **There are**, and begin some sentences with the location or position. Remember to use a comma! Also note the quantity: singular or plural.

Start with There is/*There's* and *There are* Quantity: Singular or Plural?	Start with the Location or Position Quantity: Singular or Plural?

Notice that we use prepositional phrases to indicate the location or position of people or things. These <u>prepositional phrases are underlined</u> in the sentences in the previous example box. We use prepositional phrases quite often. Some sentences even contain more than one prepositional phrase. In Chapter 2, you learned prepositions of time. Now, let's learn about **prepositions of place**!

Prepositions of Place, Position, and Movement/Direction

To indicate where someone or something is, we use prepositions and prepositional phrases. Let's first look at common prepositions of location and position.

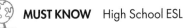

Prepositions of Location and Position					
in / inside / inside of	on	at (We're at the door.)	under / underneath / beneath / below	over / on top of / above	next to / next door to / beside
near / nearby (not: *near to*)	between A and B	behind / in back of	in front of	across from	on the corner of
at the end of	among	against	around	by	out of / outside / outside of
opposite of	before (a position preceding / in front of)	after (a position following)	past (synonym of *after* / farther than a particular place)	beyond (on or to the farther side of something)	

Now, let's look at some prepositions for movement and direction.

Prepositions for Movement and Direction			
to / toward (movement toward a destination)	into (movement toward the interior of a space)	onto (movement toward a surface)	from (movement from a destination)
down / downward	up / upward	at (He lunged <u>at</u> the dog.)	through (from one end or side of something to the other end or side)

Prepositional Phrases

Notice in the ten example sentences on page 72 that a preposition plus other words describe the location or position of people and things. The underlined words in each of these example sentences form a prepositional phrase of place, position, or movement, and two of the sentences have two prepositional phrases. What is a phrase? A phrase is two or more words that do *not* contain a subject and a verb. This group of words usually acts as *one part of speech.* For example, prepositional phrases act like prepositions, and noun phrases act like nouns. Let's learn what prepositional phrases are, how to form them, and how to use them. In the following sentences, notice the underlined prepositional phrases of location. Take a look at the <u>double underlined phrases</u>, too. These are also prepositional phrases, but they don't describe place, position, or movement.

EXAMPLES

▶ There are some fragrant flowers <u>on the wooden bistro table</u>.

▶ <u>In this art class</u>, there are 20 students.

▶ There's a substitute teacher <u>in line</u> <u>in the cafeteria</u>.

▶ <u>Above the automatic garage door</u>, there is an emergency key.

▶ Jake enjoys coffee <u>at the corner coffee shop</u>.

▶ Jake's sister prefers tea <u>from the local teahouse</u>.

▶ Michaela walks <u>around the manmade lake</u> <u>with Tina</u> every sunny Saturday morning.

▶ On Saturday evenings, the Robinson family drives <u>to their favorite church</u> <u>for the spiritual service</u>.

▶ Every Sunday morning, Sammy goes <u>to what she calls "the best brunch place ever."</u>

▶ My boyfriend and I bike <u>to the huge farmer's market</u> <u>by the lake</u> and shop <u>for healthy food</u>.

▶ Sometimes we see our friends <u>at the prepared food section</u> and eat <u>with them</u>.

▶ Do you prefer walking or biking <u>to it</u>?

What does each prepositional phrase begin with? That's correct: a preposition. Following the preposition is the rest of the prepositional phrase. We form prepositional phrases with a preposition plus some version of a noun such as a noun, pronoun, noun phrase, or noun clause. See how to form these phrases below.

Prepositional Phrase: Preposition + Object of the Preposition Object of the Preposition: Noun, Pronoun, Noun Phrase, or Noun Clause				
Preposition	Object of the Preposition			
	Noun	Pronoun	Noun Phrase (Modifier/s + noun or pronoun) modifiers = articles, adjectives, adverbs	Noun Clause (WH question word + S + V) WH question words = where, when, what, why, how, etc.
on			the wooden bistro table	
in			this art class	
in			line	
in			the cafeteria	
above			the automatic garage door	
at			the corner coffee shop	
from			the local teahouse	
around			the manmade lake	
with	Tina*			
to			their favorite church	
for			the spiritual service*	
to				what she calls "the best brunch place ever"
to			the huge farmer's market	
by			the lake	
for			healthy food*	
at			the prepared food section	
with		them*		
to		it		

Note: * Indicates a prepositional phrase that doesn't describe place, position, or movement.

Practice 3-C

Check out below some more examples of prepositional phrases used to show location, position, or movement of people and things. Underline the prepositional phrases you find. Double underline any prepositional phrases that do not describe location, position, or movement. Then, check your answers in Practice 3-C in the Answer Key.

There are some apples in the pantry.	Under the back porch, there's some firewood.
After the gas station, there's a three-way intersection.	My car is next to the red sports car.
At the crooked stop sign, take a right.	She walked toward the store entrance.
They arrived at the hospital just in time.	There's a cell phone on the desk.
My exam is in the regular classroom.	Are we walking to where he parked his car?
Take a left just before the big grocery store.	Beyond the parking lot, there is a lovely French café.

Now that you are familiar with the use of ***there is/there are***, let's look at how to form negative statements, yes/no questions, WH questions, and tag questions. Notice the use of prepositional phrases of place, position, and movement.

Forming the Negative

Sometimes, we talk about what does *not* exist or what is *not* located somewhere, so we use ***there is/there are*** in the negative form. Note that we usually use the contraction of the negative ***there is*** and ***there are*** by contracting the BE verb and ***not***.

There	BE Verb	Negative/ Contraction	Subject	Location
There	**is**	**not (isn't)**	a student	in the hallway.
There	**are**	**not (aren't)**	enough cookies	on the plate.
There	**is**	**not (isn't)**	a hair salon	on this block.
There	**are**	**not (aren't)**	any gas stations	around here.

Forming Yes/No Questions

To find out if something exists, ask a yes/no question with ***there is*** or ***there are***. Notice that *any* is used with negatives and questions.

BE Verb	There	Subject	Location
Is	there	a convenience store	near your house?
Are	there	any public restrooms	here?

Answering Yes/No Questions

When we ask a yes/no question using *there is/there are*, the answer is usually short. Notice that we often use contractions in answers unless it's affirmative, in which case we do NOT contract. See examples of answers below.

Yes/No Question with *There Is/There Are*	Answer
Is there a laptop in this classroom?	Yes, there is. (~~Yes, there's.~~)
	No, there isn't.
Are there any good movies to see?	Yes, there are. (~~Yes, there're.~~)
	No, there aren't.

Often when we give a short answer, we also provide more information or an explanation. See the following examples.

Yes/No Question with *There Is/There Are*	Answer + Additional Information/Explanation
Is there a laptop in this classroom?	No, there isn't. The teacher has the laptop in another classroom.
Are there any good movies to see?	Yes, there are. The scary one looks really good, and I want to see the latest *Star Wars* movie, too.
Excuse me. Are there any public restrooms here?	Yes, there are. At the end of this parking lot, there are restrooms.
Pardon me. Is there a library close by?	No, there isn't. The public library is on the other side of town.

Forming WH Questions of Location

When you want to locate someone or something, ask a WH question with **where**. We commonly use **there is** with **where**. Note that it's less common to use **where** with **there are**.

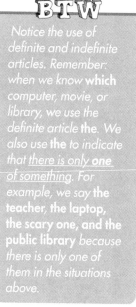

Where	BE Verb	There	Subject
Where	is	there	a grocery store?
Where	are	there	places to eat?

Sometimes, we omit **there** as in the example sentences below.

Where + *There Is*	*Where* Only
Where is there a secondhand clothing store?	Where is a secondhand clothing store?
Where is there a good coffee shop in this area?	Where is a good coffee shop in this area?

Forming WH Questions of Quantity

To count the number or amount of people or things, ask a WH question with either **how many** *or* **how much**. We use *how many* to quantify countable nouns such as books, teachers, trees, and birds. However, we use *how much* to measure uncountable nouns. Uncountable, or noncount, nouns are too difficult to count or they are in a form that must be measured. Examples of noncount nouns are tangible items such as hair, water, oil, gas, rice, flour, and sand. Noncount nouns are also intangible things such as ideas, beliefs, values, and concepts. Examples of these are freedom, love, charity, and loyalty. Use *how many* only with *there are*. Use *how much* with **all** noncount nouns. Read the examples.

How Many/ How Much	Subject	BE Verb	There	Rest of the Sentence if Necessary
How many	houses	are	there	on this boulevard?
How much	sugar	is	there	in the cupboard?

For questions with *how many*, we **always** use the plural BE verb *are*. We always ask, "How many (plural count noun) are there?" Even when we think there is only one, we ask the question in the plural form. It is grammatically incorrect to ask, "How many is there?"

 IRL Even though this question is grammatically incorrect, many Americans use it. It is common in daily life to hear "How many is there?" However, I recommend you use the correct form of this question.

Sometimes, we don't add a subject. This happens when we already know what the noun is. Here are some examples of this.

How Many/ How Much	BE Verb	There	Rest of the Sentence if Necessary	Reason
How many	are	there	on this boulevard?	The speakers already know what the subject is—houses.
How much	is	there	in the cupboard?	The speakers identified the noun (sugar) already in the conversation.

Answering Quantity Questions

To answer *how many* and *how much* questions, we use the appropriate form of *there is* or *there are*. Sometimes, we only answer with the quantity. Read the examples below:

EXAMPLES

▶ **Question:** How many houses are there on this boulevard?

▶ **Answer:** There are fourteen houses on this boulevard./There are 14. / Fourteen.

▶ **Question:** How much sugar is there in the cupboard?

▶ **Answer:** There isn't any sugar in the cupboard./There isn't any./None.*

***Note:** We never answer with only the word *any*.

Using Adjectives to Describe People, Places, and Things

Adjectives describe **nouns,** which are **people, places, and things**. An adjective precedes the noun it modifies, or it follows a stative verb. You can learn more about stative verbs in Chapter 5. See explanations and examples of adjectives in the table.

Place the **adjective before** the noun:

Adjective + noun

Example sentences:

That's a <u>colorful sweater</u>.

adj = colorful

n = sweater

We live in a <u>blue house</u>.

adj = blue

n = house

Place adjectives that **describe a state, condition, or feeling after** the stative verb:

Subject + stative verb + adjective

Example sentences:

It'<u>s good</u>.

stative verb = is

adj = good

They <u>seem angry</u>.

stative verb = seem

adj = angry

Word Order

In English, there's a prescribed order for adjectives. Most native speakers aren't aware of this word order rule, but they notice when adjectives are in the wrong order. See the table below.

Categories of Adjectives	Examples
Determiner (Learn more about determiners in Chapter 4.)	**Articles:** a, an, the **Personal pronouns:** my, your, his, our **Demonstrative adjectives:** this, that, those, these
Quantity	one, several, multiple
Opinion or observation	funny, beautiful, wondrous
Size	large, tiny, medium, short
Physical quality	crowded, thin, smooth
Shape	round, square, rectangular
Age	young, middle-aged, ancient
Color	yellow, purple, green
Origin or religion	Spanish, Egyptian Buddhist
Material	wooden, tin, silk, marble, metal
Type	multi-purpose, two-sided
Purpose or attribute noun	drinking, mixing, baking baseball, commercial, recreational

(Rows from Size through Color are grouped under the side label: Physical Description)

You may use one or many adjectives to describe a noun. If you use two or more adjectives **from the same category**, you must **separate them with a comma**. For example, *funny* and *friendly* are both adjectives from the opinion/observation category, so a comma between them is necessary. However, no comma is necessary when you use adjectives from different categories. Read the following examples.

These <u>small</u> <u>purple</u> flowers grow in spring.
    size   color

The <u>large</u> <u>crowded</u> <u>exhibit</u> hall is <u>noisy</u>.
  size   attribute   opinion
    physical quality

The <u>playful</u> <u>blue and white</u> dolphins swim all day.
 observation   color

My <u>red</u> <u>race</u> car has a <u>sexy</u>, <u>glittery</u> paint job.
  color type   opinion observation

She wants <u>large</u> <u>shiny</u> <u>gold</u> hoop earrings for her birthday.
       size   quality color/material

hoop earrings = compound noun

There is a <u>large</u> <u>grassy</u> dog park down the street.
       size   quality

dog park = compound noun

Look around you and find one person, one place, and one thing to describe. Use adjectives you know or from the categories above in the correct word order and write three sentences below. Then mark the category for each adjective. Check your comma usage. Be creative and have fun!

1. Person: _____

2. Place: _____

3. Thing: _____

Comparatives and Superlatives

It's helpful to compare and contrast people, places, and things to describe them. We use comparatives and superlatives to do this. Read the following examples and identify the comparatives and superlatives in each sentence. Check your answers in Practice 3-D in the Answer Key.

Practice 3-D

▶ Rosie is the tallest person in the room.

▶ That building is shorter than the hospital.

▶ The mansion is more ornate than the church.

▶ Main Street is wider than River Road.

▶ My sister is more fun than my brother.

▶ The ferry building is the closest one to the bay.

We provide more information when we modify comparatives and superlatives. Modifiers such as *a lot*, *much*, *slightly*, and *by far* are commonly used. Let's take a look at how to form comparatives and superlatives. Then, study the modifiers, their positions, and some examples.

Forming Comparatives		
1. adjective + -er + than	For shorter adjectives, use the –er form of the adjective	<u>stronger than</u> my boyfriend <u>older than</u> ancient ruins <u>happier than</u> my puppy
2. *more* + adjective + than	For longer adjectives, add *more* before the adjective	<u>more colorful than</u> a rainbow <u>more talented than</u> me <u>more intelligent than</u> mankind

Common Modifiers for Comparatives: a lot / much / a bit / slightly

Modifier	Comparative	Example Sentences
a lot	duller than	The vintage mirror is <u>a lot duller than</u> the new one.
much	bigger than	The skyscraper <u>is much bigger than</u> the clock tower.
a bit	sunnier than	Today is <u>a bit sunnier than</u> yesterday.
slightly	smaller than	This gemstone is <u>slightly smaller than</u> that one.

Forming Superlatives		
1. *the +* superlative *(–est)*	For shorter adjectives, add *the* + the *–est* form of the adjective	<u>the silliest</u> child <u>the brightest</u> star <u>the highest</u> mountain
2. *the most +* adjective	For longer adjectives, add *the most* before the adjective	<u>the most beautiful</u> city <u>the most delicious</u> seafood <u>the most horrendous</u> storm
3. *the best/the worst* + noun	These phrases are not followed by another adjective.	<u>the best</u> restaurant <u>the worst</u> book

Common Modifiers for Superlatives: easily / by far / one of

Modifier	Superlative	Example Sentences
easily	the tallest	In this small town, the church is <u>easily the tallest</u> building.
easily	the worst	The assigned book for this class is <u>easily the worst</u> book I've ever read.
by far	the highest	That one is <u>by far the highest</u> mountain.
by far	the most athletic	Jesse is <u>by far the most athletic</u> student here.
one of	the strongest	Gerard is <u>one of the strongest</u> guys in school.
one of	the most wonderful	<u>One of the most wonderful</u> days of my life was my high school graduation day.

Now you try it: Write down three sentences that describe people, places, and things in your life. Use comparatives and superlatives with modifiers. Be creative!

1. Person: _____

2. Place: _____

3. Thing: _____

Using *-ed* and *-ing* Forms of Adjectives

Another type of adjective is formed with **–ed** or **–ing**. Some learners of English are confused by these adjectives, so let's take a close look at how we use these different forms. Read the sentences below, which contain these types of adjectives.

EXAMPLES

▶ I'm so tired after that workout.

▶ That workout routine is tiring.

▶ They're confused by the math equation.

▶ The math equation is confusing to them.

▶ She's excited to graduate high school!

▶ Graduating high school is exciting!

▶ My cousins are bored at the party.

▶ The party is boring.

Practice 3-E

Do you notice the difference between the **–ed** and **–ing** forms of the adjectives in the example sentences above? <u>Underline</u> them. Then, check your answers in Practice 3-E in the Answer Key. How are they different? Can you guess the rules? Try to guess the rules before you continue reading.

There are two basic rules:

Rule 1	Use the *–ed* form to describe **how someone is affected** by someone or something. This means that someone **experiences a feeling**.
Rule 2	Use the *–ing* form to describe **the effect something or someone has** on someone or something. In other words, someone or something **causes an effect**.

The chart below demonstrates these rules in sentences.

Adjective Type	Example Sentences	Meaning
-ed **form**	Paul is <u>confused</u> in math class.	Paul experiences confusion in math class.
-ing **form**	Math class is <u>confusing</u>.	Math class causes confusion.
-ed **form**	We are <u>relaxed</u> on vacation.	We experience calmness and relaxation on vacation.
-ing **form**	Our vacation on the beach is <u>relaxing</u>.	A vacation on the beach causes a calm feeling.

Below are some other *–ed* and *–ing* adjectives we use.

thrilled / thrilling	amazed / amazing	annoyed / annoying
exhausted / exhausting	disgusted / disgusting	interested / interesting
shocked / shocking	depressed / depressing	amused / amusing

Using Adverbs to Intensify

We often use adverbs to **intensify an adjective**, or make the adjective stronger or weaker. When an intensifier adverb strengthens an adjective, it's called a booster or amplifier because it boosts, or amplifies, the adjective. However, when an intensifier adverb weakens an adjective, it's called a "down toner" because it tones down, or weakens, the adjective. To use an intensifier adverb with an adjective, put the adverb first. Although we regularly use intensifier adverbs in conversation, we use them less often in writing. Here are some notes of caution about using intensifiers in writing:

- Use them only when necessary in writing: Do not overuse them.

- In conversation, we repeat intensifiers to emphasize a point. However, do not double them in writing. (Example: He is very ~~very~~ happy.)

■ Some adjectives are absolute, so they do not require an intensifier. (Example: The project was ~~extremely~~ impossible to complete on time. *Impossible* is clear by itself. It's absolute: it means no possibility. Something cannot be less possible than not possible.)

See a list of common intensifier adverbs below shown in order from stronger to weaker.

Booster intensifiers:

Extremely • Incredibly • Awfully • Terribly • Very • Quite • Really • So • Rather • Fairly • Pretty

Stronger ———————————————————————→ **Weaker**

Down toner intensifiers:

A bit • A little • A little bit • A tad

See how these work in the table below.

Intensifier Adverb	Adjective	Example Sentences
extremely	dangerous	Climbing Half Dome is <u>extremely dangerous</u>.
awfully	kind	That is an <u>awfully kind</u> gesture.
pretty	big	It's a <u>pretty big</u> problem.
so	lazy	My brother is <u>so lazy</u>.
a little bit	worried	I'm <u>a little bit worried</u> about my grade.
too	short	Rex is <u>too short</u> for the rollercoaster ride.

BTW

The adverb **too** *gives an adjective a negative meaning. Check out the example sentences below that demonstrate this.*

- *This quiz is <u>too hard</u>.* = **It's more difficult than you would like. You want it to be easier.**
- *There are <u>too many</u> questions on this survey!* = **There are more questions than you want. You prefer fewer questions.**
- *My soup is <u>too hot</u>.* = **It's hotter than you prefer. You want it to cool down.**

Using Adverbs to Limit

We also use adverbs to **limit an adjective**. A limiting adverb restricts an adjective. Just as with an intensifier adverb, we generally put the limiting adverb before the adjective it modifies. Some common limiting adverbs are:

almost	nearly	merely	hardly	just	only

Notes and Tips

- These limiting adverbs can also modify verbs.

- In writing, place limiting adverbs carefully because the position can change the meaning of the sentence.

- Remember: The adverb precedes the adjective it restricts.

Limiting Adverb	Adjective	Example Sentences
nearly	20	She's <u>nearly 20</u> years old.
hardly	correct	That answer is <u>hardly correct</u>.
just	one	There's <u>just one</u> person in line.
only	happy	He's <u>only happy</u> when he gets an A.

Just and *Only*

The words *just* and *only* have several different definitions and uses. However, you can also use them interchangeably. See a few uses and definitions below.

Just and *Only* as Interchangeable Limiting Adverbs

Definition	Example Sentences
no more than	The engine died, and the car is <u>only</u> three years old.
	The engine died, and the car is <u>just</u> three years old.
	There were <u>only</u> easy questions on the test.
	There were <u>just</u> easy questions on the test.
less than desired	There are <u>only</u> 10 minutes left.
	There are <u>just</u> 10 minutes left.
	She has <u>only</u> a few cookies.
	She has <u>just</u> a few cookies.

Just as an Intensifier Adverb

positively; really	Your puppy is <u>just</u> so cute!
	Note: *Only* cannot be used here.

Note: Notice other definitions of *just* and *only*. In these cases, they are *not* interchangeable.

Part of Speech/Definition	Example Sentences
Just	
(adv) very recently	He <u>just</u> got off the plane.
(adv) exactly; precisely	That is <u>just</u> what she wanted!
Only	
(adj) singular	She's the <u>only</u> woman I love.
	I'm an <u>only</u> child.
(conjunction) means the same as *but*	We're both college students, <u>only</u> she goes to a private university.
	We're both college students, <u>but</u> she goes to a private university.

Using Imperatives

Imperatives are useful for giving directions and instructions. You find imperatives in recipes, instruction manuals, and directions to locations. When you ask for directions or instructions, most people reply with imperatives. Look at some example sentences with imperatives.

<u>Walk</u> around the park to find the coffee shop.

To order it online, <u>go</u> to the website.

When the water simmers, <u>add</u> the cinnamon sticks.

<u>Make</u> a left at the intersection.

Forming Imperatives

To form an imperative sentence, use the base form of a verb. The **base form of a verb** is a verb with **no verb endings**. For example, we do not add **–s** or **–ing** or **–ed** to the verb. Rather, we use the verb with nothing added. The subject is *you*, but we do not write or say *you*. It doesn't matter if the subject is the singular or plural *you*. Check out the following table and examples.

(Subject Pronoun *You*)	Base Form of Verb	Rest of Sentence
(You)	**Make**	a left at the intersection.

EXAMPLES

▶ (You) <u>Walk</u> around the park to find the coffee shop.

▶ When the water simmers, (you) <u>add</u> the cinnamon sticks.

▶ To order it online, (you) <u>go</u> to the website.

Here are examples of correct and incorrect imperative sentences. Notice that the correct form does **not** add any ending to the verb.

Correct: <u>Continue</u> straight until you reach the gas station.
Incorrect: ~~Continuing~~ straight until you reach the gas station.
Incorrect: ~~Continues~~ straight until you reach the gas station.

Practice 3-F

Let's practice using the imperative form. Underline the <u>imperative form of the verb</u> in each of the following sentences, and then check the answers in Practice 3-F in the Answer Key.

1. At 5:00 p.m., turn on the news.

2. To start the car, push the key in and step on the brake at the same time.

3. Bake the pizza in the oven until the cheese is slightly brown.

4. Switch the lights on, please!

5. Be nice and gentle. This glass vase is delicate.

6. Enter the theater quietly.

7. Eat all your vegetables!

8. Please go to the whiteboard and write your answers on the appropriate lines.

Forming Negative Imperatives

When we *don't* want someone to do something, we use the negative form of imperatives. We use **do not** or the contraction **don't**. Remember, the unspoken subject is **you**, so we never use **does** or **doesn't**. Check out the table.

Do	Negative	Base Form of Verb	Rest of Sentence	Example Sentences
Do	not	turn	right at the light.	Do not turn right at the light.
Do	n't	turn	right at the light.	Don't turn right at the light.

Now, let's look at some more examples.

1. Don't be late!

2. It's very valuable. Please be careful! Don't break it.

3. Don't take a right there. Take a left.

4. For the test, don't copy anyone else. Do your own work.

5. Don't forget to bring the flowers, please!

6. To beat your opponent, don't waste time.

7. Don't be silly. This is serious.

8. Don't park on the street. Park in the parking lot.

Practice 3-G

In the example sentences above, underline the <u>affirmative imperatives</u> and double underline the <u>negative imperatives</u>. See Practice 3-G in the Answer Key to check your answers.

Requesting and Giving Instructions and Directions

To learn how to do something, we ask for **instructions**. To learn how to get somewhere, we ask for **directions**. There are several expressions for requesting information such as instructions or directions, and we generally use the imperative form to give instructions and directions. Let's look at these expressions and the imperative in sample conversations below.

Asking for Instructions

Take a look at these sample expressions and conversations to see how we can ask someone for instructions on how to do something. In the situations, the requests are double underlined and the imperatives are underlined.

Useful Expressions:	Add Anytime:
How do I (+ base form of verb)?	Please
How can I (+ base form of verb)?	
How should I (+ base form of verb)?	

Situation 1: A high school science teacher gives the class an assignment, and a student in the class isn't sure how to complete the task.

Ms. Jennings: For homework, study pages 33–37 and then complete the assignment on page 38. Come to class with your work on paper, which I will collect.

Cecilia raises hand.

Ms. Jennings: Yes, Cecilia?

Cecilia: I don't understand the instructions on page 38. How can I conduct this experiment at home?

Ms. Jennings: Good question. Use your kitchen sink, a glass jar, regular food coloring, and tap water. Follow the step-by-step instructions in the book. Also, use the math equation we learned this week. Take notes on every reaction you see. Put the math and your observations on paper, so I can see all of your work: show me every step. Use a calculator if necessary, but you still need to show me every step. Otherwise, you will lose points.

Cecilia: So, it's okay to use tap water. Okay, I got it. Thank you.

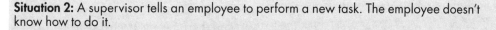

Situation 2: A supervisor tells an employee to perform a new task. The employee doesn't know how to do it.

Julio: Sean, please <u>close up</u> the store tonight. I can't be here to do it.

Sean: I've never closed before. <u>How should I</u> do that?

Julio: Oh, you've never closed? Okay, well there are instructions under the counter. Carefully <u>follow</u> all five steps. <u>Call</u> or <u>text</u> me any questions. Barry usually closes and he's around, so you can call him, too. <u>Make</u> sure to turn on the alarm before you lock the door. I receive a notification from the alarm company when it's turned on and off, so I'll know it's done. Got it?

Sean: Sure, okay. It'll be fine. I have your number and Barry's number, too, so I'm good.

Julio: You can do it, Sean. Thank you.

Asking for Directions

Take a look at these sample expressions and conversations to see how we can ask someone for directions on how to get somewhere or how to find something.

Useful Expressions: Notice the underlined alternatives within these expressions. Be creative: Try other phrases and combinations!

To get someone's attention:

Excuse me./Pardon me.

Note that "pardon me" is more formal.

Add anytime: Please

To ask a WH question about a location:

<u>Could / can</u> you tell me where there's <u>a / the</u> . . . <u>near / around</u> here?

<u>Do / Would</u> you know where the closest . . . is?

How <u>can / do</u> I get to a / the . . . ?

Where <u>can / do</u> I find a / the . . . ?

How far is the . . . from here?

(continued)

Paraphrase to check understanding:

To paraphrase is to say the same thing in another way. This is helpful to check if you understand the instructions or directions. Refer to the Paraphrasing to Check Your Understanding section later in this chapter for more information.

So, (paraphrase or repeat directions) . . . ?

So, you are saying that I <u>need to / should</u> (+ base form of verb) . . . ?

In other words (paraphrase or repeat directions) . . . ?

To ask additional information:

About how far is that?/How long will it take me to walk / drive / get there?

To state understanding:

I got it./Okay./Right—okay!

To express gratitude (smile!):

Thank you!/Thank you very much!/Thank you so much!/Thanks!

Here are some common expressions for locations:

to take / make a right / left

to turn / go right / left

to bear right / left

to stay / go / keep straight

on the / your right / left

on the right / left side of the street

to cross the street

to go to the intersection

to go through / past the intersection

just before the . . .

just after / past the . . .

Situation 3: Irving is in an unfamiliar town, and he needs to get groceries. He **pulls** his car **into*** a gas station to ask someone for directions.

*Note: *To pull into* is a phrasal verb that means to drive into an area. This is different from *to pull over*, which means to drive to the side / shoulder of the road and stop the car.

Irving: Hello, excuse me!

Person at gas pump: Yeah?

Irving: <u>Could you tell me where there's a</u> grocery store near here?

Person at gas pump: Oh yeah sure. There's a small one two blocks from here, and there's a big one just off the highway.

Irving: The small one is perfect.

Person at gas pump: Okay that's easy. Just <u>go</u> down this street for one block, and then <u>make</u> a right. <u>Drive</u> two blocks down, and it's on your right.

Irving: So, one block down here, take a right, and two more blocks?

Person at gas pump: Yup.

Irving: Thank you!

Person at gas pump: No problem.

Situation 4: Cheryl is **on foot*** in a part of town she doesn't know well. She is hungry and wants a sandwich, so she asks someone at a bus stop.

*Note: To be **on foot** means to *walk rather than to bicycle or drive.*

Cheryl: Excuse me. <u>Would you know where there's a</u> good place to get a sandwich nearby?

Person at bus stop: Yeah sure. There's a deli down there and a soup and salad place over there.

Cheryl: How about the deli?

Person at bus stop: Just <u>walk</u> a few blocks down Main Street until you see the library. The deli is across the street from the library.

Cheryl: Is the soup and salad place closer?

Person at bus stop: It's about the same. <u>Go</u> up Main, <u>turn</u> left on Aspen, and <u>walk</u> to the end of the street.

Cheryl: Okay, so Main and to the end of Aspen Street.

Person at bus stop: <u>Don't forget</u> to go *left* on Aspen.

Cheryl: Yes, left on Aspen. Thank you so much!

Person at bus stop: No worries.

> ▶ Use rising pitch when paraphrasing to elicit an answer to your question.
>
> ▶ Use falling pitch with WH questions that ask for additional information.

Practice 3-H

You learned ***there is/there are***, the imperative form, prepositions of place, and expressions for instructions and directions. Look at the situations starting on page 94 again. The requests and imperatives are already underlined. Now, identify the other items in situations 1-4: Put parentheses ( ) around the prepositional phrases, circle the prepositions, and highlight ***there is/there are***. Check your answers under Practice 3-H in the Answer Key.

Checking Your Understanding

In the last section, you saw some expressions to check understanding. Sometimes, it's difficult to understand instructions or directions for several reasons: Someone may speak too quickly or use unfamiliar vocabulary. A phone connection might be weak, so it's difficult to clearly hear words. Don't worry, though, because when you want to be sure you understand, you can check in two simple ways. One way is to ask for repetition, and another way is to paraphrase, or confirm, what you understand. First, let's practice asking for repetition.

Asking for Repetition

When we don't understand someone's words clearly, we can ask them to repeat what they said. It's common to ask for repetition, so don't be shy. I strongly recommend you frequently practice asking for repetition. When it becomes comfortable for you to ask anyone for repetition, communication will feel a lot easier. There are many ways to ask for repetition, so practice all of them. Let's look at a few expressions we can use.

Expressions to Ask for Repetition

Note: You can use *I'm sorry* or *excuse me* or *pardon me* interchangeably. *Pardon me* is more formal.

Could you please repeat that?	Excuse me, what was that?
I'm sorry. I didn't catch that. Could you repeat that, please?	Pardon me. Could you speak more slowly, please? I'm learning English. (smile)
I'm sorry. I didn't understand what you said. Could you please say that again?	Excuse me. Could you say that again, please?

PRONUNCIATION

▶ When you ask for repetition to check understanding, use rising pitch to show uncertainty. This makes it clear to the listener that you need a response. See the Appendix for other pitch changes.

▶ Use falling pitch to show understanding.

Now that you know some ways to ask for repetition, look at two example conversations with these expressions. In the following two scenarios, Lucy gives Jorge directions. He doesn't understand her directions completely, so he asks for repetition.

Example Conversations

Directions	Asking for Repetition
Lucy: Once you get to the bakery, go right and you'll see the bookstore next to the shoe store on the left.	**Jorge:** Excuse me. I didn't understand what you said. Could you say that again, please?
Lucy: Go straight through this intersection and it's on your right after the gas station.	**Jorge:** I'm sorry. Could you speak more slowly, please? I'm learning English. (smile)

Success Strategy: Naming the Elephant Revisited

In Chapter 1, you learned that an important strategy to ensure successful communication is to **name the elephant in the room**. Do you remember what this expression means? It means that you **explicitly state the obvious**. In this case, you state that you are **learning English**. You can see an example of this in the second conversation between Lucy and Jorge on the last page. Remember: it's okay to say that you are an English language learner. You can name the elephant in the room, and you can also ask for help. This is a **simple but powerful strategy for communicating successfully**. No matter what level of English you speak, when you state the situation, others can more easily support you. Here are some benefits to using this communication strategy:

1. When you state the reality of the situation, you create honesty and openness.

2. Telling others that you are learning English shows that you are responsible.

3. Stating the obvious relieves tension and gives others a greater opportunity to connect with you.

4. Using this communication strategy empowers you.

5. Over time, naming the elephant in the room will build your confidence.

What are some ways we name the elephant in the room? Do you remember from Chapter 1? Close the book now and make a list of the ways you can remember from Chapter 1. Then, look at the variety of expressions you can use below. With all these expressions, remember to smile to show you are sincere.

Expressions to Use to Name the Elephant in the Room

- I'm learning English.

- I'm practicing my English pronunciation.

- I'm practicing my English listening and speaking skills.

- My English coach / teacher / mentor / instructor / tutor wants me to ask for . . . (repetition / clarification).

- My English pronunciation coach / teacher / instructor / tutor says I should check my understanding.

Use any of these or mix them up to create your own. Experiment with different expressions and see what feels best to you. Use one of these expressions the next time you need to ask for repetition or clarification. Go for it!

Paraphrasing to Check Your Understanding

Now that you understand effective ways to ask for repetition, let's study paraphrasing to check understanding. We studied this briefly in the directions section of this chapter. You want to be sure to understand instructions or directions, so a great strategy is to paraphrase. This means to say something in another way using different words. There are several ways to begin a paraphrase. See below for some example expressions. Note that we often use **So** in informal responses.

Expressions to Paraphrase General Information		Expressions to Paraphrase Instructions/Directions
So, . . . ?	Informal	**So,** I should / need to / must . . . (base form of verb)?
Are you saying . . . ?		**Are you saying that** I should / need to / must . . . (base form of verb)?
Do you mean . . . ?		
What you mean / are saying is . . . ?		**To make sure I have this right,** I should / need to / must . . . (base form of verb)?
To make sure I have this right, . . . ?		**To make sure I understand,** I should / need to / must . . . (base form of verb)?
To make sure I understand, . . . ?		
If I understand you correctly, . . . ?	Formal	**If I understand you correctly,** I should / need to / must . . . (base form of verb)?

Now let's see these expressions in use. In the following scenario, Lou gives Sarafina directions. See three ways Sarafina can check her understanding by paraphrasing.

Three Examples of Paraphrasing

Directions	Paraphrase for Understanding
Lou: Once you reach the tennis courts, take a right and the movie theater is across from the donut shop.	**Sarafina response 1:** <u>What you mean is</u> after I take a right, the movie theater is opposite the donut shop?
	Sarafina response 2: <u>So,</u> after I make a right at the tennis courts, it's opposite the donut shop?
	Sarafina response 3: <u>So, I should</u> take a right at the tennis courts, and the movie theater is across the street from the donut shop?

Paraphrasing in Writing

Paraphrasing is a way to say or write someone else's words in a different way. In speaking, we use it to check our understanding. In writing, however, we use paraphrasing to state information from an author or other source. In other words, to use ideas from someone else's work in your own writing, you must express those ideas in a different way. It's important to give credit to the original author, too, to avoid plagiarizing. Paraphrases usually contain more words than the original statement. Here are some effective steps to paraphrasing:

Step 1: Read the original text multiple times to be sure you understand it. The writing may be a section of a book, a poem, part of an essay or article, an excerpt, or another kind of work. Be sure to understand the writer's message clearly.

Step 2: Hide the original text and write down **in your own words** your understanding of that section of writing.

Step 3: Check the accuracy of your paraphrase by referring back to the original source. Once you are certain you captured the meaning of the original writing, you can move on to the next step. It is a good idea to have an instructor, mentor, or tutor check your paraphrase, too.

Step 4: Follow these guidelines to ensure that you paraphrase rather than plagiarize:
- Change the structure of the sentences by:
  - Starting with a different point
  - Using different word order by creating and changing phrases and clauses
  - Writing more sentences instead of using multiple clauses
- Use different words by:
  - Using synonyms
  - Creating phrases that describe a key word rather than using a synonym
  - Writing different forms of key words
  - Using antonyms or opposite ideas to create contrast

Note 1: You must use both of these strategies to avoid plagiarizing.

Note 2: Paraphrases are usually longer than the original text.

Step 5: Introduce your paraphrase with a transition phrase such as:
- What XX is saying is (XX = name of author)
- XX means that . . .
- XX is making the point that . . .
- XX's message is . . .

Step 6: Be sure to integrate your paraphrase properly into your written work. Also, **cite the work** to give credit to the author. Otherwise, it is plagiarism. There are many ways to do this. Check with your instructor or educational institution to discover which writing style is preferred: MLA Style, APA Style, Chicago Manual of Style, and so on.

Study two examples of written paraphrases below.

Original Text	Paraphrased Idea
"Injustice anywhere is a threat to justice everywhere." —Martin Luther King Jr., Letter from a Birmingham Jail, 1963	What Martin Luther King Jr. is saying is that if someone is treated unjustly in one part of the world, it negatively affects justice for everyone else regardless of his or her geographic location.
"To make a great dream come true, the first requirement is a great capacity to dream; the second is persistence." —Cesar E. Chavez	Cesar Chavez's message is that two important things are required to achieve a dream. One is for a person to be able to create big dreams, and the other is to persist in making those dreams come true.

Practice 3-I

Look back at these two examples and identify the phrase that introduces each paraphrase. Then, identify which strategies helped this student paraphrase. Did he or she use synonyms, different forms of the key words, and/or more sentences to explain it? What other strategies can you find? Check your answers in Practice 3-I in the Answer Key.

Dialogue: At the Bus Station

Now that you have learned how to use the simple present verb tense with expressions of time for public transportation and set schedules, let's see how it all works together in a conversation. In this conversation, Manfred is at the bus station in Albion. He doesn't know the bus schedule, and he needs to get to Main Street in Mendocino. Read the conversation between him and a customer service agent at the bus station. Notice the use of imperatives, adjectives, prepositional phrases, verb tenses, time expressions, vocabulary, and strategies for checking understanding.

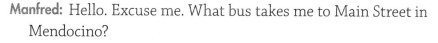

Manfred: Hello. Excuse me. What bus takes me to Main Street in Mendocino?

Customer Service Agent: When do you want to go?

Manfred: I'd like to get there by 3 p.m. today.

Customer Service Agent: It's 1 p.m. now. The #5 Albion bus leaves at 2 p.m.

Manfred: Are there any buses that leave sooner than 2 p.m.?

Customer Service Agent: Not today. It's Sunday, so the buses run on a holiday schedule. The #5 is your best option.

Manfred: Okay, thank you. Where does the bus pick up passengers?

Customer Service Agent: In the back of the station. Look for the large green sign that says "Albion #5" and wait there.

Manfred: Okay, so I need to wait at the #5 sign out back?

Customer Service Agent: You got it.

Manfred: Thanks so much! =)

Customer Service Agent: You're so welcome. =)

Practice 3-J

Can you find where the simple present is used? <u>Underline</u> every instance it's used. Do you see where the paraphrase to check understanding is? <u>Double underline</u> it. Check the answers in Practice 3-J in the Answer Key.

Lecture: Languages in the United States

Read aloud the lecture below. Highlight important points and underline new vocabulary. Make notes on any reactions you have to the content of the lecture.

Languages in the United States

Languages and language learning in America are fascinating. Although the United States doesn't have an official language, English has been widely accepted as the primary language. However, there are many other languages currently being spoken in the United States, the top five of which are Spanish, Chinese (Mandarin, Cantonese, and other dialects), Tagalog, Vietnamese, and French. Most natural-born citizens in America only speak English, which means they are monolingual. According to a 2015 report from the US Census Bureau (Source: U.S. Census Bureau, 2009–2013 American Community Survey), less than 20 percent of Americans speak English and another language at home. Though a foreign language is required in high school, most American students rarely learn and understand enough of a new language to have meaningful conversations. In contrast, many residents of the United States who were born elsewhere are bilingual, trilingual, and even multilingual, or proficient in multiple languages.

There are many reasons why most Americans use only English. One reason is shame. An example of this is my personal situation: I grew up speaking only English even though my parents grew up speaking Canadian French. They spoke French at the dinner table when they *didn't* want my siblings and me to understand what they were saying. Why didn't they speak French around us? They deliberately chose *not* to speak French to us because they felt that their dialect was "too provincial." They were ashamed of it because it sounded "uneducated." It is a dialect spoken in a coastal town of Canada, and when my grandparents immigrated to the United States, they didn't attend school to learn English. Rather, they learned it on the street.* My mother and father didn't think the French from my grandparents was proper enough for us. This is so unfortunate: I could have grown up speaking two languages! Instead, I learned French as a foreign language in high school, but I never became fluent because I only used it in French class.

Another reason many Americans only speak English is because learning a new language is not easy. For adults, learning a language is much more difficult than acquiring a language as a child. Healthy children learn languages easily and naturally, whereas adults must use their cognitive learning skills. Cognition requires deliberately focusing on learning and putting in a lot of effort, while acquiring a language as a child engages the brain's natural language learning capacity: It doesn't require much effort. Many people find learning another language challenging, as it requires hard work, dedication, and a great desire to learn the language. There are many other reasons why most Americans don't speak a second language, but we won't cover those here. I acknowledge you, dear student, for embarking on this English learning adventure. Cheers to you for learning English!

*****Note:** Learning a language *on the street* means that someone doesn't learn it in school. Rather, they learn it by using it as necessary out in the world.

Success Strategy: Reading Comprehension Through Context Clues of Contrast

Sometimes, we don't fully comprehend a reading passage. Thankfully, there are words and phrases that provide clues. We call these devices **context clues**, and they help readers understand the meaning. One type of context clue is a **context clue of contrast.** These clues provide **contrast, or difference,** to help you understand the meaning of new words, phrases, or ideas. There are many contrast clues. In this section, you will learn these context clues of contrast: ***but, however, although, though, even though, whereas, while,*** and ***on the other hand***. Study these clues and example sentences in the table below. The underlined word is the <u>unfamiliar word, phrase, or idea</u>. The **context clue that introduces the contrast** is in bold, and the *contrasted information that helps us understand the meaning* is in italics. Remember: because the context clue is expressing a contrast, you will see opposition, contradiction, or difference. Once you find the contrast clue, consider the opposite or different meaning. This will help you discover the meaning. Note that ***S+V*** stands for Subject + Verb combination. Every sentence must have a subject and a verb. You'll learn more about sentence structure in Chapter 7.

Context Clues of Contrast	Example Sentences
1. **But** S+V, **but** S+V. • Place a comma and a space before ***but,*** which is a conjunction in compound sentences. • ***But*** is a coordinating conjunction, so it connects two coordinating independent clauses (simple sentences) of equal importance or emphasis. • ***But*** is the "B" in FAN<u>B</u>OYS, a list of coordinating conjunctions. • ***But*** contrasts or contradicts an idea.	Oleksander is <u>bilingual</u> in Russian and Italian, **but** he prefers to *speak only one language*: his native Russian. We know from ***but*** that <u>bilingual</u> must mean something different from *to speak only one language*. We can guess it means speaking two languages because Russian and Italian are stated.

Context Clues of Contrast	Example Sentences
2. **However** **However,** <u>S+V</u> <u>S</u>, **however,** <u>V.</u> <u>S+V</u>; **however,** <u>S+V.</u> • Place a comma after **however** when it begins a sentence. • Place the comma before and after it when it is between the subject and the verb. • Place a semicolon and a space before **however** and a comma after it when it's in the middle of a sentence connecting two independent clauses (sentences). • **However** is a conjunctive adverb used to show opposition. • In this example, it connects two independent clauses.	Prisca is a <u>polyglot</u>; **however,** Danielle can *only use one language proficiently and thinks five languages seems impossible.* We can guess from the use of **however** that a <u>polyglot</u> contrasts with *only use one language proficiently and thinks five languages seems impossible.* We can guess that a polyglot speaks five languages. Wow!
3. **On the other hand** **On the other hand,** <u>S+V.</u> <u>S</u>, **on the other hand,** <u>V.</u> <u>S+V</u>; **on the other hand,** <u>S+V.</u> • Place a comma after **on the other hand** when it begins a sentence and when it immediately follows the subject of a sentence. • Place a semicolon and a space before **on the other hand** and a comma after it when it's in the middle of a sentence. • **On the other hand** is a conjunctive adverb used to show contrast. • In this example sentence, it connects two independent clauses.	Michiko has an <u>auditory learning style</u> with languages. Bennie, **on the other hand,** is much *better at learning visually*; he has *poor listening skills.* In this example, there's a difference between how Michiko and Bennie learn languages. An "auditory learning style" is a new vocabulary term, so let's look at Bennie's situation for contrast. Bennie is *better at learning visually,* and he has *poor listening skills.* If you know what *visual* or *visually* means ("from vision"), that helps. If you don't know *visual* or *visually,* use the "poor listening skills" to give you a clue. From this information, we can guess that an auditory learning style is related to listening.

(continued)

Context Clues of Contrast	Example Sentences
4. Although / though / even though S+V **although / though / even though** <u>S+V.</u> **Although / Though / Even though** <u>S+V</u>, S+V. • When an **although, though,** and **even though** clause begins a sentence, place a comma after that clause. • **Although, though,** and **even though** show contrast or concession. • They are subordinators that introduce subordinating (dependent) clauses. • The information in the subordinating clause is less important than the information in the main (independent) clause.	**Even though** Matthew prefers the analysis of mathematical equations, he also studies the <u>linguistics of English</u>. Can you guess what *linguistics of English* means? If it contrasts with the content of the first clause (the analysis of mathematical equations), then perhaps it means the analysis of the English language. Math deals with numbers, and English deals with words. These two ideas are often considered opposite. In this example, the emphasis is on the fact that he studies English linguistics.
5. While / whereas S+V, **while** <u>S+V</u>. | **While** <u>S+V</u>, S+V. S+V, **whereas** <u>S+V</u>. | **Whereas** <u>S+V</u>, S+V. • Always put a comma between clauses with **while** or **whereas**, no matter the position. • **While** and **whereas** are subordinating conjunctions that link two contrasting ideas. • As they are subordinators, they introduce subordinating (dependent) clauses. • The information in the **while / whereas** clause isn't as important as the information in the main clause. • As subordinators of contrast, **while** and **whereas** are used interchangeably. • **Note:** The rules here specifically refer to **while** and **whereas** as **subordinators expressing contrast**.	**While** most Americans are <u>monolingual</u>, a small percentage do *speak more than one language*. From the context clue **while**, we can guess that <u>monolingual</u> means the opposite of "speak more than one language." Therefore, it probably means "speak one language."

Practice 3-K

Now, reread the lecture on languages in the United States. As you read, find and underline the <u>context clues of contrast</u>. Are there additional contrast clues? Check your answers in Practice 3-K in the Answer Key.

EXERCISES

EXERCISE 3-1

Complete the sentences using the correct form: there is *or* there are. *Use contractions, too! Form affirmative and negative statements as well as yes/no and WH questions with* where *and* how many/how much. *Follow the examples.*

There is a supermarket next to the bank.

There aren't any students in the classroom. (negative)

Are there extra pencils here? (yes/no question)

No, there aren't. / *Yes, there are.* (answer to yes/no question)

Where is there an ATM machine near here? (*where* question)

1. _____ enough people to play the game? (yes/no question)

2. _____. (negative answer)

3. Near the Italian restaurant, _____ a great nail salon. Go there!

4. _____ milk _____ in the fridge? (*how many/much* question)

5. _____ a little bit.

6. _____ enough for my coffee? (yes/no question)

7. _____. (affirmative answer)

8. _____ a good bakery around here? (*where* question)

9. At the end of Stone River Road, _____ a really good bakery. (answer to previous where question)

10. _____ health classes _____? (*how many/much* question)

EXERCISE 3-2

Write sentences with there is *or there are and prepositions of place with the words in parentheses. Use contractions and remember to use the correct article* a *or* an *or the* if there is only one. Form affirmative/negative statements and yes/no/WH questions. *Follow the examples.*

(movie theater / Chinese restaurant / across the street from) affirmative
There's a movie theater across the street from the Chinese restaurant.

(many people / in line / at the tech store) negative
There aren't many people in line at the tech store.

(food / for lunch) how much / many question
How much food is there for lunch?

(any / pumpkin muffins / left) yes/no question
Are there any pumpkin muffins left?

1. (bakery / near here) *where* question

   _____

2. (extra salad / for me) yes/no question

   _____

3. (doctor's office / corner of Willow Street and C Road) affirmative

   _____

4. (a public library / in this small town) negative

   _____

5. (a pho restaurant / nearby) yes/no question

   _____

6. (hospitals) *how much/many* question   .

_____

7. (money / in my wallet) *how much/many* question

_____

8. (enough meat / in this sandwich) negative

_____

EXERCISE 3-3

Answer each question below with a short affirmative and negative answer.
Follow the example.

   Example: Is there a bank around here?

   Yes, there is.   _No, there isn't._

1. Are there any used bookstores?

   _____   _____

2. Is there a drive-thru coffee shop close by?

   _____   _____

3. Is there a safe place to park my car?

   _____   _____

4. Are there any good restaurants around here?

   _____   _____

5. Is there a place to buy gift cards?

_____ _____

6. In this town, are there skateboarding parks?

_____ _____

EXERCISE 3-4

Practice yes/no questions and short answers with there is/there are. Complete the sentences in the conversation below with the information given. Use the example to guide you.

Example: Excuse me. *Is there* a Buddhist temple in this town?

No, there isn't. However, there is one in Anderson Valley about 40 miles from here.

1. Excuse me. _____ a used record shop anywhere?

_____, but there is a used clothing store that sells records about a mile from here.

2. Excuse me. _____ car wash places?

_____ . My favorite place is on High Street.

3. _____ a deli to get fresh made sandwiches near here?

_____ . There's a café with a deli counter over there.

4. Hello! _____ an athletic shoe store anywhere?

_____ . I usually go to the mall about 45 minutes away from here.

5. Excuse me. In this town, _____ a garden store or nursery?

_____ . It's two towns over.

EXERCISE 3-5

Complete the questions using the words given. Use there is *or* there are *in each question. Follow the correct word order and be sure to end the sentence with a question mark. Use the example to guide you.*

Example: Where / a massage spa

Where is there a massage spa?

1. How many / much / yoga studios

_____

2. Where / a good greasy spoon* (*Note: A greasy spoon is slang for a small, cheap, run-down café or diner that serves fried food.)

_____

3. How many / much / traffic

_____

4. Where / a place to donate clothes and household items

_____

EXERCISE 3-6

Read the list of words below. Then write a sentence with the correct adjective word order to describe the noun. Use the simple present verb tense. Remember to be sure your subject and verb agree.

Example: He / have / motorcycle / Italian / black / shiny

He has a shiny black Italian motorcycle.

1. They / use / method / simple / old-fashioned / effective

   _____

2. Karla / own / dog / fluffy / big / Great Pyrenees

   _____

3. My daughter / live / apartment / spacious / Victorian

   _____

4. Joel / attend / university / British / well-known

   _____

EXERCISE 3-7

Use the information in each item to write a sentence using a comparative or superlative. Use the modifiers given. For each item, write more than one sentence. Follow the example.

adjective: tall & short; measurement = feet + inches

Rachel: 5'3"   Robbie: 5'8"

Xavier: 6'2"   Denise: 6'1"

Example: *Xavier is the tallest.*   *Xavier is a bit taller than Denise.*

Rachel is by far the shortest.   *Denise is much taller than Rachel.*

adjective: heavy & light; measurement = lbs (pounds)

science textbook: 11 lbs   math textbook: 8 lbs

French textbook: 3 lbs   history textbook: 7 lbs

_____

_____

_____

_____

adjective: hot & cool; measurement = degrees Fahrenheit

freshly poured hot green tea: 180°F   freshly brewed coffee: 205°F

steam: 215°F   boiling water: 212°F

_____

_____

_____

_____

EXERCISE 3-8

Complete the sentences by writing the correct form of the adjective. Follow the example.

> **Example:** That boy is *fascinated* with his new puzzle. (fascinated / fascinating)

1. Melody and Peter are _____ at the large amount of homework. (annoyed / annoying)

2. The dead animal on the road is _____. (disgusted / disgusting)

3. We are _____ with the long holiday weekend. (thrilled / thrilling)

4. The new amusement park ride is _____. (thrilled / thrilling)

EXERCISE 3-9

Use the words below to form a sentence in the simple present verb tense. The words are out of order, so you must put them in the correct word order. Follow the example.

> **Example:** very / Gerard / gourmet dinners / cook / tasty
>
> *Gerard cooks very tasty gourmet dinners.*

1. cloudy / It / today / a little bit / BE

   _____

2. extremely / She / an artist / BE / talented

   _____

3. ready / The muffins / nearly / BE

   _____

4. after / get / awfully / lunch / He / sleepy

   _____

EXERCISE 3-10

Draw a simple map of your downtown, neighborhood, or city. Draw streets, shops, buildings, parks, and other landmarks. It doesn't have to be fancy! Write 5 sentences about where things are located in your town and how many of something exists. Use there is/there are; prepositions of place, position, and movement; vocabulary; and the simple present verb tense. Review the appropriate sections of this chapter to help you. Write affirmative and negative statements. Be creative!

1. _____

2. _____

3. _____

4. _____

5. _____

EXERCISE 3-11

Roxie is new in town and she needs directions to different places. Use the map that you created and write directions for five different destinations. Choose a different starting point for each destination. Use prepositions, vocabulary, there is/there are, and expressions for directions.

	Starting Point	Destination	Directions
1.	_____	_____	_____
2.	_____	_____	_____
3.	_____	_____	_____
4.	_____	_____	_____
5.	_____	_____	_____

EXERCISE 3-12

Now, create conversations between Roxie and you. Write questions and answers for directions to five different destinations. Use prepositions, vocabulary, questions/ statements with there is/there are, and a variety of expressions for directions. When answering, use short answers and then give more information. Some of the questions are started for you. You may need to write more than one sentence to give directions.

1. Excuse me. Could you tell me _____ ?

   _____

2. Pardon me. _____ around here?

   _____

3. Hello there! Where _____ ?

   _____

4. Excuse me. Hi! _____ ?

   _____

5. _____ ?

   _____

EXERCISE 3-13

Read the directions that Jamie gives. Write two different questions that ask for repetition.

Jamie: Take a left at the tallest office building; then go three blocks down the road. Look for it on your right.

1. _____

Jamie: Cross the street and walk behind the pharmacy. It's next to the Greek gyro shop.

2. _____

EXERCISE 3-14

Read the directions that Cassandra gives. Write two paraphrases using two different expressions to check your understanding.

Cassandra: Take a left here and drive to the next intersection. Go past Hyacinth Ave and then half a block down the tech store is on the right.

1. _____

Cassandra: Walk up Sander Street. Make a right at the antique shop. The poke restaurant is on the left just past the candy shop.

2. _____

EXERCISE 3-15

Katrina needs directions, so she asks Tomoko, a passerby. Create a conversation between them. Use the map you created in this chapter or choose another map. Choose Katrina's starting point and destination. Is she on foot or in a car? Complete the conversation with the vocabulary, prepositions, imperatives, simple present verb tense, and repetition/paraphrasing expressions you learned in this chapter.

Starting point: _____   **Destination:** _____

Katrina: (Use a WH question to ask for directions to a destination.)

_____

Tomoko: (Give directions using the imperative.)

_____

Katrina: (Ask for repetition.)

_____

Tomoko: (Repeat directions.)

_____

Katrina: (Paraphrase for understanding.)

_____

Tomoko: (If correct, confirm Katrina's understanding. Otherwise, repeat the directions.)

_____

Katrina: (Repeat information to show understanding.)

_____

EXERCISE 3-16

Reread the lecture on languages in the United States. You already identified the context clues of contrast in Practice 3-K. Now, determine the meaning of the idea from the context clue of contrast. The idea is in italics. First, underline the <u>context clue of contrast</u>. Then, double underline the <u>information</u> that contrasts the idea in italics.

> **Example:** <u>Although</u> *the United States doesn't have an official language,* <u><u>English has been widely accepted as the primary language</u></u>.

1. Though *a foreign language is required in high school*, most American students rarely learn and understand enough of a new language to have meaningful conversations.

2. I grew up speaking only English even though *my parents grew up speaking Canadian French.*

3. *I learned French as a foreign language in high school*, but I never became fluent because I only used it in French class.

4. Healthy children learn languages easily and naturally, whereas *adults must use their cognitive learning skills.*

EXERCISE 3-17

Read the quote below from a historical figure who fought for women's rights during the women's suffrage movement in the United States in the late 1800s. Then, follow the six steps discussed in the chapter to write a paraphrase of the original. Refer back to the transition phrases and two example paraphrases.

"Woman's degradation is in man's idea of his sexual rights. Our religion, laws, customs, are all founded on the belief that woman was made for man."

—Elizabeth Cady Stanton,
Advocate for women's equal rights in
the United States in the late 1800s.

_____

_____

_____

_____

_____

_____

_____

_____

AUDIO

Flashcard
App

4 Nouns and Pronouns

- Proper nouns differ from common nouns.

- Definite and indefinite article rules are important in English.

- There are several types of pronouns used frequently in English.

- Using pronouns correctly is key to "sounding American."

ncreasing vocabulary has been one of the most common goals of my English language learners over the last twenty years. In conversation, my students are often searching for the word they need to express their ideas. It's easy to get frustrated and lose confidence. Learning and using nouns in your speech and writing is a great way to increase your vocabulary quickly. This is easier with concrete nouns, which you can detect with your five senses. Abstract nouns, on the other hand, require a bit more effort to learn. To learn more about the difference between concrete and abstract nouns, check out the mini lecture for Chapter 4 in the audio portion that accompanies this book. For now, let's learn about nouns and pronouns you can use in your speech every day.

Nouns

What are nouns? Nouns are people, places, things, and ideas. We use nouns all the time when we talk and write. They create pictures in the minds of listeners and readers; we make mini movies when we hear stories or read sentences. Nouns are useful and important because they help us imagine the situation as we hear it or read it. For example, when your friend tells you about her weekend plans, she uses nouns and you can imagine your friend's weekend in your mind. Or when you read a paragraph in a novel, your mind can "see" the characters and events. Let's learn more about nouns! Read the following paragraph. The <u>nouns</u> are underlined. Can you "see" the nouns in your mind as you read them?

EXAMPLE

> On <u>Saturday</u>, I went to the <u>beach</u> with my <u>mom</u>. We walked on the warm <u>sand</u> as the small <u>waves</u> hit the <u>shore</u>. We found <u>sea glass</u>, beautiful <u>shells</u>, and shiny <u>rocks</u>. For <u>lunch</u>, we sat down on our <u>beach blanket</u> and ate <u>sandwiches</u>. Before we finished <u>lunch</u>, the <u>seagulls</u> were swooping down and landing on the <u>sand</u> near our <u>blanket</u>. They wanted our <u>food</u>! We stayed for the <u>sunset</u>, which turned the <u>sky</u>

orange, pink, and red. The <u>sun</u> dropped below the <u>horizon</u> at about 7:00 p.m. and we left. It was magical <u>day</u>!

If we look only at the list of nouns in this account of events on Saturday, can you imagine what the story is about? Here is the list of nouns in the paragraph: Saturday, beach, mom, sand, waves, shore, sea glass, shells, rocks, lunch, beach blanket, sandwiches, lunch, seagulls, sand, blanket, food, sunset, sky, sun, horizon, day.

By reading only the nouns, can you imagine what my Saturday was like? It's amazing how nouns can create pictures in our minds. Become a moviemaker. Use nouns when you speak and write and create mini movies in others' minds!

Common Nouns vs. Proper Nouns

Common nouns are regular nouns such as *beach*, *sand*, *day*, and *mom*. Proper nouns, on the other hand, are nouns that **name** a person, place, thing, or idea. Proper nouns name a specific noun, and they are capitalized. *Saturday* is an example of a proper noun because it names the specific day. It's not just any day: it's Saturday. Notice the capital S in **_Saturday_**. Each word in a proper noun begins with a capital letter except prepositions such as **_of_**. To clarify this point, the word **_country_** is a common noun; however, when we name a specific country, such as **_Venezuela_**, we capitalize the first letter, V. Let's look at some more examples of common vs. proper nouns.

BTW

In proper nouns, prepositions and the word <u>the</u> are not capitalized. Here are some examples of this: <u>the</u> United States <u>of</u> America and <u>the</u> Gettysburg Address.

Common Noun	Proper Noun
river	the Charles River
state	North Carolina
pond	Walden Pond
sea	the Dead Sea
avenue	Harvard Avenue
school	Edison School
woman	Ruth Bader Ginsburg
city	New York City
building	the Transamerica Building

Count vs. Noncount Nouns

Nouns are countable or uncountable.

Count Nouns: When we can count a noun (for example, one person, two drinks, three spoons, 60 flowers), we call it a **count noun**. Count nouns can be singular (one boy) or plural (two daughters, 12 cents, 1,000 years).

Noncount Nouns: When we can't count the noun because it's too difficult or impossible (flour, hair, wine, sugar, rain . . .), we call it a **noncount noun**. Noncount nouns are also called **mass nouns** because they name materials (wood), liquids (water), abstract ideas (love), and other things we see as masses without clear divisions. Noncount nouns **do not have plural forms**. They only have one form: flour, hair, wine, sugar, rain. However, we can **measure noncount nouns**. For example, we say *two cups of flour, three glasses of wine,* and *a spoonful of sugar*. It's not grammatically correct to say *two flours, three wines*, or *four sugars*.

IRL Actually, in recent years English speakers have started using quantities such as "two coffees" and "three sugars" when ordering beverages and food. It's common to hear a customer say this at a café: "Hi, I'll have two large coffees with two sugars each." Before this trend began, you would hear: "Hi, I'll have two large <u>cups of</u> coffee with two <u>packets of</u> sugar each." As a language, English is continually changing and growing.

Now, let's examine some examples of count and noncount nouns.

Count Nouns	Noncount Nouns
• nouns that can be counted	• nouns that can**not** be counted
• singular or plural forms	• only one form
Examples: Person / people, book / books, desk / desks, woman / women, tooth / teeth, tomato / tomatoes, movie / movies, knife / knives, suitcase / suitcases	**Examples:** Water, rain, air, rice, salt, oil, plastic, money, music, tennis, coffee, cheese, chocolate, sugar, cream, tea, hair, paper, wood, sand, soap, happiness, freedom, cheese, fish, chicken, furniture, luggage, equipment, information, weather, bread, news, fruit, meat, health
My <u>two suitcases</u> got lost.	My <u>luggage</u> got lost. *Not:* My <u>luggages</u> got lost.
He needs the <u>tools</u>.	He needs the equipment. *Not:* He needs the <u>equipments</u>.
She bought <u>two</u> new <u>desks</u>.	Maggie researches information at work. *Not:* Maggie researches <u>informations</u> at work.
My family owns one <u>car</u>.	They completed their <u>homework</u> on time. *Not:* They completed their <u>homeworks</u> on time.

As stated previously, the English language is constantly changing. What was once ungrammatical has become acceptable. This is true for many food-related noncount nouns such as water and wine and for abstract mass nouns such as freedom. It's not uncommon to hear someone order "three waters" rather than "three bottles of water." Another example is: "Americans are entitled to many freedoms" rather than "Americans are entitled to many types of freedom." Pay attention to what you learn in this book and what you hear "on the street." In this way, you can learn English for writing, which requires proper, grammatical English, and English for speaking, which is less formal and more idiomatic.

Nouns That Can Be Either Count or Noncount Nouns

There are some words that can be both count and noncount nouns. For example, the word *cake* can be both count and noncount depending on how it is used. If we are talking about a whole, complete cake, it's countable. However, if it is divided into sections, it is noncount and you need to use quantifiers such as ***a piece of***. We'll look at more quantifiers in the next section of this chapter. For now, look at the example sentences.

Count Noun: A Cake	Noncount Noun: Cake
Marjorie baked <u>a chocolate cake</u> today. Sometimes, she bakes <u>two cakes</u> in one day!	Marjorie's husband is eating chocolate <u>cake</u> for dessert. He is eating <u>some cake</u>. He is eating <u>a piece of cake</u>.

Count Noun: A Pork	Noncount Noun: Pork
Mrs. Jenson cooks <u>a tender pork</u>.	May I have <u>some pork</u>, please? May I have <u>a slice of pork</u>, please?

Quantifiers with Noncount Nouns

When we talk about noncount nouns, we usually use quantifiers. For example, you can have <u>a glass of</u> juice, <u>a slice of</u> bread, and <u>a bowl of</u> soup. **Quantifiers are countable**. When you use quantifiers, you make the noncount noun countable, or measurable. If you have more than one, be sure to make the quantifier plural. For example, she can eat <u>a piece of</u> cake or **two pieces of** cake. Check out the short list of quantifiers below and see examples

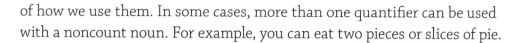

of how we use them. In some cases, more than one quantifier can be used with a noncount noun. For example, you can eat two pieces or slices of pie.

Quantifiers	Examples
two pieces of	two pieces of pie
a slice of	a slice of bread
a bag of	a bag of chips
five cans of	five cans of soda
a bottle of	a bottle of wine
a cup of	a cup of flour
two tablespoons of	two tablespoons of salt
a dish of	a dish of ice cream

Determiners with Nouns

Determiners are words such as *many, his, my, a lot of,* and *these* that precede nouns. These words help us **determine the noun**. In other words, determiners **identify or quantify a noun**. For example, in the sentence *Her book is on my desk,* **her** identifies which book. It's not *his book* or *a book*. It's *her book*. Similarly, we can determine which desk we reference in the sentence. Which desk is it? It's **my** desk. In the sentence *Several people are leaving,* **several** measures the number of people. It's not *one person* or *two people* but *several people*. Read more examples of determiners below.

Types of Determiners That <u>Identify</u> a Noun	Determiners That <u>Measure/Quantify</u> a Noun
articles: *a, an, the*	*some, any, no*
possessive adjectives: *my, your, his, her, its, our, your, their*	*each, every, either, neither*
demonstrative adjectives: *this, that, these, those*	*much, many, more, most, enough, several, (a) little, (a) few*
	all, both, half
	one, two, one hundred . . .
	other, another

Few and *a few* (countable) have different meanings. *Few* has a negative meaning. *Few* means "nearly none or less than expected." However, *a few* has a positive meaning. *A few* means "some, but not many." Look at the two sentences below that have only one word difference: **a**. Notice that the meanings of these two sentences are completely different.

- **Negative meaning:** <u>Few</u> people attended the meeting. = hardly any people / fewer people than expected
  Positive meaning: <u>A few</u> people attended the meeting. = some people / not many

Just like *few* and *a few*, *little* and *a little* (uncountable) have different meanings. *Little* has a negative meaning. It means "nearly none—not enough." However, *a little* has a positive meaning: it means "some, but not much." Look at the two sentences below that have only one word difference: **a**. Notice that the meanings of these two sentences are completely different.

- **Negative meaning:** There is <u>little</u> water in the well. = nearly none / not enough

- **Positive meaning:** There is <u>a little</u> water in the well. = some water / not much

Check out the variety of determiners in these example sentences.

▶ <u>Your</u> cousin works at <u>the</u> hospital.

▶ <u>That</u> restaurant has <u>some</u> outdoor seating.

▶ <u>This</u> cookbook has <u>many</u> vegetarian recipes.

▶ <u>My</u> mother is shopping at <u>a few</u> stores today.

How Many vs. How Much

To find out the quantity of something, we ask a WH question with either
How many or *How much*. Use **How many** to ask about **count nouns**. Use
How much to ask about **noncount nouns**. Let's study some examples below.

▶ *How Many* + **Count Nouns**

How many <u>peaches</u> are there?

How many <u>people</u> are eating with us?

How many <u>hamburgers</u> should I order?

How many <u>cans</u> of coconut water do you have?*

▶ *How Much* + **Noncount Nouns**

How much <u>peach pie</u> do you want?

How much <u>cheese</u> is needed for the recipe?

How much <u>meat</u> should I order?

How much <u>coconut water</u> do you have?

***Note:** Although <u>coconut water</u> is noncount, <u>cans</u> is countable. Therefore, we use
how many in this sentence.*

Plural Count Nouns

We indicate a **plural count noun by spelling it differently**. Regular count nouns are marked by adding an **–s** or **–es**. Irregular count nouns have a variety of spellings. Study the rules below.

Spelling Rules for Regular Count Nouns	Examples
For most nouns, add **–s**	breakfast → breakfast**s**, car → car**s**, carrot → carrot**s**
When the noun ends in a **consonant + y**, change **y** to **i** and add **–es**	ber**ry** → berr**ies**, lady → lad**ies**, baby → bab**ies**
For nouns ending in **sh, ch, tch, s, ss, x,** or **z** add **–es** **Note:** For words ending in a single –z, add zes	fox → fox**es**, match → match**es**, octopus → octopus**es** quiz → qui**zzes**
For some nouns ending in **o**, add **–es**	ech**o** → echo**es**, her**o** → hero**es**, potat**o** → potato**es**, tomat**o** → tomato**es**

What are the spelling rules for irregular countable nouns? The English language is composed of several different languages and has been influenced by several other languages. English has steadily changed and grown with the advent of new commerce, industry, and technology. As a result, there are rules, but there are also exceptions. Memorizing the spelling of irregular count nouns is a good idea because of these rules and exceptions. See a few rules for irregular count nouns below. This is not a comprehensive list. Read aloud the examples of count nouns and remember the pronunciation rules for **–s** endings. See Chapter 2 for a refresher on this.

Spelling Rules for Irregular Count Nouns	Examples
For words ending in **f** or **fe**, change the **f** to **v** and add **–es** or **–s**	calf → calves, elf → elves, half → halves, knife → knives, leaf → leaves, life → lives, loaf → loaves, self → selves, shelf → shelves, thief → thieves, wife → wives
Other irregular count nouns	child → children, foot → feet, goose → geese, man → men, mouse → mice, ox → oxen, person → people, tooth → teeth, woman → women
Some words derived from foreign languages such as Greek and Latin have irregular plurals.	analysis → analyses, appendix → appendices, bacterium → bacteria, datum → data, fungus → fungi, medium → media

Definite vs. Indefinite Articles

We use **articles with both count nouns and noncount nouns**. We'll talk more about the difference between count and noncount nouns later in this chapter. For now, it's important to know that:

- The **definite article *the*** can be used for **count** (singular and plural) and **noncount nouns**.

- The **indefinite articles** are ***a, an, some,*** and ***any.***

  Note: Some grammarians disagree that *some* and *any* are articles. Most agree that they are determiners—a larger category of words—of which articles are a part. You'll learn more about determiners later in this chapter. *Some* and *any* can also be used as pronouns. In this book, we'll treat *some* and *any* as articles when they are used with nouns.

- We use ***a*** and ***an*** for singular count nouns.

- ***Some*** is used for both plural count nouns and noncount nouns.

- ***Any*** is used in questions and negatives.

- We can **omit the article** if the noun is plural or noncount.

- We can ***never* omit the article** with singular count nouns.

Check out the table below, which illustrates these article rules.

	Count Nouns	Noncount Nouns
Singular	• Definite article: *the* • Indefinite article: *a, an* • Article required	
Plural	• Definite article: *the* • Indefinite article: *some, any* • No article (Ø)	
Unchanging form		• Definite article: *the* • Indefinite articles: *some, any* • No article (Ø)

A vs. An

What's the difference between the articles *a* and *an*? We use *a* before a word that **begins with a consonant sound**. We use *an* before a word that **begins with a vowel sound**. See the example sentences, which show when to use *a* and when to use *an*.

Example Sentences Using *a* or *an*	Explanation
She goes to **a** <u>café</u> every Saturday morning.	The word *café* begins with the consonant **c** with the sound **/k/**, so the indefinite article used is **a**.
They are enjoying lunch at **an** <u>excellent</u> café right now.	The word *excellent* begins with the vowel **e** with the sound **/ɛ/**, so the indefinite article used is **an**.
He is attending **a** <u>university</u>.	Although the word *university* begins with a vowel, it's pronounced with the sound **/y/ as in you**, so the indefinite article used is **a**.
He is attending **an** <u>I</u>vy League university.	The word *Ivy* begins with the vowel **i** and the sound **/ay/**, so the indefinite article used is **an**.

When to Use Definite and Indefinite Articles

There are two helpful rules to remember when deciding to use a definite or indefinite article. Let's take a look at them both:

1. We use **definite articles** when we talk about **specific things**. We use **indefinite articles** to talk about **general or non-specific things.** Review the example sentences below.

	Indefinite Article	Definite Article
Count noun singular	I want to eat <u>an</u> apple. (Which apple? Any apple—not a specific one.) Can I please have <u>a</u> nectarine? (Which nectarine? Any nectarine—not a specific one.)	I would like <u>the</u> apple. (There is only one apple or you know precisely which apple you are referring to.) Can I have <u>the</u> nectarine on the counter? (Which nectarine? A specific nectarine—the one on the counter.)
Count noun plural	Gerald is eating <u>some</u> desserts. (Which desserts? Nonspecific desserts.)	He is eating <u>the</u> desserts you brought to the party. (Which desserts? The desserts you brought—specific desserts.)
Noncount noun	Do you want <u>some</u> juice? Which juice? Nonspecific juice.	Do you want the juice we got this morning? (This is specific juice—the juice we got this morning.)

2. We also use definite articles to refer to something **we already know**. This means that we use an **indefinite article when we first talk about a noun**, then we use a **definite article for the same noun the next time** it is mentioned. See some examples of this below.

> **Example 1:** I am watching **a** funny movie. I downloaded **the** movie earlier today.

Example Sentences	Reason for Using a Definite or an Indefinite Article
I am watching **a** funny movie.	This is the first time I mention the movie.
I downloaded **the** movie earlier today.	We know which movie now, so we use *the* when I mention it the second time.

> **Example 2:** I am learning **a** new exercise. **The** exercise targets my core muscles.

Example Sentences	Reason for Using a Definite or an Indefinite Article
I am learning **a** new exercise.	This is the first time I mention the exercise.
The exercise targets my core muscles.	We know about the exercise now, so we use *the*.

Now, look at these example conversations to see how this works in everyday life.

EXAMPLE

▶ **Conversation 1:**

Sheila: I am reading **a** new book.

Khalid: Really? What is it?

Sheila: **The** book is *Little Women* by Louisa May Alcott.

Khalid: It sounds interesting!

Sentence	Reason for Using a Definite or an Indefinite Article
I am reading **a** new <u>book</u>.	This is the first time we talk about a book.
The <u>book</u> is *Little Women* by Louisa May Alcott.	This is the second time it's mentioned, so we use *the*.

EXAMPLE

▶ **Conversation 2:**

Noah: I am trying **a** new <u>recipe</u>.

Maya: Really? Is it from your grandmother?

Noah: I found **the** <u>recipe</u> in my new cookbook.

Maya: Are you inviting me for dinner?

Sentence	Reason for Using Definite or Indefinite Article
I am trying **a** new <u>recipe</u>.	This is the first time talking about it, so we use **a**.
I found **the** <u>recipe</u> in my new cookbook.	They are talking about the same recipe and this is the second time it's mentioned, so we use **the**.

Pronouns and Possessive Adjectives

We often use a **pronoun to replace a noun**. Remember, a **noun** is a **person, place,** or **thing**. Americans use pronouns and possessive adjectives regularly. When you learn them and skillfully use them, you will sound more "American." See the Appendix for a complete list of pronouns. Let's start with subject pronouns.

Subject Pronouns

A **subject pronoun replaces a noun in the subject position** of a sentence. As you know, the **subject** of a sentence is usually at the **beginning of a sentence before the verb**. Which subject pronouns do you know? Study the chart of subject pronouns below.

Subject Pronouns

	Singular	Plural
First person	I	We
Second person	You	You
Third person	He (male) ♂	They*
	She (female) ♀	
	It	

*****Note:** However, some individuals in the United States choose to use the more gender-neutral pronoun *they* even though it's a plural pronoun.

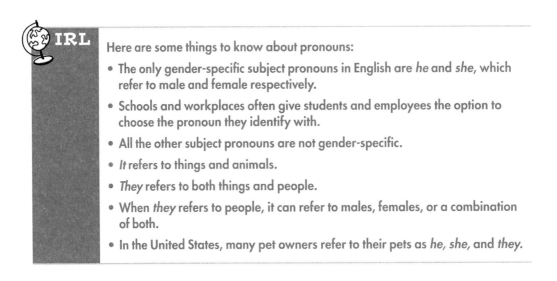

IRL

Here are some things to know about pronouns:

- The only gender-specific subject pronouns in English are *he* and *she*, which refer to male and female respectively.
- Schools and workplaces often give students and employees the option to choose the pronoun they identify with.
- All the other subject pronouns are not gender-specific.
- *It* refers to things and animals.
- *They* refers to both things and people.
- When *they* refers to people, it can refer to males, females, or a combination of both.
- In the United States, many pet owners refer to their pets as *he, she,* and *they.*

Let's take a look at some example sentences with subject pronouns.

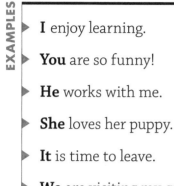

EXAMPLES

▶ **I** enjoy learning.

▶ **You** are so funny!

▶ **He** works with me.

▶ **She** loves her puppy.

▶ **It** is time to leave.

▶ **We** are visiting my grandparents.

▶ Did **they** have a good time?

Note: In English, use only a noun *or* a pronoun as the subject. Do *not* use both. Below are correct and incorrect examples of this.

Incorrect:	Sammy ~~he~~ is over there.	He ~~Sammy~~ is over there.
Correct:	Sammy is over there.	He is over there.

Object Pronouns

The difference between a subject pronoun and an **object pronoun** is that the replaced noun is in a different position in the sentence. We can replace a **noun in the object position** of the sentence with an object pronoun. Let's talk about **two types of objects**:

1. **The object of a verb**

2. **The object of a preposition**

What is the difference between these two types of object pronouns? The object of a verb (OV) follows the verb; it takes the action of the verb. However, the object of a preposition (OP) follows the preposition in a prepositional phrase. Which object pronouns do you know? Study the chart of object pronouns.

Object Pronouns (OV and OP)

	Singular	Plural
First person	me	us
Second person	you	you
Third person	him (male) ♂	them*
	her (female) ♀	
	it	

*****Note:** Just as some individuals use the subject pronoun, *they*, some people also use the gender-neutral object pronoun *them*.

Check out the example sentences below.

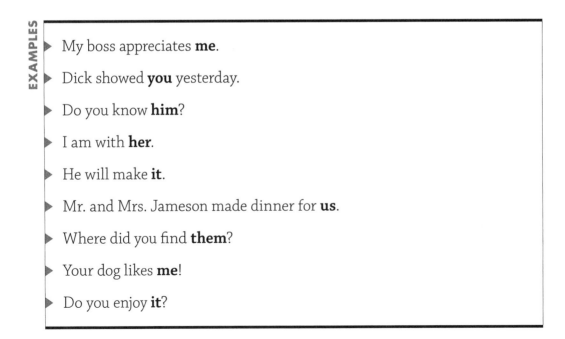

EXAMPLES

▶ My boss appreciates **me**.

▶ Dick showed **you** yesterday.

▶ Do you know **him**?

▶ I am with **her**.

▶ He will make **it**.

▶ Mr. and Mrs. Jameson made dinner for **us**.

▶ Where did you find **them**?

▶ Your dog likes **me**!

▶ Do you enjoy **it**?

How do you know what/where the object is? To find the **object of the verb** in a sentence, ask the question "What?" or "Whom?" after the verb. To find the object of the preposition, ask "What?" or "Whom?" after the preposition. Let's look at some examples.

Object of the Verb

Sentence with Object Pronoun	Verb + What or Whom?	Object Pronoun
My dog follows **me**.	Follows whom?	me
I love **you**!	Love whom?	you
They asked **him** for advice.	Asked whom?	him
My neighbor recommended **her**.	Recommended whom?	her
The kids want **it**.	Want what?	it
Our friends invited **us** over.	Invited whom?	us
We bought **them**.	Bought what?	them

You can also find the **object of a preposition** this way. Prepositions are words that show position or direction such as *in on, for, with,* and *to.* Look at the table below.

Object of the Preposition

Sentence with Object Pronoun	Preposition + What or Whom?	Object Pronoun
Mr. Pelletier looked everywhere <u>for</u> **me**. prep	For whom?	me
The phone is <u>near</u> **you**. prep	Near whom?	you
She will go <u>with</u> **him**. prep	With whom?	him
Moses talked <u>about</u> **her**. prep	About whom?	her
The ball was <u>under</u> **it**. prep	Under what?	it

(continued)

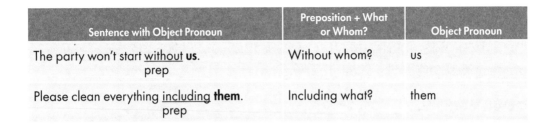

	Sentence with Object Pronoun	Preposition + What or Whom?	Object Pronoun
The party won't start <u>without</u> **us**. prep		Without whom?	us
Please clean everything <u>including</u> **them**. prep		Including what?	them

Now that you understand subject and object pronouns a bit more, why don't we study possessive adjectives?

Possessive Adjectives

What are possessive adjectives, and why do we use them? Possessive adjectives talk about possessions—things we have, or people and things that belong to us. Americans use these a lot. When you master the skill of using these, you will sound more "American." To understand this a bit better, see the example sentences below that use possessive adjectives. The underlined words are possessive adjectives.

EXAMPLES

▶ <u>My</u> kitten plays with milk jug caps.

▶ <u>Your</u> sister is really smart.

▶ <u>His</u> line of work is top secret.

▶ Did <u>her</u> car start this morning?

▶ I wonder if <u>its</u> wing is broken. The poor bird can't fly!

▶ How is <u>their</u> new house?

▶ Where should we hang <u>our</u> coats?

▶ The Sheffield Brothers are touring with <u>their</u> band.

See a list of possessive adjectives below.

Possessive Adjectives

	Singular	Plural
First person	my	our
Second person	your	your
Third person	his (male) ♂	their*
	her (female) ♀	
	its	

*****Note:** Like *they* and *them,* the more gender-neutral possessive adjective *their* can refer to an individual.

The following table shows when to use the various possessive adjectives.

People only	my, your, his, her, our, their
Things only	its
People and things	their

Possessive adjectives always precede a noun: **possessive adjective + noun.** Study the following examples from the sentences above.

EXAMPLES

▶ My kitten   Your sister

▶ His line of work   her car

▶ its wing   their new house

▶ our coats   their band

Do you think you can correctly use possessive adjectives? I think so! Think of some things you, your family, and your friends own. Which possessive adjective do you use for these nouns?

Possessive Pronouns

Now let's move on to possessive pronouns. As the name suggests, we use possessive pronouns to talk about possession—things that we have or own, and people and things that belong to us. However, they are different from possessive adjectives in their form and how they're used. Study the following forms of possessive pronouns.

	Singular	Plural
First person	mine	ours
Second person	yours	yours
Third person	his (male) ♂	theirs*
	hers (female) ♀	

***Note:** By now, you understand the use of gender-neutral pronouns. *Theirs* is often used to refer to individuals.

Now, let's see how we actually use possessive pronouns. Look at these four rules:

1. Possessive pronouns **replace a possessive adjective + a noun** such as *his car.*

2. Possessive pronouns **replace possessive nouns** such as *Laurel's* and *Aidan's.*

3. Possessive pronouns can be **subjects** and **objects**.

4. Possessive pronouns can refer to **singular** or **plural nouns.**

Let's first look at the difference between how we use possessive adjectives and possessive pronouns. Study the following example sentences that use possessive pronouns.

Possessive Adjective + Noun	Possessive Pronoun
<u>My car</u> is that silver car. (singular / subject)	**Mine** is that silver car. (singular / subject)
Those books are <u>my books</u>. (plural / object)	Those books are **mine**. (plural / object)
<u>Our house</u> is the old one. (singular / subject)	**Ours** is the old one. (singular / subject)
That game is <u>our game.</u> (singular / object)	That game is **ours**. (singular / object)
<u>Their child</u> is in the house. (singular / subject)	**Theirs** is in the house. (singular / subject)
Is this little book <u>their book</u>? (singular / object)	Is this little book **theirs**? (singular / object)

Now, let's see how possessive **pronouns** replace possessive **nouns**. Remember, possessive pronouns can be both subject and object pronouns. Look at the table below.

Possessive Noun	Possessive Pronoun
The missing parakeet is <u>Asha's</u>.	The missing parakeet is **hers**.
<u>Hee Jeong's</u> is the street on the right.	**Hers** is the street on the right.
<u>Hope and Nguyen's</u> is the restaurant over there.	**Theirs** is the restaurant over there.
This bone is <u>Rex's</u>.	This bone is **his**.

Reflexive Pronouns

A **reflexive pronoun** always **refers back to the subject of a sentence**. Which reflexive pronouns do you know and use? Study the chart of reflexive pronouns below.

Reflexive Pronouns

	Singular	Plural
First person	myself	ourselves
Second person	yourself	yourselves
Third person	himself (male) ♂	themselves*
	herself (female) ♀	
	itself	

* **Note:** The more gender-neutral reflexive pronoun *themselves* is sometimes used by individuals.

How do we use reflexive pronouns? Let's see how we actually use them. Look at the four rules below:

1. Reflexive pronouns **always refer back to the subject** of the sentence.

2. Reflexive pronouns **must have an antecedent** to make sense. The antecedent is always the subject of the sentence, which comes before the reflexive pronoun in the sentence.

3. Reflexive pronouns **are objects** of the verb or a preposition.

4. Reflexive pronouns **are necessary** to the sentence because **they complete the idea**.

Look at some example sentences with reflexive pronouns and analyze them. Remember, the reflexive pronoun always **refers back to the subject of the sentence, yet it is an object**.

▸ I sliced <u>myself</u> some sourdough bread.

▸ Did you make <u>yourself</u> some lunch?

▸ Patrick hurt <u>himself</u> at the game.

▸ She bought a silver beaded necklace for <u>herself</u>.

▸ The monitor puts <u>itself</u> to sleep after 20 minutes of idle time.

▸ My family and I are taking <u>ourselves</u> to Lake Como in Italy for vacation!

▸ My twin sisters mailed <u>themselves</u> birthday gifts.

▸ Her cousin tested the new facial cream on <u>herself</u>.

▸ The coffee maker shuts <u>itself</u> off.

Now, let's analyze how the reflexive pronoun works in a sentence **as the object of the verb**. On the left-hand side of the following table, you can see that the reflexive pronoun refers back to the subject. On the right-hand side, notice that <u>the subject of the sentence (the antecedent)</u> is underlined, the verb is highlighted, the **reflexive pronoun** is bolded, and the *direct object* is italicized. If the reflexive pronoun is the direct object, it is bolded and italicized. Observe that the reflexive pronoun in these sentences is either the direct object (DO) or the indirect object (IO). For a more on direct and indirect objects, see the appropriate section in Chapter 7.

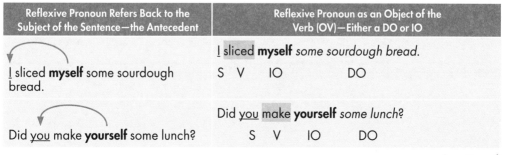

Reflexive Pronoun Refers Back to the Subject of the Sentence—the Antecedent	Reflexive Pronoun as an Object of the Verb (OV)—Either a DO or IO
I sliced **myself** some sourdough bread.	I sliced **myself** *some sourdough bread.* S V IO DO
Did you make **yourself** some lunch?	Did <u>you</u> make **yourself** *some lunch?* S V IO DO

(continued)

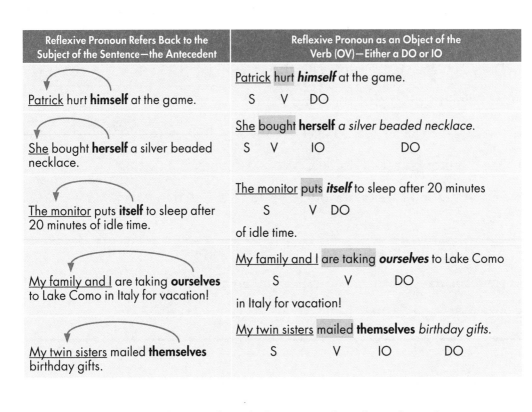

Reflexive Pronoun Refers Back to the Subject of the Sentence—the Antecedent	Reflexive Pronoun as an Object of the Verb (OV)—Either a DO or IO
Patrick hurt **himself** at the game.	Patrick hurt *himself* at the game. 　　S　　V　　DO
She bought **herself** a silver beaded necklace.	She bought **herself** a silver beaded necklace. 　S　V　IO　　　　DO
The monitor puts **itself** to sleep after 20 minutes of idle time.	The monitor puts *itself* to sleep after 20 minutes 　　S　　V　DO of idle time.
My family and I are taking **ourselves** to Lake Como in Italy for vacation!	My family and I are taking **ourselves** to Lake Como 　　S　　　　V　　　DO in Italy for vacation!
My twin sisters mailed **themselves** birthday gifts.	My twin sisters mailed **themselves** birthday gifts. 　　S　　　　V　　IO　　　DO

To expand your understanding, let's now analyze how the reflexive pronoun works in a sentence as the **object of the preposition**. A reflexive pronoun can only be used as an OP when the **OP is the *same* as the subject of the sentence**. It answers the question *prep + what/whom?* Take a look at some example sentences analyzed on the following page. The subject of the sentence (the antecedent) is underlined, the verb is highlighted, the *DO* is italicized, the **reflexive pronoun** is bolded, and the [prepositional phrase] has brackets [ ] around it.

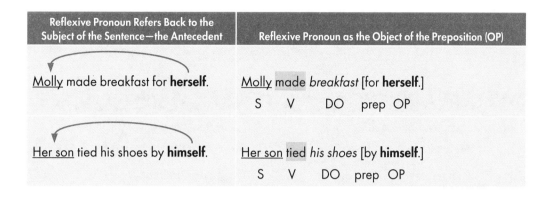

Reflexive Pronoun Refers Back to the Subject of the Sentence—the Antecedent	Reflexive Pronoun as the Object of the Preposition (OP)
Molly made breakfast for **herself**.	Molly made *breakfast* [for **herself**.] S　　V　　DO　prep　OP
Her son tied his shoes by **himself**.	Her son tied *his shoes* [by **himself**.] S　　V　　DO　prep　OP

Demonstrative Adjectives

We often use demonstrative adjectives to talk about specific things and people. Demonstrative adjectives usually **identify a noun that is near or far in distance or time**. Here are some things to remember about demonstrative adjectives:

- We use *this* and *these* to talk about things and people that are **near** in distance or time.

- We use *that* and *those* to talk about things and people that are **far** in distance or time.

- Sometimes, we point to the noun we are talking about.

- We may also indicate the noun by holding it, touching it, or looking at it.

IRL | Note that it's *not polite to point with your finger at people*. Instead, we point at people with an open hand. However, when we point at things, we can point with a finger. It's common to point with the index finger.

	Singular	Plural	Pronunciation Notes
Near	this	these	*This* rhymes with <u>kiss</u>. *These* rhymes with <u>cheese</u>.
Far	that	those	*That* rhymes with <u>hat</u>. *Those* rhymes with <u>knows</u>.

Demonstrative adjectives are great for indicating what or who we are talking about. Let's see some example sentences with demonstrative adjectives.

	Singular	Plural
Near	<u>This</u> guy is my boyfriend. My father built <u>this</u> house.	<u>These</u> students are in my science club. Do you like <u>these</u> earrings?
Far	<u>That</u> movie was hilarious! Check out <u>that</u> muscle car!	<u>Those</u> dogs are really friendly. He sewed <u>those</u> curtains.

Demonstrative adjectives act just like possessive adjectives (*her, my, your*), which we talked about earlier in this chapter. We use singular demonstrative adjectives with singular nouns and plural demonstrative adjectives with plural nouns. Study the guidelines below. Demonstrative adjectives:

1. Talk about a **specific noun**.

2. Always precede a noun: **demonstrative adjective + noun.**

3. Answer the question *Which one/s?*

4. Are **gender neutral**.

Let's examine some examples of demonstrative adjectives:

	Singular	Plural
Near in distance or time	<u>this</u> cat	<u>these</u> students
Far in distance or time	<u>that</u> textbook	<u>those</u> memories

Demonstrative Pronouns

Both demonstrative adjectives and demonstrative pronouns talk about **specific things and people**. Notice they look exactly the same as demonstrative adjectives:

	Singular	Plural
Near	this	these
Far	that	those

The difference between them is that **demonstrative adjectives *modify* nouns**. However, **demonstrative pronouns *are the nouns in pronoun form***. When we use demonstrative pronouns, it's clear what the noun is, so we don't need to name it. Check out the examples.

Demonstrative *Adjective*	Demonstrative *Pronoun*
My friend made <u>this sandwich</u>. demonstrative adjective = this noun = sandwich	My friend made <u>this</u>. demonstrative pronoun = this
How do you like <u>these eyeglasses</u>? demonstrative adjective = these noun = eyeglasses	How do you like <u>these</u>? demonstrative pronoun = these
He's buying <u>that motorcycle.</u> demonstrative adjective = that noun = motorcycle	He's buying <u>that</u>. demonstrative pronoun = that
She wrote <u>those poems</u>. demonstrative adjective = those noun = poems	She wrote <u>those</u>. demonstrative pronoun = those

Now, let's study these helpful guidelines. **Demonstrative pronouns**:

1. **Replace demonstrative adjectives + nouns**.

2. Can be a **subject** or an **object**.

3. Are **gender neutral**.

Note: It's less common to use demonstrative pronouns for people. It's more common to use demonstrative pronouns for things. Look at some example sentences with demonstrative pronouns.

Singular	Plural
This is my oldest sister.	These are in my math problems.
My grandfather painted this.	Where did you find these?
That is good news!	Those are delicious grapes.
Did you see that?	We will have those tomorrow.

In this next set of examples, notice how the demonstrative pronoun is used as a subject or object in the sentence.

	Demonstrative Pronoun as a *Subject*	Demonstrative Pronoun as an *Object*
This	Mike, this is Deb.	Yummy! Did you bake this?
That	Wow! That is so beautiful.	I knew that.
These	These are comfortable shoes.	He recommends these to everyone.
Those	Those are her challenges.	When did she invest in those?

Dialogue: The Science Lab

Read this dialogue and notice how two high school classmates use paraphrase expressions to check their understanding, which we discussed in Chapter 3. Also notice the use of demonstrative adjectives and demonstrative pronouns. Carl and Nancy are working on a biology project in the science lab. They already know each other, and they have been partners for a couple of weeks.

Nancy: Carl, can you come over here and help me with this?

Carl: Sure, what's up?

Nancy: I can't figure out where the bacteria are in this petri dish. I hate this microscope! It's so frustrating!

Carl: Let's see here. (Looks through microscope.) Yah, it's blurry. Hard to see anything. Did you adjust the focus? That's how you sharpen the image.

Nancy: I tried, but it just won't focus. I can't see the bacteria, and we have to check the bacteria's growth every day to log our observations. If I can't see them, I can't observe anything.

Carl: So, we're supposed to observe and log every day? I thought it was every *week*!

Nancy: The teacher said every day because these are fast-growing bacteria. Didn't she?

Carl: Let me check with Ms. Quilici to make sure. (Goes to biology teacher.)

Ms. Quilici: What can I help you with, Carl?

Carl: I wanted to clarify the assignment for this experiment. Should we be making and logging our observations of the bacteria every day? Or every week?

Ms. Quilici: It depends on the type of bacteria you are growing in the petri dish. Do you have Type A or Type B?

Carl: I'm not sure. I need to double-check that.

Ms. Quilici: If it's Type A, you need to check and log observations every day. If it's Type B, you do it once a week on the same day of the week for three weeks.

Carl: Oh okay! That makes sense. Thank you, Ms. Quilici.

Ms. Quilici: You're welcome, Carl.

Nancy: What did she say?

Carl: It depends on what kind of bacteria we have. Which one do we have? Type A or B?

Nancy: Oh wow. I didn't realize there were two types! How do we find out?

Carl: Maybe we check the label on the petri dish?

Nancy: Yes, look! We've got Type A. What does that mean?

Carl: With Type A, we check and log our observations every single day.

Nancy: That's what I thought! Phew! Okay, so now how do I focus this microscope?

Carl: Here. Turn this knob while you're looking at the petri dish, but you have to turn it little by little because it's loose and it's easy to go too far.

Nancy: Are you saying I turn this knob here? Oh my goodness! I've been turning the wrong knob!

Lecture: *Star Wars*

A Commercial Success: *Star Wars*

The movie series, *Star Wars*, has become quite a commercial success in the United States. The first movie in this motion picture franchise came out in 1977. American filmmaker George Lucas had to invent machinery and new tools to get the special effects he wanted. The film begins with these words: "A long time ago in a galaxy far, far away. . . ."

It's the story of a young man named Luke Skywalker who finds himself in the unlikely position of becoming a great interplanetary warrior known as a Jedi Knight. His charge is to save the galaxy from the "evil empire" controlled by Darth Vader. Luke gets his warrior training from an 800-year-old Jedi Master named Yoda. Yoda is wise and teaches Luke how to understand and harness "The Force" within him. With the help of a princess (Princess Leia), a smuggler (Han Solo), a tall furry ape-like animal (Chewbacca), two robots (C-3PO and R2-D2), and a variety of other intergalactic characters, Luke Skywalker saves the galaxy.

Even though the technology used in 1977 to create flying ships and the battles was cutting edge then, by today's standards it seems ancient. Technology has come so far and so have the other nine pictures in this series. Almost 45 years later, the *Star Wars* franchise is still commercially popular and successful. Major cities all over the world host *Star Wars* conventions, where fans dress up as *Star Wars* characters and celebrate. *Star Wars* is quite a phenomenon. Watch the series starting with the original film and see for yourself what it's like!

EXERCISES

EXERCISE 4-1

Look at the list below and circle the proper nouns.

Salvator	street	teacher	house
the White House	school	Dedham High School	bank
city	River Street	Prof. Schertle	store
Caesar's Market	Wareham Bank	Brooklyn	

EXERCISE 4-2

Think of three proper nouns that you know. Write a sentence using each of these proper nouns. Use the simple present verb tense form. See the examples below.

Examples: <u>**Austin** is a city in **Texas**.</u>

<u>We see our dentist, **Dr. Perry**, twice a year.</u>

<u>The foghorn on the **Pigeon Point Lighthouse** sounds almost every night.</u>

1. _____

2. _____

3. _____

EXERCISE 4-3

Read the sentences below. Complete each sentence with an indefinite article
(a, an, some) or the definite article the. Follow the example.

> **Example:** I am trying _a_ new recipe. _The_ recipe is from my new
> cookbook.

1. My sisters received _____ invitation to the graduation party. They
   accepted _____ invitation.

2. His birthday party was at _____ bowling alley. _____ bowling alley
   plays rock and roll music.

3. My mother is shopping for _____ new purse. She wants _____ purse to
   be leather.

4. Manny wants _____ costume party. _____ party is for his birthday.

5. Olga is getting _____ puppy. She is getting _____ puppy from the
   rescue shelter.

EXERCISE 4-4

Read the sentences below. Circle the correct article for each sentence. The symbol Ø
means no article is needed.

1. Do you like _____ cookies I baked?   the   Ø

2. Are you eating _____ leftovers from last night?   an   Ø

3. I wouldn't like _____ syrup on my pancakes, thank you.   any   some

4. Are they enjoying _____ swimming pool at the resort?   the   some

5. My brother is buying _____ used car.   a   Ø

EXERCISE 4-5

Now you try it. Write one sentence for each category. Use the correct definite or indefinite article for count and noncount nouns. Follow the spelling rules for plural count nouns.

Count noun singular

1. Indefinite Article: _____

2. Definite Article: _____

Count noun plural

3. Indefinite Article: _____

4. Definite Article: _____

Noncount noun

5. Indefinite Article: _____

6. Definite Article: _____

EXERCISE 4-6

Write the correct spelling of the plural for each count noun below. Some of these nouns are regular and some are irregular.

    Example: peach → *peaches*

1. fork → _____
2. tooth → _____
3. knife → _____
4. baby → _____
5. child → _____
6. quiz → _____
7. bowl → _____
8. slice → _____
9. tomato → _____
10. octopus → _____
11. cup → _____
12. goose → _____

EXERCISE 4-7

Read the sentences below. Circle the (count nouns) *you see. Underline the* noncount nouns*. Follow the example.*

    Example: I am shopping for <u>tea</u>, <u>honey</u>, (lemons), and (persimmons).

1. I bought all the ingredients to make my favorite tea.
2. Would you like coffee, tea, or juice?
3. My hair is color damaged, so I bought special shampoo.
4. The sand on this beach is soft and white.
5. Lily won't eat this soup because she doesn't like chicken.

EXERCISE 4-8

Match the appropriate noncount noun to the quantifier. There may be multiple answers for some items. Follow the example.

Noncount Nouns			
pie	salt	ice cream	milk
water	sugar	bread	chips

Example: a slice of *bread*_____

1. two pieces of _____

2. a bottle of _____

3. a cup of _____

4. a glass of _____

5. a bag of _____

6. two pinches of _____

7. a bowl of _____

EXERCISE 4-9

Read the sentences below. Write **How many** *or* **How much** *on the line to correctly complete each sentence. Follow the example.*

Example: *How much* money do you need?

1. _____ cereal should I buy?

2. _____ quarters do you have?

3. _____ fruit should I buy?

4. _____ rice does the recipe call for?

5. _____ varieties of apples are in this pie?

6. _____ kinds of music do you like?

EXERCISE 4-10

Now you try it. Write two questions using **How many** *and two questions using* **How much.** *Follow the spelling rules for plural count nouns.*

How many . . . ?

1. _____

2. _____

How much . . . ?

3. _____

4. _____

EXERCISE 4-11

Read the sentences below. Underline all of the <u>determiners</u> you find.

1. Many people in my class got an A on the test.

2. Several dogs are playing in the neighborhood dog park.

3. Three chairs at the kitchen table are broken.

4. Every French teacher gives a midterm and final exams.

5. My sister is cooking some beef stew for the family.

6. That kid is a great baseball pitcher!

EXERCISE 4-12

Circle the correct subject pronoun for each sentence. Follow the example.

Example: Alexandra (female)   (She) He It   works at the library.

1. Dick and Jane (male + female)   We   They   You   attend Grover High School.

2. Musaka and I (male + male)   We   They   You   went to the rally.

3. Robert (male)   She   He   It   has four children.

4. Patty (female)   She   He   It   plays BINGO on Sunday nights.

5. My book (gender neutral)   She   He   It   is interesting.

6. Steve and Robin (male + female)   We   They   You   work every weekday.

EXERCISE 4-13

Complete the sentences below with the correct subject pronoun. Study the names of people in the conversation. Follow the example.

Prof. Banks (male)	Jim (male)	Ms. Couris (female)	Dr. Aguirre (female)
Mick (male)	Mrs. Fowler (female)	Ella (female)	Wendy (female)

Example 1: Prof. Banks → Jim (about Jim)   <u>You</u> are in my class.

Example 2: Jim → Mrs. Fowler (about Wendy)   <u>She</u> is my wife.

1. Mick → Ms. Couris (about Ella and Jim)

   _____ are my coworkers.

2. Ella →Wendy (about Prof. Banks)

   _____ is my professor.

3. Dr. Aguirre → Ms. Couris (about Mrs. Fowler)

   _____ is my neighbor.

4. Dr. Aguirre → Jim (about Jim)

   _____ need to exercise more.

5. Prof. Banks → Mick (about Mick)

   _____ passed the class.

6. Wendy → Ella (about Wendy and Ella)

   _____ should go out tonight.

EXERCISE 4-14

Write sentences with subject pronouns. Study the people below and talk about their jobs. Follow the example.

Miguel (male, student)	Jun Li (female, poet)	Melinda (female, chef)	Blake (male, mechanic)
Fallon (female, student)	Travis (male, computer engineer)	Dexter (male, police officer)	Cersei (female, dog walker)

Example 1: Fallon → Cersei (about Travis)   *He's a computer engineer.*

1. Jun Li → Cersei (about Blake)

   _____

2. Miguel → Blake (about Miguel and Fallon)

   _____

3. Travis → Melinda and Jun Li (about Cersei)

   _____

4. Cersei → Fallon (about Cersei)

   _____

5. Dexter → Travis (about Dexter)

   _____

EXERCISE 4-15

Circle the object pronoun in each sentence. Follow the example.

   Example: Oliver noticed (it.)

1. She brought him to the party.

2. Joseph played baseball with him.

3. They spent a lot of money on it.

4. We gave them to the used clothing store.

5. I heard you.

6. My niece loved it!

7. Text me!

8. The manager showed us the sale rack.

EXERCISE 4-16

Read the sentences below. In each sentence, there is an object of the verb or an object of the preposition. Rewrite the sentence, replacing the underlined object noun with an object pronoun. Follow the example.

   Example: She drove to <u>the farmers market</u>.

   She drove to it.

1. Katie shopped for <u>her nephew</u>.

   _____

2. She often attends <u>community lectures</u>.

   _____

3. My sister got a good deal on <u>her house.</u>

_____

4. I am friends with <u>Ava</u>.

_____

5. Carolina found a gift for <u>Dan</u>.

_____

6. She bought <u>the tickets</u> yesterday.

_____

EXERCISE 4-17

Underline the possessive adjectives in the sentences below. There may be more than one possessive adjective in each sentence. Follow the example.

Example: He hiked the trails on <u>his</u> property.

1. Her kids are in their treehouse.

2. My family enjoys skiing in the mountains.

3. His cat brought home a mouse.

4. His children like drinking your homemade lemonade at your summer parties.

5. Her classmates sang in their church celebration.

6. Noah came to my house.

7. We strolled in the park at the end of my road.

8. Our neighbors swam in the pond behind our house.

EXERCISE 4-18

Underline the possessive pronouns in the sentences below. Highlight any possessive adjectives you find in the sentences. Follow the example.

Example: The book on the table is <u>mine</u>.

1. Look at all the sweaters the knitting club made! His is the green one.

2. My brother has a bountiful vegetable garden. It's much more productive than mine.

3. See that old pickup truck over there? It's theirs.

4. Their paintings are in that gallery. Theirs are the colorful, abstract paintings.

5. Is this money yours?

6. Here is a black purse. Is it hers?

EXERCISE 4-19

Write sentences using possessive pronouns to replace the underlined words. Follow the example.

Example: The basketball is <u>Stewart's</u>. → *The basketball is his.*

1. <u>Our house</u> was the small one over there. → _____

   It's not <u>our house</u> anymore. We sold it. → _____

2. Those socks are <u>Pam's</u>. → _____

3. The birds in the cage are <u>his birds</u>. → _____

4. The two with red hats are <u>our kids</u>. → _____

EXERCISE 4-20

Look at the list of demonstrative adjectives with nouns in the box below and then answer the questions.

| Near in distance or time | <u>this</u> cupcake | <u>these</u> paintbrushes |
| Far in distance or time | <u>that</u> person | <u>those</u> bicycles |

1. Which nouns are singular? _____

2. Which demonstrative adjectives are singular? _____

3. Which nouns are plural? _____

4. Which demonstrative adjectives are plural? _____

EXERCISE 4-21

Write three sentences about things and people that are near to you or far from you right now. Use the demonstrative adjectives **this, that, these,** *and* **those.**

1. _____

2. _____

3. _____

EXERCISE 4-22

Underline the <u>demonstrative pronouns</u> in the sentences below.

1. Those are the good guys.

2. I can't believe this!

3. Have you been to that?

4. These are so fun!

5. You can't have that. It's too dangerous.

6. That is very bad news.

7. This is trending right now.

8. What is this?

EXERCISE 4-23

Write sentences using demonstrative pronouns. Replace the demonstrative adjectives and nouns with demonstrative pronouns. Follow the example.

Example: <u>This water</u> is Chloe's. → *This is Chloe's.* _____

1. I don't like <u>this project.</u> → _____

2. <u>Those papers</u> are Kammie's. → _____

3. <u>These movies</u> are scary. → _____

4. <u>Those teenagers</u> are mine. → _____

AUDIO 🔊

Talking About Ongoing Activities

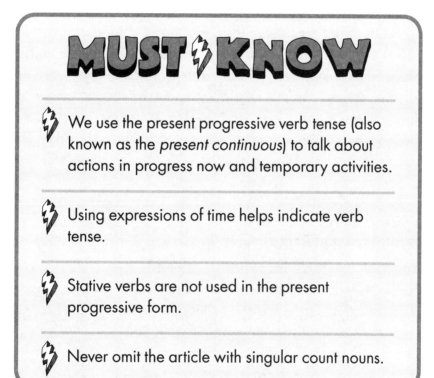

MUST KNOW

- We use the present progressive verb tense (also known as the *present continuous*) to talk about actions in progress now and temporary activities.

- Using expressions of time helps indicate verb tense.

- Stative verbs are not used in the present progressive form.

- Never omit the article with singular count nouns.

hat <u>are</u> you <u>doing</u> right now? You are reading this sentence. You are studying the English language. You are learning about the present progressive verb tense. We often talk about activities that we <u>are doing</u> either in the moment of speaking or in progress temporarily. These actions began before the moment of speaking or writing and continue, or progress, in the moment of speaking or writing.

Present Progressive Verb Tense

Temporary actions in progress are different from habitual actions, which we learned about in Chapter 2. We perform habitual actions regularly, such as every day, every week, every Sunday, every month, every winter, and every year. As you know from Chapter 2, we use the simple present tense for routines, customs, and schedules. However, actions in progress at the moment of speaking require the **present progressive verb tense**. This verb tense indicates that the action is in progress. Let's take a look at how we form and use the present progressive tense.

Forming the Present Progressive Tense

We use this verb tense to talk about things we do over time. These activities are happening right now, or they are happening temporarily for a length of time including now. Look at some example sentences of actions that are in progress. These actions are not complete. We use the present progressive to talk about **temporary activities that have a short or a long duration**. Notice the use of time words and phrases to indicate when we are doing these things. The time words and phrases are underlined.

We also use this verb tense to talk about future plans. You will learn more about this and the future verb tense in Chapter 8.

EXAMPLES

▶ Sherry **is walking** her dog <u>now</u>.

▶ Josephine and her mother **are shopping** for groceries <u>this morning</u>.

▶ I**'m taking** physics and chemistry classes <u>this semester</u>.

▶ She**'s watering** the plants <u>right now</u>.

▶ They**'re exercising** every morning <u>this summer</u>.

▶ Teachers **are giving** too much homework <u>these days</u>.

Expressions of Time

Notice the time phrases in the example sentences above. ***Now*** and ***right now*** indicate that the speaker is doing the action <u>in the moment of speaking</u>. However, time phrases with the pronoun ***this*** <u>indicate a period of time that is still in progress</u>. Examples of these time phrases are ***this semester***, ***this summer***, and ***this month***. Each of these time phrases indicate that the action is still in progress. So, when we use ***this week***, the week is not finished. Similarly, ***this month*** indicates that the month is still in progress: it's not complete. In the second example sentence, ***this morning*** indicates that it is still morning: it is not noon yet. The last example expression uses the idiomatic expression ***these days***, which indicates <u>a current trend</u>. A similar expression is ***nowadays***. Let's learn how to form this verb tense.

Present Progressive Tense: Forming the Affirmative

How do we form the present progressive in affirmative statements? Here's how we form **dynamic (action) verbs** in the present progressive affirmative.

How to Form the Affirmative Present Progressive Verb Tense

Subject or Subject Pronoun	Appropriate Form of the BE Verb	Main Verb: –ing Form of the Verb (Present Participle)	Example Sentences
I	am	running	I am running around the track right now.
You / We / They	are	studying	At this moment, you / we / they are studying for the test.
He / She / It	is	working	He / She / It is working today.

Spelling Rules

There are some spelling rules to know when writing the present participle form of a verb. Look at these spelling rules:

1. Add *–ing* to the base form of the verb. Example: work → working

2. If the verb ends in a **silent e**, drop the *e* and add *–ing*. Example: tak<u>e</u> → taking

3. When the last three letters are a **consonant-vowel-consonant** (CVC) in a one-syllable word, double the last consonant and add *–ing*.
Example: <u>r u n</u> → run<u>n</u>ing
            CVC

4. Exception: Do <u>not</u> double the final consonant if it is a *w*, *x*, or *y*.
Example: <u>show</u> → sho<u>w</u>ing

Present Progressive Tense Timeline

Let's look at the timeline for this verb tense.

Example 1: Marcus is pitching in the baseball game right now.

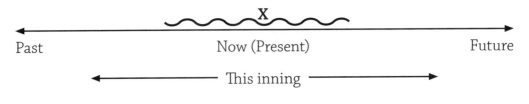

In this inning, Marcus is pitching for his team. It is a temporary activity because he's not the regular pitcher for the team. He started this activity a few minutes ago, and it will last for the whole inning. During this inning, he is pitching. He may not be the pitcher for the next inning, but right now, he's pitching. It's a temporary activity that lasts for a period of time.

Example 2: Angela is working at the used bookstore this summer.

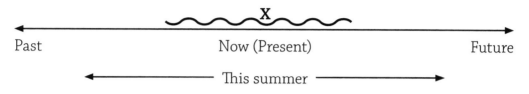

Angela is working at the used bookstore for the summer. She started working there at the beginning of the summer, and she will continue until the end of the summer. It's still summer, so Angela's job is not complete. It's a temporary activity because it's a job only for the summer.

Example 3: My brother and his wife are taking an online business course.

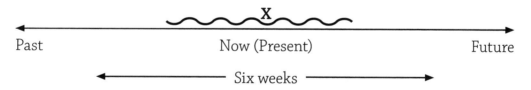

It's 7:00 a.m. on Sunday morning and my brother and his wife are sleeping. We say ***they are taking an online course*** even though at this moment they are sleeping. They are taking the online course over six weeks. The course already started and will end in a few weeks. We use the present progressive because the course is temporary. The fact that they are sleeping at the moment I am talking about them is irrelevant. This activity (online class) is occurring for six weeks. It is in progress.

Expressions of Time

Here are some common time expressions we use with the present progressive.

When to Use These Expressions	Expressions to Use with the Present Progressive Verb Tense			
In the moment of speaking	now	right now	at this moment	
In a period of time that is not complete	this week	this weekend	this month	this semester
	this season	this quarter	this year	today
Describing trends	these days	nowadays	currently	

Present Progressive Tense: Forming the Negative

How do we form the present progressive in negative statements? To form the negative present progressive verb tense, use **not**. Check out the table on the next page.

How to Form the Negative Present Progressive Verb Tense

Subject or Subject Pronoun	Appropriate Form of the BE Verb	Negative	Main Verb: –ing Form of the Verb (Present Participle)	Example Sentences
I	am	not	bring*ing*	I **am not bringing** my daughter. I'm bringing my son.
You / We / They	are	not	talk*ing*	You **are not talking** about breakfast. You're talking about lunch.
				We **are not talking** about food for the party. We're talking about beverages.
				They **are not talking** about the house. They're talking about the apartment.
He / She / It	is	not	study*ing*	He **is not studying** for the biology quiz. He's studying for the English exam.

Forming Negative Contractions

As you know, we usually use contractions when we speak. The present progressive verb tense requires the verb BE; therefore, we can make a negative contraction two different ways. One way is to combine the subject and the BE verb. Another way is to combine the BE verb and *not*. We also learned these contraction strategies in Chapter 2. Check out the following charts.

1. Contractions with the Subject Pronoun + BE Verb

Subject Pronoun + Appropriate Form of BE Verb	Negative	Main Verb: -ing Form of the Verb (Present Participle)	Example Sentences
I'm	not	singing	I'm **not singing**. However, I'm dancing.
You're	not	dancing	You're **not dancing** very well. You're off beat.
We're			We're **not dancing** salsa. This is zumba!
They're			They're **not dancing** in the school play because it was cancelled.
He's	not	playing	He's **not playing** chess right now because he's sick.
She's		working	She's **not playing** well. Her shoulder hurts.
It's			It's **not working**. I think it needs a tune-up.
John's			John's **not working** today because he's on vacation.

2. Contractions with the Negative BE Verb (BE + Negative)

Subject or Subject Pronoun	Appropriate Form of BE Verb + Negative	Negative	Main Verb: -ing Form of the Verb (Present Participle)	Example Sentences
I	am **Note:** We do *not* contract *am* and *not*.	not	kidding	I **am not kidding**: She's giving a test today!
You / We / They	aren't		cooking	You **aren't cooking** today. We **aren't cooking** dinner. We have dinner reservations. They **aren't cooking** pasta.
He / She / It	isn't		writing	He **isn't writing** his research paper at the moment. She **isn't writing** in her diary these days. It **isn't writing** smoothly. I think my pen is running out of ink.

Present Progressive Tense: Forming Yes/No Questions

In conversation, we often ask questions about what people are doing. We use **yes/no questions** to ask what is happening, and we answer yes/no questions with either *yes* or *no*. For yes/no questions in the present progressive, we **invert the subject and the BE verb**. This means we switch the order of the subject and the BE verb. The appropriate form of the BE verb begins the sentence and the subject comes after the BE verb. Let's review how we form these questions.

Appropriate Form of BE Verb	Subject or Subject Pronoun	Main Verb: -ing Form of the Verb (Present Participle)	Rest of the Sentence	Example Sentences
Am	I	**driving**	too slowly?	**Am** I **driving** too slowly?
Are	you	**listening**	to the coach?	**Are** you **listening** to the coach?
	we		to classical music?	**Are** we **listening** to classical music?
	they		carefully?	**Are** they **listening** carefully?
Is	he	**growing**	vegetables this season?	**Is** he **growing** vegetables this season?
	she		her hair out?	**Is** she **growing** her hair out?
	it		quickly?	**Is** it **growing** quickly?

Reminder: Use rising pitch at the end of yes/no questions to indicate you are looking for an answer. See the pitch chart in the Appendix for more information.

Answering Yes/No Questions

We usually answer yes/no questions with complete answers or short answers when we are talking with teachers, parents, bosses, colleagues, and coworkers. With peers and friends, short answers are more common. Note the BE verb is stressed in affirmative answers and the negative is stressed in negative answers. In the chart below, the stressed words are in bold. Note that in negative answers, the BE part of the BE-not contraction is the stressed syllable. This is underlined. We usually do not contract the affirmative answer. Rather, we stress the BE verb in the affirmative answer by pronouncing it a bit stronger and louder.

Complete Answers

Yes/No Question	Affirmative Answer	Negative Answer
Are you studying right now?	Yes, I **am** studying right now.	No, I'm **not** studying right now.
Is she meeting us here?	Yes, she **is** meeting us here.	No, she **isn't** meeting us here. No, she's **not** meeting us here.
Are they enjoying the holiday?	Yes, they **are** enjoying the holiday.	No, they **aren't** enjoying the holiday. No they're **not** enjoying the holiday.

When giving a negative answer, we sometimes offer more information for clarity and accuracy. For example, we might say *No, I'm not cleaning the house. I'm cooking supper*. Sometimes, we offer an explanation. For example, we might say *No, I'm not cleaning the house because I cleaned yesterday.* When the answer is negative, we may omit the negative answer and instead correct and clarify with the word *actually*. For example, we might say *Actually, I'm cooking supper*.

Short Answers

Yes/No Questions	Affirmative Answer*	Negative Answer
Are you having fun at the park?	Yes, I am.	No, I'm not.
Is he playing golf today?	Yes, he is.	No, he isn't.
		No, he's not.
Are they working on the computer?	Yes, they are.	No, they aren't.
		No, they're not.

***Remember:** We don't contract affirmative short answers.

Quick Answers to Yes/No Questions

A quick *yes* or *no* answer to these questions is okay, too. However, be sure to use a polite tone of voice. Otherwise, a quick answer may sound abrupt and rude. With friends, it's common to answer with slang. Review the slang expressions for *yes* and *no* in Chapter 1.

PRONUNCIATION

▶ For long affirmative answers, stress the BE verb when not contracted:

  Yes, he *is* taking the exam.

▶ For short affirmative answers, stress the BE verb:

  Yes, he *is.*

▶ For long negative answers, stress *not*:

  No, he's *not* taking the exam.

▶ For short negative answers with contractions of the BE verb and *not*, stress the BE form.

  No, he *is*n't.

  No, they *are*n't.

▶ **Important:** Do not stress the quick answers.

Active vs. Stative Verbs

We use the present progressive verb tense primarily with action verbs. We *rarely* use stative, or nonaction, verbs with the present progressive verb tense. What exactly are stative verbs? Stative verbs describe states: conditions or situations that exist. They are not verbs of physical or physiological activity. Stative verbs describe mental states, emotional states, senses, perceptions, possession, and measurement. For example, we *remember, know, forget,* and *understand* things, and these are all *mental activities.* Don't use stative verbs with the present progressive. Rather, **use stative verbs with the simple present verb tense even if the action is ongoing.** See a list of commonly used stative verbs in the table below.

appear	appreciate	belong	believe	consist	cost
desire	dislike	doubt	equal	forget	hate
have	know	like	matter	mean	need
owe	own	possess	prefer	realize	recognize
remember	resemble	seem	suppose	understand	want

Examples of States: Existing Conditions and Situations

Let's look at some example sentences with stative verbs. The timeline shows an existing state. Even though the state happens over time, we use the simple present—*not* the present progressive—for these situations.

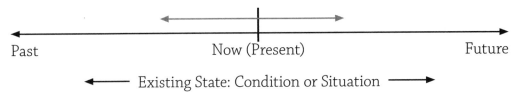

Past   Now (Present)   Future

⟵ Existing State: Condition or Situation ⟶

1. He <u>likes</u> his job.

2. You <u>dislike</u> your boss.

3. She <u>appreciates</u> everything you are doing for this project.

4. It really <u>matters</u> to me.

5. The kit <u>consists</u> of everything you need to build a model airplane.

6. I <u>forget</u> her name.

7. I <u>remember</u> her name now!

8. That dog <u>belongs</u> to him.

9. Five plus five <u>equals</u> ten.

10. We <u>need</u> a long vacation on a tropical island.

Verbs That Can Be Stative or Active

Some stative verbs also have dynamic meanings. When the verb has a stative meaning, do not use the progressive verb tense. However, when the meaning **is dynamic, or active, it is used in the progressive form** of the verb tense. The following verbs can be stative (non-action) or dynamic (action) verbs, depending on how they are used.

Thoughts and opinions	doubt	forget	guess	imagine	mean	mind
	remember	see	think	want		
Emotions and feelings	like	love				
Senses and perception	feel	hear	look	see	smell	taste
Possession	have					
Measurement	weigh					
Other existing states	appear	be	cost	include	look	sound

IRL In prescriptive grammar, *like* and *love* are stative verbs all of the time. However, this has changed recently. Sometimes, we use *like* and *love* as dynamic verbs. This is especially trendy with young adults. Using *like* and *love* in a progressive form shows emphasis of the feeling in the moment of speaking. Let's look at some example sentences:

- I'm <u>loving</u> that dress! Where did you get it?
- He's <u>not liking</u> his math teacher right now. He failed the exam.

Stative and Dynamic Verbs: Examples of Use

To understand how these verbs can be both stative and dynamic, see the example sentences in the following table.

Stative Verb	Meaning	Dynamic Verb	Meaning
I <u>see</u> what you mean.	I **understand** you.	I <u>am seeing</u> the doctor tomorrow morning.	I am **meeting** with the doctor tomorrow.
She <u>looks</u> amazing!	She **appears** amazing.	She <u>is looking</u> at her calendar.	She is **directing her eyes** at her calendar.
They <u>have</u> a new car.	Possession: They **own** a new car.	They <u>are having</u> a good time.	They are **experiencing** a good time.
He <u>is</u> clever.	**Permanent quality** or state	He <u>is being</u> silly.	He is **behaving** this way **temporarily**.
That soup <u>tastes</u> so good!	Sensory perception or experience of **flavor**	My mom <u>is tasting</u> the soup.	She is **using her taste buds to assess** the flavor.
Joan <u>feels</u> satin is better than silk.	Mental state: Joan **thinks** satin is better than silk.	Joan <u>is feeling</u> the silky fabric.	Joan is **physically touching** the fabric.
Dinner <u>smells</u> delicious!	**Olfactory sensory perception**	They <u>are smelling</u> the roses in the garden.	They are **putting their noses close** to the flowers to **breathe in and experience** fragrance.

Present Progressive Tense: Forming WH Questions

We briefly studied this in Chapter 1, but let's revisit WH questions in the present progressive verb tense.

To ask questions about what people are doing, we use WH questions to ask about time, location, manner, and reason for an action. Remember from Chapter 1 that WH questions begin with WH question words or phrases such as *who, what, when, where, why, how, what kind, which one, how long, how many*, and *how much*. The table below shows how to form these questions.

WH Question Word/Phrase	Appropriate Form of the BE Verb	Subject or Subject Pronoun	Main Verb: *-ing* Form of the Verb (Present Participle)	Rest of the Sentence	Example Sentences
When	am	I	meeting	your new boyfriend?	**When am** I **meeting** your new boyfriend?
Where	are	you	walking	right now?	**Where are** you **walking** right now?
		we	playing		**Where are** we **playing** Frisbee?
		they	picnicking		**Where are** they **picnicking**?
Why	is	he	wearing	a sweater	**Why is** he **wearing** a sweater? It's hot out!
		she	wearing	a tutu	**Why is** she **wearing** a tutu?
		it	making	that strange sound?	**Why is** it **making** that strange sound?
Who/Whom (object)	is	she	talking to	right now?	**Who is** she **talking** to?
					To **whom is** she **talking**?

We usually use **falling pitch at the end of WH questions**. However, if you don't hear or understand some information and **you need repetition, use rising pitch** as in the second example. Look at the pitch patterns below.

1. Stress the proper syllable in the last content noun—noun, verb, adjective or adverb—and use falling pitch for most WH questions:

How many people are attending the **sem**inar?

2. Stress the WH question word and use rising pitch to check that you understand the question correctly and to express that you need repetition:

Why is she wearing a silly hat?

Note: Pitch patterns are shown above, below, and through the words of sentences to illustrate that our pitches change as we speak.

Forming *Who* Questions

When **Who** is the subject of the sentence, **we do not add another subject**. We do not add *I, you, we, they, he, she,* or *it*. See the table below with examples of this.

Who (Subject of Sentence)	BE Form = is	Main Verb: –ing Form of the Verb (Present Participle)	Rest of the Sentence	Example Sentences
Who	is	**watching**	the baby?	**Who is watching** the baby?
Who	is	**baking**	the cake?	**Who is baking** the cake?

Note: The BE form for the WH question word **who** is always **is**.

For all WH questions, we can give long, short, or quick answers. The long answer is a complete sentence. The short answer provides essential information + the BE verb. The quick answer gives only the essential information that answers the question.

POP QUIZ!

Which verb tense do we use to talk about things we are doing in the moment of speaking and temporary, ongoing actions? If you said the present progressive verb tense, you are correct!

Which verb tense do we use when we are talking about states or conditions that are ongoing? Did you answer simple present? If so, you are correct!

Present Progressive Tense: Using Tag Questions

In Chapter 2, you learned how to use tag questions at the end of statements to verify information or seek agreement. We can use tag questions with the present progressive verb tense, too. With present progressive forms of the verb, use tag questions with the BE verb. You must choose the appropriate form of the BE verb, which depends on the subject of the sentence. So, if the subject is **she**, then the tag question will use **isn't she**. Check the example sentences below to understand this rule:

EXAMPLES

▶ I'm going with you, aren't I?

▶ You're having fun, aren't you?

▶ She's learning Spanish, isn't she?

▶ He's making an appointment for the dentist, isn't he?

▶ It's working well now, isn't it?

▶ We're enjoying this vacation, aren't we?

▶ They're eating lunch now, aren't they?

Using Intonation with Tag Questions

In Chapter 2, you learned that we use tag questions in two ways: **to verify information and to seek agreement**. See examples of these tag questions and their pitch patterns below.

Statement with Tag Question to Verify Information

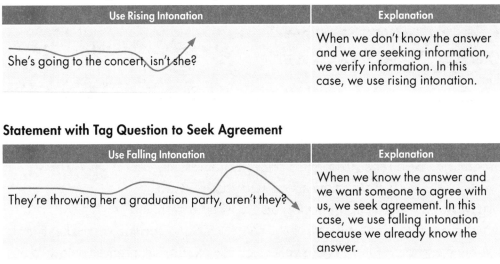

Use Rising Intonation	Explanation
She's going to the concert, isn't she?	When we don't know the answer and we are seeking information, we verify information. In this case, we use rising intonation.

Statement with Tag Question to Seek Agreement

Use Falling Intonation	Explanation
They're throwing her a graduation party, aren't they?	When we know the answer and we want someone to agree with us, we seek agreement. In this case, we use falling intonation because we already know the answer.

Forming Affirmative and Negative Tag Questions

As you learned in Chapter 2, when we have an affirmative statement, the tag question is negative and vice versa. Here are some helpful notes to remember:

- Even though the statement is in the present progressive verb tense, the **tag question and the answer only use the BE verb**.

- In affirmative answers, do not contract.

- In negative statements and in the negative answers, either contraction works well.

- Even though a certain answer is expected, answer accurately.

Check out the table below for example sentences.

Affirmative Statement	Negative Tag Question	Expect Affirmative Answer
I'm making good time,	aren't I?	Yes, you are.
She's throwing a party,	isn't she?	Yes, she is.
They're graduating this year,	aren't they?	Yes, they are.
We're winning the game,	aren't we?	Yes, we are.
She's having fun,	isn't she?	Yes, she is.
They're exercising,	aren't they?	Yes, they are.

Negative Statement	Affirmative Tag Question	Expect Negative Answer
I'm not failing,	am I?	No, you're not.
She isn't eating now,	is she?	No, she isn't. No, she's not.
They're not watching the movie,	are they?	No, they aren't. No, they're not.
We aren't planning anything right now,	are we?	No, we aren't. No, we're not.
He's not partying these days,	is he?	No, he isn't. No, he's not.
They aren't singing along,	are they?	No, they aren't. No, they're not.

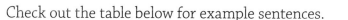

BTW

Even when there is an expected answer to a question, you must answer truthfully. To illustrate this, look at the first example, for which an affirmative answer is expected: **I'm making good time, aren't I? Yes, you are.** *If the reality is that you are NOT making good time, then the answer should be negative:* **No, you're not.**

You can start with these words to soften the unexpected answer: **actually, honestly, truthfully,** *or the trendy expression with young adults* **I'm not gonna lie.** *Sometimes, the* **yes** *or* **no** *is omitted. Here are a few examples of unexpected answers:*

* *Actually, no, you're not./Actually, you're not.*

* *Honestly, you're not.*

* *I'm not gonna lie: you're not.*

Using Articles

We learned articles in Chapter 4; however, it's so important that we'll review one particular rule here. For many English language learners, articles are confusing because there are multiple rules and many specific situations. One point to master is this: **We must always use an article (or determiner) with a singular count noun.** In other words, we can *never* omit the article with singular count nouns. Review articles in general below and note this important rule in bold.

	Count Nouns	Noncount Nouns
Singular	Definite article: *the* Indefinite article: *a, an* **Article required**	
Plural	Definite article: *the* Indefinite article: *some, any* **No article**	
Unchanging form		Definite article: *the* Indefinite articles: *some, any* **No article**

Let's look at example sentences that follow this rule. Notice that every singular count noun is preceded by an article or determiner.

- We're attending **the science fair** this week.
- I'm using **your pen** right now.
- He's eating **a** delicious **dinner**.
- She's juggling **two jobs** this summer.
- They're not taking **the exam** right now.
- You're preaching to **the choir**.*

*__Note:__ *To preach to the choir* is an idiom that means to speak to people who already agree with your point.

Dialogue: The Internship

David and Jennifer are coworkers at a local restaurant. They are chatting while they prepare for the dinner rush. Notice the use of the present progressive verb tense, time words and phrases, and articles and determiners.

David: What are you doing?

Jennifer: I'm folding some napkins. What are you doing? Can you help me?

David: I'm not doing anything yet. Yeah, I can help.

Jennifer: So, what's going on with you?

David: Nothing much, really. Well, actually, I'm applying for an internship this semester.

Jennifer: Wow, that's great! Where's the internship?

David: It's at a nonprofit business near my dad's house.

Jennifer: What kind of business?

David: It's an intercultural exchange organization that promotes cross-cultural experience and understanding. It's really cool.

Jennifer: Is the organization big?

David: No yeah no, it's really big, and it's expanding its services this year.

Jennifer: What position are you applying for?

David: I'm applying for the host family development internship.

Jennifer: Really! Do you think you'll get it?

David: I hope so! I am a graduate of the program. I loved it.

Jennifer: I didn't know that. Did you travel?

David: Yup, I stayed with a family in Greece. It was awesome. I learned so much.

Jennifer: I want to do that!

Practice 5-A

To check your understanding, reread the dialogue and identify the elements we learned in this chapter. Circle the (present progressive verb tense,) underline the time words and phrases, and highlight the article and determiners. See the answers in Practice 5-A in the Answer Key.

Lecture: Carhenge

Carhenge: A Unique Place to Visit

One of the most unique tourist destinations in the United States is Carhenge. This manmade sculpture is one of a kind because it is the only known replica of Stonehenge in existence in the United States constructed entirely of cars! A year before the creation of Carhenge, an artist in Ontario, Canada, erected Autohenge, a similar replica, for an automobile commercial. However, it was dismantled soon after, and it no longer exists. Carhenge, located on the High Plains near Alliance, Nebraska, still stands, and this popular landmark attracts thousands of visitors a year.

Although it is now an international tourist sensation, this quirky structure had humble beginnings. In 1987, Jim Reinders, inspired by England's Stonehenge, and 35 of his family members gathered to build and erect this memorial to his father on the family's property. They found abandoned cars from the 1950s and 1960s on nearby farms and junkyards and designed an exact replica of Stonehenge. It took 39 of those vintage cars to complete it. Some of the cars were half-buried in five-foot pits; some cars were placed on their sides; and others were scattered to perfectly match the original "henge." To replicate the arches, multiple cars were piled on top of one another and welded together. Eventually, the finished product was spray-painted grey to better resemble the stones in Stonehenge.

Carhenge was officially dedicated on the summer solstice in June 1987. At that time, the residents of Alliance despised the appearance of it and wanted to build a fence around it to hide it. Once they saw how it attracted growing numbers of tourists, however, they appreciated Carhenge. Reinders donated the site to the Friends of Carhenge, and today, it includes several additional car-art sculptures and a gift shop. More than 30 years later, this peculiar American monument still brings joy to thousands of visitors every year.

Success Strategy: Using Tracking

You learned about shadowing in Chapter 2. The next step in building your listening skills is *tracking*.

Tracking is similar to singing along with your favorite song when you know the words. The singer is singing the song, and you are listening and singing the same words at the same time in the same rhythm. This is tracking. Do this with the audio files and transcript that accompany this book. Practice by listening to each audio file several—three to seven—times to become familiar with the "song" of the sentence or dialogue or mini lecture. Then sing along with your voice. If you get off track, that's okay. Just keep doing it until you can track the voices on the audio files.

How to Track

Follow these steps after listening multiple times to the audio:

1. Listen and speak along with the voice you hear—at the same time.

2. If the audio is too fast or slow, pause your speech and jump back in wherever you can.

3. Repeat this many times until you know the "song" of the voice on the audio file and can imitate it accurately.

Support step: If the speech feels too fast, you can **hum along** instead of saying all the words. Get the melody of the speech first. Then, after you listen and hum multiple times, speak the words. Articulate as many words as you can while you stay with the audio. Eventually, you will keep the rhythm as you say each word.

There are only three steps, but it takes some time to track well. This listening strategy is simple, yet effective and powerful. You can use it for any kind of audio file that also has a transcript. For example, audio books with hard copy books are great for tracking. Other sources are online video recordings of talks and interviews both short and long. Do this with your favorite shows and use closed captioning (cc). Be sure you can pause the show so you can practice.

Advanced step: Once you master tracking, try the next-level technique: different speaking styles. Examples of different speaking styles are news, dramas, songs, famous speeches, narrated documentaries, and sitcoms— situation comedies. There are many speaking styles, and you can explore them. Practice tracking different styles so you can expand your pitch range and strengthen your speaking skills and build confidence.

EXERCISES

EXERCISE 5-1

Choose the correct form of the BE verb in the present progressive verb tense. Follow the example.

Example: Marty _____ **making** a poster for the school project.   am   are   (is)

1. Mercedes _____ **growing** flowers on her back porch.   am   are   is

2. Mr. and Mrs. Gilbert _____ **raising** chickens.   am   are   is

3. Professor Tufo _____ **teaching** chemistry this year.   am   are   is

4. Right now, we _____ **getting** coffee to go.*   am   are   is

5. I _____ **thinking** about my weekend plans.   am   are   is

Note: Food *"to go"* means that you do not eat in the restaurant. Rather, you go to the restaurant or café, buy food or beverages, and *take it out of the restaurant to eat or drink it elsewhere.*

EXERCISE 5-2

Spell the progressive form of the verb below correctly.

1. share → _____

2. cry → _____

3. make → _____

4. shop → _____

5. put → _____

6. walk → _____

EXERCISE 5-3

Complete the sentences below with the correct form of the BE verb and the verb in parentheses. Follow the example.

Example: Ms. McKinley *is grading* our tests right now. (grade)

1. They _____ to the movie theater right now. (drive)

2. At this moment, Cole _____ the doctor's office to make an appointment. (call)

3. Right now, Suzanna _____ live music at the park. (enjoy)

4. Dionne _____ her daughter how to count from one to five. (teach)

5. My nephew _____ a special meal for his wife's birthday. (cook)

6. We _____ money to buy a new car this year. (save)

EXERCISE 5-4

Write sentences with the present progressive verb tense about what you, your friends, and your family are doing right now or as temporary ongoing activities. Use all forms of the BE verb: am, is, and are. Each of these is listed on a line below.

1. _____ (am)

2. _____ (is)

3. _____ (are)

EXERCISE 5-5

Choose the correct negative form of the present progressive verb. Follow the example.

Example: Deb ***isn't*** **cleaning** the kitchen tonight. It's Mike's turn.   'm not   isn't   aren't

1. Mycah _____ **working** part time. She's working full time.   'm not   isn't   aren't

2. My cousins _____ **studying** German. They're studying French.   'm not   isn't   aren't

3. Dr. Mitchell _____ **seeing** patients today. It's a holiday.   'm not   isn't   aren't

4. I _____ **teaching** this winter. I'm taking a sabbatical.   'm not   isn't   aren't

5. Steve and Michelle _____ **eating** out* because Steve is cooking.   'm not   isn't   aren't

6. We _____ **worrying** about the storm. Our house is safe and secure.   'm not   isn't   aren't

*__Note:__ *To eat out* and *to go out* for a meal mean to dine at a restaurant.

EXERCISE 5-6

Use the negative form of the present progressive verb tense. Write sentences about what you and your friends and family are __not__ doing right now or as temporary ongoing activities. Use all forms of the BE verb: am, is, and are. These are listed on a line below. Do not use contractions.

1. _____ (am)

2. _____ (is)

3. _____ (are)

EXERCISE 5-7

Form sentences describing what people are doing. Use the present progressive verb tense in the affirmative and the words provided. Then, write the negative form of the sentence using the two different ways to make a contraction for all except "I" sentences. Review the spelling rules in the chapter. Follow the example.

Example: Jeanne / visit / her sister / this week.

Jeanne is visiting her sister this week.

Jeanne isn't visiting her sister this week.

She's not visiting her sister this week.

1. Jackie / play / soccer right now.

_____

_____

_____

2. I / study / Spanish this year.

_____

_____

_____

3. Jean Claude and Sofie / argue / at this moment.

_____

_____

_____

4. My dog / eat / the new dog food.

_____

_____

_____

5. Sue and I / talk / on the phone.

_____

_____

_____

EXERCISE 5-8

Use the negative contraction with the present progressive verb tense. Write sentences about what you and your friends and family are not doing right now or as temporary ongoing activities. Use all forms of the BE verb: am, is, and are. Use both kinds of contractions wherever possible.

1. _____ (am)

2. _____ (is)

3. _____ (are)

EXERCISE 5-9

Form yes/no questions with the present progressive verb tense using the words provided. Then write long, short, and quick answers to the question. Answer the questions affirmatively (Yes) or negatively (No). Follow the examples below.

Example 1: BE verb / Hiro / take / swim lessons this summer? (Yes.)

Question: *Is Hiro taking swim lessons this summer?*

Long answer: *Yes, he is taking swim lessons this summer.*

Short answer: *Yes, he is.*

Quick answer: *Yes.*

Example 2: BE verb / Heidi and Duncan / raising / hens in their backyard? (No.)

Question: *Are Heidi and Duncan raising hens in their backyard?*

Long answer: *No, they aren't raising hens in their backyard. / No, they're not raising hens in their backyard.*

Short answer: *No, they aren't. / No, they're not.*

Quick answer: *No.*

1. BE verb / George / build / cabinets for his kitchen? (Yes.)

   Question: _____

   Long answer: _____

   Short answer: _____

   Quick answer: _____

2. BE verb / Marcia / read / your research paper right now? (No.)

   Question: _____

   Long answer: _____

   Short answer: _____

   Quick answer: _____

3. BE verb / they / work / at the hardware store? (No.)

   Question: _____

   Long answer: _____

   Short answer: _____

   Quick answer: _____

4. BE verb / you / study / at the university? (Yes.)

   Question: _____

   Long answer: _____

   Short answer: _____

   Quick answer: _____

5. BE verb / Bethany / paint / an original mural? (Yes.)

Question: _____

Long answer: _____

Short answer: _____

Quick answer: _____

EXERCISE 5-10

Form WH questions with the present progressive verb tense using the words provided. Form long and short answers using the information in the parentheses. Follow the examples below.

Example 1: Where / BE verb / Junko / take / swim lessons? (at the Parkland Pool)

Question: *Where is Junko taking swim lessons?*

Long answer (complete sentence): *She's taking swim lessons at the Parkland Pool.*

Short answer (not a complete sentence): *At the Parkland Pool.*

Example 2: Why / BE verb / Joey / make / brunch for his neighbors? (he enjoys cooking)

Question: *Why is Joey making brunch for his neighbors?*

Long answer (complete sentence): *He's making brunch because he enjoys cooking.*

Short answer (not a complete sentence): *Because he enjoys cooking.*

1. When / BE verb / Olivia / go / to school? (at night)

   Question: _____

   Long answer: _____

   Short answer: _____

2. How many magazines / BE verb / Ella / read / at lunch? (three)

   Question: _____

   Long answer: _____

   Short answer: _____

3. How often / BE verb / the professor / give / pop quizzes this semester?
   (every week)

   Question: _____

   Long answer: _____

   Short answer: _____

4. Why / BE verb / she / study / at the community college? (it's convenient
   and affordable)

   Question: _____

   Long answer: _____

   Short answer: _____

5. How / BE verb / Bethany / progress / on her painting? (very well)

   Question: _____

   Long answer: _____

   Short answer: _____

EXERCISE 5-11

Form who questions with the present progressive verb tense using the statements given. Form long, short, and quick answers using the information in parentheses. Notice that the questions and long answers are often shortened. Follow the example below.

Example: _____ BE form practicing American English pronunciation right now? (Leticia)

Question: *Who is practicing American English pronunciation right now?* **or** *Who is practicing American English pronunciation?*

Long answer (complete sentence): *Leticia is practicing American English pronunciation.*

Short answer (essential information + BE verb): *Leticia is.*

Quick answer (essential information only): *Leticia.*

1. _____ BE form taking a shower? (Max)

Question: _____

Long answer: _____

Short answer: _____

Quick answer: _____

2. _____ BE form driving to the cinema? (Shahila and her son)

Question: _____

Long answer: _____

Short answer: _____

Quick answer: _____

3. _____ <u>BE form</u> preparing Thanksgiving dinner? (Elena's mother)

Question: _____

Long answer: _____

Short answer: _____

Quick answer: _____

4. _____ <u>BE form</u> buying sandwiches at the local café? (Cheryl and her friends)

Question: _____

Long answer: _____

Short answer: _____

Quick answer: _____

5. _____ <u>BE form</u> packing for a trip to Paris? (Charlene and Jim)

Question: _____

Long answer: _____

Short answer: _____

Quick answer: _____

EXERCISE 5-12

Read the sentences below. Circle the correct article for each sentence. Follow the example. The symbol Ø means no article is necessary.

Example: I am trying _____ new Persian restaurant.   ⓐ any

1. Do you like _____ dollhouse we made?   the Ø

2. We are all eating _____ sushi that you bought.   any the

3. I don't want _____ spaghetti, thank you. I'm not hungry.   any some

4. Is she enjoying _____ new toy?   the some

5. My aunt and uncle are buying _____ lottery tickets.   a Ø

EXERCISE 5-13

Now you try it. Write a true sentence about your life for each category. Use the correct definite or indefinite article for count or noncount nouns. Follow the spelling rules for plural count nouns. Remember that for singular count nouns, an article (or determiner) is required.

Count noun singular

1. Indefinite Article _____

2. Definite Article _____

Count noun plural

3. Indefinite Article _____

4. Definite Article _____

Noncount noun

5. Indefinite Article _____

6. Definite Article _____

AUDIO 🔊

6 Talking About Past Activities

MUST KNOW

- We use the simple past verb tense to talk about actions completed in the past—any time before now.

- Irregular verbs do not follow the spelling rules.

- There are three different ways to pronounce the *–ed* ending in past tense verbs.

- You can figure out the meaning of new vocabulary by looking at nearby words.

hat did you do yesterday? Where did they go for lunch? Who went to the party on Friday? These are questions about past actions, events and situations. We often ask questions like these in conversation with friends. In school, we may use the simple past verb tense to discuss homework assignments or projects. For example, your instructor might ask questions like these: *Did you finish the homework? What was difficult about the assignment? When did you submit the essay?* Let's take a closer look at this verb tense.

Simple Past Verb Tense

When we talk about things that happened in the past, which is any time before this moment, we use the past tense. Specifically, when the action, event, or situation is **completed**, we use the **simple past** form of the verb tense. An action, event, or situation is completed when it is 100 percent done. For example, if we talk on Monday about what we did the previous weekend, we usually use the simple past verb tense because the weekend is completed: it's finished. Let's look at some example sentences with **verbs in the simple past form** in bold. Notice the <u>time words and phrases that indicate when these things happened</u>. These are underlined.

EXAMPLES

▶ We **visited** my grandparents <u>two weeks ago</u>.

▶ <u>On Friday night,</u> Jenny and her three friends **went** to the movies.

▶ She **didn't finish** her homework <u>last night</u>.

▶ Griffin and Kay **had** a great time at the concert in the park <u>Saturday afternoon</u>.

▶ My computer **died** <u>this past weekend</u>, so my parents **bought** me a new one.

▶ My cousins **came** to visit us <u>for the weekend</u>. It **was** fun!

▶ **Did** you **see** the sunset <u>this past Sunday night</u>? It was beautiful.

▶ Why **did** they **cancel** the party <u>last weekend</u>?

Simple Past Tense Timeline

Let's look at the timeline for this verb tense.

Example 1: <u>Yesterday</u>, I **ate** a big lunch.

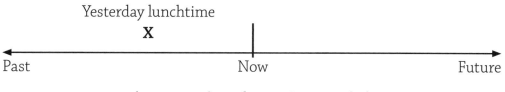

(moment of speaking = 8 a.m. today)

Lina states that she did something before this moment of speaking (or writing). The time of speaking is 8 a.m. today. She did something in the past and it is a completed action. Lunch yesterday is finished. What did she do and when did she do it? She ate a big lunch yesterday.

Example 2: Brad **rode** his bike to school <u>this morning</u>.

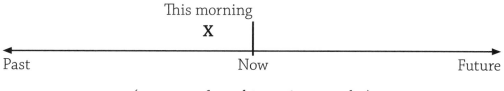

(moment of speaking = 1 p.m. today)

When we talk about the past, it is about *any* time before the moment of speaking. It may be just one minute before. In this case, Brad's brother is talking to a friend at 1 p.m. today about what Brad did earlier in the morning. The action—riding his bike—is completed, so Brad's brother uses the simple past verb form.

Example 3: They **attended** the seminar <u>on Saturday</u> and really <u>liked</u> it.

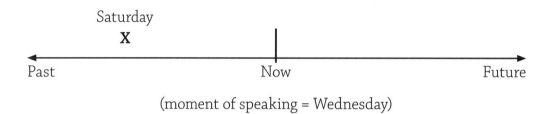

(moment of speaking = Wednesday)

It's Wednesday and I am talking about what my parents did on Saturday, four days earlier. The seminar is over, so it's a completed action and it's in the past. The simple past form is the appropriate verb tense for this statement.

Example 4: They **sold** their house <u>in the 1980s</u> and **moved** to Costa Rica.

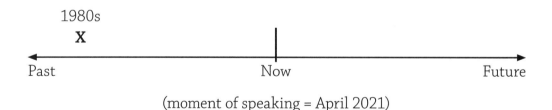

(moment of speaking = April 2021)

In April 2021, Jack stated what his grandparents did: they sold their house and they moved to another country. As this happened approximately 40 years earlier and the actions are completed, using the simple past form is the best verb tense for this statement.

Expressions of Time

In the following table are some common words and phrases used with the simple past verb tense. Study them and read the example sentences.

Time Word/Phrase	Example Sentences
on + day	<u>On Sunday</u>, we **watched** the Super Bowl.
for + time period	We **went** to the lake <u>for the weekend</u>.
over + time period	They **rehearsed** for the play <u>over the weekend</u>.
all + time period (the whole time)	We **hung out** <u>all weekend</u>.
yesterday, yesterday morning, yesterday afternoon, last night	<u>Yesterday morning</u>, Charlene **cooked** a big breakfast for us.
last Monday, Tuesday, Wednesday, etc. (describes the previous week)	He finally **passed** his driving test <u>last Tuesday</u>.
last week / weekend / month / year	Larry and Sandy **graduated** from college <u>last month</u>.
this past weekend / specific day / week / month / year (describes most recent time period)	<u>This past weekend</u>, I **stayed** in bed because I **didn't feel** well.
specific amount of time + ago	She **got** her dog <u>two days ago</u>.
this morning (it's after the morning)	<u>This morning</u> **was** totally chaotic.
earlier today / this week / this month	I **submitted** my essay <u>earlier this week</u>.

Simple Past Tense: Regular vs. Irregular Verbs

The difference between regular verbs and irregular verbs is that regular verbs have an **–ed** ending in the simple past form. Irregular verbs, on the other hand, do not follow this rule. The simple past form of irregular verbs does *not* have an **–ed** ending. Instead, they have a variety of endings that indicate past form. To understand this better, see the examples.

Regular verbs

Base Form of the Verb	Simple Past Form (With -ed Ending)
stop	stopp<u>ed</u>
learn	learn<u>ed</u>
bake	bake<u>d</u>

Irregular verbs

Base Form of the Verb	Simple Past Form (Irregular Spelling)
eat	ate
forget	forgot
sleep	slept

The Most Common Irregular Verbs

Take a look at the most commonly used irregular verbs below. Note that the best way to learn these is to memorize them.

Base Form of Verb	Simple Past Form	Base Form of Verb	Simple Past Form	Base Form of Verb	Simple Past Form
be (am / is / are) →	was / were	catch →	caught	drive →	drove
become →	became	choose →	chose	eat →	ate
begin →	began	come →	came	fall →	fell
bite →	bit	cost →	cost	feed →	fed
blow →	blew	cut →	cut	feel →	felt
break →	broke	deal →	dealt	fight →	fought
bring →	brought	do →	did	find →	found
build →	built	draw →	drew	fly →	flew
buy →	bought	dream →	dreamed	forget →	forgot
		drink →	drank	forgive →	forgave

Base Form of Verb	Simple Past Form	Base Form of Verb	Simple Past Form	Base Form of Verb	Simple Past Form
freeze →	froze	pay →	paid	steal →	stole
get →	got	put →	put	stick →	stuck
give →	gave	quit →	quit	strike →	struck
go →	went	read →	read	swear →	swore
grow →	grew	ride →	rode	sweep →	swept
have →	had	ring →	rang	swim →	swam
hear →	heard	rise →	rose	swing →	swung
hide →	hid	run →	ran	take →	took
hit →	hit	say →	said	teach →	taught
hold →	held	see →	saw	tear →	tore
hurt →	hurt	sell →	sold	tell →	told
keep →	kept	send →	sent	think →	thought
know →	knew	set →	set	throw →	threw
lay →	laid	shake →	shook	understand →	understood
lead →	led	shine →	shone / shined		
leave →	left			wake →	woke
lend →	lent	shoot →	shot	wet →	wet
let →	let	shut →	shut	win →	won
lie →	lay	sing →	sang	withdraw →	withdrew
light →	lit	sit →	sat	write →	wrote
lose →	lost	sleep →	slept		
make →	made	speak →	spoke		
mean →	meant	spend →	spent		
meet →	met	spread →	spread		
		stand →	stood		

Examples of Irregular Verbs in Sentences

Let's look at some example sentences with irregular verbs in the simple past form.

EXAMPLES

▶ He **ate** an ice cream sundae <u>after dinner last night</u>.

▶ **Did** you **take** the job?

▶ She **felt** thankful for your help <u>yesterday</u>.

▶ The flowers **made** me so happy!

▶ Where **did** you **go** <u>last night</u>?

▶ Jim **got** angry with his sister <u>last week</u>.

▶ I **ran** to school <u>this morning</u>.

▶ <u>This past Saturday</u>, they **lost** the game.

▶ **Did** you **understand** the physics lesson <u>today</u>?

▶ He **kept** his lucky rock in his pocket <u>all day yesterday</u>.

Simple Past Tense: Forming the Affirmative

How do we form the simple past in affirmative statements? To see how we do this, review the following table with example sentences.

Affirmative Form of the Simple Past Verb Tense

Subject or Subject Pronoun	Verb: –ed Form of the Regular Verb or the Correct Form of the Irregular Verb	Example Sentences
I	**walked**	I **walked** six miles <u>yesterday</u>!
You	**donated**	<u>Last week</u>, you **donated** so much time to the project.
We		We already **donated** two gift baskets to the fundraiser.
They		<u>Last night</u>, they **donated** money to their favorite charity.
He	**ran**	<u>Last year</u>, he **ran** a marathon.
She		She **ran** for class president <u>last semester</u>.
It		The car **ran** smoothly <u>today</u>.

Forming Regular Verbs

To correctly spell the simple past form of regular verbs, there are four rules to remember:

1. If the base form of the verb ends in **–e** → add **–d.**

   Examples: lik<u>e</u> → lik**ed** | chas<u>e</u> → chas**ed** | refin<u>e</u> → refin**ed**

2. If the base form of the verb ends in one vowel + one consonant → double the consonant and add **–ed.**

   Examples: st<u>op</u> → stop**ped** | j<u>og</u> → jog**ged** | tr<u>ip</u> → trip**ped**

3. If the base form of the verb ends in a consonant + **–y** → change **–y** to **–i** and add **–ed.**

   Examples: stud<u>y</u> → stud**ied** | cr<u>y</u> → cr**ied** | clarif<u>y</u> → clarif**ied**

4. In all other cases, add –ed.

   Examples: start → start**ed** | play → play**ed** | show → show**ed**

Three Different Sounds for *–ed* Endings for Regular Verbs

Many students make the mistake of pronouncing every simple past regular tense verb the same way. However, there are three different ways we pronounce the *–ed* endings. In most cases, this is simply a case of incorrect pronunciation, but for native speakers of English it sounds like a grammar mistake. Let's learn about the three different *–ed* ending sounds, so you can pronounce past tense verbs correctly.

How do you know which *–ed* ending to use?
The sound of the *–ed* ending is determined by the **last consonant sound in the base form of the verb**. This is similar to the rules for the three *–s* endings you learned in Chapter 2. Let's look at the rules for the three *–ed* endings:

1. Only Air = Voiceless (Also Known as Unvoiced)

For the first *–ed* ending sound /t/, the last consonant sound of the base form of the verb must be **voiceless**. This means that we **use *only air*** to make this sound. We do not engage our vocal cords. An example of this is the verb **wor<u>k</u>**. The final consonant sound in **wor<u>k</u>** is /k/, which is a voiceless sound because only air is released when we make the /k/ sound. Therefore, the sound of the *–ed* ending will also be voiceless. It will sound like /t/ as in <u>t</u>ime. The regular verb **work** in the past—**worked**—sounds like */workt/*.

2. Vibration = Voiced (Vocal Cords Activated)

For the second *–ed* ending sound **/d/**, the last consonant sound of the base form of the verb must be **voiced**. This means that we **engage our vocal cords**. An example of this is the verb *move*. The final consonant sound in *move* is **/v/**, which is a voiced sound because we activate the vocal cords to make the **/v/** sound. Try it: say the **/v/** sound as you hold the palm of your hand on your throat. Do you feel your throat vibrating? This is what it feels like to engage your vocal cords. It's similar to strumming a guitar: The string vibrates and makes sound. When the final consonant sound of the base form of a verb is voiced, the sound of the *–ed* ending is also voiced. It will sound like **/d/** as in *dog*. The regular verb *move* in the past—*moved*—sounds like */moovd/*.

Note: Do not add a syllable here!

3. Add a Syllable = /ɪd/

The third *–ed* ending sound is only for verbs whose final consonant sound is either **/t/** as in *start* or **/d/** as in *decide*. Again, the *–ed* ending is determined by the final consonant sound in the base form of the verb. It adds the syllable */ɪd/* and it is illustrated like this: **/ɪd/**. The important thing to remember here is that we *add a syllable* for this *–ed* ending. Look at the examples in the following table. The simple past form of the verb *start* (one syllable) is *started* (two syllables), and the simple past form of the verb *decide* (two syllables) is *decided* (three syllables).

See the following table for a list of sounds, rules, and examples.

Final –ed Sounds

	/t/ Voiceless Sounds	/d/ Voiced Sounds	/ɪd/ Add a Syllable!
Examples	miss → missed /t/ laugh → laughed /t/ skip → skipped /t/ walk → walked /t/ match → matched /t/ wish → wished /t/	assume → assumed /d/ design → designed /d/ raise* → raised /d/ love → loved /d/ scrub → scrubbed /d/ hug → hugged /d/ mill → milled /d/ snow → snowed /d/ pry → pried /d/ ping → pinged /d/ cure → cured /d/ judge → judged /d/ breathe → breathed /d/	post → posted /ɪd/ shift → shifted /ɪd/ want → wanted /ɪd/ divide → divided /ɪd/ guide → guided /ɪd/ fold → folded /ɪd/
Final consonant sounds	/s/ /f/ /p/ /k/ /θ/ (voiceless /th/) /ʧ/ (/ch/) /ʃ/ (/sh/)	/m/ /n/ /z/ /v/ /b/ /g/ /l/ /w/ /y/ /ŋ/ (/ng/) /r/ /dʒ/ /ʒ/ (/zh/) /ð/ (voiced /th/) all vowel sounds	/t/ /d/
Rules and notes	This **–ed** ending sounds like the **/t/** in **time**. It is a **voiceless sound**. We use **only air** to make it. Put your hand on your throat when you make this **/t/** sound. There is **no vibration**.	This **–ed** ending sounds like the **/d/** in **dog**. It is a **voiced sound** because it **engages the vocal cords**, which vibrate. Put your hand on your throat and feel the vibration when you make the **/d/** sound.	This ending **adds a syllable** to the word. It is **pronounced like id**, and it rhymes with **did**. It is a voiced sound.

*Note that the s in raised actually has a /z/ sound, so it's voiced.

Simple Past Tense: Forming the Negative

How do we form the simple past in negative statements? To form it, you must use the appropriate form of the DO auxiliary verb plus the negative word **not**. The past tense of DO is **did**, so use this in all negative statements with the simple past. **Note that because the past time frame is indicated in the auxiliary verb did, the main verb is not in the past tense form. Rather, the main verb is in its base form.** Check out the table below.

How to Form the Negative Simple Past Verb Tense

Subject or Subject Pronoun	Appropriate Form of the Auxiliary DO Verb = did	Negative (not)	Main Verb: Use the Base Form of the Verb (Note: The past tense is in *did*.)	Example Sentences
I	did	not	taste	I **did not taste** the dessert yet. I'm still eating dinner.
You / We / They	did	not	find	You **did not find** it yet, did you? We **did not find** the restaurant last night. We got lost! They **did not find** the man guilty.
He / She / It	did	not	show	Yesterday, the professor **did not show** the math scores. She **did not show** me her new car. It **did not show** anything: the screen was blank.

Forming Negative Contractions

As you know, we usually use contractions in English. To contract the negative simple past form, we combine the auxiliary **did** verb and the negative word **not.**

Contractions with *Did + Not*

Subject or Subject Pronoun	Auxiliary *did* + Negative *not = didn't*	Main Verb: Use the Base form of the Verb	Example Sentences
I	didn't	eat	I **didn't eat** anything last night for dinner.
You / We / They	didn't	like	You **didn't like** the sandwich?
			We **didn't like** the video.
			They **didn't like** the lake because the water was too cold.
He / She / It	didn't	bake	He **didn't bake** her a birthday cake.
			She **didn't bake** the cookies long enough.
			It **didn't bake** all the way through, so I put it back in the oven.

Simple Past Tense: Forming Yes/No Questions

To get to know someone or to nurture a friendship, we often ask questions about what people did. We use **yes/no questions** to ask what happened, and we usually answer yes/no questions with *yes* or *no* or some version of yes/no. To form yes/no questions in the simple past, we **invert the subject and the auxiliary *did***. This means we change the order of the subject and *did*, so *did* begins the sentence and the subject follows it. Remember: Because the past time frame is indicated in the auxiliary *did*, the main verb is *not* in the past tense form. Instead, the main verb is in its *base* form. Review how to form these questions in the table.

Did	Subject or Subject Pronoun	Main Verb: Use the Base Form of the Verb	Rest of the Sentence	Example Sentences
Did	I	**do**	that homework assignment already?	**Did** I **do** that homework assignment already?*
Did	you	**enjoy**	the beach party?	**Did** you **enjoy** the beach party?
	we		our anniversary celebration?	**Did** we **enjoy** our anniversary celebration?
	they		the flight?	**Did** they **enjoy** the flight?
Did	he	**make**	the appointment?	**Did** he **make** the appointment?
	she		it in time?	**Did** she **make** it in time?
	it		sense to you?	**Did** it **make** sense to you?

* When we ask ourselves a question, we are usually thinking aloud or repeating someone else's question.

Answering Yes/No Questions

As we learned in earlier chapters, we usually answer yes/no questions with complete answers or short answers when we are talking with teachers, parents, supervisors, colleagues, and coworkers. With peers and friends, short or quick answers are more common. Note that **_did_** is stressed in both affirmative (**_did_**) and negative (**_did_**n't) answers. The stressed syllables are underlined. Remember: We don't contract the affirmative answer.

Complete & Short Answers

Yes/No Question	Affirmative Answers	Negative Answers
Did you **see** the movie in class yesterday?	Yes, I **did** see the movie.	No, I **didn't** see the movie.
	Yes, I **did.**	No, I **didn't.**
Did the presentation go well?	Yes, it **did** go well!	No, it **didn't** go well.
	Yes, it **did.**	No, it **didn't.**
Did they have fun at the museum last week?	Yes, they **did** have fun. The activities were interactive!	No, they **didn't** have fun. They thought it was boring.
	Yes, they **did.**	No, they **didn't.**

When answering, we sometimes offer more information or provide an explanation. For negative answers, we may omit *no* and correct and clarify with the word *actually* instead. For example, we might say, *Actually, I didn't like the museum. It was really boring.*

Quick Answers to Yes/No Questions

A quick **yes** or **no** answer to these questions is acceptable, too. However, be sure to use a polite tone of voice. Otherwise, a quick answer may sound abrupt and rude. With friends, it's common to answer with slang. See the slang ways to say **yes** and **no** in Chapter 1.

Simple Past Tense: Forming WH Questions

To ask questions about what people did, we use WH questions to ask about time, location, manner, and reason for an action. As mentioned in Chapter 1, WH questions begin with WH question words or phrases such as *who, what, when, where, why, how, what kind, which one, how long, how many*, and *how much*. See how to form these questions in the table below.

WH Question Word/Phrase	Did	Subject or Subject Pronoun	Main Verb: Base Form of the Verb	Rest of the Sentence	Example Sentences
When	did	I	see	him last?	When **did** I **see** him last?
Which one	did	you	like	better?	Which one **did** you **like** better?
		we	choose	?	Which one **did** we **choose**?
		they	buy	?	Which one **did** they **buy**?
How long	did	he	stay	last night?	How long **did** he **stay** last night?
		she	stay	?	How long **did** she **stay**?
		it	last	?	How long **did** it **last**?

As we learned in Chapter 5, falling pitch is usually used at the end of WH questions. However, if you don't hear or understand some information and you need repetition, use a "fast rising" pitch. This pitch differs from a regular rising pitch because the rise begins earlier in the sentence and continues to increase in pitch to the end. A regular rising pitch only rises toward the end of the sentence. Look at the pitch patterns below and see the pitch chart in the Appendix for more information.

1. Use falling pitch for most WH questions:

Which one did you like better?

2. Use rising pitch to check your understanding and to express that you need repetition:

How long did he stay last night?

Forming *Who* Questions

When ***Who*** is the subject of the sentence, **we do not add another subject**. We do not add *I, you, we, they, he, she,* or *it*. See the following examples of this.

Who (Subject of Sentence)	Main Verb: –ed Form of the Verb (or Irregular)	Rest of the Sentence	Example Sentences
Who	**attended**	the Philosophy Club meeting?	**Who attended** the Philosophy Club meeting?
Who	**went**	to the party?	**Who went** to the party?

As you learned in Chapter 5, WH questions can be answered in a variety of ways. The two best ways are the long and quick answers. The long answer is a complete sentence, whereas the quick answer gives only the essential information that answers the question. See examples below of answers to the **Who** questions.

Who Question with Simple Past Verb Tense	Answer to Question
Who attended the Philosophy Club meeting?	**Long:** The three of us attended the Philosophy Club meeting.
	Quick: The three of us.
Who went to the party?	**Long:** The whole family went to the party.
	Quick: The whole family.

Simple Past Tense: Using Tag Questions

In Chapters 2 and 5, you learned how to use tag questions at the ends of statements to verify information or seek agreement. Tag questions can be used with all verb tenses. In simple past sentences, use tag questions with **did**. Check the example sentences below to understand this rule.

EXAMPLES

▶ I got here on time, **didn't I**?

▶ You finished the homework, **didn't you**?

▶ She took German last year, **didn't she**?

▶ He didn't complete it yet, **did he**?

▶ It didn't break, **did it**?

▶ We had fun on vacation, **didn't we**?

▶ They didn't go to the beach yet, **did they**?

Using Intonation with Tag Questions

As you know by now, we use **rising intonation to verify information**, and we use **falling intonation to seek agreement**. See these pitch patterns in the example sentences below. Also, see the Appendix for more information on the pitches we use in American English.

Statement with Tag Question to Verify Information

Use Rising Intonation	Explanation
She went to the class, didn't she?	When we don't know the answer, we verify information. In this situation, we use rising intonation. Drop your pitch on the *did/didn't* and glide your pitch up on the pronoun.

Statement with Tag Question to Seek Agreement

Use Falling Intonation	Explanation
They enjoyed the concert, didn't they?	When we want someone to agree with us, we use falling intonation. Go up in pitch on the *did/didn't* and glide down on the pronoun.

Note: Pitch patterns are shown above, below, and through the words of sentences to illustrate that our pitches change as we speak.

Forming Affirmative and Negative Tag Questions

Remember: when we have an affirmative statement, the tag question is negative and vice versa. Notice that the statement is in the simple past verb tense, yet the tag question and the answer only use **_did_**, not the main verb. Use a comma before the tag question. Check out the chart for example sentences.

Affirmative Statement	Negative Tag Question	Expect Affirmative Answer
I did a good job,	**didn't** I?	Yes, you did.
She made the cookies,	**didn't** she?	Yes, she did.
They performed well,	**didn't** they?	Yes, they did.
We debated logically,	**didn't** we?	Yes, we did.
It worked well,	**didn't** it?	Yes, it did.

Negative Statement	Affirmative Tag Question	Expect Negative Answer
I didn't say that correctly,	**did** I?	No, you didn't.
She didn't pass her driver's test,	**did** she?	No, she didn't.
They didn't give the presentation,	**did** they?	No, they didn't.
You didn't make our spa appointments,	**did** you?	No, I didn't.
He didn't care about that,	**did** he?	No, he didn't.

PRONUNCIATION

▶ Conversational speech doesn't often sound like it's spelled. That is the case with *did you*, *did he*, and *didn't I*.

▶ In regular relaxed speech, ***did you*** is often pronounced *didjoo*. This is similar with *education* and *graduation*, which are usually pronounced *edjoocation* and *gradjoowation*.

▶ For ***did he***, we normally drop the /h/ in *he* and link the two words, so it sounds like *diddee*.

▶ In ***didn't I***, we drop the /t/ sound and link the /n/ sound with the word *I*, so it sounds like *didnI*.

▶ As you go about your day, see what other pronunciation patterns you notice.

Dialogue: What Did You Do Last Weekend?

Marcia and Greg are friends at school. It's Monday, and they are eating lunch in the cafeteria. They are talking about what they did over the weekend. Read their conversation. Which verb tense is used to talk about completed actions in the past?

Marcia: Hey, Greg! How's it going?

Greg: Hiya! Really good. You?

Marcia: Same old thing. How was your weekend?

Greg: Oh man, it was so fun!

Marcia: Cool! What did you* do?

Greg: My family celebrated my little brother's birthday. What a blast it was!

Marcia: How did you* celebrate?

Greg: Well, my dad took us on a "mystery ride," so we had no idea where we were going. Then, we arrived at this really big warehouse. I thought maybe it was a paintball course, but it wasn't. When we got inside, I saw people flying!

Marcia: What the heck?

Greg: Yah, it was a skydiving simulation place. My little brother screamed! He was so excited.

Marcia: Skydiving simulation?

Greg: I know—crazy! I felt super nervous at first. My dad and little brother flew first.

Marcia: What do you mean? Did they fly on cables?

Greg: No, it was in an air-filled chamber that simulated falling from an airplane.

Marcia: Oh my gosh. That is crazy!

Greg: My little brother didn't hesitate. He put on the flying suit and walked right into that flight chamber ready to go. It was awesome! The instructor led him with a harness and guided him. Then, he let my brother go. My brother flew! He laughed the whole time. He really enjoyed it.

Marcia: Did you* do it, too?

Greg: Yup! After my brother went, I wasn't so nervous. The instructor guided me at first, and then I hollered just like my brother when he let me do it alone. Best thing I've ever done!

Marcia: You're making me want to do it!

Greg: Oh, you have to! Let's do it together!

Marcia: Uh . . . okay! I'm nervous!!

Greg: It's an event you will never forget, and I can't wait to do it again!

Marcia: Okay, let's do it!

Greg: *Yes!*

*Note: Remember that *did you* is usually pronounced *didjoo*.

Lecture: The California Gold Rush

The California Gold Rush

The Gold Rush of 1849 forever altered the future of California in several ways. One significant change that resulted from this historic event was California's population: it increased and different ethnicities became residents. In January 1848, when gold was discovered in Coloma on John Sutter's property, the population was only about 160,000, most of whom were Native Americans. Coloma is located along the American River approximately 50 miles east of Sacramento. On January 24 of that year, Sutter's carpenter, James Marshall, found gold flakes in the streambed.

Sutter and Marshall agreed to become partners in gold mining and to keep the discovery a secret. However, news of gold spread rapidly to the East Coast of the United States. Very quickly, hundreds of prospectors, people who search for mineral deposits such as gold and oil, from the eastern part of America packed their bags and set out for California. At that time, California was a territory, not yet a state of the Union. The first gold miners—approximately 4,000—arrived in August 1848. Most of them were white Americans from the East Coast; others were from China, Europe, and South America. Although the bulk, or majority, of the miners arrived over the next few years, 80,000 arrived in 1849. These fortune seekers, also known as '49ers, had to travel treacherous, untested overland routes or go by sea around Cape Horn. Those that made it to California alive were a tough, hardy bunch. By 1855, 300,000 gold miners were panning for gold.

To "strike it rich," a man had to find enough gold to compensate him for his time and expenses. Mining for gold was backbreaking work. It required digging and moving heavy dirt from riverbeds, sifting through the dirt for hours to search for gold, and standing in streams and rivers from sunrise to sundown six days a week. It was not easy. Many men died from disease, poor living conditions, and harsh weather.

During those Gold Rush years, the methods of mining improved. Most individuals, however, continued to pan for gold—to wash and separate gravel from gold in a wide, open metal dish. As the gold mining industry grew, new and more efficient methods of panning were invented. One example is the sluice box, aka a sluicer, which enabled much more dirt to be washed and separated at one time. Eventually, businesses grew and companies controlled most of the gold mining in California.

All of this activity in California caught the attention of the federal government, and as a result, California was accepted into the Union as an official state in 1850. The Gold Rush changed the composition of the population, ushered in corporate enterprise, expedited California's statehood, and ultimately put an isolated territory on the map of the United States. The Gold Rush was an important historic event for California.

Success Strategy: Building Your Vocabulary

Building your vocabulary boosts your confidence and gives you more freedom to say exactly what you mean. When we read, we often encounter new words and phrases that we don't understand. People use different strategies in this situation. What strategy do you usually use? **Do you:**

1. Skip over the word (ignore it)?

2. Try to guess the meaning?

3. Look up every word you don't know in the dictionary?

4. Ask someone for the definition?

Good readers use a variety of strategies. You may be able to ignore the word if it is only used once and you understand the main idea of the passage. If a word or phrase is repeated often, look it up in the dictionary or check the definition with an English speaker. However, there is an alternative strategy: You can guess the meaning from the context, or the words near it. There are several ways to do this. Let's look at five of these context clue strategies.

Use Context to Discover the Meanings of Words and Phrases

Context Clues	Example Sentences
1. Or Form: _____, or _____. There is a comma after the new word or phrase, then the word **or** + definition or synonym, followed by a period if it's the end of the sentence or a comma if it's in the middle of the sentence.	A good source of plant protein can be found in legumes, **or beans and peas**. Legumes, **or beans and peas,** are a good source of plant protein.
2. Commas Form: _____, _____, There is a **comma** after the new word or phrase and **another comma** after the definition or synonym. If it's at the end of the sentence, a period is used instead of the second comma.	Temperate regions, **areas with moderate temperatures,** are what I prefer. We prefer to live in temperate regions, **areas with moderate temperatures.**
3. Dashes Form: _____ – _____ – Similar to the commas, there's a **dash** after the new word or phrase and **another dash** after the definition or synonym. However, if the synonym is at the end of the sentence, the second dash is omitted.	It's been found that mitochondria—**tiny organic structures found in our cells**—play a critical role in converting food into energy. Critical components for food-to-energy conversion are mitochondria—**tiny organic structures found in our cells.**
4. Parentheses Form: _____ (_____) There is an **opening parenthesis** after the new word or phrase and **a closing parenthesis** after the definition or synonym. If it's at the end of the sentence, closing parenthesis is followed by a period.	Deciduous trees **(trees that shed their leaves)** grow abundantly in my neighborhood. Trees that grow abundantly in my neighborhood are deciduous trees **(trees that shed their leaves).**
5. Also called, also known as, aka Form: _____, **also called** _____, Form: _____, **also known as** _____, Form: _____, **aka** _____, There is **a comma** after the new word or phrase, then **also called** or **also known as** or **aka** + definition or synonym, followed by **another comma.** If it's at the end of the sentence, the second comma is replaced with a period.	Artificial intelligence, **also called AI,** is a burgeoning field of robotics. Artificial intelligence, **also known as AI,** is a burgeoning field of robotics. Artificial intelligence, **aka AI,** is a burgeoning field of robotics. Many innovative companies are experimenting with artificial intelligence, **aka AI.**

EXERCISES

EXERCISE 6-1

Let's practice forming the simple past verb tense with regular verbs. Complete the sentences below with the simple past form of the verb given in parentheses. Follow the example.

Example: (play) Vivek ___*played*___ beach volleyball all weekend.

1. (watch) Joan _____ a new science fiction movie Friday night.

2. (try) On Sunday, Monish _____ a new exercise routine. He loved it!

3. (create) Ruby _____ Valentine's Day gifts for her classmates.

4. (jog) The whole team _____ 10 miles to raise money.

5. (hike) Cheryl and Pete _____ their favorite trail last Wednesday.

6. (dance) We _____ all night and it was so fun! The music was great!

7. (cook) This past weekend, my parents _____ for the neighborhood party.

8. (move) My best friend _____ to Chicago. I miss her so much!

EXERCISE 6-2

Now, let's practice forming the simple past verb tense with irregular verbs. Complete the sentences below with the simple past form of the irregular verb given in parentheses. Follow the example.

Example: (give) Luna ___*gave*___ me a beautiful bracelet for my birthday.

1. (shake) We _____ hands because it was our first time meeting.

2. (drink) I _____ eight glasses of water yesterday. I feel healthier already!

3. (eat) Last Tuesday afternoon, we _____ a big salad for lunch.

4. (bring) Kammie _____ her friend to the party.

5. (sleep) She _____ all weekend because she felt sick.

6. (understand) Jon _____ the math problem, but I didn't.

7. (meet) He _____ his teammates after school yesterday for practice.

8. (make) Shay _____ it on time to class this morning.

EXERCISE 6-3

Write sentences with the simple past verb tense. Use the words provided. Remember to put a period at the end of the sentence. Follow the example.

Example: Myron / drive / 100 miles / last weekend

Myron drove 100 miles last weekend.

1. Deb and Tina / have / a good time / at the party

   _____

2. She / bike / to her grandmother's house / last week

   _____

3. On Friday, / Joe / study / all night / for his online exam

   _____

4. Earlier this week, / Carrie / get / a new car

   _____

5. I / download / a new yoga app / yesterday afternoon

_____

6. The Zumba class / be / really fun / on Sunday morning.

_____

EXERCISE 6-4

Complete the sentences with the correct negative form of the simple past. Follow the example. Write contractions in every sentence.

Example: (sing) Merlin _didn't sing_ at Karaoke last night, but his buddies did.

1. (freeze) It was very cold last night, but it _____ .

2. (sell) The kids _____ a lot at the bake sale.

3. (catch) Professor Asti _____ any students cheating.

4. (come) Last night, Melody _____ to the rehearsal.

5. (grow) The vegetables in the garden _____ much in the last week.

6. (like) My husband and I _____ the new restaurant.

EXERCISE 6-5

Write sentences using the words provided. First, write the negative form. Then, write it using a contraction. Follow the example.

Example: Michelle / NEGATIVE / see / the movie.

*Michelle **did not see** the movie.*

*Michelle **didn't see** the movie.*

1. Vera / NEGATIVE / have / a good time.

   _____

   _____

2. Roberto and his wife / NEGATIVE / buy / the house.

   _____

   _____

3. You / NEGATIVE / get / an A on the essay.

   _____

   _____

4. I / NEGATIVE / pay / full price for the clothes. They were on sale.

   _____

   _____

EXERCISE 6-6

Form yes/no questions with the simple past verb tense using the words provided. Remember to use the appropriate form of the auxiliary DO verb. Then write long, short, and quick answers to the question. Answer the questions affirmatively (Yes) or negatively (No). Follow the examples below. For quick questions, you can write more information as appropriate.

Example 1: DO / Cathy / tour / the gardens / yet? (Yes)

Question: *Did Cathy tour the gardens yet?*

Long answer: *Yes, she did tour the gardens.*

Short answer: *Yes, she did.*

Quick answer: *Yes. She loved them!*

Example 2: DO / Mr. Howell / finish / the apple pie? (No)

Question: *Did Mr. Howell finish the apple pie?*

Long answer: *No, he didn't finish the apple pie.*

Short answer: *No, he didn't.*

Quick answer: *No. There's one piece left if you want it.*

1. DO / Elysa / take / the train / to work / this morning? (Yes)

Question: _____

Long answer: _____

Short answer: _____

Quick answer: _____

2. DO / they / manage / the store / well / while I was gone? (Yes)

Question: _____

Long answer: _____

Short answer: _____

Quick answer: _____

3. DO / Ms. Jolly / know / about the problem? (No)

Question: _____

Long answer: _____

Short answer: _____

Quick answer: _____

4. DO / you / sit / close to the stage / at the concert? (Yes)

Question: _____

Long answer: _____

Short answer: _____

Quick answer: _____

5. DO / Angela / enroll / in college classes yet? (Yes)

Question: _____

Long answer: _____

Short answer: _____

Quick answer: _____

EXERCISE 6-7

Form WH questions with the simple past verb tense using the statements given. Form long and short answers using the information in parentheses. Follow the examples below.

Example 1: Prisca and Philippe travelled to Belgium. (Where)

Question: *Where did Prisca and Philippe travel?*

Long answer (complete sentence): *They travelled to Belgium.*

Short answer (essential information only): *To Belgium.*

Example 2: Judy had a baby a month ago. (When)

Question: *When did Judy have a baby?*

Long answer (complete sentence): *She had a baby a month ago.*

Short answer (essential information only): *A month ago.*

Example 3: Jasper and Griffin played basketball in the championship. (Who)

Question: *Who played basketball in the championship?*

Long answer (complete sentence): *Jasper and Griffin played basketball in the championship.*

Short answer (essential information only): *Jasper and Griffin.*

1. Paul took his wife to *Phantom of the Opera* on Sunday evening. (When)

Question: _____

Long answer: _____

Short answer: _____

2. Shelby got in a car accident last night, but she's okay. (Who)

   Question: _____

   Long answer: _____

   Short answer: _____

3. Rocky opened his new gym last month. (What)

   Question: _____

   Long answer: _____

   Short answer: _____

4. The Thompsons took a cruise to Alaska last summer. (Where)

   Question: _____

   Long answer: _____

   Short answer: _____

5. The yoga retreat in Costa Rica was for two weeks. (How long)

   Question: _____

   Long answer: _____

   Short answer: _____

EXERCISE 6-8

Look at the sentences below. Find and underline the <u>definition</u> of the bolded word by using the context clues you learned in this chapter. Follow the example.

> Example: **Electrolytes**—<u>salts and minerals that conduct electrical impulses in the human body</u>—generate energy and help our muscles contract.

1. **Constellations** (a group of stars that form a design) in the night sky often guided travelers centuries ago.

2. The carpenter made a **jig**, or a device for guiding the cutting tool, for the benches he built to ensure they were uniform.

3. **Sequoias**, also called redwoods, can grow as tall as 385 feet.

4. Steam rooms, ice baths, and infrared saunas are great examples of **hormesis**, a slightly stressful situation that benefits the human body by building a healthy stress response.

5. The **ampere**—a basic unit measuring electrical current—is named after a French physicist who is considered the father of electromagnetism.

EXERCISE 6-9

Go back and read "The California Gold Rush" lecture in this chapter. Find and underline all the <u>definitions</u> you find that follow the strategies outlined in the Success Strategy: Building Your Vocabulary section. How many did you find?

EXERCISE 6-10

Write sentences about your recent past activities. Look at the example below and use the prompts to help you.

   Example: (fun activity) <u>On Saturday night, we had game night at my house.</u>

1. (fun activity) _____

2. (group activity—with friends or family) _____

   _____

3. (boring activity) _____

4. (exciting activity) _____

5. (relaxing activity) _____

EXERCISE 6-11

Time to practice writing sentences! Write 10 sentences about the activities, events, tasks, and situations you experienced any time in the past. Use the simple past verb tense and time expressions you learned in this chapter. Use both regular and irregular verbs. Write affirmative and negative sentences. Be sure that every sentence begins with a capital letter and ends with a period if it is a statement, a question mark if it is a question, and an exclamation point if it's an interjection.

1. _____

2. _____

3. _____

4. _____

5. _____

6. _____

7. _____

8. _____

9. _____

10. _____

AUDIO 🔊

Flashcard App

7 Simple Sentences

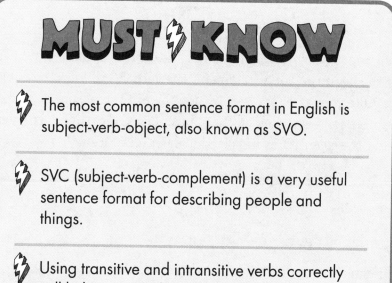

MUST KNOW

- The most common sentence format in English is subject-verb-object, also known as SVO.

- SVC (subject-verb-complement) is a very useful sentence format for describing people and things.

- Using transitive and intransitive verbs correctly will help you speak more clearly.

The primary sentence format in English is subject-verb-object, or SVO. The subject (S) comes first, the verb (V) follows the subject in a statement, and finally there is an object of the verb (O or OV) in this sentence structure. Note that not all statements follow this structure. In many cases, the sentence structure may only contain a subject and a verb, or SV. Also, some sentences may contain a **complement (C)** rather than an object. This sentence structure is known as subject-verb-complement, or SVC. Let's take a closer look at these sentence structures and how they work.

Subject-Verb-Object (SVO)

In English, most <u>statements</u> follow this structure. The subject (S) usually comes at the beginning of a statement; the verb (V) follows the subject; and an object (O) comes after the verb. Study the SVO structure by reviewing some example sentences below. The <u>subject</u> (S) is underlined, **the verb** (V) is bolded, and the *object* (O) is italicized in each sentence.

EXAMPLES

▶ <u>Marlena</u> **rides** *her bike* to work every day.

▶ <u>Xavier and John</u> **got** *As* on their tests.

▶ <u>My cat</u> **caught** *a mouse* yesterday.

▶ <u>We</u> **are bringing** *an appetizer* to the party.

▶ <u>Alex</u> **is drawing** *a butterfly* in his sketchbook.

▶ Tomorrow, <u>the neighborhood organization</u> **will email** *an announcement* about the meeting.*

▶ <u>Dawn and her husband</u> **have contributed** *time and energy* to their favorite charity for many years.**

▶ <u>Kyle and his brothers</u> **have been selling** *new and used cars* since the 1980s.**

*See Chapter 8 to learn more about the future verb tenses.

**Chapter 9 explains the present perfect and present perfect progressive tenses.

How to Identify the SVO

Now that you have seen a few example sentences with the SVO structure, do you see a pattern? Consider and answer these questions:

The object of the verb is also known as the **direct object**. We'll talk about direct objects later in this chapter.

1. Where is the subject (S) in these example statements?

2. What position in the sentence is the verb (V)?

3. Where is the object of the verb (O or OV) in relation to the S and V?

Sometimes, it's easy to identify the S, the V, and the O. However, other times it's not so obvious. How do we find the subject, verb, and object in a sentence? Follow these three steps:

Step 1: First, **find the verb**. Even though the subject comes before the verb in statements, it's easier to first locate the verb. The verb is usually the <u>action</u> of the sentence. You can ask the question ***What is the action?***

Step 2: Second, **look for the subject**. The subject is the noun or pronoun that comes before the verb in a statement. You can ask the question ***Who/What* + verb?**

Step 3: Third, **locate the object**. The object of the verb follows the verb. To find it, ask the question **verb + *what/whom?***

What's the difference between a sentence and a statement? A statement is a type of sentence. There are **four sentence types:** A **statement** ends with a period (.); a **question** ends with a question mark (?); and an **exclamation** ends with an exclamation point (!). There are also **imperatives**, which we also call **commands**.

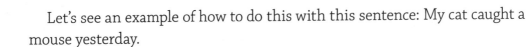

Let's see an example of how to do this with this sentence: My cat caught a mouse yesterday.

Step	Question to Ask	Answer
Step 1: Find the verb. Ask the question, What is the action of this sentence?	What is the action of this sentence?	The verb: **caught**
Step 2: Look for the subject. The subject is the noun or pronoun before the verb in a statement. Ask the question, *Who/What* + verb?	Who/what caught?	The subject: **My cat**
Step 3: Locate the object. The object of the verb usually follows the verb. Ask the question, **Verb + what/whom?**	Caught what?	The object of the verb: **a mouse**.

<u>My cat</u> **caught** *a mouse* yesterday.
   S   V   O

One more time! Let's be sure you understand how to identify the S, V, and O of a sentence. Try the steps on this sentence: Alex is drawing a butterfly in his sketchbook.

Step	Question to Ask	Answer
Step 1: **Find the verb.**	What is the action of the sentence?	V: **is drawing**
Step 2: Look for the subject.	Who/what is drawing?	S: **Alex**
Step 3: Locate the object.	Is drawing what?	O: **a butterfly**

<u>Alex</u> **is drawing** *a butterfly* in his sketchbook.
  S   V   O

Practice 7-A

Let's check your understanding of the SVO sentence. Follow the steps above and identify the S, V, and O of each sentence below. Underline the <u>S</u>, highlight the V, and circle the (O.) Follow the example. See Practice 7-A in the Answer Key for answers.

    Example: <u>Jeremy and his brother</u> are learning (Mandarin.)

1. Pamela bought new ice skates.

2. We played board games last night.

3. It printed my ticket.

4. The sales clerk sells shoes.

5. My parents rented a beach house for vacation.

6. You spelled my name correctly.

    Now that you learned the basic SVO structure of a sentence in English, let's look more closely at the object of the verb. There's more to uncover here.

Direct vs. Indirect Objects

The object of the verb (O or OV) in a sentence **can be either a direct object (D.O.) or an indirect object (I.O.).** What is the difference between a direct and an indirect object? Let's find out.

Direct Objects (D.O.)	Indirect Objects (I.O.)
• Direct objects are nouns or pronouns that **take the action** of a transitive verb.	• Indirect objects are nouns or pronouns that **receive the direct object**.
• In other words, the D.O. is the **object of the action verb**.	• The I.O. is the **recipient of the direct object**.
• An easy way to remember the direct object's role is to know that it is *directly* affected by the action verb.	• To find the indirect object, ask the question **direct object + *to/for whom/what?***
	• Indirect objects **always precede the direct object**.
• To find the D.O., ask the *question* **verb + *what/whom?***	• Indirect objects rarely have the word "to" or "for" stated.

What do direct objects and indirect objects look like in a sentence? Let's see in the following tables. First, study the example sentences that have **direct objects only**.

1. Read the example sentences.

2. To find the direct object, ask and answer the question **verb + *what/whom?***

Example Sentences with Direct Objects Only	Verb + What/Whom?	What Is the Direct Object?
I grow daisies in my garden.	Grow what?	daisies
Did Karl bring her?	Bring whom?	her
My brother operates the machine at work.	Operates what?	the machine
When are they baking the cake?	Baking what?	the cake
She wants it.	Wants what?	it
The neighbors threw a block party.	Threw what?	a block party
We discussed the plan already.	Discussed what?	the plan
Dave and Mindy moved the furniture in the living room.	Moved what?	the furniture

Now, study the example sentences that have **both direct objects and indirect objects**. Follow these steps:

1. Read the example sentences.

2. To find the **direct object**, ask and answer the question **verb + *what/ whom*?**

3. To find the **indirect object**, ask and answer the question **verb + direct object + *to/for whom/what*?**

Example Sentences with Direct and Indirect Objects	Verb + What/ Whom?	What Is the Direct Object?	Verb + Direct Object + to/for Whom/What?	What Is the Indirect Object?
Jack sang me a song.	Sang what?	a song	sang a song to whom?	me
Monty gave his girlfriend an engagement ring.	Gave what?	an engagement ring	gave an engagement ring to whom?	his girlfriend
The supervisor sent us all the update.	Sent what?	the update	sent the update to whom?	us all
Josephine kicked Beth the soccer ball.	Kicked what?	the soccer ball	kicked the soccer ball to whom?	Beth

Another way to identify the indirect object is to ask the question like this:

Subject   Verb   the direct object   *to/for whom/what*?

Here's an example using this question to find the indirect object: Monty gave his girlfriend an engagement ring.

Question: Monty gave an engagement ring to whom?

Answer: To his girlfriend = indirect object

Transitive vs. Intransitive Verbs

Some verbs require an object, and some verbs don't make sense with an object. Verbs that require an object are **transitive verbs**, and verbs that do not require an object are **intransitive verbs**. There are also verbs that can either take an object or not. A common mistake that English language learners make is to omit an object with a transitive verb. For example, look at this incorrect statement: **I need.** This is incorrect because "need" is a transitive verb, which requires an object. A correct way to say this is **I need it**. When you use transitive and intransitive verbs skillfully, you will speak more clearly. Let's learn more about these kinds of verbs. Notice in the table below that the <u>subject is underlined</u>, the verb is highlighted, and the *object is italicized*.

Type of Verb	Characteristics	Example Sentences
Intransitive verbs	• These are **action verbs** (not linking verbs). • They **don't transfer their actions** to anyone or anything else. • They **do not need an object** to complete their meaning. • They **are complete** verbs. • You can modify the verb with adverbs and prepositional phrases.	<u>She</u> spoke clearly. <u>That bird</u> chirps every morning. <u>The dog</u> is barking. <u>We</u> will travel to Rome next summer.

Type of Verb	Characteristics	Example Sentences
Transitive verbs	• These are **action verbs** (not linking verbs). • They **must transfer their actions** to someone or something else. • They **require an object** to complete their meaning. • They are incomplete verbs without an object.	Pip brought *the birthday cake* to the party. It doesn't make sense to write: *Pip brought to the party.* We think, "brought what?!" We sent *the gift.* It doesn't make sense to write: *We sent.* We wonder, "sent what?!" She enjoys *chocolate.* You can't write only *She enjoys* because you must indicate *what* or *who* she enjoys to complete the idea.
Verbs that go both ways	These verbs can be either transitive or intransitive depending on whether they take an object or not.	She ate yesterday. She ate *the last piece of the apple pie.* She sang *her favorite song.* She didn't sing.

Now that you understand a little bit more about transitive and intransitive verbs, let's see a list of some common ones.

Common Intransitive Verbs Note: Linking Verbs Are Intransitive	Common Transitive Verbs	Common Verbs That Can Be Both Intransitive and Transitive
agree	bring	change
arrive	buy	close
become	get	continue
belong	give	cost
cry	have	eat
depend	leave	do
die	lend	drink
fall	make	drive
go	offer	grow
happen	owe	live
laugh	pass	open
learn	pay	play
listen	promise	read
look	refuse	return
move	send	run
pray	show	set
sit	take	sing
sleep	teach	understand
smile	tell	write
stand	wear	
stay		
wait		
wake		
walk		
work		

Subject-Verb-Complement (SVC)

Now that you understand the SVO sentence, let's look at the SVC sentence. These structures have similarities and differences. Let's first look at their similarities. How are SVO and SVC sentences similar?

- The subject (S) comes before the verb in a statement

- The verb (V) follows the subject in a statement

How are SVO and SVC sentences different?

- In SVC sentences, the verb isn't an *action* verb. Rather, the verb is a **linking verb (LV)**.

- In SVC sentences, there isn't an object. Instead, there's a **complement (C)**.

Study the examples of SVC sentences below. In each sentence, the subject (S) is underlined, the linking verb (LV) is highlighted, and the complement (C) is double underlined. They are also labeled with an S, an LV, and a C.

Example SVC Sentences

Their last name is Knapp.
    S   LV C

Cheryl is a first-time mom!
  S LV   C

These two children are brother and sister.
     S   LV   C

Cole seems tired today.
  S LV   C

They are excited for the new school year.
 S LV   C

Olivia is sad because her pet rabbit died.
   S LV C

What do you notice about the verbs in these sentences? They are not action verbs. Rather, they are **linking verbs**.

How to Identify an SVC Sentence

The verb in the SVC structure is **a linking verb**. A linking verb **links, or connects, two or more things**. In the SVC sentence, the linking verb **links the subject (S) and the complement (C).** Here is a list of common linking verbs:

be	become	seem	appear	look	feel	taste	smell	sound

Linking verbs are like an equal sign. The complement describes the subject.

Their last name is Knapp.➔ Their last name = Knapp

Cheryl is a first-time mom! ➔ Cheryl = a first-time mom

These two children are brother and sister. ➔ These two children = brother and sister

Cole seems tired today. ➔ Cole = tired

They are excited for the new school year. ➔ They = excited

Olivia is sad because her pet rabbit died. ➔ Olivia = sad

Now, how can we find the subject, linking verb, and complement in a sentence? It is similar to the SVO strategy. Follow these three steps to find the S, LV, and C of a sentence:

> **Step 1:** First, **find the linking verb** (LV).
>
> **Step 2:** Next, **identify the subject**. The subject is the noun that usually comes before the linking verb in a statement.
>
> **Step 3:** Then, **locate the complement**. The complement follows the linking verb and **describes the subject**.

Let's see how to find the SVC with this sentence: Rani is absent from school today.

Step	Question to Ask	Answer
Step 1: Find the linking verb. • The linking verb connects the subject and complement. • See the list provided above to help you.	What is the linking verb in this sentence?	The linking verb: **is**
Step 2: Look for the subject. • The subject precedes the linking verb in a statement. • Ask the question, *Who/What* + **linking verb?**	Who <u>is</u>?	The subject: **Rani**
Step 3: Locate the complement. • It follows the linking verb. • Ask the question **linking verb** + *what or whom?*	Is what?	The complement: **absent**

<u>Rani</u> is <u>absent</u> from school today.
  S   V   C

Practice 7-B

Let's check your understanding of the SVC sentence. Follow the steps above and identify the S, V, and C of each sentence below. Underline the <u>S</u>, highlight the V, and double underline the <u>C</u>. Follow the example. See Practice 7-B in the Answer Key for answers.

Example: <u>They</u> seem <u>happy</u> today!

1. She is really tall.

2. Marty is Sherry's brother.

3. Harry and Marisol are newlyweds.

4. He became a dentist.

5. The apple pie tastes delicious!

6. That music sounds wonderful!

Simple Sentences

A simple sentence has only **one** S-V combination. It may have more than one subject before the verb, and it may have more than one verb after the subject. However, a simple sentence only has **one S-V combination**. It can be short or long. The number of words in a sentence doesn't determine whether it's simple. The important thing to know is that **for a simple sentence to be grammatical, it must satisfy these three requirements**:

1. It must **have a subject**.

2. It must **have a verb**.

3. It must **express a complete thought**.

Note: A simple sentence may also have an object of the verb or a complement as we learned earlier in this chapter with SVO and SVC sentences.

Here are some examples of correct simple sentences:

EXAMPLES

▶ Charlie and Victoria are classmates.

▶ Sebastian goes to high school.

▶ Marion is wearing a suit today.

▶ She had a great time.

▶ It isn't working.

▶ My mother and I are going to get a manicure.

▶ Mick and Toby fish and hunt every winter.

▶ Jerry, Bob, and Theo look alike.

▶ Sapphire does her homework every day and then makes dinner.

> He teaches.

> We completed the project and went to dinner.

> I love dancing anywhere but hate singing in public.

Let's analyze a simple sentence to be sure it's grammatical. Follow the three steps below:

Step 1: Is there a verb? Find and highlight the verb. Label it V if it's an action verb and label it LV if it's a linking verb. Determine whether the verb is transitive or intransitive, too. If you find more than one verb after the subject of the sentence, it is a ***compound predicate***.

Step 2: Is there a subject? Find and underline the subject. Label it S. Be sure to underline the whole subject. If you find more than one subject before the verb in the sentence, it is a ***compound subject***.

Step 3: Does it express a complete thought? This question is a bit tricky to answer. Essentially, the sentence must contain all the necessary information to complete the idea.

Let's see a demonstration of how to check whether a simple sentence is complete. We'll use the following sentence: Marion is wearing a suit today.

Step	Question to Ask	Answer
Step 1: Is there a verb? • Find the verb. • Is the verb an action or linking verb? • Is it transitive or intransitive? Your answers to these questions help you in Step 3.	What is the verb in this sentence?	The verb: **is wearing**
Step 2: Is there a subject? • Find it. • Ask the question, **Who/What + verb?** • It may be a compound subject.	Who/what <u>is wearing</u>?	The subject: **Marion**
Step 3: Does it express a complete thought? • To help you determine this, check for objects and complements. • If the verb is transitive, it requires an object. • You can ask the question, **verb + what or whom?** • Once you find all the required elements, ask the question **Is this a complete idea?**	<u>Is wearing</u> what? *Wear* is transitive, so it must have an object and it does.	The object: **a suit** This is a complete thought. It is a simple sentence because it has all three necessary elements: a subject, a verb, and a complete idea.

Remember, a simple sentence does not need an object to be complete. The sentence may be complete with only a subject and a verb. Let's look at the grammatical elements of some simple sentences. The <u>subject</u> is underlined; the verb or linking verb is highlighted, the *object* is italicized, and the <u>complement</u> is double underlined. Does the sentence have a compound subject or compound predicate? We'll discuss these in the next section.

1. <u>Charlie and Victoria</u> are <u>classmates</u>.
    S   S   LV   C

2. <u>Sebastian</u> goes to high school.
    S   V

3. <u>Marion</u> is wearing *a suit* today.
    S   V   O

4. <u>She</u> had *a great time*.
    S V   O

5. <u>It</u> isn't working.
    S   V

6. <u>My mother and I</u> are going to get a manicure.
        S   S   V

7. <u>Mick and Toby</u> fish and hunt every winter.
     S   S   V   V

8. <u>Jerry, Bob, and Theo</u> look <u>alike</u>.
    S   S   S LV C

9. <u>Sapphire</u> does *her homework* every day and then makes *dinner*.
     S   V   O   V   O

10. <u>He</u> teaches.
    S   V

11. <u>We</u> completed *the project* and went to dinner.
     S   V   O   V

12. <u>I</u> love *dancing* anywhere but hate *singing* in public.
    S V   O   V   O

Compound Subjects and Predicates

Although they are called "simple sentences," they are not so simple. Remember, simple sentences must have three things: a subject, a verb, and a complete thought. However, a simple sentence can also have multiple subjects, verbs, objects, and complements. You can see explanations and examples of these in the "Patterns of a Simple Sentence" section of this chapter.

What is a predicate? A predicate is everything in a simple sentence that isn't the subject. It includes the verb, and it may also include the object of the verb, the complement, adjectives, adverbs, prepositional phrases, and more. Let's take a closer look at predicates. See simple sentences below with the <u>subject</u> underlined and the ***predicate*** bolded and italicized.

EXAMPLES

▶ <u>He</u> ***teaches***.
Subject   Predicate

▶ <u>Jerry, Bob, and Theo</u> ***look alike***.
  Compound Subject   Predicate

▶ <u>Sapphire</u> ***does her homework every day and then makes dinner***.
  Subject   Compound Predicate

▶ <u>Mick and Toby</u> ***fish and hunt every winter***.
Compound Subject   Compound Predicate

Study the four patterns we can use in a simple sentence below.

Patterns of a Simple Sentence

In the example sentences on the next page, the <u>subject</u> is underlined, the verb/linking verb is highlighted, any *object* is italicized, and any <u>complement</u> is double underlined.

Patterns	Notes	Example Sentences
1. S V	This pattern has **one subject** and **one verb**.	The kids ran around the block today.
2. S S V	This pattern has **more than one subject** and **only one verb**.	Jolene and Carrie found *a silver ring* on the street today.
3. S V V	This pattern has **only one subject** and **more than one verb**.	Dr. Northrup diagnosed *the patient's condition* and prescribed *bed rest.*
4. S S V V	This pattern has **more than one subject** and **more than one verb**.	Marjorie and Robyn were hungry and felt sick.

As you learned earlier, simple sentences are not so simple. They are called simple to contrast them from compound, complex, and compound-complex sentences, which you will learn about in Chapter 10 of this book. However, at this point, you should understand the distinction between a simple sentence and a compound sentence. Students of English often confuse these two sentence structures. Let's see how they differ.

Simple Sentences vs. Compound Sentences

As we noted, simple sentences must have **one SV combination**. On the other hand, **compound sentences have two or more SV combinations**. Let's see how this plays out in the table below.

Simple Sentence Pattern	Example Sentences	Compound Sentence Pattern	Example Sentences
S S V	Jolene and Carrie found *a silver ring* on the street today.	S V + S V	Jolene and Carrie found *a silver ring* on the street today, and I found *a gold earring!*
S V V	Dr. Northrup diagnosed *the patient's condition* and prescribed *bed rest.*	S V + S V	Dr. Northrup diagnosed *the patient's condition,* and she prescribed *bed rest.*
S S V V	Marjorie and Robyn were hungry and felt sick.	S V + S V	Marjorie was hungry, but Robyn felt sick.

Notice that in all of the compound sentence examples, the two SV combinations are separated by a comma and the conjunction *and* or *but*. This is the distinction between a simple sentence and a compound sentence. Be sure you understand these two different sentence structures.

Lecture: The Grand Canyon

POP QUIZ!

What is the difference between a simple sentence and a compound sentence?

Remember, a simple sentence has one SV combination, while a compound sentence has at least two SV combinations.

A Natural Wonder in the United States: The Grand Canyon

The Grand Canyon, widely accepted as one of the Natural Wonders of the World, is one of the most amazing places to visit in the United States. It is an immense national park located in Arizona measuring 277 miles long, 18 miles wide, and 1 mile deep. The Grand Canyon was formed by the Colorado River, which carved its way through the rock over six million years ago. Over time, the constant flow of the river wore down the rock and created natural structures including rivulets, waterfalls, and caves. In fact, there are an estimated 1,000 caves in the Grand Canyon, but only 335 caves are recorded.

There are many ways to experience this national treasure, such as hiking, bicycling, off-roading, and even flying over it in a helicopter! Most tourists, however, only visit one of two places, the North Rim or the South Rim, to see the view and take photos. A small percentage of visitors hike the one-mile descent to the bottom of the canyon. A variety of activities like canyon mule rides, river-rafting, and overnight camping are available to the public on the canyon floor.

Because the Grand Canyon is such a popular tourist attraction, visitors who want to river-raft or camp should make reservations far in advance. For example, overnight campers should reserve a campsite a few months in advance.

It's also important to consider which time of year to go to the Grand Canyon. Every season offers its own beauty, but the ideal times to visit are during the spring and autumn months, when the days are cool and there aren't too many people. The other seasons are not ideal. Summertime, for instance, is the park's peak tourist season, so crowds of people fill the viewing stations, and daytime temperatures are hot. In the winter months, much of the park is closed and it gets quite cold.

No matter when you go to the Grand Canyon, it is sure to be an unforgettable experience to witness its breathtaking views.

Success Strategy: Discovering Meaning with Context Clues for Examples

What do you do when you find an unfamiliar word while reading? In Chapter 6, you discovered how to find the meaning of a new word from definition context clues. In this chapter, we will learn another way to find the meaning of a word—from **example context clues**. Example context clues provide **examples or details to help you understand the meaning** of new words, phrases, and ideas. Let's focus on five of these example context clues: *for example, for instance, including, such as,* and *like*. In the example sentences, the underlined word is the <u>new word or phrase</u>. The **phrase that introduces an example** is in bold, and the *example that helps us understand the meaning of the new word* is in italics.

Context Clues for Examples	Example Sentences
1. **For example,** _____ • Place a comma after *For example* at the beginning of a sentence. • When *for example* begins a sentence, it is followed by an independent clause, which is a simple sentence. • *For example* can also follow a noun or other part of speech. When it does, place a comma before and after *for example*.	Ecotourism promotes environmental conservation. **For example,** it encourages *walking, bicycling, canoeing, and other environmentally friendly transportation methods.*
2. **For instance,** _____ • Put comma after *For instance* at the beginning of a sentence. • When *for instance* begins a sentence, it is followed by an independent clause. • *For instance* can also follow a noun or other part of speech. When it does, place a comma before and after *for instance*.	Ecotourism also empowers local communities. **For instance,** it *helps fight poverty among the area's residents.*
3. _____, **including** • We sometimes use a comma before *including*. • Nouns, noun phrases, or noun clauses follow *including*.	Ecotourism encourages greater understanding of the area's natural treasures, **including** *its nature, local community, and its culture.*
4. _____, **such as** • *Such as* implies inclusion. • We often use a comma before *such as*. • Nouns, noun phrases, or noun clauses follow *such as*.	Ecotourism respects indigenous people's sacred traditions, **such as** *spiritual ceremonies and dance rituals.*
5. **like** • *Like* implies comparison. • We usually don't use a comma with *like*. • Nouns, noun phrases, or noun clauses follow *like*. • *Like* is informal and mostly used in conversation rather than academic writing.	Ecotourism encourages environmentally sustainable activities **like** *walking, hiking, and bicycling.*

Practice 7-C

Reread the lecture on the Grand Canyon and find five different example context clues. Underline the context clue and highlight the examples these context clues introduce. See Practice 7-C in the Answer Key for answers.

EXERCISES

EXERCISE 7-1

Read the sentences below. Use the three steps you learned in this chapter to find the S, the V, and the O in each sentence. Highlight the verb, underline the <u>subject</u> and circle the⟨object.⟩ Follow the example. Under each sentence, label these items.

Example: <u>Serena</u> drives⟨her new car⟩to work every day.
      S   V   O

1. Sonja enjoys her book collection.

2. This afternoon, Peter is going to kick the ball around.

3. Dr. Price attends medical conferences every year.

4. Last night, my cousins visited us.

5. You enjoyed the concert, didn't you?

6. Steve and Michele get coffee every morning together.

7. This year, my son is taking advanced placement classes.

8. The Quilici family sends holiday cards every year.

EXERCISE 7-2

Write SVO sentences. Use the simple present verb tense (learned in Chapter 2) to talk about habits, routines, regular activities, and customs. Use a variety of vocabulary. Get creative! Practice everything you are learning. Be sure that every sentence follows the SVO formula, which means you can't use linking verbs. After you write the sentence, use the three steps to check that you have a subject, verb, and object and label them. Use the words provided in the exercise to guide you. Follow the example.

Example: (weekly activity – simple present)

Every Tuesday afternoon, I babysit my brother.

                    S   V   O

1. (daily activity – simple present)

2. (how you commute to school or work – simple present)

3. (bus or train schedule information – simple present)

4. (a custom in your city – simple present)

5. (yearly event/custom – simple present)

EXERCISE 7-3

Practice finding the subject (S), linking verb (LV), and complement (C) in these sentences. Use the steps in this chapter to help you. Highlight the verb, underline the <u>subject</u>, and double underline the <u>complement</u>. Follow the example.

    Example: <u>Randy</u> looks <u>angry</u>.

1. Genevieve seems worried.

2. Mel and his wife are happy.

3. My lab partner is Rachel.

4. My aunt and uncle are funny.

5. Learning English is a challenge.

6. This house smells so good!

7. My brother-in-law appears confident.

8. Ruby and Luna are sisters.

EXERCISE 7-4

Read the sentences in Exercise 7-3. Find the complement in each sentence. What part of speech is the complement? Is it a noun, pronoun, or adjective? Write the complement on the line below. Then, label it n (noun), pro (pronoun), or adj (adjective). The first one is done for you.

1. *worried - adj* _____

2. _____

3. _____

4. _____

5. _____

6. _____

7. _____

8. _____

EXERCISE 7-5

Write sentences about your life, your friends, your family, and your situation.
Use the linking verbs provided below. Write one sentence for each linking verb.
Use the correct verb tense and verb form. Be sure that every complement is a
noun (n), pronoun (pro), or adjective (adj). Every sentence must follow the
SVC formula. After you write the sentences, review the three steps in this chapter
to check that you have a subject, linking verb, and complement. Label them S, LV, and
C. Label the part of speech the complement is. Follow the example.

Example: (be) <u>*My youngest daughter is an engineer.*</u>

 S   LV   C   (n)

1. (be) _____

2. (taste) _____

3. (seem) _____

4. (appear) _____

5. (look) _____

6. (feel) _____

7. (taste) _____

8. (smell) _____

9. (sound) _____

EXERCISE 7-6

Read the sentences. Then find and underline the direct and indirect objects. Not every sentence has an I.O. Use the strategies you learned in this chapter to identify the D.O. and I.O. Follow the example.

> **Example:** She mailed <u>me</u> <u>the package</u>.
>   I.O.   D.O.

1. When did she send you the book?

2. Nora gave Bentley the presentation slides.

3. Danielle and Mike threw their friends a party.

4. Shelby made homemade vanilla ice cream. It was delicious!

EXERCISE 7-7

Read the sentences and determine whether the verb is transitive or intransitive. Circle **trans** *or* **intrans**. *Then explain how you know on the line.*

1. The work continued into the early morning.   trans   intrans

_____

2. All weekend, he read.   trans   intrans

_____

3. She is changing her clothes.   trans   intrans

_____

4. I understand.   trans   intrans

_____

5. She wrote the book in six months.   trans   intrans

_____

6. They closed the shop early.   trans   intrans

_____

EXERCISE 7-8

Underline the <u>subject(s)</u>, highlight the verb(s), and double underline the <u>object(s) and</u> <u>complement(s)</u>. Label these in each sentence. Then, circle if it's a⟨simple⟩ sentence or ⟨compound⟩ _sentence. Write how you got your answer on the line. Follow the example._

> **Example:** <u>Sara and Joe</u> took <u>Madison and Owen</u> to the park.
>   S   V   O
>
>   _Simple Sentence. This sentence has only one S-V combination._

1. Catherine and Ken built a new house and moved   simple   compound
   in last summer.

   _____

2. Jim and Sue are watching the babies   simple   compound
   Saturday night.

   _____

3. JoAnne and Virginia are sisters, but they grew   simple   compound
   up separately.

   _____

4. The Young Family and the Pinna Family got   simple   compound
   together for Christmas and ate a big dinner.

   _____

EXERCISE 7-9

Look at the sentences below. The new word, phrase, or idea is in bold. Underline the example context clue and highlight the examples that describe the new word, phrase, or idea. See the example for guidance.

> **Example:** The discovery of **cultural artifacts,** <u>including</u> weaponry, pottery, and artwork, shows evidence of ancient civilizations.

1. **Cultural relics**, such as the Great Pyramids of Egypt and the Great Wall of China, are immovable national treasures.

2. One way to appreciate the history of a place is to go on a **heritage tour**. For example, you can walk through a house built by an early American settler in Massachusetts, or you can watch the reenactment of a battle in South Carolina.

3. My favorite part of the tour was watching **the reenactment of the American Revolutionary War**. In this reenactment, for instance, hundreds of men in traditional American and British uniforms fought with authentic weapons at the site of the battle in Lexington, Massachusetts.

4. **National historic landmarks in the United States**, such as objects, buildings, structures, sites, and districts, are protected by the US government.

Flashcard App

Talking About Future Activities

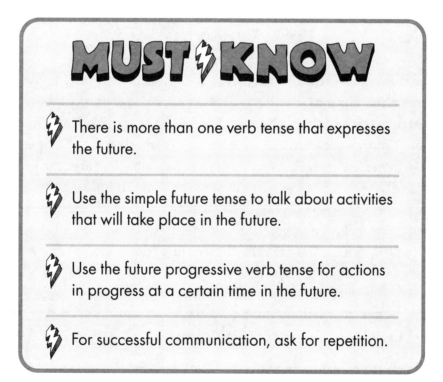

MUST KNOW

⚡ There is more than one verb tense that expresses the future.

⚡ Use the simple future tense to talk about activities that will take place in the future.

⚡ Use the future progressive verb tense for actions in progress at a certain time in the future.

⚡ For successful communication, ask for repetition.

What time will we meet tomorrow? Where are you going on vacation this summer? Who will be going to the meeting next week? These are questions about activities that will take place in the future. We often ask questions like these in conversation with friends. In school, we may use the simple future tense to discuss homework assignments or exams. For example, your instructor might say: *Your essay will be due next Wednesday* or *While you are taking the exam, I will be reading your essays.* Let's take a closer look at this verb tense.

Simple Future Verb Tense

When we talk about future actions, events, and situations, which is **any time after this moment**, we use the future tense. Specifically, we use the **simple future** form of the verb tense. For example, if we talk on Wednesday about our plans for the upcoming weekend, we usually use the simple future verb tense because the weekend is in the future. Let's look at some example sentences with verbs in the simple future verb tense in **bold**. However, notice that there are two non-simple future verb tenses represented in two of the sentences below. Can you find and identify them? Notice the time words and phrases that indicate the future time frame. These time words and phrases are <u>underlined</u>.

EXAMPLES

- I **am going to see** the doctor <u>on Wednesday</u>.

- Fabiola and June **are going to drive** to the mountains <u>this weekend</u>.

- She **will finish** her project <u>by the due date</u>.

- Sven and Lynn **are flying** to Amsterdam <u>next week</u>.

- He **isn't going to** make the party <u>Saturday night</u>. He has other plans.

- That idea **won't work**.

▶ **Are you going to cook** dinner <u>tonight</u>?

▶ **Will** Darius **apply** for the job?

▶ Why **are** they **buying** a new car?

▶ How **is** she **going to finish** her homework <u>on time</u>?

▶ Our train **leaves** <u>in one hour</u>.

▶ <u>In five years</u>, I**'m going to retire** and **move** to Santa Fe, New Mexico.

▶ I**'m going to be** on a retreat in the Yucatan <u>this summer</u>.

Simple Future Tense Timeline

Let's look at the timeline for this verb tense. Notice that these actions, events, and situations are in the future—<u>any moment after now</u>.

Example 1: *BE going to*—Tina**'s going to have** lunch with her boyfriend <u>today</u>.

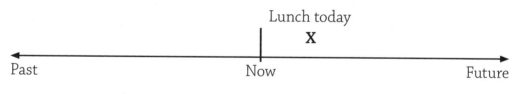

Lunch today

X

Past   Now   Future

(now: moment of speaking = 10 a.m. today)

When we talk about the future, it is for *any* time after the moment of speaking. It may be just one minute later. In this case, the moment of speaking is 10 a.m., and Tina plans to have lunch with her boyfriend today. The **plan**—to have lunch—is after 10 a.m., so we use the simple future verb tense with ***BE going to*** to talk about the plan.

Example 2: *Will*— I'**ll go** to the store with you. Let's go!

(now: moment of speaking = 3:30 p.m.)

At 3:30 p.m., I **spontaneously decide** to join my friend who's going to the store, so I use the simple future verb tense with *will*. This is one of the ways we use *will* with the simple future.

Example 3: *Present progressive*—<u>Tomorrow</u>, my friends **are working** at the street fair.

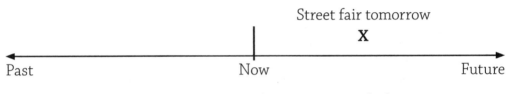

(now: moment of speaking = 4 p.m. today)

My friends have a **plan** to work at the street fair tomorrow. Because it's a **plan for a scheduled event**, we can use the present progressive verb tense.

Example 4: *Simple present*—The train **comes** <u>in 10 minutes</u>.

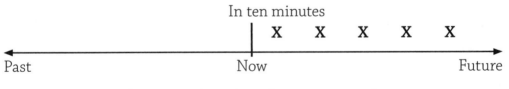

(now: moment of speaking = 7:00 a.m.)

This is a **train schedule**, so we use the simple present verb tense. We learned how to form the simple present verb tense in Chapter 2. In Chapter 3, you learned how to use the simple present verb tense to discuss set schedules, such as bus and train schedules, movie schedules, and store hours.

Expressions of Time

What are some common time expressions for the future verb tense? See some examples underlined in sentences below. They can come at the beginning of the sentence or as part of the predicate. Usually, if the time expression begins the sentence, we follow it with a comma.

Time Expressions	Example Sentences
in + amount of time (a week, 10 minutes, four years)	The play begins <u>in 20 minutes</u>. <u>In 20 minutes</u>, the play begins.
this + morning, afternoon, evening, day, week, month, year . . .	He's going to have fun <u>this summer</u>. <u>This summer</u>, he's going to have fun.
next + name of day, week, month, year	I'll be there <u>next week</u>. <u>Next week</u>, I'll be there.
tonight	We're going to make dinner <u>tonight</u>. <u>Tonight</u>, we're going to make dinner.
tomorrow	She's studying for the exam all day <u>tomorrow</u>. <u>Tomorrow</u>, she's studying for the exam all day.
later	I'll do that <u>later</u>. I'm busy right now. <u>Later</u>, I'll do that. I'm busy right now.
soon	He'll finish <u>soon</u>. <u>Soon</u>, he'll finish.
by + date / time / day **Note:** usually used with promises	We'll be done with the project <u>by May 15</u>. <u>By May 15</u>, we'll be done with the project.
before + event / time	I'm going to check the website <u>before the meeting</u>. <u>Before the meeting</u>, I'm going to check the website.
after + event / time	I'm going to see her <u>after the show</u>. <u>After the show</u>, I'm going to see her.

Choosing Which Form to Use

We use the **simple future** verb tense to talk about *actions, events, and situations in the future.* There are four ways to show future time, and we use these for different reasons. Study the table below.

	Future Verb Tense	Uses & Examples
1.	BE *going to* + base form of the main verb	a. to talk about plans or intentions We**'re going to see** a concert on Thursday night. b. to make predictions for the immediate future from evidence in the moment of speaking Watch out! You**'re going to fall** into the hole! **Note:** For plans, we often use the simple future **BE** *going to* and the present progressive interchangeably.
2.	*will* + base form of the main verb	a. to make predictions You**'ll pass** the test. Don't worry! b. to make promises I **won't disappoint** you. c. to make offers I**'ll take** you to the store. I have to go, too. **Note:** We do *not* use **will** to talk about plans.
3.	present progressive: BE + verb *–ing*	a. to talk about plans already arranged We**'re attending** a musical on Thursday night. **Note:** We usually use present progressive instead of **BE** *going to* when the main verb is **go**. It's easier! As an example, we'd say, She**'s going** to the mall tomorrow rather than, She**'s going to go** to the mall tomorrow.
4.	simple present verb tense	a. for set schedules such as transportation schedules and store hours The bus **leaves** tomorrow morning at 8:00 a.m.

Simple Future Tense: Forming the Affirmative

How do we form the simple future in affirmative statements? To see how we do this, look at the notes and example sentences in the tables below.

Forming Affirmative Statements with *will*

Subject or Subject Pronoun	*will* +	Base Form of the Main Verb	Example Sentences
I / You / We / They / He / She / It	will	look	I **will look** for your wallet while you pack the car! (offer)
		help	We **will help** you clean the house tomorrow. (promise)
		carry	You **will** really **like** this movie. I just know it! (prediction)

Forming Contractions with *will*

Subject or Subject Pronoun	+ *will* =	Contraction	Base Form of the Main Verb	Example Sentences
I +		**I'll**	do	**I'll do** my homework after dinner.
You +		**You'll**	be	**You'll be** fine. Don't worry.
We +		**We'll**	have	**We'll have** a lot of fun at her party!
They +	will =	**They'll**	walk	**They'll walk** to your car with you.
He +		**He'll**	finish	**He'll finish** the test on time. I just know it.
She +		**She'll**	perform	**She'll perform** well in the musical.
It +		**It'll**	take	**It'll take** two weeks to get the test results.

▶ Many English language learners avoid using contractions. Native speakers, on the other hand, almost always use contractions when speaking. It's a good idea for you to become familiar with them and practice pronouncing them, so you can use them more often in your speech. Fortunately, some of these **subject pronoun + will** contractions sound like other vocabulary words. Let's check these out and practice pronouncing them.

Contraction	Sounds Like
I'll →	aisle, isle – rhymes with *file*
We'll →	wheel – rhymes with *meal*
It'll →	rhymes with *little*

Contraction	Sounds Like
You'll →	yule – rhymes with *cool*
He'll →	heel, heal – rhymes with *meal*

Forming Affirmative Statements with *BE going to*

Subject or Subject Pronoun	BE *going to* (use correct form of *be*)	Base Form of the Main Verb	Example Sentences
I	**am going to**	**get**	I **am going to get** a kitten at the shelter this weekend! (plan / intention)
You / We / They	**are going to**	**cook**	Shelly and Mom **are going to cook** all day tomorrow for the party. (plan / intention)
He / She / It	**is going to**	**snow**	Look at that white sky. It **is going to snow** soon. (prediction from evidence)

Remember to use the correct form of BE, so there is subject-verb agreement.

Please note that native American English speakers sometimes say *going to* quickly and it sounds like **gonna, gonnu, gointa,** *or* **gointu**.

Forming Contractions with *BE going to*

Subject or Subject Pronoun	BE	Contraction	Going to	Base Form of the Main Verb	Example Sentences
I +	am =	I'm	going to (gonna)	sell	I'm **going to sell** my bike. (plan / intention)
You + We + They +	are =	You're We're They're	going to (gonna)	make	They**'re going to make** dessert for the potluck. (plan / intention)
He + She + It +	is =	He's She's It's	going to (gonna)	be	Look at that bright blue sky. It**'s going to be** sunny today! (prediction from evidence)

▶ Just like contractions with *will*, some of the **subject pronoun + BE** contractions sound like other words. See the examples below.

Contraction	Sounds Like	Contraction	Sounds Like
I'm →	rhymes with *time*	They're →	There, their – rhymes with *share*
You're →	Your – rhymes with *for*	It's →	its – rhymes with *fits*
He's / She's→	rhymes with *peas, keys, fees*		

Simple Future Tense: Forming the Negative

Now that you are familiar with the simple future verb tense and how we use it, let's see how to form negative statements. Remember, we usually use contractions in conversation because it's less formal. Note that there is only one way to contract the negative future verb tense with *will*. Study the table on the next page.

Forming Negative Statements and Contractions with *will*

Subject or Subject Pronoun	*will*	*not*	Contraction	Base Form of the Main Verb	Example Sentences
I / You / We / They / He / She / It	will +	not =	won't	carry	You **won't carry** any burdens in your life. (prediction)
				fail	I **won't fail** the driver's test! (promise / refusal*)

* *Will* + *not* can mean refusal. For example, *I will not/won't fail the driver's test* can mean *I refuse to fail the driver's test.*

Forming Negative Statements and Contractions with *BE going to*

There are two ways to construct negative statements in the simple future verb tense with *BE going to*. You learned these two types of contraction in Chapter 1. Below is a review.

Negative Contraction 1: *BE going to* Using *BE* + *not*

Subject or Subject Pronoun	BE	*not*	Contraction	*going to*	Base Form of the Main Verb	Example Sentences
I	am	not =	No contraction	going to	get	I'm **not going to get** that car. It's too expensive.
You / We / They	are +	not =	aren't	going to	need	You **aren't going to need** a coat. It's really warm today.
He / She / It	is +	not =	isn't	going to	watch	She **isn't going to watch** the movie because it's scary.

Negative Contraction 2: *BE going to* Using Subject Pronoun + *BE*

Subject or Subject Pronoun	BE		not	going to	Base Form of the Main Verb	Example Sentences
I +	am =	I'm	not	going to	mention	I'm **not going to mention** the bad news.
You + We + They +	are =	You're We're They're	not	going to	find	You're **not going to find** the keys in that drawer.
He + She + It +	is =	He's She's It's	not	going to	let	He's **not going to let** a little rain ruin his day.

Note: BE + *not going to* can also mean refusal. For example, *I am not going to panic before the test* can mean *I refuse to panic before the test*.

Please note that when we use this type of contraction – subject pronoun + BE verb—the word *not* is usually stressed.

Simple Future Tense: Forming Yes/No Questions

In conversation, we commonly ask questions about actions, events, and situations in the future. One type of question we ask is the **yes/no question**. As you know from previous chapters, we answer yes/no questions with either **yes** or **no**. See how to form these types of questions on the next page.

We often make requests with *will*. In the first chart, notice that we use *will* with every subject pronoun and the form of *will* doesn't change.

Forming Yes/No Questions with *will*

Will	Subject or Subject Pronoun	Base form of the Main Verb	Rest of Sentence	Example Sentences
Will	I / you / we / they / he / she / it	**want**	tickets to the outdoor concert?	**Will** they **want** tickets to the outdoor concert?
Will		**hold**	my bag for a moment, please?	**Will** you **hold** my bag for a moment, please? (request)

Forming Yes/No Questions with *BE going to*

BE Verb	Subject or Subject Pronoun	*going to*	Base Form of the Main Verb	Rest of Sentence	Example Sentences
Am	I	**going to**	**see**	you this weekend?	**Am** I **going to see** you this weekend?
Are	you / we / they	**going to**	**have**	a party for Sara this weekend?	**Are** they **going to have** a party for Sara this weekend?
Is	he / she / it	**going to**	**give**	a donation to the school?	**Is** she **going to give** a donation to the school?

PRONUNCIATION

> Remember to use rising pitch at the end of yes/no questions because yes/no questions indicate uncertainty. See the pitch chart in the Appendix for more information. Notice the dip in pitch before the rise. In order to go up in pitch, we must begin from a lower point. The words that are "dipped" are stressed words (important to the meaning of the sentence.) The pitch rise occurs on the last content word of the sentence. Content words are nouns, verbs, adjectives, or adverbs.

Am I going to see you this weekend?   Is she going to give a donation to the school?

Note: Pitch patterns are shown above, below, and through the words of sentences to illustrate that our pitches change as we speak.

Answering Yes/No Questions

As you know from previous chapters we answer yes/no questions in a few different ways. One way is to give long answers by repeating the complete verb tense and all parts of the sentence. Another way is to give short answers, which include only part of the verb tense. A third way to answer is to give a very quick answer with only *yes* or *no*. All of these are acceptable. With quick answers, however, be sure to use a polite tone of voice. Also, we often add an explanation if more information is needed. Read the examples below.

Yes/No Questions and Answers: Example with *will*

Will Nora get a job this summer?		
Affirmative Answers		
Long:	Yes, she ***will*** get a job this summer.	
Short:	Yes, she **will**.	Quick answer: Yes.*
Negative Answers		
Long:	No, she **won't** get a job this summer.	
Short:	No, she **won't**.	Quick answer: No.*
	No, she will **not**.	
	Note: We use *will not* (without contraction) for emphasis.	

*Note that you can also use alternative expressions for **yes** and **no**. See Chapter 1 for these.

Yes/No Question and Answers: Example with *BE going to*

Is Nora going to get a job this summer?		
Affirmative Answers		
Long:	Yes, she **is going to get** a job this summer.	
Short:	Yes, she **is**.	**Quick answer:** Yes.
Negative Answers		
Long:	No, she **isn't going to get** a job this summer.	
Short:	No, she **isn't going to**.	**Quick answer:** No.
	No, she **isn't**.	
	No, she**'s not going to**.	
	No, she's **not**.	

 IRL When the answer is negative, we sometimes provide a reason or cause. Look at this example: *No, she isn't going to get a job this summer because she's attending summer school.* Or *No, because she's attending summer school.*

Short answers follow these two rules:

- Omit the main verb in short answers.

- Do not contract the affirmative short answer.

Short Answers to Yes/No Questions with *will*

Yes or No + Comma	Subject or Subject Pronoun	*will*	Negative	Negative Contraction
Yes,		will	–	Yes, they **will**. ~~Yes, they'll.~~
No,	I / you / we / they / he / she / it	will	not	No, it **will not**.
			won't	No, it **won't**.

Short Answers to Yes/No Questions with *BE going to*

Yes or No + Comma	Subject or Subject Pronoun	BE	Negative	Negative Contraction
Yes,	I	am	-	Yes, I **am**. ~~Yes, I'm.~~
No,	I	am	not	No, I**'m not**.
Yes,	you / we / they	are	-	Yes, we **are**. ~~Yes, we're.~~
No,	you / we / they	are + not = aren't		No, we **aren't**.
		're + not		No, we**'re not**.
Yes,	he / she / it	is	-	Yes, it **is**. ~~Yes, it's.~~
No,	he / she / it	is + not = isn't		No, it **isn't**.
		's + not		No, it**'s not**.

Simple Future Tense: Forming WH Questions

When we need more information, we ask **WH questions,** or information questions, about the time, location, manner of, and reason for actions, events, and situations in the future. WH questions begin with WH question words or phrases such as *who, what, when, where, why, how, how long, how many,* and *how much.* Let's study how to form these questions using the simple future tense in the following table.

Forming WH Questions with *will*

WH Question Word	*will*	Subject or Subject Pronoun	Base Form of the Main Verb	Example Sentences
Where			be	**Where will she be** in 20 minutes?
How long			stay	**How long will you stay** at your grandmother's next week?
What	will	I / you / we / they / he / she / it	have	**What will you have** for dinner tonight?
Why			need	**Why will he need** more money tomorrow?

For WH questions in which **who** is the subject, we do not add another subject. See the examples below.

Who (Subject of Sentence)	*will*	Base Form of the Main Verb	Example Sentences
Who	will	help	**Who will help** me with the house cleaning?
Who	will	be	**Who will be** his partner for the next game?

PRONUNCIATION

Remember, we usually use falling pitch at the end of WH questions. However, if you don't hear or understand some information and you need repetition, use a "fast rising" pitch. This pitch differs from a regular rising pitch because the rise begins earlier in the sentence and continues to increase in pitch to the end. A regular rising pitch only rises toward the end of the sentence and doesn't rise too much. Look at the pitch patterns below for guidance.

1. **Use falling pitch for most WH questions:**

2. **Use fast rising pitch to check your understanding and to express that you need repetition:**

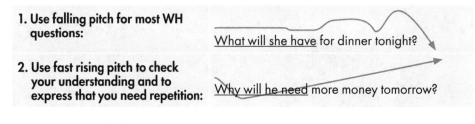

Forming WH Questions with -BE *going to*

WH Question Word	BE Verb	Subject or Subject Pronoun	*Going to*	Base Form of the Main Verb	Example Sentences
Where	am	I	going to	find	**Where am** I **going to find** edamame?
How long	are	you /we /they	going to	study	**How long are** you **going to study** for the history test?
What	is	he / she / it	going to	get	**What is** she **going to get** for her birthday?
Why	are	you / we / they	going to	order	**Why are** they **going to order** dinner from the Thai place?

Just like yes/no answers, we can answer WH questions in different ways. We give long answers, which are complete sentences, and we give short answers with only the essential information to answer the question. See some examples below.

WH Question and Answers: Example with *will*

Question: When will Marjorie write her book report?

Long answer (complete sentence): She'll write her book report this weekend.

Short answer (essential information only): This weekend.

WH Question and Answers: Example with *BE going to*

Question: How long are you going to be on vacation?

Long answer (complete sentence): I'm going to be on vacation for two weeks.

Short answer (essential information only): Two weeks.

Simple Future Tense: Using Tag Questions

As you learned in previous chapters, tag questions are used at the end of statements to verify information or seek agreement. With simple future forms of the verb, use tag questions with the appropriate form of the auxiliary verb: either **will** or **BE**. See example sentences below to understand this rule.

EXAMPLES

▸ You'll accept my invitation, <u>won't</u> you?

▸ She'll join us, <u>won't</u> she?

▸ This plan won't work, <u>will</u> it?

▸ They'll tell us the news soon, <u>won't</u> they?

▸ We won't get there late, <u>will</u> we?

▸ We're going to like this movie, <u>aren't we</u>?

▸ She's not going to be here today, <u>is</u> she?

▸ He's going to make us dinner, <u>isn't</u> he?

▸ We aren't going to order yet, <u>are</u> we?

▸ They're going to finish on time, <u>aren't</u> they?

▸ It isn't going to help us, <u>is</u> it?

▸ You're going to enjoy the party, <u>aren't</u> you?

How to Use Tag Questions

There are four important things to know about tag questions:

1. We use tag questions in two ways: **to verify information** and **to seek agreement**.

2. We use **rising intonation to verify information**, and we use **falling intonation to seek agreement**. Check out the pitch patterns in the example sentences below.

3. When speakers make affirmative statements with tag questions, they expect the answer to be affirmative. The opposite is also true: when speakers make negative statements with tag questions, they expect the answer to be negative. However, the question should be answered truthfully regardless of the expectation.

4. We can verify information and seek agreement with both affirmative and negative statements.

Statement with Tag Question to *Verify Information*

Use Rising Intonation: When we think we understand something but we want to be certain, we verify information.

It isn't going to help us, is it?   You're going to enjoy the party, aren't you?

Statement with Tag Question to *Seek Agreement*

Use Falling Intonation: When we know the answer and we want someone to agree with us, we seek agreement.

It isn't going to help us, is it?   You're going to enjoy the party, aren't you?

Forming Affirmative and Negative Tag Questions

When the statement is affirmative, the tag question is negative and vice versa. Notice that the statement is in the simple future verb form, yet the tag question and the answer **only use the auxiliary verbs *will*** or ***BE***. Be sure to use the correct form of the appropriate auxiliary verb. A comma is required after the statement and after *yes* and *no* in the answer. Note that we do *not* contract affirmative answers. Check out the table below for examples.

> **POP QUIZ!**
>
> Which verb tense do we use to talk about future actions, events, and situations? If you said the simple future verb tense, you are correct!

Affirmative Statement	Negative Tag Question	Expect Affirmative Answer
You**'ll accept** my invitation,	**won't** you?	Yes, I **will**. / ~~Yes, I'll.~~
She**'ll join** us,	**won't** she?	Yes, she **will**. / ~~Yes, she'll.~~
They**'ll tell** us the news soon,	**won't** they?	Yes, they **will**. / ~~Yes, they'll.~~
We**'re going to like** this movie,	**aren't** we?	Yes, we **are**. / ~~Yes, we're.~~
He**'s going to make** us dinner,	**isn't** he?	Yes, he **is**. / ~~Yes, he's.~~
They**'re going to finish** on time,	**aren't** they?	Yes, they **are**. / ~~Yes, they're.~~
You**'re going to enjoy** the party,	**aren't** you?	Yes, I **am**. / ~~Yes, I'm.~~

Negative Statement	Affirmative Tag Question	Expect Negative Answer
This plan **won't work**,	**will** it?	No, it **won't**.
We **won't get** there late,	**will** we?	No, we **won't**.
She**'s not going to be** here today,	**is** she?	No, she **isn't**. / No, she**'s not**.
We **aren't going to order** yet,	**are** we?	No, we **aren't**. / No, we**'re not**.
It **isn't going to help** us,	**is** it?	No, it **isn't**. / No, it**'s not**.

Future Progressive Verb Tense

When we talk about future actions and events that are continuous, or progressive, we use the future progressive verb tense. We also call this verb tense the *future continuous*. Why do we use the progressive form of the future rather than the simple form? As you've already learned, the simple future form is for actions, events, and situations that occur in the future. However, the **future progressive form is specifically used for:**

1. Actions and events that are **in progress** at a definite time in the future.

2. An action that will be **in progress** when another action occurs.

3. Emphasizing the **duration** of the future action.

Let's look at some sentences with verbs in the **future progressive form** in bold. Notice the underlined time words and phrases that indicate the future time frame.

EXAMPLES

▶ I **will be talking** with my professor <u>next Tuesday</u>.

▶ Hidalia and Rafael **will be attending** the seminar <u>all weekend</u>.

▶ She **is going to be working** on her project <u>for the rest of the month</u>.

▶ Amy and Olaf **are going to be traveling** through Europe <u>this summer</u>.

▶ Oleksandr **won't be coming** with us to the party <u>Saturday night</u>. He's working.

▶ **Will you be making** a birthday cake for the party <u>this weekend</u>?

▶ When **will** they **be buying** a new house?

▶ The bus **will be coming** <u>soon</u>. Grab your backpack.

▶ They**'ll be vacationing** in the Italian Riviera <u>in the spring</u>.

Choosing Between Simple Future and Future Progressive

When do we use the simple future instead of the future progressive verb tense? How do we know which one is correct? See some guidelines and examples below to help you determine which is most appropriate for you. The **verb tense** is bolded, and the <u>time expressions</u> are underlined.

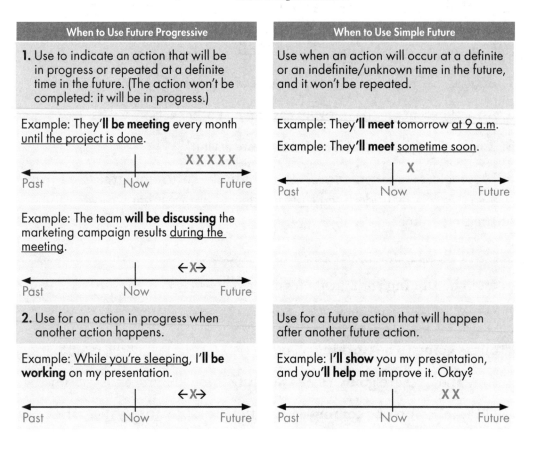

When to Use Future Progressive	When to Use Simple Future
1. Use to indicate an action that will be in progress or repeated at a definite time in the future. (The action won't be completed: it will be in progress.)	Use when an action will occur at a definite or an indefinite/unknown time in the future, and it won't be repeated.
Example: They**'ll be meeting** every month <u>until the project is done</u>.	Example: They**'ll meet** tomorrow <u>at 9 a.m.</u> Example: They**'ll meet** <u>sometime soon</u>.
Example: The team **will be discussing** the marketing campaign results <u>during the meeting</u>.	
2. Use for an action in progress when another action happens.	Use for a future action that will happen after another future action.
Example: <u>While you're sleeping</u>, I**'ll be working** on my presentation.	Example: I**'ll show** you my presentation, and you**'ll help** me improve it. Okay?

When to Use Future Progressive	When to Use Simple Future

3. Use to emphasize the <u>duration</u> of a future action (usually long).

Example: I**'ll be studying** for the exam <u>all week</u>.

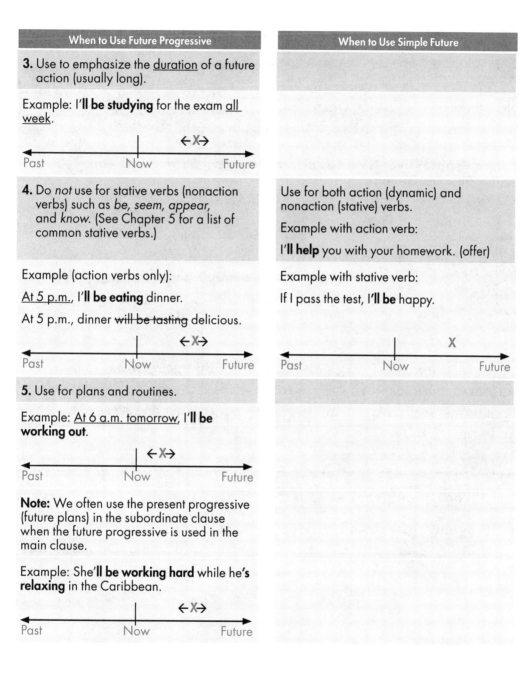

Past — Now — Future

4. Do *not* use for stative verbs (nonaction verbs) such as *be, seem, appear,* and *know*. (See Chapter 5 for a list of common stative verbs.)

Use for both action (dynamic) and nonaction (stative) verbs.

Example with action verb:

I**'ll help** you with your homework. (offer)

Example (action verbs only):

<u>At 5 p.m.</u>, I**'ll be eating** dinner.

At 5 p.m., dinner ~~will be tasting~~ delicious.

Example with stative verb:

If I pass the test, I**'ll be** happy.

Past — Now — Future

Past — Now — Future

5. Use for plans and routines.

Example: <u>At 6 a.m. tomorrow</u>, I**'ll be working out**.

Past — Now — Future

Note: We often use the present progressive (future plans) in the subordinate clause when the future progressive is used in the main clause.

Example: She**'ll be working hard** while he**'s relaxing** in the Caribbean.

Past — Now — Future

Future Progressive Tense: Forming the Affirmative

Now that you understand when we use the future progressive, let's learn how to form it in affirmative statements. Look at the table below.

Future Progressive: How to Form Affirmative Statements with *will* + *BE* + Verb *–ing*

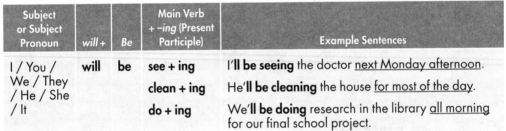

Subject or Subject Pronoun	*will* +	*Be*	Main Verb + *–ing* (Present Participle)	Example Sentences
I / You / We / They / He / She / It	will	be	see + ing	I'**ll be seeing** the doctor <u>next Monday afternoon</u>.
			clean + ing	He'**ll be cleaning** the house <u>for most of the day</u>.
			do + ing	We'**ll be doing** research in the library <u>all morning</u> for our final school project.

We can also form the future progressive with "***BE*** + ***going to be***," but it's seldom used because it's awkward and long. Read the sentences below with both forms. They have the same meaning, but the first one is easier to say and write.

EXAMPLES

▶ He'**ll be cleaning** the house for most of the day.

▶ He'**s going to be cleaning** the house for most of the day.

Future Progressive Tense: Forming the Negative

Now that you know how to form affirmative statements in the future progressive verb tense, let's discover how to form negative statements.

Forming Negative Statements and Contractions with *will not* + BE + Verb *–ing*

Subject or Subject Pronoun	*will not* or *won't*	*Be*	Main Verb + *–ing* (Present Participle)	Example Sentences
I / You / We / They / He / She / It	will not / won't	be	play + ing move + ing hike + ing	I **won't be playing** in the game <u>this weekend</u>. I hurt my shoulder. She **won't be moving** into her new apartment <u>until the first of the month.</u> They **won't be hiking** the Appalachian Trail <u>this year</u> because Judy broke her leg.

Note: Check the spelling rules for verb + ing in Chapter 5.

Future Progressive Tense: Forming Yes/No Questions

How do we form *yes/no questions* using the future progressive tense? See how to form yes/no questions with affirmative and negative forms of *will* on the next page. What's the difference between them? We ask *will* yes/no questions when we don't know the answer, and we ask *won't* yes/no questions when we expect the answer to be *yes*.

Will (Affirmative)	Subject or Subject Pronoun	be	Main Verb + –ing (Present Participle)	Example Sentences (We don't know the answer.)
Will	I / you / we / they /he / she / it	be	register + ing	**Will** you **be registering** for classes <u>soon</u>?
			care + ing for	**Will** they **be caring for** John's dogs <u>while he's traveling</u>?

Won't (Negative)	Subject or Subject Pronoun	be	Main Verb + –ing (Present Participle)	Sentences (We expect the answer to be *yes*.)
Won't	I / you / we / they /he / she / it	be	register + ing	**Won't** you **be registering** for classes <u>soon</u>?
				Expected answer: Yes.
			care + ing for	**Won't** they **be caring for** John's dogs <u>while he's traveling</u>?
				Expected answer: Yes.

Answering Yes/No Questions

See examples below of the different ways to respond to yes/no questions in the future progressive form.

Will you **be registering** for classes <u>soon</u>?	
Affirmative Answers	
Long:	Yes, I **will / I'll be registering** for classes soon. Probably next week.
Short:	Yes, I **will**. Probably next week.	**Quick answer:** Yes. Probably next week.
Negative Answers	
Long:	No, I **will not / won't be registering** for classes soon. I have to choose my major first.
Short:	No, I **will not / won't**. I have to choose my major first.	**Quick answer:** No. I have to choose my major first.

Future Progressive Tense: Forming WH Questions

As we know, we use WH questions to ask for more information. Let's see how to form these questions using the future progressive tense. The **WH question word and verb phrase** are bolded and the <u>time phrase</u> is underlined.

WH Question Word	*will*	Subject or Subject Pronoun	*be*	Main Verb + *-ing* (Present Participle)	Example Sentences
Where			be	go + ing	**Where will** they **be going** <u>over the holiday</u>**?**
How long	will	I / you / we / they / he / she / it	be	study + ing	**How long will** you **be studying** <u>tonight</u>**?**
What				do + ing	**What will** we **be doing** <u>for summer vacation this year</u>**?**
Why				work + ing	**Why will** she **be working** <u>this weekend</u>**?**

Just as you learned for the simple future verb tense, we do not add another subject with **who** questions when **who** is the subject of the sentence. See examples below.

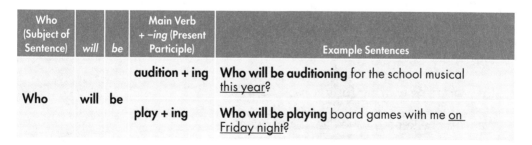

Who (Subject of Sentence)	*will*	*be*	Main Verb + *-ing* (Present Participle)	Example Sentences
Who	will	be	audition + ing	**Who will be auditioning** for the school musical <u>this year</u>**?**
			play + ing	**Who will be playing** board games with me <u>on Friday night</u>**?**

Answering WH Questions

Let's look at some ways to answer WH questions. See examples below.

---

1. Question: Where will they be going over the holiday?

Long answer (complete sentence): They**'ll be visiting** friends in Florida.

Short answer (essential information only): Florida.

2. Question: Why will she be working this weekend?

Long answer (complete sentence): She**'ll be working** this weekend because her coworker is sick, and she has to cover the shift.

Short answer (essential information only): Because her coworker is sick.

Future Progressive Tense: Using Tag Questions

To form tag questions in the future progressive verb tense, use **_will_** or **_won't_**. See some example sentences below.

EXAMPLES

▶ You'll be going to the party Saturday night, <u>won't</u> you?

▶ She'll be joining us, <u>won't</u> she?

▶ In the fall, her children will be attending that private school, <u>won't</u> they?

▶ They won't be waiting for her, <u>will</u> they?

▶ We won't be keeping the lizard, <u>will</u> we?

▶ He won't be going to study group tonight, <u>will</u> he?

Forming Affirmative and Negative Tag Questions

Remember, there are four important things to know about tag questions. Review the section of this chapter on the simple future for these rules. Check out the table below for examples.

Affirmative Statement	Negative Tag Question	Expect Affirmative Answer
You**'ll be going** to the party Saturday night,	**won't** you?	Yes, I **will be**. / Yes, I **will**.
She**'ll be joining** us,	**won't** she?	Yes, she **will be**. / Yes, she **will**.
In the fall, her children **will be attending** that private school,	**won't** they?	Yes, they **will be**. / Yes, they **will**.

Negative Statement	Affirmative Tag Question	Expect Negative Answer
We **won't be keeping** the lizard,	**will** we?	No, we **won't be**. / No, we **won't**.
They **won't be waiting** for her,	**will** they?	No, they **won't be**. / No, they **won't**.
He **won't be going** to study group tonight,	**will** he?	No, he **won't be**. / No, he **won't**.

Success Strategy: Asking for Repetition

Whether we're learning English or we already know the language, it's common to not understand speakers sometimes. As you learned in Chapter 3, asking for repetition is an important way to understand someone. No matter why the message isn't clear, asking questions helps create successful communication for everyone. It's perfectly acceptable to ask a question when you need something repeated. In fact, it's your **responsibility to be sure you understand what the speaker said**. In the United States, we say that "communication is a two-way street," which means that it takes both the speaker and listener together to find clarity and understanding. Let's take another look at this successful communication strategy.

Here are some expressions we use to ask for repetition. The list below goes from informal to more formal.

- *Excuse me* is typically American.

- *Pardon me* is formal.

- *Sorry* is less common in the United States, but it's often used in United Kingdom.

- *Please* in a polite tone of voice is a great addition.

Mix it up and try a few different combinations!

Expressions for Asking for Repetition

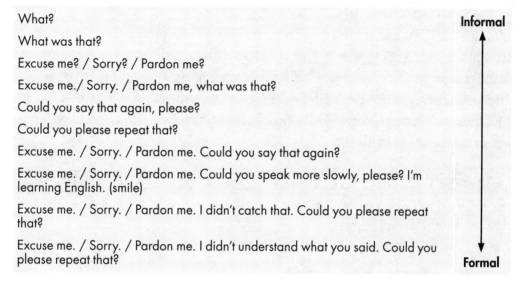

What?   **Informal**

What was that?

Excuse me? / Sorry? / Pardon me?

Excuse me./ Sorry. / Pardon me, what was that?

Could you say that again, please?

Could you please repeat that?

Excuse me. / Sorry. / Pardon me. Could you say that again?

Excuse me. / Sorry. / Pardon me. Could you speak more slowly, please? I'm learning English. (smile)

Excuse me. / Sorry. / Pardon me. I didn't catch that. Could you please repeat that?

Excuse me. / Sorry. / Pardon me. I didn't understand what you said. Could you please repeat that?   **Formal**

PRONUNCIATION

▶ When you ask for repetition, use rising pitch to show uncertainty. This means that you raise the pitch of your voice toward the end of your question. We usually begin questions at a pitch level of 2 and our voice rises to a high 3 at the end of the question. See the Appendix for more information on pitch changes.

Dialogue: Project Planning

Melanie and James are having a conversation on the phone about a project they are working on together. They work in different departments at the same company. They met once before, but they don't know each other well. They are acquaintances, not friends. Follow the conversation between Melanie and James below. Notice how future tenses are used and how James asks for repetition to clarify.

Melanie on the Phone	James on the Phone
Hi, James. It's nice to talk to you again. It's been a long time.	Hi there, Melanie. Yes, it has been a long time. How are you?
I'm well, thank you. And you?	Doing pretty good.
Great! Do you have time now to discuss the timeline for the project?	I sure do.
I <u>was under the impression</u>* that this project should be ready for the all-staff company meeting in June, and you and I will preview the rollout of the new customer management system. ***Note: *to be under the impression*:** to believe or assume something	<u>I'm sorry, I didn't quite catch what you said. Could you repeat that, please?</u>
Sure. The CEO will be discussing the new customer management system at our next all-staff meeting in June. The project you and I are working on should be done by then. By June 15, right?	Ah, okay! Right. Yes, we should be done with the project by June 15.
Okay good. What do you think? Will you be able to handle this timeline?	Oh yes. I will. Shall we **nail down*** progress deadlines? *** Note: *To nail down something*** is a phrasal verb, which means to make a final decision on something. You can *nail something down* or *nail down something*. If you use the pronoun *it*, it must come between *nail* and *down* like this: *nail it down*.
Absolutely! Great idea.	Fantastic. I'll get my calendar.

EXERCISES

EXERCISE 8-1

Complete the sentences below with the simple future form of the verb given in parentheses. Use the clue to guide you. Follow the examples.

Example 1: Prediction from evidence: (step) Be careful! You *are going to step* on my foot!

Example 2: Promise: (email) I *will email* you later with the information.

Example 3: Arranged plan: (take) He *is taking* archery lessons this summer.

Example 4: Schedule: (open) The store *opens* at 10 a.m.

1. Plan/intention: (go) Aidan _____ to his house after school.

2. Prediction: (be) Psychic: You _____ very happy in life!

3. Prediction from evidence: (fall) Watch out! You _____ into that ditch!

4. Arranged plan: (meet) Niles _____ with his boss tomorrow morning.

5. Offer: (watch) I _____ your dog for you while you're on vacation.

6. Prediction from evidence: (rain) What a dark sky! It _____ soon.

7. Promise: (complete) Jenna _____ the assignment by 5 p.m. tonight.

8. Prediction: (find) Fortune cookie: You _____ great happiness this year.

9. Plan/intention: (lead) Jamillah and Alicia _____ the class meeting later today.

10. Schedule: (arrive) The train _____ in about 10 minutes.

EXERCISE 8-2

Let's practice contractions with the simple future in the affirmative form. Refer to the sentences in Exercise 8-1. Complete the sentences using contractions. If the subject is not a pronoun, make it a pronoun. For example, in sentence #1 Aidan = he. Follow the examples that refer to Exercise 8-1.

Example 1: Be careful! You're *going to step* on my foot!

Example 2: I'll *email* you later with the information.

EXERCISE 8-3

Now that you know some time expressions used for the simple future, practice identifying them. Go back to Exercise 8-2 and highlight the time expressions in each sentence. Some sentences may not have a time expression.

EXERCISE 8-4

Form sentences with the affirmative simple future verb tense using the words in parentheses. Follow the examples. Use contractions in sentences with subject pronouns.

Example 1: (Promise) Maya / ride / to school / with you / this week
Maya will ride to school with you this week.

Example 2: (Arranged plan) Tammy and Rocky / start / ping pong lessons / next month
Tammy and Rocky are starting ping pong lessons next month.

1. (Promise) I / complete / the report / by Monday night

   _____

2. (Schedule) The train / arrive / in an hour

   _____

3. (Offer) I / give / you / money / for college textbooks

   _____

4. (Plan/intention) This weekend, / we / make / brunch / for our parents

   _____

5. (Prediction) Father: You / succeed / in life

   _____

6. (Intention/plan) Esperanza / collaborate / with her classmate / in class on Friday

   _____

EXERCISE 8-5

Now you try it! Form sentences using the simple future verb tense. Write about your own future activities, events, plans, tasks, and situations. Write about your friends and your family, too. Use time expressions. Be creative!

1. (Promise) _____

2. (Plan/intention) _____

3. (Prediction) _____

4. (Arranged plan) _____

5. (Offer) _____

6. (Schedule) _____

EXERCISE 8-6

Complete the following sentences with the negative form of the correct simple future verb tense. Don't use contractions. Follow the examples.

Example 1: (study – be going to) Dung *is not going to study* for the exam this weekend.

Example 2: (go – will) Jane *will not go* to that mall. It's too crowded.

1. (be – will) Ariana _____ at the party Saturday. She is visiting her cousins.

2. (buy – be going to) My sister-in-law _____ any more clothes online. It's too expensive.

3. (take notes – be going to) The secretary _____ at the meeting because it's being recorded.

4. (sell – will) Chuck _____ his vintage motorcycle. It's too sentimental.

5. (read – will) Nacho _____ online news. He prefers to read a real newspaper.

6. (prescribe – will) The doctor _____ any more medication until I get a checkup.

EXERCISE 8-7

Let's practice negative contractions with the simple future verb tenses. Look at the sentences you wrote in Exercise 8-6. Rewrite those sentences below using all possible contractions for that future verb tense. Change subjects to subject pronouns. Follow the examples.

Example 1: (study – be going to) Dung *is not going to study* for the exam this weekend.
She isn't going to study for the exam this weekend.
She's not going to study for the exam this weekend.

Example 2: (go – will) Jane *will not go* to that mall. It's too crowded.
She won't go to that mall. It's too crowded.

1. _____

2. _____

3. _____

4. _____

5. _____

6. _____

EXERCISE 8-8

Write sentences using the words below. Form sentences with <u>all forms</u> of the negative contraction. Change the subject to a subject pronoun where possible. Follow the examples.

Example 1: (BE going to) Victoria has no money. She / NEGATIVE / buy / new clothes / for a while
She's not going to buy new clothes for a while.
She isn't going to buy new clothes for a while.

Example 2: (will) Tami and Billy are busy. They / NEGATIVE / have time / for dinner / tonight
They won't have time for dinner tonight.

1. (BE going to) Barry is sick. He / NEGATIVE / make it / to the party / today

   _____

   _____

2. (BE going to) She is home in Japan for two weeks. She / NEGATIVE / practice / English / every day / there

   _____

   _____

3. (BE going to) I am studying tonight for the test tomorrow. I / NEGATIVE / attend / the concert / at the school / tonight

   _____

   _____

EXERCISE 8-9

Form yes/no questions with the simple future verb tense using the words given. Then write long, short, and quick answers to the question. Answer the questions affirmatively or negatively as indicated. Add a reason to the sentence when the answer is negative. Follow the examples.

Example 1: *will*

Affirmative answer: Will / Decker / take / tennis lessons / this summer?

Question: *Will Decker take tennis lessons this summer?*

Long answer: *Yes, he will take tennis lessons this summer.*

Short answer: *Yes, he will.*

Quick answer: *Yes.*

Negative answer: Will / Decker / take / tennis lessons / this summer? (No – he's working full time)

Question: *Will Decker take tennis lessons this summer?*

Long answer: *No, he will not/won't take tennis lessons this summer. He's working full time.*

Short answer: *No, he will not. / No, he won't. He's working full time.*

Quick answer: *No. He's working full time.*

Example 2: *BE going to*

Affirmative answer: BE going to / Decker / take / tennis lessons / this summer?

Question: *Is Decker going to take tennis lessons this summer?*

Long answer: *Yes, he is going to take tennis lessons this summer.*

Short answer: *Yes, he is.*

Quick answer: *Yes.*

Negative answer: BE going to / Decker / take / tennis lessons / this summer? (No – he's working full time)

Question: *Is Decker going to take tennis lessons this summer?*

Long answer: *No, he's not/he isn't going to take tennis lessons this summer. He's working full time.*

Short answer: *No, he's not./No, he isn't. He's working full time.*

Quick answer: *No. He's working full time.*

1. Will / they / have / fun / at the event / this weekend? (No – they're grounded)

   Question: _____

   Long answer: _____

   Short answer: _____

   Quick answer: _____

2. BE going to / Mace / need / a new car / for his new job? (No – he's getting a company car)

   Question: _____

   Long answer: _____

   Short answer: _____

   Quick answer: _____

3. Will / you / please / show / me / some examples? (Yes)

   Question: _____

   Long answer: _____

   Short answer: _____

   Quick answer: _____

4. BE going to / Maximillian and Tara / rent / a shuttle / for the party? (Yes)

Question: _____

Long answer: _____

Short answer: _____

Quick answer: _____

EXERCISE 8-10

Form WH questions with the simple future verb tense using the statements given. Use the question word in parentheses. Form long and short answers with the information in parentheses. Use subject pronouns and contractions. Follow the examples.

Example 1: *will*: Harry will research topics for his essay. (When) (during sixth period)

Question: *When will Harry research topics for his essay?*

Long answer (complete sentence): *He'll research topics for his essay during sixth period.*

Short answer (essential information only): *During sixth period.*

Example 2: *BE going to*: I am going to pick the kids up later. (Where) (at Sheila's house)

Question: *Where are you going to pick the kids up later?*

Long answer (complete sentence): *I'm going to pick the kids up at Sheila's house.*

Short answer (essential information only): *At Sheila's house.*

1. My dad will fix the toy bike. (Where) (in the garage)

   Question: _____

   Long answer: _____

   Short answer: _____

2. Margi is going to finish her school project. (When) (later tonight)

   Question: _____

   Long answer: _____

   Short answer: _____

3. Miles is going to register for summer school. (Why) (he failed math)

   Question: _____

   Long answer: _____

   Short answer: _____

4. Jeanette and Daniel will buy a new TV. (Why) (theirs is broken)

   Question: _____

   Long answer: _____

   Short answer: _____

EXERCISE 8-11

Practice forming sentences with the future progressive verb tense in the affirmative form using the words given. Then, write the contraction. Change subjects to subject pronouns. Follow the examples.

Example 1: Alma / drive / herself / to school / tomorrow morning / with her own car

Alma will be driving herself to school tomorrow morning with her own car.

She'll be driving herself to school tomorrow morning with her own car.

Example 2: His two sisters / visit / him / at the university / over the long holiday

His two sisters will be visiting him at the university over the long holiday.

They'll be visiting him at the university over the long holiday.

1. Manira / work / late / every night this week

   _____

   _____

2. The seminar / start / in 10 minutes

   _____

   _____

3. I / get / a massage / once a month / for the next six months

   _____

   _____

4. Next week, / Mr. Wu / substitute / for Mrs. Singh / because she's ill

_____

_____

5. My mother / sew / my Halloween costume / for the party Sunday

_____

_____

6. Faby / graduate / at the top of her class / this year

_____

_____

EXERCISE 8-12

Complete the following sentences with the correct negative form of the future progressive verb tense. Use the full form and then write the sentence with a contraction. Follow the example.

> **Example:** (play) Nick *will not be playing* in the volleyball game today. He hurt his knee in practice.
>
> Nick *won't be playing* in the volleyball game today.

1. (attend) Mr. Schiffer _____ the engagement party this Sunday evening. He's got plans.

_____

2. (grade) My math professor _____ our exams till next week.

_____

3. (take care of) My neighbor _____ my plants while I'm gone because she's on vacation, too.

   _____

4. (babysit) I _____ my little cousins this summer because I'll be in Spain.

   _____

5. (present) Facundo _____ the new ad campaign at the client meeting as he's out of town.

   _____

6. (go) Shandra _____ to her primary care physician next week. Her doctor is booked next week.

   _____

EXERCISE 8-13

Form yes/no questions with the future progressive verb tense using the words given. Then write long, short, and quick answers to the question. Answer the questions affirmatively or negatively as indicated. Add a reason to the sentence when the answer is negative. Follow the examples.

Example 1: your husband / make / plans / for your anniversary / this summer? (Yes)

Question: *Will your husband be making plans for your anniversary this summer?*

Long answer: *Yes, he will be making plans for our anniversary this summer.*

Short answer: *Yes, he will.*

Quick answer: *Yes.*

Example 2: your husband / make / plans / for your anniversary / this summer? (No – we're postponing the celebration until he's better)

Question: _Will your husband be making plans for your anniversary_ _this summer?_

Long answer: _No, he will not/won't be making plans for our anniversary_ _this summer. We're postponing the celebration until he's better._

Short answer: _No, he will not. / No, he won't. We're postponing the_ _celebration until he's better._

Quick answer: _No. We're postponing the celebration until he's better._

1. they / attend / the conference / next week? (No – they have other plans)

   Question: _____

   Long answer: _____

   Short answer: _____

   Quick answer: _____

2. your boss / give / you / a raise / this year? (Yes)

   Question: _____

   Long answer: _____

   Short answer: _____

   Quick answer: _____

3. Alana / introduce / me / at the company meeting? (No – Tran will)

   Question: _____

   Long answer: _____

   Short answer: _____

   Quick answer: _____

4. Cora / arrange / a ride / from the airport / for us? (Yes)

Question: _____

Long answer: _____

Short answer: _____

Quick answer: _____

EXERCISE 8-14

Form WH questions with the future progressive. Each statement gives information about what the subjects must do. Use that information and the question word in parentheses to write a question. Then, use the information in parentheses to form long and short answers. Use subject pronouns and contractions in the answers. Follow the examples.

Example 1: Julie and Aria have to work on a company presentation. (When) (all weekend)

Question: *When will Julie and Aria be working on the company presentation?*

Long answer (complete sentence): *They'll be working on the company presentation all weekend.*

Short answer (essential information only): *All weekend.*

Example 2: Berto has to fly to another country. (Where) (Bulgaria)

Question: *Where will Berto be flying?*

Long answer (complete sentence): *He'll be flying to Bulgaria.*

Short answer (essential information only): *To Bulgaria.*

1. My aunt has to go to the doctor. (Why) (she has migraine headaches)

   Question: _____

   Long answer: _____

   Short answer: _____

2. Annie and David have to sell their house. (When) (this summer)

   Question: _____

   Long answer: _____

   Short answer: _____

3. My nephew has to take driving lessons. (Where) (at the driving school on Willow Street)

   Question: _____

   Long answer: _____

   Short answer: _____

4. Josh and Jerry have to buy a new car. (What kind of car) (a rugged, off-road vehicle)

   Question: _____

   Long answer: _____

   Short answer: _____

EXERCISE 8-15

Complete the sentences with the correct form of the verb in parentheses, using the most appropriate verb tense for future actions, events, and situation. More than one may be appropriate. Follow the example.

> **Example:** repetitive future activity: (perform) Robin and Jamie <u>will be performing</u> every Saturday night in March.

1. Planned event: (perform) My twin sisters _____ this Saturday night at school.

2. Future activity over time: (discuss) My family _____ our vacation over the weekend.

3. Future situation: (be) I _____ happy when the school year is over.

4. Routine: (jog) Nora and Gray _____ tomorrow morning, so they can't drive you.

5. Promise: (do) I _____ the dishes tonight.

6. Offer: (hold) Do you need help? I _____ your books for you.

7. Emphasize duration: (write) We _____ this book for the rest of the year.

8. Prediction based on evidence: (trip) Watch out! You _____ over that log.

EXERCISE 8-16

Read the instructions on the left-hand column of the table below. In the right-hand column, ask for repetition. Use a variety of expressions to ask for repetition.

Instructions	Questions That Ask for Repetition
Supervisor to employee: Before you lock up the store, please turn the new alarm on. Make sure you use the correct code.	1.
Teacher to students in class: For homework, turn in the essay by midnight Friday and the book report by Monday 9 a.m.	2.
Customer service representative to customer: To get a refund, you need to complete the form and email it back. Write the problem with the product in the box at the bottom of the form.	3.

9 Connecting the Past and the Present

MUST KNOW

 To make a connection to a past action and now, use the present perfect verb tense.

 To connect the past, present, and future, you can use the present perfect progressive verb tense.

Supporting your position on a topic is important and demonstrates critical thinking skills.

You can disagree without being disagreeable using certain expressions.

hen do we use the present perfect verb tense? This is a question many English language learners struggle to answer. A simple way to remember is this: We use the present perfect to talk about a past action that has a connection to right now. Let's dive deeper into the present perfect to understand this concept.

Present Perfect Verb Tense

We use the present perfect verb tense to talk about something that **occurred in the past but has relevance now**. Specifically, the action, event, or situation is **completed**; however, it has a **connection to the moment of speaking**. For example, an hour ago, Katie ate lunch. It's a completed action and lunch is finished, so we use the simple past verb tense for *eat* —*ate*— to describe the fact that it's finished. Then her friend, Julie, asks Katie to join her for lunch. How does Katie reply? She uses the present perfect verb tense because although lunch is done, Katie is still full: she is still feeling the effects of eating when she replies to Julie. Look at their conversation.

Fact: Katie **ate** lunch 30 minutes ago. (Lunch is finished. Katie is not eating now.)

Julie: Katie, do you want to have lunch with me?

Katie: Oh, I'd love to, but I**'ve eaten** lunch already. (Lunch is finished, and Katie isn't hungry now. Here is the connection: Although Katie *ate* lunch, the effect is relevant *now*.)

Let's look at more examples of sentences with verbs in the present perfect form in **bold**. Notice the time words and phrases we often use with the present perfect verb tense:

EXAMPLES

▶ She **has** <u>already</u> **finished** the exam.

▶ My parents **have been** to Paris <u>twice</u>.

▶ **Have** you <u>ever</u> **driven** across the United States?

▶ My car **has broken down** <u>three times in the last month</u>.

▶ Gloria **hasn't taken** driving lessons <u>yet</u>.

▶ Vivian and Soroya **have** <u>never</u> **seen** the sunrise. They are night owls.

▶ When **have** I <u>ever</u> **lied** to you?

▶ Her aunt and uncle **have been** married <u>for 20 years</u>.

▶ <u>This is the first time</u> I**'ve performed** for a large crowd.

▶ She**'s baked** this delicious cake <u>twice</u>. I hope she bakes it again!

▶ **Has** this <u>ever</u> **happened** <u>before</u>?

▶ This **has** <u>never</u> **happened** to me <u>before</u>!

Deciding When to Use the Present Perfect Tense

In general, we use the present perfect to demonstrate completed actions or events that are relevant to this moment. We also use it to show duration of an activity, for certain states, and for occasional events. The present perfect also indicates a completed action in the past when the time of the action is unknown or unimportant. Finally, it expresses a repeated action over a time period that is not complete. Let's look at these guidelines more closely and study examples.

Reasons to Use the Present Perfect	Examples, Timelines + Explanations
1. Past events relevant now: • To show **a completed action that has relevance now – in the moment of speaking or writing**	I**'ve seen** that movie <u>already</u>. 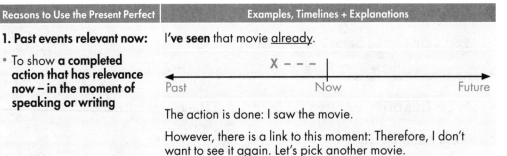 The action is done: I saw the movie. However, there is a link to this moment: Therefore, I don't want to see it again. Let's pick another movie.
2. States: • To talk about certain ongoing states and to show **existence, mental states, and possession** with these verbs: **to be, to know**, and **to have** • These **states began in the past, have connection to now, and will most likely continue into the future.** • We can use the present perfect with **dynamic and stative verbs**.	I**'ve been** a dentist <u>for five years</u>. I became a dentist in the past; I am still a dentist now; and I will continue to be a dentist in the future. We**'ve known** each other <u>for 30 years</u>! We met 30 years ago, we are still in each other's lives, and we'll continue to be friends. She**'s had** allergies to pollen <u>ever since</u> she moved to Northern California. The allergies began in the past; they still occur; and while she is in Northern California, they will probably continue to affect her.

Reasons to Use the Present Perfect	Examples, Timelines + Explanations

3. Occasional events:

- To show an action **done in the past with the possibility or expectation that it will occur again in the future**

We**'ve salsa danced** <u>once so far</u>.

The first time is complete, but we expect to do it again. *So far* expresses "up to this point" and suggests the likelihood that it will happen again in the future.

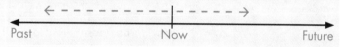

My best friend, Raj, **has ridden** that crazy roller coaster <u>six times</u>! He loves it!

Raj rode it six times in the past, and there's a very good possibility that he'll ride it again in the near future.

```
         X       |- - - X - - X - - →
◄────────────────┼───────────────────►
Past            Now             Future
```

<u>This is the first time</u> she**'s gone** to the doctor's office alone.

She went alone to the doctor's office. The action is complete, but she will most likely do it again more times in her life.

4. Long-term continuing action:

- For the **long-term duration of a continuing action or event** that **shows a specific time duration up to the present**

- Used with **states** and **for**

- Used for **frequent activities with a reference to start time**—*since*

Often used with states and *for*:

```
   ← - - - - - - - - - -|- - - - - →
◄────────────────────────┼──────────────►
Past                    Now           Future
```

My sister and her boyfriend **have been** together <u>for many years</u>.

BE indicates a state. They started a relationship many years ago, and they are still together. It started in the past, includes now, and will likely continue.

Also used for frequent activities with a reference to start time—*since*:

```
   XXXXXX|- - X - X- X -X -X - →
◄────────────────┼───────────────────►
Past            Now             Future
```

We **have attended** this game <u>every Saturday since 1987</u>.

We started going to this game in 1987, we continue to go every Saturday, and we intend to go every Saturday in the future. *Every Saturday* indicates frequency.

Choosing Among Present Perfect and Other Verb Tenses

Whenever you write or speak, you choose which verb tense is best for the situation and your intention. Take a look at the contrasting uses of different verb tenses below. This will help you choose the most appropriate verb tense.

Reasons to Use the Present Perfect	Contrasted with Another Verb Tense	Examples, Timelines + Explanations
Present Perfect vs. Simple Past		
To show **a completed action that affects something that is relevant now**	**Simple past:** To show a completed action with **no perceived connection to the present**	X — Past — Now — Future I **saw** that movie <u>last night</u>. The simple past shows the activity is finished. A specific time is given: last night. ?X – – Past — Now — Future She's **seen** that movie <u>already</u>. There is no specific time when the action occurred, and it doesn't matter. The relevance is that because she saw the movie, she doesn't want to see it again.
To talk about an **action in the past when the time of the action is unknown or unimportant**	For a **single, finished action** in the past	X — Past — Now — Future <u>Last June</u>, my friends and I **walked** the Camino de Santiago from Portugal to Spain. The time of the action is significant in this sentence. It's a completed action in the past at a certain time. ? Past — Now — Future We**'ve walked** the Camino de Santiago from Portugal to Spain. It was unforgettable! The time of the action is not important. The fact that we walked this trail is the significant information in this sentence.

Reasons to Use the Present Perfect	Contrasted with Another Verb Tense	Examples, Timelines + Explanations
To express an **action or the repeated action that is finished, but** *the period of time* in which it happened *is unfinished*	**Simple past:** To express an **action or repeated action that is finished, and the period of time** in which it took place *is finished*	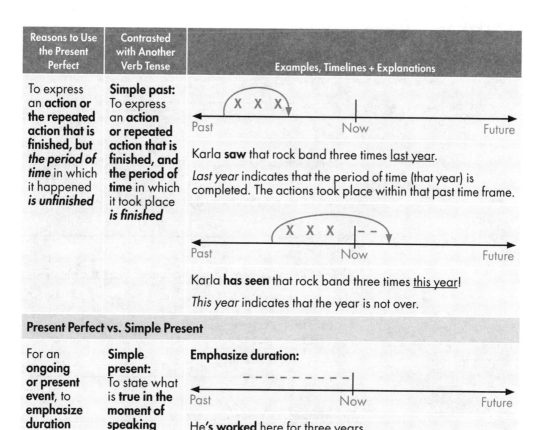

Karla **saw** that rock band three times <u>last year</u>.

Last year indicates that the period of time (that year) is completed. The actions took place within that past time frame.

Karla **has seen** that rock band three times <u>this year</u>!

This year indicates that the year is not over.

Present Perfect vs. Simple Present

For an **ongoing or present event**, to emphasize duration *or* To show **the event may be repeated—with stative and dynamic verbs**	**Simple present:** To state what is **true in the moment of speaking with no indication of when the action began or of its duration**	**Emphasize duration:**

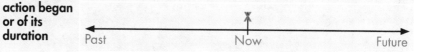

He**'s worked** here <u>for three years</u>.

The present perfect **emphasizes how long** he has worked here: for three years.

He **works** here.

The simple present shows what is true **now**. From this sentence, we don't know when he started working there or for how long he's worked there.

Event may be repeated with stative verbs:

She**'s felt** nauseous <u>several times recently</u>.

The present perfect shows that this has happened a certain number of times up to now.

(continued)

Reasons to Use the Present Perfect	Contrasted with Another Verb Tense	Examples, Timelines + Explanations
		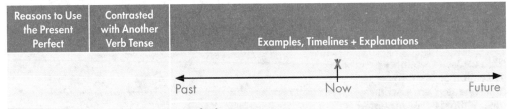

She **feels** nauseous.

The simple present shows what is true **now**: At this moment, she has nausea.

Event may be repeated with dynamic verbs:

XXXXXX|– – – –

Past   Now   Future

<u>All her life</u>, she**'s visited** her grandparents <u>every Christmas</u>.

The present perfect shows that this activity has happened every year since she was born. It is a repeated activity and "all her life" indicates that she will continue this activity because the period of time "all her life" is not complete.

X X X X X X

Past   Now   Future

She **visits** her grandparents <u>every Christmas</u>.

This is a tradition, so we use the simple present. We don't know the start time of this activity nor the duration.

Reasons to Use the Present Perfect	Contrasted with Another Verb Tense	Examples, Timelines + Explanations
Present Perfect vs. Present Progressive		
To show the **event finished in the past but is still relevant to this moment**	**Present progressive:** • To describe an **action or event that is ongoing or repeated over a period of time** • The action or event **started and it is continuing.**	X – – | ←——————————————————→ Past Now Future They**'ve washed** and **dried** the dishes. The actions are complete, but the result is relevant to me **at this moment** because now I don't have to do the dishes. Yay! **Activity in progress:** – – | – – ←——————————————————→ Past Now Future They**'re washing** and **drying** the dishes. They are in the process of this activity. They started and they are not done: They are still doing the dishes now.

With certain verbs, we use the simple past to indicate the start of an action or state, but we use a different verb in the present perfect to talk about the duration or continuation of that same action or state. We indicate the start of the activity (simple past) with a word or phrase for a specific point in time. However, to talk about the duration of the activity (present perfect), we use time words and phrases that express the length of time. As a writer and speaker, it's up to you to choose which verb and verb tense fits your intended meaning best. See the following table for some of these special verbs and examples of how they're used.

Simple Past Verbs That Change in the Present Perfect

Simple Past	Present Perfect	Example Sentences
find out →	know	He **found out** how to do research in the library databases <u>at the beginning of the semester</u>. He**'s known** how to do research in databases <u>all semester.</u>
meet →	know	They **met** <u>25 years ago</u>. They**'ve known** each other <u>for 25 years</u>.
become →	be	She **became** a doctor <u>in 1999</u>. She**'s been** a doctor <u>since 1999</u>.
get (receive, buy, obtain) →	have / own	We **got** our marriage license <u>last week</u>. We**'ve had** our marriage license <u>for almost a week</u>.
learn →	know	I **learned** graphic design <u>in college</u>. I**'ve known** graphic design <u>since college</u>.
put on →	wear	He **put** the dog sweater **on** his dog Rex <u>this morning</u>. Rex **has worn** the sweater <u>all day</u>.
join →	belong to	Camilla **joined** the Pilates gym <u>on January 1</u>. Camilla **has belonged** to the Pilates gym <u>since the New Year</u>.

Expressions of Time

Here are some common words and phrases used with the present perfect verb tense. Study them and read the example sentences.

Time Word/Phrase + Meaning	Use + Notes	Example Sentences
When the Exact Time of the Action Is Unknown		
ever: not at any time in his/her/their lifetime	• Used most often in yes/no questions and negative statements • Placement: Before the main verb • Can also be used at the end of a sentence for emphasis.	**Have** you <u>ever</u> **toured** the White House? She **hasn't** <u>ever</u> **toured** the White House. I **haven't been** to the White House <u>ever</u>!
never: *Never* is negative. not ever/not up to this point in time	• Mostly used in statements. • Yes/no questions with *never* are a bit awkward. It's more common to use a statement with rising pitch. • This question expresses surprise and/or shock, so fast rising pitch is usually used.	I'**ve** <u>never</u> **swum** in the Pacific Ocean. He'**s** <u>never</u> **swum** with dolphins. *Less common:* **Have** you <u>never</u> **swum** in the Pacific?! *More typical:* You'**ve** <u>never</u> **swum** in the Pacific?!
yet: Expresses expectation of an activity's completion before now. **Note:** *Yet* has many definitions in English. For the present perfect, this is the meaning.	• Used in yes/no questions and negative statements • Placement: *Yet* usually goes at the end of the sentence, but it can also go immediately before the main verb.	**Have** they **bought** a new house <u>yet</u>? They **haven't bought** a new house <u>yet</u>. They **haven't** <u>yet</u> **bought** a new house. Why **haven't** they **bought** a new house <u>yet</u>?

(continued)

Time Word/Phrase + Meaning	Use + Notes	Example Sentences
still: before now/up to now **Note:** *Still* has many definitions and is used in several different ways in English. For the present perfect, this is the meaning.	• Used in negative statements • Implies that the activity should be completed, but it is not. • Placement: *Still* is placed just before the auxiliary verb *have/has* in the sentence.	My brother <u>still</u> **hasn't applied** to college. We <u>still</u> **haven't heard** from the bank. My car <u>still</u> **hasn't started**. I think the engine is dead.
already: before now/up to now Suggests that the activity happened earlier than expected	• Used in affirmative statements and questions • Placement: At the end of the sentence or before the main verb	**Has** the seminar **started** <u>already</u>? It's <u>already</u> **started**. It **has started** <u>already</u>.
When the Exact Time of the Action Is Unknown *But Close to Now*		
lately: not long ago **recently:** not long ago	• *Lately* and *recently* are used interchangeably. • They are used with questions and affirmative and negative statements. • Placement: Usually at the end of the sentence; occasionally at the beginning	Where **have** you **been** <u>lately</u>? We **haven't eaten** out <u>lately</u>. <u>Lately</u>, we **haven't eaten** out. **Have** you **seen** Jenny <u>recently</u>? No, I **haven't seen** her <u>recently</u>.
just: *very close* to this moment—closer than *lately* and *recently* *Just* has several meanings, and it is used in different ways in English. Use this definition for the present perfect.	• Typically used for questions and affirmative statements • Placement: Immediately preceding the main verb	Careful! I'**ve** <u>just</u> **washed** the floor. Take your shoes off, please. **Hasn't** she <u>just</u> **taken** the test? Congratulations! You'**ve** <u>just</u> **won** $200!

Time Word/Phrase + Meaning	Use + Notes	Example Sentences
To Talk About the Duration or Start Time		
for: for + amount of time for two minutes for a few weeks for several years	• Indicates length of an action or state • Placement: Usually at the end of the sentence, but also at the beginning	I**'ve had** this rash <u>for two weeks</u>. <u>For nine days</u>, I**'ve waited** for you. We**'ve had** our cat <u>for eleven years</u>. I**'ve been** overweight <u>for too long</u>.* *too long = a complaint
since: since + time, day, date, a point in time since 10 a.m. since the 1980s since you arrived since she quit eating sugar	• Expresses the point in time when the action or state started • Placement: At the beginning and end of the sentence • *Since* is often used in time clauses (*since* SV).	She**'s commuted** to work <u>since she got the job.</u> <u>Since you arrived</u>, I**'ve been** happy! It**'s been** cloudy <u>since this morning</u>. <u>Since she quit eating sugar</u>, she**'s lost** 30 pounds. He**'s lived** on this land <u>since 1962</u>.
When the Period of Time Isn't Complete		
this: this morning, this semester, this year, etc.	• The morning, semester, year, etc. is not finished. • The period of time is still in progress. • Placement: At the beginning or end of sentence	We**'ve been** home <u>this morning</u>. <u>This morning</u>, we**'ve been** home. He**'s visited** us <u>this summer</u>. <u>This summer</u>, he**'s visited** us.
all: all morning, all afternoon, all day, all month, all year, all my life, etc.	• The period of time is still in progress. • Placement: At the beginning or end of sentence	Philippe **has worked** overtime <u>all week</u>. <u>All day</u> Joyce and Leigh **have been** in the library.

(continued)

Time Word/Phrase + Meaning	Use + Notes	Example Sentences
past: the past week, the past month, this past year, etc. **Note:** With <u>the simple past</u>, we use <u>last</u> week, <u>last</u> month, <u>last</u> year, etc.	• The period of time isn't complete. • Placement: At the beginning or end of sentence	Athena **has studied** a lot <u>this past year</u>. They say that junior year is the hardest. <u>In the past month,</u> Tara and Amy **haven't had** any soda.
so far: unknown starting point to now with an expectation of continuing into future	• Used with affirmative and negative statements and questions • Placement: At the beginning or end of sentence	<u>So far</u>, we **haven't met** his parents. We**'ve washed** half the laundry <u>so far</u>. Which part **have** you **liked** the most <u>so far</u>?
up until now: from an unknown start point in the past to this moment	• Used with affirmative and negative statements and questions • Placement: At the beginning or end of sentence	He**'s been** satisfied <u>up until now</u>. <u>Up until now</u>, I**'ve been** confused. Now I understand! <u>Up until now</u>, we**'ve had** dinner at a restaurant every Friday night. Now, it's too expensive.

Present Perfect Tense: Forming the Affirmative

How do we form the present perfect in affirmative statements? Let's check it out.

Affirmative Form of the Present Perfect Verb Tense

Subject or Subject Pronoun	Auxiliary *Have or Has*	Main Verb: Past Participle	Example Sentences
I	**have**	**hiked**	I **have hiked** that mountain <u>recently</u>.
You	**have**	**been**	You **have been** to Disneyland, haven't you?
We			We **have been** to that restaurant <u>before</u>.
They			They **have been** here <u>since 5:00 p.m.</u>
He	**has**	**eaten**	He **has** <u>already</u> **eaten** all the dessert.
She			She **has eaten** frog legs <u>several times</u>.
It			It **has eaten** all the birdseed in the feeder.

Forming Past Participles: Regular Verbs

We form the present perfect with the auxiliary *have/ has* plus the past participle of the main verb. With regular verbs, the past participle is the same as the simple past form of the verb. So, if the verb is **walk,** the simple past form is **walked** and the past participle form is **walked**, too. Likewise, if the verb is **study**, the simple past form is **studied** and so is the past participle. This is easier to remember than the past participles of irregular verbs.

BTW

*We do not repeat the auxiliary **have/has** when the sentence contains a compound verb. Here are a few examples of this:*

- *Ella **has played** and **coached** softball all her life.*

- *Mr. Chabre **has cooked** and **eaten** his dinner every night since Sunday.*

- *George and Jana **have come** and **gone** already.*

Forming Past Participles: Irregular Verbs

Study the past participles of the most commonly used irregular verbs below. One way to become familiar with them is to memorize them all. However, an easier way is to learn the common patterns. The common patterns are AAA, ABA, AAB, ABB, and ABC. To clarify, "AAA" indicates that the present, past, and past participle forms are the same. In contrast, "ABC" indicates that all forms are different. See these in the tables. Please note that the "Present" columns in the table do not include the third person singular. For example, the verb *bet* doesn't include "bets," which is the he/she/it form.

AAA Pattern

Present	Past	Past Participle
bet	bet	bet
cost	cost	cost
cut	cut	cut
hit	hit	hit
hurt	hurt	hurt
let	let	let
put	put	put
quit	quit	quit
read / riyd /	read / rɛd/	read / rɛd/
set	set	set
shut	shut	shut
wet	wet	wet

ABA Pattern

Present	Past	Past Participle
become	became	become
come	came	come
run	ran	run

AAB Pattern

Present	Past	Past Participle
beat	beat	beaten

ABB Pattern

Present	Past	Past Participle
bring	brought	brought
build	built	built
buy	bought	bought
dream	dreamed / dreamt	dreamed / dreamt
feed	fed	fed

(continued)

ABB Pattern

Present	Past	Past Participle
feel	felt	felt
fight	fought	fought
find	found	found
have	had	had
hear	heard	heard
hold	held	held
keep	kept	kept
leave	left	left
lose	lost	lost
make	made	made
meet	met	met
pay	paid	paid
say	said	said
send	sent	sent
sit	sat	sat
sleep	slept	slept
stand	stood	stood
teach	taught	taught
tell	told	told
think	thought	thought
understand	understood	understood

ABC Pattern

Present	Past	Past Participle
begin	began	begun
break	broke	broken
choose	chose	chosen
do	did	done
drink	drank	drunk
drive	drove	driven
eat	ate	eaten
fly	flew	flown
forbid	forbade	forbidden
forget	forgot	forgotten
get	got	gotten / got*
give	gave	given
go	went	gone
grow	grew	grown
know	knew	known
ride	rode	ridden
see	saw	seen
sing	sang	sung
speak	spoke	spoken
throw	threw	thrown
wear	wore	worn
withdraw	withdrew	withdrawn
write	wrote	written

Note: *Gotten* is the past participle used in the United States. *Got* is the past participle most often used in British English.

Present Perfect Tense: Forming the Negative and Contractions

How do we form the present perfect in negative statements? As you probably guessed, we use **not**. In the table below, you can see the negative form and the contraction. Notice the time words used with the present perfect.

Subject or Subject Pronoun	Auxiliary Have/Has + Not =	Negative Contraction Haven't/ Hasn't	Main Verb: Past Participle	Example Sentences
I	have + not =	**haven't**	**found**	I **haven't found** the right outfit for my party <u>yet</u>.
You / We / They	have + not =	**haven't**	**gone**	They **haven't gone** to the farmers market <u>lately</u>.
He / She / It	has + not =	**hasn't**	**shown**	He **hasn't shown** you his new motorcycle, has he?

Present Perfect Tense: Forming Yes/No Questions

How do we form yes/no questions with the present perfect verb tense? To form yes/no questions, we **invert the subject and the auxiliary *have* or *has***. This means we change the order of the subject and *have* or *has*. **Have** or **has begins the sentence and the subject follows it.** We must use the past participle form of the main verb. Review how we form these questions in the chart on the next page.

Appropriate Form of the Auxiliary *Have or Has*	Subject or Subject Pronoun	Past Participle of the Main Verb	Rest of the Sentence	Example Sentences
Have	I	**done**	that yet?	**Have** I **done** that yet?
Have	you	**chosen**	a major yet?	**Have** you **chosen** a major yet?
	we		which outfit to wear?	**Have** we **chosen** which outfit to wear?
	they		the movie for tonight?	**Have** they **chosen** the movie for tonight?
Has	he	**made**	the appointment yet?	**Has** he **made** the appointment yet?
	she		the brownies already?	**Has** she **made** the brownies already?
	it		sense to you at all?	**Has** it **made** sense to you at all?

Reminder: Use rising pitch at the end of yes/no questions because this shows that we are looking for an answer. See the pitch chart in the Appendix for more information.

Answering Yes/No Questions

Just as with other verb tenses, we answer yes/no questions with complete answers or short answers when talking with teachers, parents, supervisors, colleagues, and coworkers. With peers and friends, short answers are more common. In complete answers, contractions are common. Which words are stressed in answers? In the examples below, the <u>stressed words or syllables</u> are double underlined. The <u>time words and phrases</u> are underlined.

Complete Answers

Yes/No Question	Affirmative Answer	Negative Answer
Have you **seen** my wallet? I can't find it.	Yes, I **have** **seen** your wallet. Yes, I**'ve** **seen** your wallet.	No, I **have** **not** **seen** your wallet. No, I **haven't** **seen** your wallet.

(continued)

Yes/No Question	Affirmative Answer	Negative Answer
Has she **hiked** on Catalina Island <u>yet this year</u>?	Yes, she **has** hiked on Catalina Island <u>this year</u>. Yes, she**'s hiked** on Catalina Island <u>this year</u>. **Note:** We don't include *yet* in the affirmative answer.	No, she **hasn't** hiked Catalina Island <u>yet this year</u>.
Have they <u>already</u> **decided** where to go for vacation?	Yes, they **have** <u>already</u>* **decided** where to go for vacation. Yes, they**'ve** <u>already</u> **decided** where to go for vacation. **Note:** For the affirmative and negative answers, *already* can be omitted.	No, they **have** **not** decided where to go for vacation. No, they **haven't** decided where to go for vacation.

When giving an affirmative or negative answer, we usually offer more information or provide an explanation. As you learned in previous chapters, when the answer is negative, we sometimes omit the negative part of the answer and instead correct and clarify with the word *actually*. For example, to the question, *Have you eaten lunch today?*, we might reply with *Actually, I've been too busy to take a break, and I'm so hungry!*

Short Answers

Yes/No Questions	Affirmative Answer Note: Don't contract these.	Negative Answer
Have you **eaten** lunch today?	Yes, I **have**.	No, I **haven't**. Actually, I'm starving! Want to go to lunch?
Have we **reached** our destination <u>yet</u>?	Yes, we **have**.	No, we **haven't**. We're very close, though.
Has my package **arrived** <u>yet</u> <u>today</u>?	Yes, it **has**.	No, it **hasn't**. When was it shipped?

Quick Answers to Yes/No Questions

As you learned in previous chapters, a quick *yes* or *no* answer to these questions is acceptable, too. However, be sure to use a polite tone of voice. Otherwise, a quick answer may sound abrupt and rude. With friends, it's common to answer with slang. See some slang ways to say *yes* or *no* in Chapter 1.

Present Perfect Tense: Forming WH Questions

Let's discuss WH questions in the present perfect verb tense. To ask questions about what people have done or haven't done, we use WH questions to ask about time, location, manner, and reason for an action. You may remember that WH questions begin with WH question words or phrases such as *who, what, when, where, why, how, what kind, which one, how long, how many*, and *how much*. Use the following table to study how to form these questions.

WH Question Word/ Phrase	*have* or *has*	Subject or Subject Pronoun	Past Participle Form of the Main Verb	Rest of the Sentence	Example Sentences
Where	**have**	I	**seen**	your keys?	Where **have I seen** your keys?
Which one	**have**	you	**chosen**	to wear?	Which one **have** you **chosen** to wear?
		we	**talked about**	?	Which one **have** we **talked about**?
		they	**purchased**	?	Which one **have** they **purchased**?
How long	**has**	he	**decided**	to stay?	How long **has** he **decided** to stay?
		she	**been**	here?	How long **has** she **been** here?
		it	**been**	broken?	How long **has** it **been** broken?

PRONUNCIATION

▶ Look at the pitch patterns below and see the pitch chart in the Appendix for more information.

▶ Use the standard falling pitch for most WH questions:

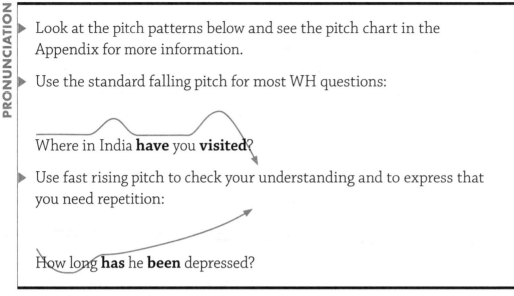

Where in India **have** you **visited?**

▶ Use fast rising pitch to check your understanding and to express that you need repetition:

How long **has** he **been** depressed?

Note: Pitch patterns are shown above, below, and through the words of sentences to illustrate that our pitches change as we speak.

Forming *Who* Questions

When **who** is the subject of the sentence, we do not add another subject. We do not add *I, you, we, they, he, she,* or *it.* See examples of this below.

Who (Subject of Sentence)	has	Past Participle Form of the Verb	Rest of the Sentence	Example Sentences
Who	**has**	**registered**	for classes <u>already</u>?	Who **has registered** for classes <u>already</u>?
Who	**has** <u>already</u>	**volunteered**	to work on parent-teacher conference night?	Who **has** <u>already</u> **volunteered** to work on parent-teacher conference night?

Answering WH Questions

As you have learned already, we can answer WH questions in a variety of ways. The long answer is a complete sentence, the short answer provides the answer with the auxiliary, and the quick answer gives only the essential information that answers the question (who). See examples below of answers to the *Who* questions. Notice the subject in the answer is stressed.

Who Question with the Present Perfect Verb Tense	Answer to the Question
Who **has registered** for classes <u>already</u>?	**Long:** <u>We</u> have registered for the classes <u>already</u>. **Short:** <u>We</u> have. <u>**Mary, Jake,**</u> and <u>**me**</u>.* **Quick:** <u>**Mary, Jake,**</u> and <u>**me**</u>.
Who **has** <u>already</u> **volunteered** to work on parent-teacher conference night?	**Long:** <u>**The Leadership Club**</u> has <u>already</u> volunteered to work on parent-teacher conference night. **Short:** <u>**The Leadership Club**</u> has. **Quick:** <u>**The Leadership Club**</u>.

*Note that "Mary, Jake, and I" is grammatically correct, but most Americans will say "me" instead of "I" because it sounds formal and strange.

Present Perfect Tense: Using Tag Questions

In previous chapters, you learned how to use tag questions at the end of statements to verify information or seek agreement. We can do this with the present perfect verb tense, too. With present perfect forms of the verb, use tag questions with the appropriate form of the auxiliary—***have*** or ***has***. Check the example sentences below to understand this rule.

POP QUIZ!

True or False: we only use the present perfect to discuss complete actions or events that are relevant to this moment. False! Think about it and head back to the "Reasons to Use the Present Perfect" table for a refresher.

EXAMPLES

▶ He's been there before, **hasn't he**?

▶ You've reported the crime, **haven't you**?

▶ It hasn't been easy, **has it**?

▶ They haven't left yet, **have they**?

> I haven't done anything wrong, **have I**?

> We've eaten too much, **haven't we**?

> She hasn't dropped the class, **has she**?

Using Intonation with Tag Questions

Remember from previous chapters that we use tag questions in two ways: **to verify information** and **to seek agreement**. We use **rising intonation to verify information**, and we use **falling intonation to seek agreement**. See these pitch patterns in the example sentences.

Statement with Tag Question to Verify Information

Explanation: When you don't know the answer but you need it, verify information. **Use rising intonation.**

She's gone to the store, hasn't she?

Statement with Tag Question to Seek Agreement

Explanation: When you know the answer and want someone to agree with you, **use falling intonation.**

I've overstepped my boundaries, haven't I?

Forming Affirmative and Negative Tag Questions

Remember: when we have an affirmative statement, the tag question is negative and vice versa. Notice that the statement is in the present perfect verb tense, yet the tag question and the answer only use the auxiliary **have** or **has**. Also notice the placement of the required comma before the tag question. Remember that even though a certain response is expected, you should answer truthfully. Check out the chart for example sentences.

Affirmative Statement	Negative Tag Question	Expect Affirmative Answer
I've **savored** every bite of this meal,	**haven't** I?	Yes, you **have**.
You've **told** me that already,	**haven't** you?	Yes, I **have**.
They've already **moved** to New England,	**haven't** they?	Yes, they **have**.
We've **been** very patient,	**haven't** we?	Yes, we **have**.
It's **felt** like a very long day,	**hasn't** it?	Yes, it **has**.

Negative Statement	Affirmative Tag Question	Expect Negative Answer
I **haven't emailed** you that information yet,	**have** I?	No, you **haven't**.
Jenna **hasn't decided** her degree program,	**has** she?	No, she **hasn't**.
They **haven't forgotten** your birthday,	**have** they?	No, they **haven't**.
Everett **hasn't** ever **flown** on a plane,	**has** he?	No, he **hasn't**.
You **haven't cleaned** your room yet,	**have** you?	No, I **haven't**.

Present Perfect Progressive Verb Tense

Now that you are familiar with the present perfect verb tense, let's look at the **present perfect *progressive*** verb tense. We use this verb tense to talk about something that **began in the past and is still in progress now or just finished**. The emphasis is on the duration or hardship of the action. We **cannot use stative verbs** with this progressive verb tense. Let's look at examples of this verb tense in action.

EXAMPLES

▶ I've **been waiting** for you for hours! Where have you been?

▶ You've **been studying** all day for this exam. I hope you ace it!

▶ Toni **has been cramming** for her exams, too.

▶ Geoffrey**'s been working** on his final project all week. He's almost done.

▶ It**'s been raining** all day. Will it ever stop?

▶ Tami and Billy **have been living** in South Lake Tahoe for a few years.

▶ We**'ve been cooking** all day. Are you coming over for dinner?

Deciding When to Use the Present Perfect Progressive Tense

We use the present perfect progressive to talk about actions (not states) that began in the past and (1) are in still progress at the moment of speaking or (2) have just recently finished. This verb tense is often used to emphasize the duration of an activity or the fact that this activity has caused hardship. It expresses a continuous activity as well as a repeated action over a period of time.

Here are a few things to remember with the present perfect progressive:

- The action can be **continuous or periodically repeated**.

- The length of time of the action is usually important: this verb tense **emphasizes duration**.

- It can also **emphasize the *process* of an action**. In this case, the length of time is not important.

- Usually, the **action is still in progress in the moment of speaking**; however, if the action is over, **it finished *very close to now***.

- If the action has already finished, it often **has significance in the moment of speaking**.

- With the verbs *live, work, study,* and *teach,* the present perfect and present perfect progressive can be used interchangeably.

■ **Stative verbs** cannot be used with the present perfect progressive. Instead, **use the present perfect to describe states**.

■ **Common time words and phrases** are *all morning / day / week / year*, *for / since*, *lately / recently*, and *in the past week / month*.

Let's take a closer look at some of these points in the table.

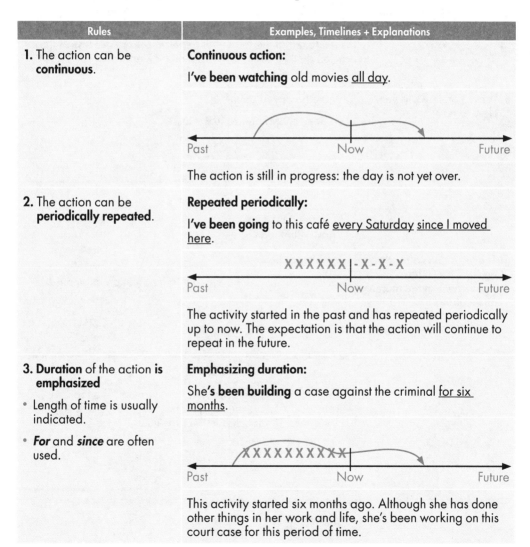

Rules	Examples, Timelines + Explanations
1. The action can be **continuous**.	**Continuous action:** I've **been watching** old movies <u>all day</u>. Past — Now — Future The action is still in progress: the day is not yet over.
2. The action can be **periodically repeated**.	**Repeated periodically:** I've **been going** to this café <u>every Saturday</u> <u>since I moved here</u>. X X X X X X	- X - X - X Past — Now — Future The activity started in the past and has repeated periodically up to now. The expectation is that the action will continue to repeat in the future.
3. Duration of the action **is emphasized** • Length of time is usually indicated. • *For* and *since* are often used.	**Emphasizing duration:** She**'s been building** a case against the criminal <u>for six months</u>. X X X X X X X X X X Past — Now — Future This activity started six months ago. Although she has done other things in her work and life, she's been working on this court case for this period of time.

(continued)

Rules	Examples, Timelines + Explanations
4. The process of the action **is emphasized**. • The precise length of time isn't important. • Rather, the subject is expressing the experience or process of the action.	**Emphasizing the process:** I**'ve been thinking** about which universities to apply for. 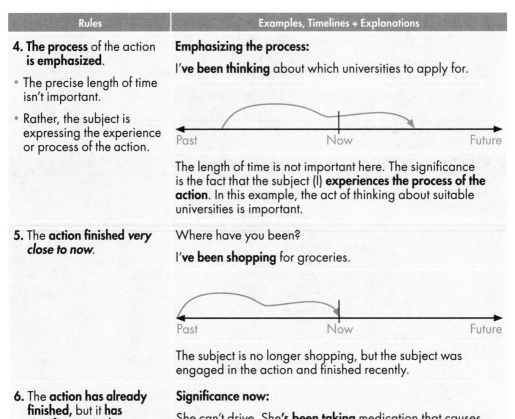 The length of time is not important here. The significance is the fact that the subject (I) **experiences the process of the action**. In this example, the act of thinking about suitable universities is important.
5. The **action finished** *very close to now*.	Where have you been? I**'ve been shopping** for groceries. The subject is no longer shopping, but the subject was engaged in the action and finished recently.
6. The **action has already finished,** but it **has significance in the moment of speaking.**	**Significance now:** She can't drive. She**'s been taking** medication that causes drowsiness.  She is not taking medication at this moment: she took it previously. However, the effects of the medication—drowsiness—impact her in the present.

Rules	Examples, Timelines + Explanations
7. With the **verbs** *live, work, study,* and *teach,* the present perfect and present perfect progressive have the same meaning when *since* or *for* is used.	**Live, work, study, teach:** She**'s lived** here <u>for 20 years</u>. She**'s been living** here <u>for 20 years</u>. They**'ve worked** at that restaurant <u>since 2010</u>. They**'ve been working** at that restaurant <u>since 2010</u>. They**'ve studied** U.S. history <u>for years</u>. They**'ve been studying** U.S. history <u>for years</u>. Mr. Vanos **has taught** microbiology <u>for the past decade</u>. Mr. Vanos **has been teaching** microbiology <u>for the past decade</u>.

Present Perfect Progressive Tense: Forming the Affirmative

How do we form the present perfect progressive in affirmative statements? Let's check it out, and then we'll look at some rules for using this verb tense.

Affirmative Form of the Present Perfect Progressive Verb Tense

Subject or Subject Pronoun	Auxiliary *Have* or *Has*	*been*	Main Verb *–ing* Form	Example Sentences
I	have	been	playing	I **have been playing** video games <u>since I woke up</u>.
You	have	been	driving	You **have been driving** <u>all day</u>. You must be exhausted.
We			working	We **have been working** on this puzzle <u>for hours</u>!
They			listening	They **have been listening** to musicals <u>since this morning</u>.
He	has	been	watching	He **has been watching** TV <u>for too long</u>.
She			worrying	She **has been worrying** about you <u>all night</u>.
It			making	My car **has been making** that funny sound <u>since I started it today</u>.

Present Perfect Progressive Tense: Forming Yes/No Questions

Just like with the present perfect, to form yes/no questions, we **invert the subject and the auxiliary *have* or *has*.** Review how we form these questions below.

Auxiliary *Have* or *Has*	Subject or Subject Pronoun	*been*	Main Verb *–ing* Form	Example Sentences
Have	I	been	performing	Have I **been performing** well <u>lately</u>?
Have	you	been	babysitting	Have you **been babysitting** for the neighbors <u>all week</u>?
	we		pretending	Have we **been pretending** that everything is fine?
	they		composing	Have they **been composing** music for the school play?
Has	he	been	performing	Has he **been performing** well <u>during practice</u>?
	she		paying	Has she **been paying** the bills <u>all day</u>?
	it		wasting	Has it **been wasting** your time?

Answering Yes/No Questions

We answer yes/no questions in the present perfect progressive similarly to that of the present perfect. In the following charts, the <u>stressed words or syllables</u> are double underlined. <u>The time words and phrases</u> are underlined.

Complete Answers

Yes/No Question	Affirmative Answer	Negative Answer
Have you **been hanging out** with Tad <u>this past week</u>?	Yes, I **have** been hanging out with Tad.	No, I **have** <u>**not**</u> been hanging **out** with Tad.
	Yes, I'**ve been** <u>**hanging out**</u> with Tad.	No, I **haven't** been hanging **out** with Tad.
Has she **been going** to that health center <u>for a long time</u>?	Yes, she **has** been going to that health center <u>for a long time</u>.	No, she **has** <u>**not**</u> been going to that health center <u>for a long time</u>.
	Yes, she'**s been** <u>**going**</u> to that health center <u>for a long time</u>.	No, she **hasn't** been going to that health center <u>for a long time</u>.
Have they **been reading** the newspaper together at breakfast since they got married?	Yes, they **have** been reading the newspaper together at breakfast since they got married.	No, they **have** <u>**not**</u> been **reading** the newspaper together at breakfast since they got married.
	Yes, they'**ve been** <u>**reading**</u> the newspaper together at breakfast since they got married.	No, they **haven't** been **reading** the newspaper together at breakfast since they got married.

Remember that when we answer the question, we often offer more information or provide an explanation. Now let's look at short answers. Note that we don't contract when we have affirmative answers.

Short Answers

Yes/No Questions	Affirmative Answer	Negative Answer
Have you **been hanging out** with Tad <u>this past week</u>?	Yes, I **have**.	No, I **haven't**.
Has she **been going** to that health center <u>for a long time</u>?	Yes, she **has**.	No, she **hasn't**.
Have they **been reading** the newspaper together at breakfast since they got married?	Yes, they **have**.	No, they **haven't**.

Quick Answers to Yes/No Questions

A quick **yes** or **no** answer to these questions is acceptable, too. However, be sure to use a polite tone of voice.

Present Perfect Progressive Tense: Forming WH Questions

Check out how to form WH questions in the present perfect progressive verb tense. Notice the difference in the following two charts.

WH Question Word/ Phrase	*have* or *has*	Subject or Subject Pronoun	*been*	Main Verb *–ing* Form	Example Sentences
Where	**have**	I	**been**	**going**	Where **have I been going** after school?
Why	**have**	you	**been**	**baking**	Why **have you been baking** cookies <u>all day</u>?
		we		**worrying**	Why **have we been worrying** about the test when it's a take-home?
		they		**writing**	Why **have they been writing** letters <u>all morning</u>?
How long **Note:** With **how long**, no time word/ phrase is used.	**has**	he	**been**	**attending**	How long **has he been attending** that private school?
		she		**stressing out**	How long **has she been stressing out** about college applications?
		it		**fluttering**	How long **has** that butterfly **been fluttering** around those daisies?

Who (Subject of Sentence)	*has*	*been*	Main Verb *–ing* Form	Example Sentences
Who	**has**	**been**	**getting**	Who **has been getting** my emails?
Who	**has** <u>already</u>	**been**	**considering**	Who **has** <u>already</u> **been considering** auditioning for the school musical?

Answering WH Questions

Take a look at some sample WH questions along with both long and quick answers to the questions.

WH Question with the Present Perfect Progressive Verb Tense	Answer to the Question
Why **have** you **been baking** cookies <u>all day</u>?	**Long:** I've **been baking** <u>all day</u> because the bake sale is in two hours! **Quick:** Because the bake sale is in two hours!
How long **has** he **been attending** that private school?	**Long:** He's been attending St. Joseph's High School <u>since</u> his freshman year. **Quick:** <u>Since</u> his freshman year.

Present Perfect Progressive Tense: Using Tag Questions

We use the same tag questions for the present perfect progressive as we do for the present perfect. Check it out:

▶ He's been enjoying his senior year, **hasn't he**?

▶ You've been thinking about the science project, **haven't you**?

▶ It hasn't been operating properly, **has it**?

▶ They haven't been worrying about their children, **have they**?

▶ I haven't been doing my homework on time, **have I**?

▶ We've been eating too much pasta lately, **haven't we**?

▶ She hasn't been lying to you, **has she**?

Forming Affirmative and Negative Tag Questions

Now, look at example sentences with tag questions and responses in the present perfect progressive verb tense.

Affirmative Statement	Negative Tag Question	Expect Affirmative Answer
I**'ve been doing** these math problems correctly,	**haven't** I?	Yes, you **have**.
You**'ve been thinking** about the science project,	**haven't** you?	Yes, I **have**.
They**'ve been donating** to the women's shelter monthly,	**haven't** they?	Yes, they **have**.
We**'ve been eating** too much pasta lately,	**haven't** we?	Yes, we **have**.
It**'s been snowing** for so long,	**hasn't** it?	Yes, it **has**.

Negative Statement	Affirmative Tag Question	Expect Negative Answer
I **haven't been doing** your laundry lately,	**have** I?	No, you **haven't.**
She **hasn't been lying** to you,	**has** she?	No, she **hasn't.**
They **haven't been worrying** about their children,	**have** they?	No, they **haven't.**
It **hasn't been operating** properly,	**has** it?	No, it **hasn't.**
You **haven't been cleaning** your room,	**have** you?	No, I **haven't.**

Choosing Among Present Perfect Progressive and Other Verb Tenses

How do you know which verb tense is best for the situation? Take a look at the contrasting uses of the present perfect progressive and other verb tenses below. This will help you choose the most appropriate verb tense.

Present Perfect Progressive vs. Past Progressive

Which One: The Present Perfect Progressive or the Past Progressive?

The present perfect progressive and the past progressive clearly differ: **the present perfect progressive expresses actions that are still in progress now or just recently finished**, while the **past progressive happened over time in the past and is already finished**. See the timelines and examples below.

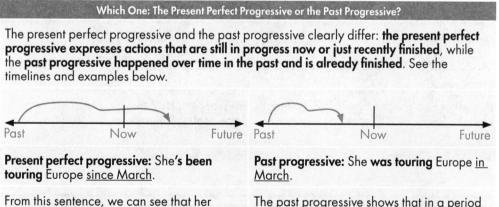

Present perfect progressive: She**'s been touring** Europe <u>since March</u>.

From this sentence, we can see that her travels started in March and they are still in progress today. She's not finished: she's still touring Europe. We don't know the end point of her travels.

Past progressive: She **was touring** Europe <u>in March</u>.

The past progressive shows that in a period of time in the past (March), she was doing something: She was touring Europe. It's now complete. The month of March and the action of touring are in the past.

(continued)

In the last chart it's clear that the time frames are different. However, **there is an instance when both verb tenses can be used: for a recently completed action in progress.** Let's take a closer look at this. For the following example sentences, it's now 6 a.m. in the morning. Read the sentences.

Past   Now   Future

Present perfect progressive: I've been cramming all night. I'm exhausted! (The process of cramming, which is finished, has an effect right now.)

Past progressive: I was cramming all night. (The process is complete.)

In both instances, the night has recently finished and the action (cramming) has also recently finished. **The intention of the speaker, however, is different.** The speaker uses the present perfect progressive to express that the completed process has an effect or significance in the moment of speaking. For example, the speaker might use the present perfect progressive to explain an effect that cramming all night had on him or her: This is why he or she is tired now. Whereas, when the speaker uses the past progressive, he or she isn't making a direct connection to the moment of speaking.

Note: In many cases, the further we get from the action, the less appropriate the present perfect progressive becomes. However, the speaker chooses the verb tense based on his/her intention, so you can decide what's most appropriate.

Present Perfect Progressive vs. Present Perfect

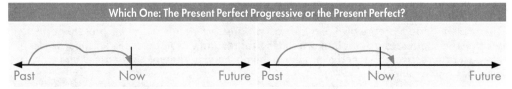

Past   Now   Future   Past   Now   Future

Present perfect progressive: When the **length of the action is what's important.** The action is most likely still in progress.

Present perfect: When the **action is what's important** and usually the action is finished

They**'ve been waiting** for two days for the delivery.

They**'ve waited** for two days for the delivery.

Meaning: The act of waiting is important, and what's **more important is the length of time that this action has been in progress.** We can assume that they are still waiting; the package has not yet been delivered.

Meaning: The act of waiting is important, and we can assume that the action is finished. The package has arrived.

Which One: The Present Perfect Progressive or the Present Perfect?	
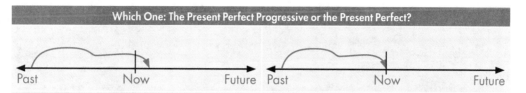	
Present perfect progressive: When the <u>process</u> **of the action is what's important.** The action is still in progress.	**Present perfect:** When the <u>completion</u> **of the action is what's important**
I**'ve been researching** information for my argumentative essay.	I**'ve researched** information for my argumentative essay.
Meaning: I've **started the research process** and I'm still doing it. I'm not done.	**Meaning:** I'm done with the research (yay!) and I'm ready to make a detailed outline of the essay.

Present perfect progressive: Not used for quantity.	**Present perfect:** To talk about **how much or how many**
	We**'ve** each **eaten** four bagels already this morning!
	We**'ve had** at least four bagels each this morning!
	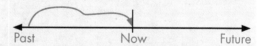
Present perfect progressive: Not used for stative verbs.	**Present perfect:** To **express states**
	They**'ve been** together for seventeen years.
	I**'ve had** a stomachache for two days.

(continued)

Which One: The Present Perfect Progressive or the Present Perfect?

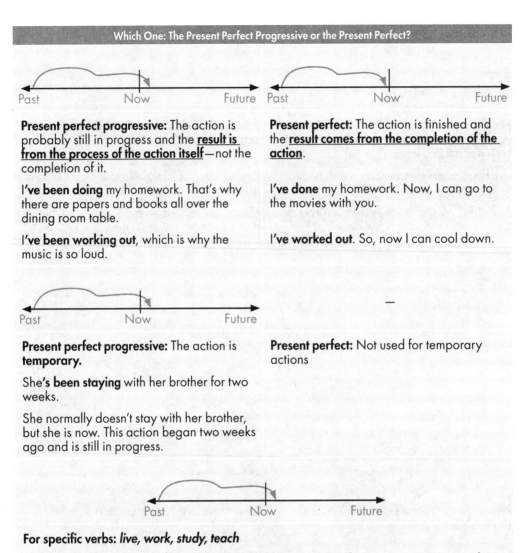

Present perfect progressive: The action is probably still in progress and the <u>result is from the process of the action itself</u>—not the completion of it.

I**'ve been doing** my homework. That's why there are papers and books all over the dining room table.

I**'ve been working out**, which is why the music is so loud.

Present perfect: The action is finished and the <u>result comes from the completion of the action</u>.

I**'ve done** my homework. Now, I can go to the movies with you.

I**'ve worked out**. So, now I can cool down.

Present perfect progressive: The action is **temporary**.

She**'s been staying** with her brother for two weeks.

She normally doesn't stay with her brother, but she is now. This action began two weeks ago and is still in progress.

Present perfect: Not used for temporary actions

For specific verbs: *live, work, study, teach*

- As noted previously, the **present perfect** and **the present perfect progressive are used interchangeably** with these verbs with **no difference in meaning**.

- We**'ve lived** here for five years. = We**'ve been living** here for five years.

- You**'ve studied** environmental science for two years already, haven't you? = You**'ve been studying** environmental science for two years already, haven't you?

- I**'ve worked** in the hospitality business my whole career. = I**'ve been working** in the hospitality business my whole career.

- Ms. McKinley **has taught** drama at this school since I can remember. = Ms. McKinley **has been teaching** drama at this school since I can remember.

Success Strategy: Agreeing and Disagreeing Politely

Knowing how to assert your ideas is important in discussions, but how can you disagree politely in conversations? Let's look at ways to agree as well as politely disagree so you can engage in deeper discussions.

Ways to Agree

Agreeing with someone is straightforward. When you agree with someone, it's a good idea to give reasons why you agree. The (S+V) indicates that a Subject and Verb clause is required to grammatically complete the statement.

Expressions to Agree	Example Sentences
• I agree with (name) about (topic / idea) because _____ (S+V).	• I agree with Charlene about the dangers of consuming sugary beverages because too much can lead to obesity.
• I agree with (name) that _____ (S+V).	• I agree with Dana that sugary beverages cause obesity.
• That's a good point. (Say more about the point stated.)	• That's a good point. When vending machines full of sugary beverages are removed from schools, students are less tempted to just grab a soda anytime during the school day.
• I agree with (name)'s / that point. It's true that _____ (S+V).	• I agree with Olaf's point. It's true that about an hour after drinking a soda, I get tired.
• She's / He's / They're right: _____. (Say why you agree with them / the idea.)	• They're right: sports drinks with electrolytes also contain lots of sugar or sugar substitutes.
• I think (name) has the right idea. (Say more about the point stated and why you agree.)	• I think Mandy has the right idea. Sugar substitutes are sometimes worse for our bodies and metabolism than real cane sugar.
• I agree with what (name) said because _____ (S+V).	• I agree with what Delia said because sugar substitutes are made from synthetic compounds.
• I feel / think the same way as (name) because _____ (S+V).	• I feel the same way as Charley because some sugar substitutes are too sweet and they have a chemical taste.

(continued)

Importance of Disagreeing

In discussion, it's important to articulate your thoughts when they differ because a diversity of ideas is essential. To do this, you need to be able to disagree politely. This is a great skill to have, so let's work on it. Be sure that when you disagree, you disagree with the idea rather than the person. This is a more socially acceptable way to disagree. Let's look at some expressions to use.

Two Ways to Disagree

There are two ways to disagree: completely or partially. Either way, be respectful and be sure to honor the other point of view. Note that (S+V) indicates that a Subject and Verb clause is required to complete the expression.

Expressions to Partially Disagree	Example Sentences
• I agree that _____ (S+V), but _____ (S+V).	• <u>I agree that</u> sodas are unhealthy, <u>but</u> students should have a choice of beverages.
• I see your point, but /; however, _____ . (State your opinion S+V.)	• <u>I see your point; however,</u> it's a free market. Soda companies should be able to sell their products anywhere.
• That's a good point, but I have a slightly different opinion. I think that _____ (S+V).	• <u>That's a good point, but I have a slightly different opinion. I think that</u> although it's a free market society, public schools have a responsibility to offer healthy meal options, which include beverages.
• Although you make a good point, I believe that _____ (S+V).	• <u>Although you make a good point, I believe that</u> public schools should offer only healthy choices for lunch, and parents should be part of the decision on what's provided in the cafeteria.
• It seems to me that <u>(topic / idea)</u> would be too <u>(adjective)</u>.	• <u>It seems to me that</u> healthy school lunch options <u>would be too</u> expensive.
• I'm afraid I don't agree. I think that _____ . (State your viewpoint S+V.)	• <u>I'm afraid I don't agree. I think that</u> students who play sports should be given academic credit for their time and energy in practice and in games.

Expressions to Completely Disagree	Example Sentences
• Respectfully, I have to disagree with the point / idea that _____ (S+V). I believe / think / feel that _____. (State your viewpoint S+V.)	• <u>Respectfully, I have to disagree with the point that</u> athletes should be treated the same as every other student. <u>I believe that</u> students do earn academic credit for playing sports because they can use sports as an extracurricular activity on their college applications.
• I disagree with that because _____ (S+V).	• <u>I disagree with that because</u> students who play sports in high school invest a lot of time and energy every day as athletes and that should be recognized in high school while they're doing it.
• No, I don't think that's true. Actually, _____. (State your viewpoint S+V.)	• <u>No, I don't think that's true. Actually,</u> students who play high school sports gain many skills that can be used later in life such as discipline, sportsmanship, and collaboration.
• I see your point, but /; however, _____ (S+V).	• <u>I see your point, but</u> then that means that students who participate in the school play and music concerts should also get academic credit for performing outside of school hours.
• Perhaps you're right about <u>(topic / idea)</u>, but I don't agree with that. I think / feel / believe that _____ (S+V).	• <u>Perhaps you're right about</u> athletes gaining skills that are useful later in life, <u>but I don't agree with that. I believe that</u> we as students also gain those kinds of skills in math and history class, and we earn academic credit for those classes.
• Perhaps you're right that _____ (S+V), but I think / feel / believe that _____ (S+V).	• <u>Perhaps you're right</u> that any student who engages in extracurricular activities should earn academic credit for their engagement, <u>but I feel that</u> these students already gain many advantages in life by involving themselves in after-school activities. Academic credit becomes superfluous.

> Be sure to use a polite tone of voice when disagreeing so that your ideas are heard. You can do this by keeping your voice at an appropriate volume, making your intonation melodic, and by using soft falling pitch at the end of your statement. If you speak too loudly, use a flat tone, and fall too fast at the end, you may sound aggressive. Your goal is to be assertive but not aggressive.

Success Strategy: Supporting Your Ideas

Once you agree or disagree, the next thing to do is support your ideas with reasons, explanations, and rationales. Your support should be clear and logical. Let's look at some expressions you can use to do that.

Ways to Support Your Ideas

Expressions to Support Your Ideas	Example Sentences
• From what I've seen / read, _____ (S+V). (State your viewpoint and explanation.)	• <u>From what I've seen,</u> high schoolers who wear the same uniform still suffer from bullying. To have all the students wear the same thing doesn't truly level the playing field. There's still discrimination.
• Let me give you an example of what I mean. _____ (S+V). (State your viewpoint and explanation.)	• <u>Let me give you an example of what I mean.</u> Yesterday I saw a group of girls make fun of a classmate's hairstyle, and they excluded her from a small group discussion. They were all wearing exactly the same clothes.
• In my experience, it isn't true that _____ (S+V). Rather, _____ (S+V). (State your viewpoint and explanation.)	• <u>In my experience, it isn't true that</u> school uniforms make students equal. <u>Rather,</u> they give a false comfort to school administrators and parents. Every high school student is aware of inequity among the student body.

Expressions to Support Your Ideas	Example Sentences
• I think / feel / believe that _____ (S+V) because _____ (S+V).	• <u>I think that</u> school uniforms make life easier <u>because</u> I don't have to spend time selecting an outfit or worrying about what to wear. I put on pretty much the same clothes every school day and that saves me precious time and energy.
• It seems to me that if _____ (S+V), then _____ (S+V).	• <u>It seems to me that if</u> school uniforms don't prevent discrimination among the students, <u>then</u> they shouldn't be required. Students should have the right to choose what they wear.
• According to this article / (name of publication), _____ (S+V). Therefore, _____ (S+V).	• <u>According to this article,</u> school uniforms may not completely eliminate discrimination in school. <u>Therefore,</u> it doesn't make sense to require uniforms.

Dialogue: Class Discussion on School Uniforms

Ms. Blake's English class is discussing the school uniform issue. One small group had the following discussion. Note the language used for agreeing, disagreeing politely, and supporting one's ideas.

Marcy: So, what do you guys think of the school uniform requirement? Do you think it's a good idea or not?

Ben: Well I, for one, don't think it's a good idea. It seems to me that if the school required uniforms, then students would rebel because they'd feel their freedom of choice was taken away. I wouldn't want to have to wear something I didn't choose myself.

Reno: I agree with Ben that students would feel restricted in their choices. If I want to wear a uniform to school, I'd pick my own: a black T-shirt, jeans, and athletic shoes.

Cody: Perhaps you're right that students wouldn't be able to choose their clothes every day, but I think that would actually be a benefit.

Wouldn't it save us a lot of time and energy wondering what to wear every day? As it is, I never have enough clean clothes: I can't keep up with my laundry.

Britanny: I disagree with that because whether you choose your own clothes or wear a uniform, you still have to do laundry. I mean, I agree that keeping up with laundry is time-consuming and difficult, but that only means that every student would need at least a few uniforms in order to have a clean one every day. Between the expense of the uniforms and the time doing laundry, it doesn't seem like an advantage to require uniforms.

Samantha: Respectfully, I have to disagree with the idea that uniforms would eliminate discrimination or bullying. Even though I'm totally against judging people based on their appearance and I'm vehemently against bullying, uniforms won't change people's behaviors. If you take away someone's choice of clothing, there are still so many other things that people judge, including how someone looks, the way they talk, and the way they act. Uniforms are not the cure-all for discrimination and bullying. It's a way bigger issue than clothing.

Marcy: I don't know. I'm still on the fence. I see both advantages and disadvantages of wearing uniforms. For me, the jury's still out.*

*If the "jury's (still) out" on a topic, then the speaker hasn't committed to a position on a subject. Usually, more information or research is needed to make a decision.

Lecture: School Uniforms

School Uniforms: To Be or Not to Be

School uniforms have been debated for decades. The question is this: Should schools require students to wear school uniforms or not? Traditionally in the United States, private schools and parochial schools—private schools supported by churches—have required school uniforms. Since the 1990s, however, some public schools have made uniforms mandatory.

Those on both sides of the school uniform debate state myriad reasons for their viewpoints. Proponents of school uniforms argue that when all students wear the same uniform, instances of discrimination and bullying decrease. Opponents, on the other hand, insist that regardless of what a student wears, discrimination and bullying still exist. Clothing is only one aspect of physical appearance that invites ridicule. There are many others, including hair, shoes, makeup, and body type.

To further their argument, those in favor of school uniforms report that school uniforms level the socioeconomic playing field because if everyone is wearing the same outfit, no one will know whether someone is socioeconomically disadvantaged or not. Those opposing school uniforms respond to this argument by citing the fact that the majority of public schools requiring school uniforms reside in socioeconomically disadvantaged areas, so uniforms actually act like a sign on students' backs announcing their socioeconomic status.

Another reason proponents support school uniforms is that they believe uniforms give students a feeling of belonging. School uniforms increase the student body's school spirit, cohesiveness, and feelings of community. The opposing viewpoint is that school uniforms prevent students from making their own choices, which violates their right to choice and freedom. When one's right to choose is restricted, it can lead to negative feelings of self-worth. Additionally, opponents claim that when students are forced to wear uniforms, their individuality isn't honored.

Both sides feel strongly and have many reasons for their beliefs. Proponents and opponents make several claims for or against the requirement of school uniforms. Whether you are a fence-sitter (someone who hasn't taken a side), a proponent, or an opponent of the school uniform mandate, the debate continues.

EXERCISES

EXERCISE 9-1

Complete the sentences below with the present perfect form of the verb given in parentheses. Write both the full form as well as the contraction wherever possible. Remember to use the past participle form of the verb. Follow the example.

Example: (eat) Manika **_has eaten_** her lunch already.

1. (adapt) Meredith's new cat _____ to its new home quickly.

2. (conclude) I _____ that exercising in the morning rather than at night is better for me.

3. (approach – negative) Luna and Estelle _____ this problem with patience and diligence.

4. (clarify) The professor _____ already _____ the homework instructions, so now I understand.

5. (acquire) _____ she _____ her real estate license yet?

6. (confirm) The hotel _____ just _____ our reservations for next weekend. Woohoo! I can't wait for vacation!

7. (be) For how long _____ he _____ sick with a fever?

8. (have) Since the beginning of spring, I _____ a runny nose and watery eyes. I must have allergies.

9. (go) For the last three summers, Michaela _____ to Moab, Utah, for vacation. She loves it there!

10. (discuss) Owen and Madison _____ already _____ this issue, and they just made a final decision.

EXERCISE 9-2

Write sentences with the present perfect verb tense. Use the words provided. Remember to use the past participle form of the verb. Spelling counts! Follow the example.

Example: Rebekah / be / doctor / since 2000.

Rebekah has been a doctor since 2000.

1. Ann and Francis / live / in the South of France / for five years already

   _____

2. Andrea / ride / her mountain bike / on that trail / every Saturday this summer

   _____

3. Since Tuesday, / Taryn / have / a cold

   _____

4. Alessandra and Stanley / get / breakfast / at that café / every morning / since they moved here

   _____

5. Since I was a kid, I / be / afraid of dogs

   _____

6. My laptop / make / a weird sound / ever since I dropped it

   _____

EXERCISE 9-3

Complete the sentences with the correct negative form of the present perfect verb tense. Use contractions wherever possible. Follow the example.

Example: (enjoy) Marlette *hasn't enjoyed* her time in Mexico this
summer. She thinks it's too hot and humid.

1. (go) My parents _____ ever _____ on
   a two-week vacation. They've only gone on vacation for two to five days
   at a time.

2. (tell) She _____ us the truth yet.

3. (grade) Professor Sullivan _____ the homework yet.

4. (detect – never) Since we bought it, the smoke detector
   _____ smoke in this house. I think it's broken.

5. (grow) I _____ my own vegetable garden before. I've
   always lived in small apartments with no yard.

6. (invest) We _____ in a new parcel of land for
   retirement yet.

EXERCISE 9-4

Form yes/no questions with the present perfect verb tense using the words provided. Then write long, short, and quick answers to the question. Answer the questions affirmatively (Yes) or negatively (No). Follow the examples below. For quick questions, you can write more information as appropriate. Be creative with this!

Example 1: Donna and Mike / ever / be / to Tuscany (Yes)

Question: *Have Donna and Mike ever been to Tuscany?*

Long answer: *Yes, they have been to Tuscany. Yes, they've been to Tuscany.*

Short answer: *Yes, they have.*

Quick answer: *Yes. They loved it and they plan on going back some day.*

Example 2: He / finish / his fieldwork / yet (No)

Question: *Has he finished his fieldwork yet?*

Long answer: *No, he hasn't finished his fieldwork.*

Short answer: *No, he hasn't.*

Quick answer: *No. It's not due for another week.*

1. Elliot / drive / across the country / before (Yes)

   Question: _____

   Long answer: _____

   Short answer: _____

   Quick answer: _____

2. Your daughter / ever / do / an internship (Yes)

   Question: _____

Long answer: _____

Short answer: _____

Quick answer: _____

3. The baby / eat / real food / yet (No)

Question: _____

Long answer: _____

Short answer: _____

Quick answer: _____

4. You / ever / get / an A / in all your classes (Yes)

Question: _____

Long answer: _____

Short answer: _____

Quick answer: _____

5. Jean and Seamus / get dressed / for the black-tie gala* / yet (Yes)

*A gala is a fancy social event with special performances and entertainment. Black-tie means that attendees dress up in elegant clothing.

Question: _____

Long answer: _____

Short answer: _____

Quick answer: _____

EXERCISE 9-5

Form WH questions with the present perfect verb tense using the words given. Form long and short answers using the information in parentheses. Use contractions wherever possible. Follow the example below.

Example 1: Romeo and Juliet / be (Where) (forest)

Question: *Where have Romeo and Juliet been?*

Long answer (complete sentence): *They've been in the forest.*

Short answer (essential information only): *In the forest.*

1. Amy and Mark / go (Where) (to bed)

   Question: _____

   Long answer: _____

   Short answer: _____

2. Steve / be / all day (Where) (in the library)

   Question: _____

   Long answer: _____

   Short answer: _____

3. Attend / the funeral service (Who) (Jacob)

   Question: _____

   Long answer: _____

   Short answer: _____

4. Lucy and Ethel / package / candy / this past week (Where) (in the candy factory)

   Question: _____

   Long answer: _____

   Short answer: _____

5. Ricky / think about / recently (What) (the consequences of his actions)

   Question: _____

   Long answer: _____

   Short answer: _____

6. Fred and Barney / move (Where) (to a new neighborhood)

   Question: _____

   Long answer: _____

   Short answer: _____

EXERCISE 9-6

Complete the sentences below using the present perfect progressive. Write both the full form as well as the contraction wherever possible. Follow the example.

> **Example:** (play) Tabitha *has been playing / Tabitha's been playing* soccer all day.

1. (wonder) Jeremiah _____ about his future lately.

2. (think about) I _____ what you said this morning. You were right: I was wrong.

3. (shelter) We _____ in place for too long.

4. (evaluate) The professor _____ our in-class participation this whole week.

5. (discriminate) In the novel, the blue people _____ against the green people since the beginning of time.

6. (contradict) You _____ me ever since this morning. Why?

7. (erode) The ocean _____ the coastline for millennia.

8. (equip) That athletic wear company _____ all the high schools with sports uniforms since the 1950s.

9. (guarantee) The company _____ the quality of its work for 20 years.

10. (build) We _____ an extension on the house for three months.

EXERCISE 9-7

Write sentences with the present perfect progressive verb tense. Use the words provided. Spelling counts! Remember to begin with a capital letter and end with a period. Follow the example.

Example: Teachers / interact / with their students / on video conferencing software / for two years / already

Teachers have / They've been interacting with their students on video conferencing software for two years already.

1. Peter Greenfield / network / with potential customers / for a few years now.

   _____

   _____

2. Politicians / manipulate / scientific data / for a long time

   _____

   _____

3. Since last year, / we / try / to maximize our investments

   _____

   _____

4. Carolyn and Stacey / resist / change / at their company / for years

   _____

   _____

5. Since the beginning of the year, Lexi / transfer / data / into new databases

   _____

   _____

6. Maggie / live / in a hotel / since the earthquake ruined her house

   _____

   _____

EXERCISE 9-8

Complete the sentences with the correct negative or affirmative form of the present perfect progressive tense verb. Follow the example. Write both the full form and contractions for every sentence.

> **Example:** (work – negative) Dolly <u>has not been working</u> / <u>hasn't been working</u> in this job for a long time.

1. (respond – negative) Denna: You _____ to my emails for weeks, Paul. Why not?

2. (research – affirmative) Paul: I'm sorry, Denna. I _____ historic information for my new novel.

3. (transform – affirmative) Wow! I haven't seen your house since last year. You _____ it so much. What a beautiful new addition!

4. (promote – negative) The company _____ our services as much because they cut our advertising budget.

5. (publish – negative) The university _____ our research lately. I don't know why.

6. (regulate – negative) The city _____ the use of leaf blowers, but they're talking about it.

EXERCISE 9-9

Form yes/no questions with the present perfect progressive verb tense using the words provided. Then write long, short, and quick answers to the question. Answer the questions affirmatively (Yes) or negatively (No). Follow the examples below. For quick questions, you can write more information as appropriate. Be creative with this!

Example 1: They / do / homework / on time / lately (Yes)

Question: *Have they been doing their homework on time lately?*

Long answer: *Yes, they have / they've been doing their homework on time lately.*

Short answer: *Yes, they have.*

Quick answer: *Yes. And their grades are improving, too.*

Example 2: Josefina / submit / her timesheets / every day (No)

Question: *Has Josefina been submitting her timesheets every day?*

Long answer: *No, she has not / hasn't been submitting her timesheets every day.*

Short answer: *No, she hasn't.*

Quick answer: *No. I will ask her why.*

1. Timothy / assist / you / with your work / this week (Yes)

   Question: _____

   Long answer: _____

   Short answer: _____

   Quick answer: _____

2. Nancy / accompany / you / to church services / this month (No)

   Question: _____

   Long answer: _____

   Short answer: _____

   Quick answer: _____

3. Your academic advisor / counsel / you / on college applications (Yes)

   Question: _____

   Long answer: _____

   Short answer: _____

   Quick answer: _____

4. You / dispose of / your trash / every week (No)

   Question: _____

   Long answer: _____

   Short answer: _____

   Quick answer: _____

5. You / exceed / the storage limit / on the computer / lately (Yes)

   Question: _____

   Long answer: _____

   Short answer: _____

   Quick answer: _____

EXERCISE 9-10

Form WH questions with the present perfect progressive verb tense using the words given. Form long and short answers using the information in parentheses. Use contractions wherever possible. Follow the example.

Example: The Jetsons / live (Where) (in space)

Question: *Where have the Jetsons been living?*

Long answer (complete sentence): *They've been living in space.*

Short answer (essential information only): *In space.*

1. The Rubbles / go / every weekend (Where) (to their grandmother's house)

   Question: _____

   Long answer: _____

   Short answer: _____

2. Mr. Flintstone / work / this year (Where) (at the quarry)

   Question: _____

   Long answer: _____

   Short answer: _____

3. Wilma and Betty / disappear to / every Friday morning (Where) (the massage parlor)

   Question: _____

   Long answer: _____

   Short answer: _____

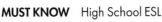

4. The children / get / their schooling (Where) (at home with a tutor)

Question: _____

Long answer: _____

Short answer: _____

5. Mr. Howell / dream about (What) (getting off the island)

Question: _____

Long answer: _____

Short answer: _____

6. Ginger and Mary Ann / live (Where) (on an island)

Question: _____

Long answer: _____

Short answer: _____

EXERCISE 9-11

In this exercise, choose the most appropriate verb tense for each sentence. Consider the timeline of the action or state, the verb itself, any time expression used, and the intention of the speaker. Follow the example and use the explanation below to help you.

Example 1: Last night, Zack _did_ his homework very quickly.
(did / has done)

Explanation: Because the time is a specific time in the past, the action is completed. As far as we know, there is no relevance to now, so we use the simple past.

1. Oh my gosh! Marjorie just _____ about the surprise party we're planning for her. I'm so disappointed! (found out / has been finding out)

2. My little brother _____ all week with the flu. He better not give it to me! (is sick / has been sick)

3. In the movie, Glinda the good witch _____ Dorothy her wish to go home to Kansas. (granted / has been granting)

4. Over the years, the pharmaceutical company _____ innocent patients' needs to decrease pain. Will they ever stop? (exploited / has been exploiting)

5. ABC Corporation _____ around since 1945. That's a long time! (is / has been)

6. Announcer at the Olympics: This young athlete _____ as a top contender for the gold medal since this event began. We'll know soon if he wins it! (emerged / has emerged)

7. Mateo _____ joining the Marines, but he decided against it. He wants to go to an Ivy League school instead. (was considering / has been considering)

8. Raleigh and Jana _____ that movie twice so far. They'll see it again, I'm sure. (have seen / have been seeing)

EXERCISE 9-12

Write sentences about your life using the present perfect and the present perfect progressive verb tenses. Talk about states you have experienced and actions you have taken. Use appropriate time words and phrases, too. Let the questions below guide you. Then create your own sentences. Follow the example.

Example: What have you been doing lately?

I've been waking up early all this week.

1. What have you done recently?

   _____

2. Where have you gone lately?

   _____

3. Who have you been hanging out with since school started?

   _____

4. Where have you been going regularly for a long time?

   _____

5. Who has been helping you with homework?

   _____

6. How have you been?

   _____

EXERCISE 9-13

AUDIO 🔊

Read Dialogue: Class Discussion on School Uniforms again and identify the expressions that the students use to agree, disagree, and support their opinion. Underline these expressions.

Flashcard App

10

Compound, Complex, and Compound-Complex Sentences

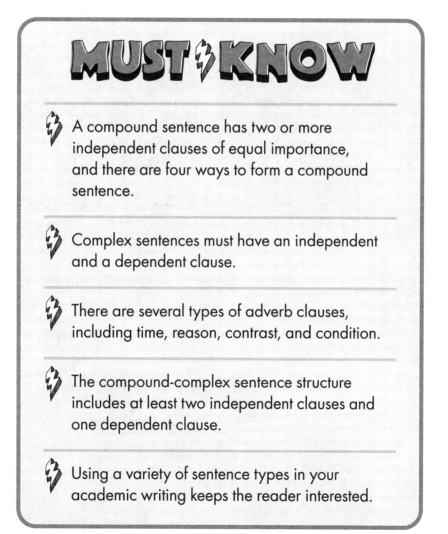

MUST KNOW

⚡ A compound sentence has two or more independent clauses of equal importance, and there are four ways to form a compound sentence.

⚡ Complex sentences must have an independent and a dependent clause.

⚡ There are several types of adverb clauses, including time, reason, contrast, and condition.

⚡ The compound-complex sentence structure includes at least two independent clauses and one dependent clause.

⚡ Using a variety of sentence types in your academic writing keeps the reader interested.

389

You learned in Chapter 7 that the primary sentence format in English is subject-verb-object (SVO) or subject-verb-complement (SVC). As a quick refresher, there are three things necessary for a simple sentence to be complete: a subject, a verb, and a complete idea. A statement requires statement word order (SV). In a question, the BE verb or auxiliary precedes the subject (VS). In this chapter, we'll examine how to build on the simple sentence structure to create compound, complex, and compound-complex sentences. Let's get started!

Compound Sentences

Compound sentences were introduced in Chapter 7, so let's add to that knowledge. A compound sentence is two or more simple sentences, also known as independent clauses, connected in a grammatical way. There are four ways to form a compound sentence, which we'll get to in a minute. First, here are some examples.

EXAMPLES

▶ Vladimir went to a clothing store on Saturday, and he ran into* a friend there.

▶ Rashid and his sister really enjoy camping, but they don't like camping in the rain.

▶ I don't like watching baseball games; I prefer to watch basketball games.

▶ She doesn't feel well; she's not going to school today.

▶ Neela is devoted to charity: She volunteers at the community center every Saturday.

▶ I never have enough time for fun during the week: I'm in school for eight hours, have three to five hours of homework, and then have swim practice for two hours every weekday.

▶ My aunt loves coffee; however, she dislikes coffee-flavored food.

▶ The students in this history class participate enthusiastically in group activities; they don't, however, enjoy writing essays.

*Note: *To run into* is a phrasal verb that means to meet someone accidentally. In other words, there was no plan to meet this person.

How to Identify a Compound Sentence

You may recall that simple sentences (SV, SVO, and SVC) are also called independent clauses. Now that you have seen a few example compound sentences, do you notice patterns?

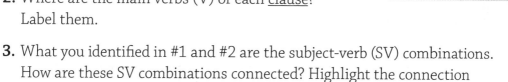

Practice 10-A

Let's warm up with some questions.

1. Where are the subjects (S) of the <u>clauses</u> in each of the example sentences? Find and label them.

2. Where are the main verbs (V) of each <u>clause</u>? Label them.

3. What you identified in #1 and #2 are the subject-verb (SV) combinations. How are these SV combinations connected? Highlight the connection devices for each compound sentence.

Check your answers to Practice 10-A in the Answer Key.

Let's look at the formulas for the four ways we can form compound sentences. Examples sentences on the prior page demonstrate how each pattern is used:

1. SV, [FANBOYS] SV.

2. SV; SV.

3. SV: SV.

4. SV; [conjunctive adverb,] SV.

Let's dive deeper into each compound sentence pattern.

1. In the first formula **(SV, [FANBOYS] SV.)**, the independent clauses are equal in importance and a <u>coordinating conjunction (FANBOYS) connects them</u>. This is the most common way of combining simple sentences. The way to remember the seven coordinating conjunctions is to see the acronym they create: FANBOYS. The first letter of each of these conjunctions spells out FANBOYS: *for, and, nor, but, or, yet*, and *so*. The four most common ones are *and, but, so,* and *or*.

 **IRL** Although the rules require a comma before the FANBOYS coordinating conjunction, we sometimes don't use a comma if both clauses are short. A comma should clarify meaning, not confuse the reader. Follow all the comma rules, but also experiment with them in compound sentences. As your sentences become longer and more complex, commas become extremely useful. Remember to use them properly by following the rules, but do not overuse them.

Example 1: Vladimir went to a clothing store on Saturday**, and** he ran into a friend there.

Example 2: Rashid and his sister really enjoy camping**, but** they don't like camping in the rain.

What do the seven different coordinating conjunctions mean and how do we use them? Study the table below to find out.

	Coordinating Conjunction	Meaning and Use
F	for	• Meaning: similar to *because* • The second clause is the <u>reason</u> for the first clause. • More formal • Beware: *For* has many definitions and uses in English.
A	and	• Meaning: adds another idea • The idea in the second clause may mean: • an idea of equal importance • the next event in a sequence • the result of an action in the first clause • Very common • Never begin a sentence with *and* in academic writing.
N	nor	• Meaning: *and not* • The first clause is negative with *never* or *neither*. The second clause is also negative using *nor*. • Warning: The independent clause that follows *nor* requires <u>inverted word order.</u> • SV, *nor* VS. • The V in the second clause is an auxiliary.
B	but	• Meaning: contrast or opposite idea • Very common • Never begin a sentence with *but* in academic writing.
O	or	• Meaning: alternative idea • Very common • Sentences can also begin with this word.
Y	yet	• Meaning: indicates an unexpected idea • Sentences can also begin with this word.
S	so	• Meaning: *therefore; for the purpose of* • Sentences can also begin with this word.

2. In the second formula **(SV; SV.)**, the two independent clauses are connected by **a semicolon**. You can connect two independent clauses with a semicolon **when they are closely related**. The relationship between the two clauses is so clear that neither a coordinating conjunction nor a conjunctive adverb are necessary.

Example 3: I don't like watching baseball games; I prefer watching basketball games.

Example 4: She doesn't feel well; she's not going to school today.

3. In the third formula **(SV: SV.)**, the two independent clauses are connected by **a colon**. In this case, the clause after the colon **explains or illustrates the first clause**. Grammarians disagree on the capitalization rules for the second clause: <u>S</u>ome say a capital letter is required and some say it's not. I recommend capitalizing the second clause. You can see an example of this in the preceding sentence in which <u>*Some*</u> is capitalized. See more example sentences below.

Example 5: Neela is devoted to charity<u>: S</u>he volunteers at the community center every Saturday.

Example 6: I never have enough time for fun during the week<u>: I</u>'m in school for eight hours, have three to five hours of homework, and then have swim practice for two hours every weekday.

4. In the last formula **(SV; conjunctive adverb, SV.)**, the two independent clauses are connected by **a semicolon, a conjunctive adverb, and a comma**. In this formula, these three elements are required. There are, however, other ways of forming a compound sentence using conjunctive adverbs. We use different conjunctive adverbs for different purposes. Study the conjunctive adverbs in the following chart. Note that some conjunctive adverbs have multiple meanings and can therefore be used in different ways. For example, *finally* can be used to indicate a time/sequence as well as a summary.

Common Conjunctive Adverbs

Cause and Effect	Therefore	Then	Accordingly	Hence	Thus
	As a result	In effect	-	-	-
Addition	Also	Additionally	In addition	Furthermore	Moreover
Contrast	However	Nevertheless	Nonetheless	Otherwise	Conversely
	On the other hand	In contrast	Alternatively	Rather	Instead
Time/Sequence	Since	Meanwhile	Simultaneously	Previously	Subsequently
	First / Firstly / First of all	Second / Secondly / Second of all	Then / Next	To begin with	In the beginning
	Before	Currently	Eventually	Later / After that	Immediately
	At that time	Thereafter	In the end	Lastly	Finally
Comparison	Likewise	Similarly	Equally	In the same way	In a similar way
Illustration / Clarification	For example	For instance	Namely	Notably	Such as
	In particular	Specifically	As an illustration	To illustrate this	-
Emphasis	Certainly	Definitely	Indeed	Of course	Naturally
	In fact	Undoubtedly	Above all	Especially	-
Generalizing	Overall	In general	Ultimately	On the whole	As a rule
Summary	Finally	In conclusion	In summary	To sum up	In brief
	Overall	In the end	All in all	All things considered	-

Be aware that in this type of compound sentence, the **conjunctive adverb (ca) can move around** in the second clause. The most common formula is the one already given: **(SV; conjunctive adverb, SV.).** Here are two more formulas that illustrate where you can position the conjunctive adverb: **(SV; S Auxiliary, ca, V.)** and **(SV; SV, ca.).**

Example 7: My aunt loves coffee; **however,** she dislikes coffee flavored food.

Example 8: The students in this history class participate enthusiastically in the group activities; they don't, **however,** enjoy writing essays.

POP QUIZ!

Before we learn the next type of sentence, let's do a quick review! What is a compound sentence? What are the elements that compose a compound sentence? Jump back to the previous section if you can't remember.

Complex Sentences

The next advanced sentence structure is the complex sentence. This structure is composed of an independent clause, also called **the main clause**, and a dependent clause, aka **a subordinate clause**. The dependent clause cannot stand alone as a sentence because it begins with a subordinating conjunction or another word or phrase. Subordinating conjunctions are words or phrases that link a main and subordinate clause. A complex sentence can begin with either the main clause or the subordinate clause.

Practice 10-B

Check out some example complex sentences on the next page. Can you identify both the main and subordinate clauses in each sentence? Can you also find the subordinating conjunctions or other transition words? Underline the main clause and put brackets around the [subordinate clause]. Highlight the subordinating conjunction. Then, check your answers to Practice 10-B in the Answer Key.

1. Zehra is in line for the Mega-Rollercoaster because she loves fast, scary rides.

2. Even though she prefers fast rides, she also likes the silly ones like the Fun House.

3. Zehra's brother, who is afraid of roller coasters, only goes on the water rides.

4. The water ride that he likes the most is the Super Flume.

5. When Zehra and her brother Zane go to the amusement park together, they bring friends.

6. Some of their friends like the crazy fast rides, while some others prefer the slow rides.

7. Before they go to the amusement park, they invite at least one friend to hang out with.

8. Zehra is always excited when the amusement park opens for the season.

9. Do you know what the park hours are?

10. Since Zehra and Zane go to the park every summer, they know all the ride operators by name.*

***Note:** *By name* means they can identify a person and they know his or her name.

How to Identify a Complex Sentence

Similar to a compound sentence, a complex sentence has at least two clauses. However, in complex sentences, **one clause is dependent and therefore cannot stand alone**. This subordinate clause depends on the independent, or main, clause. Look at the examples on the next page and the explanations to understand this concept better.

Incorrect	Because she loves fast, scary rides.
Problem	It's an incomplete sentence because it's a subordinate clause. It's incomplete because it begins with a subordinating conjunction (*because*) and it's not attached to an independent clause. An incomplete sentence is also known as *a fragment*. It's a fragment (or part) of a whole sentence.
Explanation	A dependent clause must link to an independent clause in written English. In this sentence, the clause is **an adverb clause of reason**.
How to fix it	Attach this dependent clause to an appropriate and logical independent clause to form a complete complex sentence.
Correct	Zehra is in line for the Mega-Rollercoaster because she loves fast, scary rides.

Let's analyze another incomplete sentence.

Incorrect	Who is afraid of roller coasters.
Problem	This is an incomplete sentence; therefore, it is a fragment.
Explanation	It's incomplete because it begins with a relative pronoun (*who*) and it's not attached to an independent clause. A dependent clause cannot stand alone in written English. In this case, it's an adjective clause, also known as a relative clause. **Note:** This is not a question, and we know this because the end punctuation is a period.
How to fix it	Attach this dependent clause to an appropriate, logical independent clause to form a complete complex sentence that makes sense: Zehra's brother only goes on the water rides.
Correct	Zehra's brother, who is afraid of roller coasters, only goes on the water rides.

Let's look at the three different **types of dependent clauses in complex sentences**:

1. **Adverb clauses:** Adverb clauses give information about time, manner, reason, condition, and more. These clauses add relevant information to the main clause.

2. **Adjective clauses:** Adjective clauses are also known as **relative clauses**, and they describe nouns in the main clause. These clauses modify nouns of any kind—people, places, things, and ideas— in any position of the sentence, such as subjects and objects.

3. **Noun clauses:** Noun clauses act like nouns in sentences. Wherever a noun exists in a sentence, a noun clause can go in place of a simple noun or noun phrase. For example, a noun clause can be the subject, the object of the verb, the object of the preposition, and the subject complement in a sentence.

BTW

The key feature to remember is that in a complex sentence, **the clauses have unequal importance** in the mind of the speaker or writer. The main clause is the most important information in the sentence, and the subordinating clause provides additional information.

Now, let's dive deeper into the dependent clauses that form complex sentences. We'll start with adverb clauses.

Adverb Clauses

As you now know, the main clause of a complex sentence provides the most important information. Adverb clauses add relevant information such as when, how, why, or under which conditions the information in the main clause happened. Here is a list of the different types of information that adverb clauses add.

Type of Information Added	Example Subordinating Conjunctions to Use	Example Sentences
Time – it answers the question "when?"	before, after, while, since, as soon as, when, until, once, by the time	Martin deviated from his exercise routine **when he fell and hurt his ankle**.
Place – it answers the question "where?"	where, wherever, anywhere, everywhere	Dominic's dog follows him **wherever** he goes.
Reason – it answers the question "why?" or "for what reason?"	because (common; focuses on reason) since (informal; weaker than *because*) as (more formal; focuses on result)	The Taylors declined the party invitation **because they'll be out of town**.
Purpose – it answers the question "why?" or "for what purpose?"	so, so that in order that (usually requires a modal in the adverb clause)	Jeremy and his science lab partner monitored the beaker **so that the liquid didn't burn**.
Concession – it answers the question "how is this unexpected or surprising?"	although, though, even though (They all have the same meaning. *Although* is more formal.)	**Even though she didn't have the money to buy a new car**, she researched the best models and gave them a test drive.
Direct contrast	while, whereas (Use a comma between the clauses no matter which clause begins the sentence.)	**Whereas Mr. Pinna gives a lot of homework every week**, Ms. Shattuck gives very little.
Manner – it answers the question "how? In what manner?"	as though, as if (must follow main clause)	Judith studied for the test **as though her life depended on it**.
Condition – it answers the question "under what condition?"	if, whether, whether or not, unless, provided that, only if, even if	**Whether or not Pete passes this calculus test**, he'll earn a passing grade for the class.

The Adverb Clause Formula

Now that you have seen some example sentences that contain different types of adverb clauses, let's study how to formulate a complex sentence that contains an adverb clause. There are essentially **two formulas** (note that "sc" stands for **subordinating conjunction**):

1. Main clause [sc adverb clause].

2. [Sc adverb clause], main clause. (Take note that when you begin a sentence with an adverb clause, it's followed by a comma.)

Practice 10-C

Let's look at some examples of adverb clauses. In each sentence, put brackets around the [adverb clause], highlight the subordinating conjunction, and identify what kind of adverb clause it is. Then check your answers to Practice 10-C in the Answer Key.

1. After Marnie graduates from high school, she's going to take a gap year and study real estate.

2. As soon as you are done, call me.

3. Text me once class is over.

4. By the time you complete the project, I'll be gone.

5. Wherever you go for lunch, we will meet you there.

6. She'll exercise anywhere there is enough space to do jumping jacks.

7. I'm taking a multimedia class since I have to take an elective.

8. My guidance counselor helped me research college scholarships because I have a limited college budget.

9. As that university requires a high SAT score, I'm taking many practice SAT tests.

10. I have to get at least an 85 on this test so that I can earn an A+ for the class.

Now that you know about adverb clauses and how we form them, let's look deeper into two types in particular: adverb clauses of time and adverb clauses of condition.

POP QUIZ!

Let's do a quick review. What is a complex sentence? What are the elements that compose a complex sentence? Refer back to the previous section if you can't remember.

Adverb Clauses of Time

Adverb clauses of time are commonly used adverb clauses in speaking and writing, so it's important for you to learn how to use them. Look at some of the words and phrases we use to introduce adverb clauses of time. Take note of the key rules and verb tenses, too.

Common time words and phrases: after, as, as long as, before, by the time, every time, once, since, the first / last / next time, till, until, when, while

Talking about the future: When we talk about the future time frame using time clauses, the verb tense in the time clause is actually **the present tense**! This is counterintuitive. See some examples below of how we use time clauses to talk about the future. Notice the future verb tenses in the main clauses and the simple present verb tense in the time clauses.

Practice 10-D

As you read the following sentences, draw brackets around the [time clause], highlight the word that begins the time clause, and underline the verb in the main clause and the verb in the time clause. Then, check your answers to Practice 10-D in the Answer Key.

1. After I do the homework, I'll watch a movie with you.

2. My sister is going to buy a new car before she starts her new job.

3. Jacob is leaving for Lake Tahoe as soon as he talks to his boss.

4. Once we finish lunch, we'll go to Grandma's house.

5. I will never forget this birthday party as long as I live.

6. When Ms. Ray arrives, the test will begin.

7. By the time the mail comes, he'll already be gone.

8. The next time I see her, I'm going to tell her about it.

Talking about the past: When we talk about events in the past, the verb tense in the main clause and the time clause **are usually past tense verbs**. Below are some examples of how we use time clauses to talk about past events.

Practice 10-E

As you read the following sentences, draw brackets around the [time clause], highlight the word that begins the time clause, and underline <u>the verb in the main clause and the verb in the time clause</u>.

Notice the verb tenses used in each clause. The last two examples don't follow the general rule: they use the present perfect verb tense in the main clause. You already learned about *since* with the present perfect verb tense in Chapter 9, so you are familiar with this type of time clause. Check your answers to Practice 10-E in the Answer Key.

1. After he took the test, he felt better.

2. Before Sharla began her summer vacation, she cleaned out her school locker.

3. Once Ron learned how to drive, he never asked anyone for a ride.

4. We left the building when it stopped raining.

5. When Julianna stayed with her cousin in Nebraska, she visited Carhenge.

6. While we were waiting for you, we finished our homework assignments.

7. I stayed till it got dark out.

8. She had already left for the party by the time you called.

9. My brother hasn't gone to school since he got sick.

10. Since she finished her big project, she's had relaxing evenings.

You can see that the past tense verbs in these sentences are the simple past, the past progressive, and the past perfect, and as we mentioned, the last two are in the present perfect. You may remember that the present perfect verb tense talks about an action, event, or situation in the past that has some relevance to the moment of speaking or writing. If necessary, revisit Chapter 9 to review how we use the present perfect verb tense.

Helpful tips on time words and phrases: Whether the time frame is the past, present, or future, the use of the time words and phrases illustrated in the following table holds true.

Time Word or Phrase	Helpful Tips and Timelines
After, as soon as, Once	• **The action, event, or situation in the time clause (X) that begins with *after, as soon as,* or *once* <u>occurs first on the timeline</u>, and the event in the main clause (Y) happens after that.** This is true regardless of the order in which the clauses are spoken or written. • When we use the time word *after*, we don't necessarily know how much time occurs between the two events; however, with *as soon as* and *once*, the two events occur very close together. • Meaning of *as soon as* and *once*: when one action, event, or situation occurs, another one happens soon after [**After** I do the homework,] <u>I'll watch a movie with you.</u> [**Once** we finish lunch,] <u>we'll go to Grandma's house.</u> <u>I'll watch a movie with you</u> [**after** I do the homework.] <u>We'll go to Grandma's house</u> [**once** we finish lunch.] X = do homework; finish lunch Y = watch a movie; go to Grandma's house [**After** he took the test,] <u>he felt better.</u> [**Once** Ron learned how to drive,] <u>he never asked anyone for a ride.</u> <u>He felt better</u> [**after** he took the test.] <u>He never asked anyone for a ride</u> [**once** Ron learned how to drive.] X = took test; learned how to drive Y = felt better; never asked anyone for a ride

(continued)

Time Word or Phrase	Helpful Tips and Timelines
Before, by the time	• **The action, event, or situation in the main clause (X) <u>occurs before the event in the time clause (Y)</u> that begins with *before* or *by the time*.** This is true no matter in which order the clauses are spoken or written. • We may not know exactly how much time occurs between the two actions. The important information is that one action occurs and then another happens. • Meaning of *by the time*: before; one action, event, or situation is complete before another one occurs <u>My sister is going to buy a new car</u> [**before** she starts her new job.] <u>He'll already be gone</u> [**by the time** the mail comes,] [**Before** she starts her new job,] <u>my sister is going to buy a new car.</u> [**By the time** the mail comes,] <u>he'll already be gone.</u> <pre> X Y | ◄─────────────────► Past Now Future</pre> X = she buys a new car; he goes Y = she starts her new job; the mail comes [**Before** Sharla began her summer vacation,] <u>she cleaned out her school locker.</u> [**By the time** you called,] <u>she had already left for the party</u>. <u>She cleaned out her school locker</u> [**before** Sharla began her summer vacation.] <u>She had already left for the party</u> [**by the time** you called.] <pre> X Y | ◄─────────────────► Past Now Future</pre> X = she cleaned out locker; she left Y = began vacation; you called

Time Word or Phrase	Helpful Tips and Timelines
When, the first / next / last time	• We use *when* and time phrases like *the next time* in time clauses to show **actions, events, and situations in the time clause (X) that <u>occur at the time of or just before the event in the main clause (Y)</u>**. • *When* can mean *at that time* • In cases in which *when* means *at that time*, one action usually happens immediately before another; they usually don't happen **exactly** at the same time. [**When** Ms. Ray arrives,] <u>the test will begin</u>. [**The next time** I see her], <u>I'm going to tell her about it.</u> <u>The test will begin</u> [**when** Ms. Ray arrives.] <u>I'm going to tell her about it</u> [**the next time** I see her.] X/Y timeline: Past — Now — Future X = she arrives; see her Y = test begins; tell her about it <u>We left the building</u> [**when** it stopped raining.] <u>I was delighted</u> [**the first time** I went to New York.] [**When** it stopped raining,] <u>we left the building</u>. [**The first time** I went to New York,] <u>I was delighted</u>. X/Y timeline: Past — Now — Future X = stopped raining; went to New York Y = left the building; was delighted

(continued)

Time Word or Phrase	Helpful Tips and Timelines
While, as, as long as	• We use *while, as,* and *as long as* in time clauses to show **actions, events, and situations in the main clause (X) that occur during the time of the event in the time clause (Y).** • Meaning of *while/as*: during that time • Meaning of *as long as*: for that duration of time emphasizing from beginning to end <u>I will never forget this birthday party</u> [**as long as** I live.] 　　　　　　　　X　　　　　　　　　　　　　　　　Y **Note:** *As long as I live* = for the whole time that I am alive starting from the moment of speaking 　　　　　　　　　　　　　　　　|-X + Y- - - - - - - - - - ◄──────────────┼──────────────► Past　　　　　　　　Now　　　　　　　Future X = never forget birthday party Y = I live [**While** we were waiting for you,] <u>we finished our homework assignments.</u> 　　　Y　　　　　　　　　　　　　　　X **Note:** In this case, one action **(Y)** happened over time and during that time, another action **(X)** occurred. This is how we use the past progressive verb tense—to show that during the course of one action or time period, another action occurs. 　　　　　　　　　YYYXYYY | ◄──────────────┼──────────────► Past　　　　　　　　Now　　　　　　　Future Y = we wait for you X = we finished homework

Time Word or Phrase	Helpful Tips and Timelines

Until, till	• **The action, event, or situation in the main clause (X) stops when the action in the time clause (Y) begins.**
	• Meaning of *until/till*: up to that time and no longer
	• *Till* is used often in spoken English, but it's seldom used in formal or academic written English.
	
	[**Until** he retired,] <u>my uncle worked at only one company</u>.
	    Y X
	
	<u>I stayed</u> [**till** it got dark.]
	    X Y
	
	X Y
	
	Past Now Future
	
	X = worked at one company; stayed
	Y = he retired; it got dark

Adverb Clauses of Condition

We often use adverb clauses of condition in spoken and written English. Let's learn the different types of conditionals and the verb tenses required for each.

Practice 10-F

First, read the sentences below. Can you identify the adverb clauses of condition? Draw brackets around [the adverb clauses of condition] and then underline the main clause. Check your answers to Practice 10-F in the Answer Key.

1. When the sun sets, it's in the west.

2. If it's 6:00 p.m. on a weekday, Gerald is home from work.

3. If I pass this calculus test with at least a B, I'll earn an A for the class!

4. Whenever the teacher is sick, we get a substitute teacher, and the class is more fun.

5. My mom and dad will buy me a car if I make the honor roll in my junior and senior years.

6. Should it rain, we'll have the party indoors.

7. If it doesn't rain, we'll have the party in the backyard.

8. Provided I pass the driving test, I'll drive myself to school every day.

9. Unless he stretches after running, his leg muscles won't become flexible.

10. If I were you, I'd study every night for a week to prepare for the final exam.

11. If you could carry this big box, I'd be so grateful.

12. It would help me a lot if you could do the laundry tonight.

The adverb clause of condition is also known as the **IF clause**, and the main clause is also called the **result clause**. Study the following guidelines for conditionals. Notice the **verb tenses** in bold and the shaded words, which indicate a condition. There are also key notes for you to study. You can learn more about modals in following sections in this chapter.

POP QUIZ!

Let's check what you know about adverb clauses. What are some common time words and phrases in time clauses? Name as many as you can! Jump back into the previous section to see them.

Situation/Type of Conditional	Condition/*If* Clause Verb Tense	Main/Result Clause Verb Tense	Notes
<u>True</u> **in the present: facts and general truths** Also known as *zero conditionals* and *real conditionals*	**Simple Present** **Example 1:** When the sun **sets**, (Fact: Every time the sun sets . . .) **Example 2:** If it**'s** 6:00 p.m. on a weekday,* (General truth: At 6 p.m. on every weekday . . .)	**Simple Present** it**'s** in the west. (. . . it sets in the west.) Gerald **is** home from work. (. . . it's expected that Gerald will be at home.)	• In real conditionals, the condition always has the same result. • With facts and general truths, *if* can be replaced with *when* or *whenever*. • ***Note:** This is referred to as *an inference* because it's <u>assumed</u> that Gerald is at home based on past habits and routines.
<u>True</u> **in the future** Also called *first conditionals* and *future conditionals*	**Simple Present** **Example 1:** If I **pass** this calculus test with at least a *B*, (In the case that I pass the test—which is in the future—with a B grade or better . . .) **Example 2:** If it **doesn't rain**, (In the case that it does not rain in the future for this party . . .)	**Simple Future with *Will* or *BE going to* + Base Form of the Verb** I**'ll earn** an A for the class! (The result will be a grade of A for the class.) we**'ll have** the party in the backyard. (. . . the party will be in the backyard)	• *Will* + *BE going to* indicate certainty or a plan. You can also use modals of ability and possibility such as *can*, *may*, and *might*. • Even though the verb in the *if clause* is in the simple present tense, it's referring to a future action, event, or situation.

(continued)

Situation/Type of Conditional	Condition/*If* Clause Verb Tense	Main/Result Clause Verb Tense	Notes
<u>Untrue</u> in the present + future Also referred to as **second conditionals**, **unreal conditionals**, and **hypothetical conditionals**	**Simple Past** The condition is not true. **Example 1:** If she **gave** you a ride, (She did <u>not</u> give you a ride.) **Example 2:** If you **could carry*** this big box, **Example 3:** If I **were** you, (I'm not you, but this is what I would do.)	***Would* + Base Form of the Verb** Therefore, the result is not true. you **would be** here already. (Therefore, you are <u>not</u> already here.) I**'d be** so grateful. I**'d study** every night for a week to prepare for the final exam. (This is my advice.)	• In the result clause, you can use other modals, such as *should, could, may, might*, etc. • We use this conditional for **polite requests**. • *****Note:** We sometimes add a modal in the ***if clause***, which is unusual. • It is grammatically correct to use **were** for *all* people singular or plural. • We use this conditional to give advice, too. In this case, we say *"If I were you"* in the ***if clause*** in academic and formal writing. In casual conversation, however, *"If I <u>was</u> you"* is often used.
<u>Untrue</u> in the past, Also know as **third conditionals** and **past unreal conditionals**	**Past Perfect** The condition is not true. **Example 1: Had** she **left** earlier, (She did <u>not</u> leave earlier.) **Example 2:** If I **had studied** more, (I did <u>not</u> study enough.)	**Would/Could Have + Past Participle** Therefore, the result is not true. she **wouldn't have hit** so much traffic. (Therefore, she <u>did hit</u> a lot of traffic.) I **would have gotten** a better grade. (Therefore, I did <u>not</u> get a better grade.)	• This type of conditional is mostly used to express regret or a missed opportunity. • For *all* types of conditionals, both affirmative and negative verbs can be used in both clauses as long as it makes sense.

Practice 10-G

Now that you are a bit familiar with the different kinds of conditionals, go back to the example sentences with adverb clauses of conditions in Practice 10-F. Write the conditional type and how it's used for each sentence. For example, for the first sentence in 10-F, it's a zero/real conditional and it's a fact. Check your answers in Practice 10-G in the Answer Key.

As you can see from the example sentences and guidelines above, there are multiple ways to compose conditionals. Let's take a closer look at these.

Grammatical Notes on Conditionals:

- In factual conditionals, you can substitute *if* with *when* or *whenever* because it means **every time**.

- *As long as* is another phrase you can use to indicate a condition.

- *Unless* means *If . . . not.* For example, the two sentences below mean the same thing.

EXAMPLES

▶ <u>Unless he stretches</u> after running, his leg muscles won't become flexible.

▶ <u>If he doesn't stretch</u> after running, his leg muscles won't become flexible.

- You can use *whether or not* a couple of different ways:

    1. Whether S+V or not: **Whether it's foggy or not**, we're going to the beach.

    2. Whether or not S+V: I'm going to register for salsa dance lessons **whether or not Darcy registers.**

- We never use "if or not." It's ungrammatical.

- ***Provided (that)*** is used to mean ***if X happens*** or ***in the case that X happens.*** Here's an example:

> Provided I pass the driving test, I'll drive myself to school every day.

- ***If*** can sometimes be omitted. We can omit if and invert the subject and auxiliary verb instead. Here are some examples:

> **Should it** rain, we'll have the party indoors. (If it should rain . . .)
>
> **Had she** left earlier, she wouldn't have hit so much traffic. (If she had left earlier . . .)

- We can use the progressive verb tense but only for non-stative verbs. Let's look at some examples of the past, present, future, and past perfect progressive verb tenses in condition and result clauses:

> If I **am presenting** tomorrow in class, I will rehearse tonight.
>
> If I **were working** in the bagel shop, I wouldn't have weekends free. (Notice that the *BE* verb is ***were*** not ***was***.)
>
> If her alarm **had gone off**, she **wouldn't be missing** class right now.
>
> If Madeleine **hadn't been hurrying**, she would have remembered to bring the keys.
>
> If my family **had been living** in Brazil in 2020, my father **would have been working** in construction.

- The imperative can be used in the result clause in future conditionals. Let's see examples of this:

> If Vladimir comes, **tell** him I'll be right back.

> When Rosemary calls, **let** me know.

> When you hear the oven timer go off, please **call** me.

Mixed Time Conditionals

The last type of conditional to discuss is *mixed time conditionals*. These unreal conditional sentences are formed with a different time frame in the condition clause and in the result clause. Let's look at these two types of mixed conditionals with examples and explanations below.

Mixed Time (Unreal) Conditionals

Time Frame for the Condition Clause	Time Frame for the Result Clause
Present	**Past**
simple past verb tense	**would/could have + past participle**
If I **weren't** so tired,	I **would have cooked** dinner for you.
(Truth: I am so tired.)	(Truth: I didn't cook dinner for you.)
If Jolene **liked** big dogs,	she **would have pet** your dog.
(Truth: She doesn't like big dogs.)	(Truth: She didn't pet your dog.)
Past	**Present**
past perfect verb tense	**would + base form of the verb**
If I **hadn't drunk** so much soda,	I **wouldn't feel** so nauseous right now.
(Truth: I drank a lot of soda.)	(Truth: I feel nauseous right now.)
If Robby **had spent** more time on his project,	he **might have** a better grade in the class.
(Truth: He did not spend enough time on his project.)	(Truth: He doesn't have a satisfactory grade.)

Practice 10-H

Read more examples of mixed time conditionals below. Put brackets around the [condition clause], underline <u>the result clause</u>, and highlight the verb structures in each clause. Identify which time frame is indicated in each clause. Then check your answers to Practice 10-H in the Answer Key.

1. If they weren't so busy moving this week, they would have come to game night.

2. Lloyd and Charley wouldn't be sleeping right now if they hadn't stayed up so late last night.

3. She could have joined you in the sing-along if she didn't have a sore throat.

4. Had we not seen that movie already, we would go with you to the cinema.

5. If the Perry family had brought dessert, we would be eating homemade blackberry pie right now.

6. We wouldn't have seen any stars in the sky if it were foggy.

Modals

We use modal auxiliaries with verbs to express attitudes toward actions, events, and situations. Take a look at the example sentences below. Notice that the <u>modals</u> in each sentence are underlined. Do you know any of these?

EXAMPLES

1. All employees <u>must</u> wash their hands before returning to work.

2. You <u>should</u> go to the meeting today.

3. It <u>will</u> help you understand the job better.

4. We're <u>supposed to</u> have a holiday on Monday.

5. <u>Can</u> you check the schedule, please?

6. He'<u>d better not</u> forget his folder.

7. She <u>ought to</u> speak to the boss.

8. <u>Are</u> you <u>able to</u> join me today?

9. <u>Would</u> you hand me that stack of papers, please?

10. We'<u>ve got to</u> get to a gas station soon, or we'll run out of gas.

11. I <u>might</u> go to the gym after work.

12. I <u>may be able to</u> join you, but I'm not sure yet.

13. They <u>have to</u> consult with their supervisor.

14. We <u>used to</u> go to dinner all the time, but now we're too busy.

15. <u>Can</u> you come here for a minute?

16. He <u>was going to</u> take the job, but he went back to school instead.

Notice that some of the modals require an infinitive (to + base form of verb) and some do not. We can express modals with single words and phrases, too. Look at the guidelines, definitions, and explanations for modals below. These will help you understand how to use them. Please note that in different regions of the United States, modal usage and meanings may differ, and I recommend you investigate how English speakers use them in your area. Here are modals that vary by strength or degree.

Use of Modal	Intended Meaning of Modal Auxiliary by Strength or Degree	
Modals for necessity	Stronger	Weaker
	←—————————————————————————————→	
	must/have got to	have to/need to
Modals for certainty	100% certainty	0% certainty
	←—————————————————————————————→	
	will may	might could
Modals for ability	Stronger	Weaker
	←—————————————————————————————→	
	can/be able to could	should/may/might be able to
Modals for permission	Formal	Informal
	←—————————————————————————————→	
	may	can
Modals for advice	Stronger	Weaker
	←—————————————————————————————→	
	had better have got to	should/ought to could
Modals for suggesting	Formal/less direct	Informal/more direct
	←—————————————————————————————→	
	shall I/we . . . ? should . . . ? could why don't we . . . ? can let's	
	Note: . . . ? indicates it is used in questions	
	Note: *Could* and *can* indicate possibility, but we also use them to make suggestions.	
Modals for requests	Stronger/more direct/ less formal	Weaker/less direct/ more formal
	←—————————————————————————————→	
	will can could would may I would you mind shall I/we	

Here are some more modals and notes to to help explain.

Use of Modal	Intended Meaning of Modal Auxiliary and Notes
Modals for past habits	• used to / would: used for repeated actions and routines **Example of repeated actions in the past:** When I was a little girl, my father *used to/would take* us on a "mystery ride" to get ice cream every Sunday. • used to: used for past habits not repeated **Example of habits in the past:** I *used to* eat vanilla ice cream sundaes.
Modals for expectations	• be supposed to/ought to/should: used to indicate certainty **Example:** The movie is supposed to start at 7 p.m. (certainty based on movie schedule) • ought to/should: used to make an inference based on knowledge and past actions, events, and situations. **Example:** She ought to/should pass the final exam with flying colors!* (inference based on past behaviors) **with flying colors:* This idiomatic phrase means easily/with ease.
Modal for preference	• *Would rather:* Used to indicate a clear preference • We use this phrasal modal to politely disagree with a choice. **Example:** **John:** Why don't we go to the gym tomorrow morning around 7? **Azre:** I'*d rather* go to the gym tonight and sleep late tomorrow morning.

Modals followed by the *base form of a verb*:

Can, could, had better, may, might, must, shall, should, will, would, would rather

Modals followed by the *infinitive* (to + base form of verb):

Be able to, be going to, be supposed to, have to, have got to, ought to, used to

More Notes on Modals:

- All modals can be used in the negative.

- The negatives of some modals change the meaning completely.

- Some modals have more than one definition, and you must understand the meaning from context.

- Modals illustrate the strength of the speaker's or writer's attitude.

- We use modals frequently in both speaking and writing.

- Some modals are more informal and better for speaking.

- We often use modals in the result clause of conditional sentences.

  He <u>might</u> earn a B for the class if he passes this final exam.

  If we leave now, we <u>should</u> get there on time.

  It <u>will</u> be fun if you come with me!

Adjective Clauses

Another way to form a complex sentence is to add an adjective clause (also known as a *relative clause*) to an independent clause. Adjective clauses are subordinate clauses that act like adjectives by modifying nouns, noun phrases, and pronouns in a sentence. An adjective clause describes the noun by answering the question **which one** or **what kind**. These dependent clauses describe nouns and pronouns found in any position in the sentence, such as the subject, the object of a verb, and the object of a preposition. Adjective clauses usually begin with one of these relative pronouns: **that, which, who, whom**, or **whose**.

Practice 10-1

In the example sentences below, underline the <u>main clause</u> and put brackets around the [adjective clause]. Highlight the relative pronoun in the adjective clause. Can you guess which noun the adjective clause is modifying? Double underline <u>that noun</u> and then check your answers in Practice 10-1 in the Answer Key.

1. The books that you lent me are really interesting.

2. Mr. Hopper, who lives next door, walks in the park every day after lunch.

3. I'm really enjoying the dinner you brought home for me.

4. She bought all the items on your list, which was difficult to read.

5. Did Marty buy you these flowers, which smell so good?

6. Ask the professor, who is over there.

7. My car, which I bought used, has been running really well.

8. Is that the guy that you were talking about?

9. The family owns the house that is at the end of the street.

10. Is this your dog that's wearing the pink fuzzy collar?

11. They are walking on a beach that has soft, white sand.

12. The children, who range in age from four to seven years old, are well behaved.

13. That's the person whose car is neon orange.

BTW

We can also form adjective clauses with **relative adverbs** such as **when** (to describe time), **where** (to describe place), and **why** (to describe a reason). Here are some example sentences:

• I remember a time **when** I enjoyed roller coasters. Now I don't like them.

• This is the place **where** my husband proposed to me.

• I don't know the reason **why** she doesn't like me.

14. Ms. Del Campo talked about the company that popularized the electric typewriter.

15. My cousin, whose wife is a famous hypnotist, has just arrived.

16. I've been thinking about my childhood friend with whom I used to play every day.

Did you notice that **the adjective clause immediately follows the noun or pronoun it modifies**? Follow this general rule. One common error is putting too many words between the adjective clause and the noun it modifies. This creates confusion. Don't make this mistake!

Helpful Notes About Adjective Clauses

- Like any clause, an adjective clause must have a subject and a verb.

- An adjective clause cannot stand alone: it is dependent on the main clause to be complete.

- In academic writing, an adjective clause unattached to a main clause is a *fragment*.

- An adjective clause can provide restrictive or nonrestrictive information about the noun it describes. See the discussion of restrictive and nonrestrictive clauses starting on page 430.

- For nonrestrictive clauses, commas are required.

- The relative pronoun *that* is used for people and things in restrictive adjective clauses.

- *Who* and *which* are used in nonrestrictive adjective clauses.

- *Whose* is used in both restrictive and nonrestrictive adjective clauses.

- We use adjective clauses to add necessary and/or additional information and to vary sentence structures in academic writing.

Reasons to Use Adjective Clauses

As mentioned in the bulleted list above, one reason to form adjective clauses is to provide necessary or additional information regarding a noun in the sentence. Another reason to use adjective clauses in sentences is to create variety in academic writing. A paragraph with only simple sentences will bore the reader. Writing with a variety of simple, compound, and complex sentences, however, creates a rhythm in writing that keeps the reader interested. The pace and rhythm of writing can be compared to a song whose pace and rhythm changes from beginning to end. This creates variety for the listener, just as different sentence structures create variety in writing. As the saying goes: variety is the spice of life! So, be sure to express your ideas by forming different types of sentences.

How to Form Adjective Clauses

So, how do we form adjective clauses? An adjective clause is formed in three basic ways:

1. [relative pronoun + S + V]

2. [relative pronoun as the subject + V]

3. [no relative pronoun + S + V]

The modified noun will determine how the adjective clause is formed and where in the sentence it belongs. One way to think about how to form adjective clauses is this: **When you have two sentences that refer to the same noun, you can combine the two sentences with an adjective clause.** Let's examine this.

Step 1: Find the common noun in the sentences.

A. Mary is driving a new **car**.
B. The **car** is red and sporty.

What noun is common to both sentences? You are correct: *car*. Therefore, we can combine these two sentences by referring to the car only once. We are essentially overlapping the two sentences.

Step 2: Omit one reference of the common noun.
To decide which reference to omit, determine which information is more important for the listener or reader. Ask yourself these questions:

- What is my intended message?

- What information is most important?

In this case, the important information is that Mary is driving a new car, so sentence A.

A. Mary is driving a new **car**.
B. ~~The **car**~~ is red and sporty.

Step 3: Replace the second reference with an appropriate relative pronoun.

A. Mary is driving a new **car** that is red and sporty.

Step 4: Place the adjective clause immediately after the noun it modifies.

A. <u>Mary is driving a new</u> **car** [that is red and sporty.]

Step 5: Determine if the information in the adjective clause is essential (restrictive) or nonessential (nonrestrictive).
This will tell us if we need commas: if it's nonessential, we must use commas. In this case, the <u>car is not identified</u>, so the information **is essential** to tell us **which one**—or **which car**—she is driving. Thus, we don't use commas.

Step 6: Identify the subject (S) and verb (V) in each clause.

Mary is driving a **car** [that is red and sporty.]
  S   V   S V

Main clause: S = *Mary* | V = *is driving*
Adjective clause: S = the relative pronoun *that* | V = *is*

     Let's follow these steps again to form a complex sentence with an adjective clause using the following two sentences.

A. Ms. Mancuso won a prestigious award.
B. She teaches anthropology.

Step 1: Find the common noun in the sentences.

A. **Ms. Mancuso** won a prestigious award.
B. **She** teaches anthropology.

Step 2: Omit one reference of the common noun.
Remember to ask yourself these questions to determine the most important information to convey to the listener or reader:

- What is my intended message?

- What information is most important?

     In this case, the fact that she won an award is the important message. That she teaches anthropology is additional information. Therefore, make sentence B the adjective clause.

A. **Ms. Mancuso** won a prestigious award.
B. **She** teaches anthropology.

Step 3: Replace the second reference with an appropriate relative pronoun.

A. Ms. Mancuso won a prestigious award.
B. who teaches anthropology

Step 4: Place the adjective clause immediately after the noun it modifies.

<u>Ms. Mancuso</u> [who teaches anthropology] <u>won a prestigious award</u>.

Step 5: Determine if the information in the adjective clause is essential or nonessential.

Because Ms. Mancuso has a name, the noun is defined: she is identified. The information in the adjective clause doesn't help us define—or identify—her. This means that it's **additional rather than necessary information**. In other words, we don't need the information in the adjective clause to determine who Ms. Mancuso is because she is already named in the main clause. If we omitted the adjective clause, we still know which person, or **which one**, the sentence is talking about. Thus, we know the adjective clause is nonessential, so we must use commas:

Ms. Mancuso, who teaches anthropology, won a prestigious award.

Step 6: Identify the subject (S) and verb (V) in each clause.

<u>Ms. Mancuso</u>, [who teaches anthropology,] <u>won a prestigious award</u>.
   S   S   V   V

Main clause: S = *Ms. Mancuso* | V = *won*
Adjective clause: S = the relative pronoun *who* | V = *teaches*

Relative Pronouns

Let's dive deeper into relative pronouns. How do you know which relative pronoun to use in an adjective clause? Study the guidelines below, and note that **R stands for restrictive** and **NR stands for nonrestrictive.**(See the IRL sidebar on the next page discussing *that* vs. *which*.)

What Kind of Noun?	Subject Relative Pronouns	Object Relative Pronouns
People	that (R only); who (NR) relative pronoun = required because it replaces the subject of the original sentence	that (R only); who (NR) no relative pronoun (Ø) (R only) whom (academic/formal – R + NR) preposition + whom (academic/formal – for objects of the preposition – R + NR)
Replaces pronouns:	*I, you, she, he, it, we, they*	*me, you, her, him, it, us, them*
Example sentences:	The family owns the house that is at the end of the street. Mr. Hopper, who lives next door, walks in the park every day after lunch.	Is that the guy that you were talking about? I'm really enjoying the dinner (Ø) you brought home for me. I've been thinking about my childhood friend with whom I used to play every day.
Things	that (R only); which (NR)	that (R only); which (NR) no relative pronoun (Ø) (R only)
Replaces pronouns:	*it, they*	*it, them*
Example sentences:	Ms. Del Campo talked about the company that popularized the electric typewriter. Did Marty buy you these flowers, which smell so good?	The books that you lent me are really interesting. The books (Ø) you lent me are really interesting. My car, which I bought used, has been running really well.

(continued)

What Kind of Noun?	Subject Relative Pronouns	Object Relative Pronouns
Possession: **people + things**	whose + noun (R + NR) required: cannot be omitted	
Replaces possessive adjectives:	*my, your, her, his, its, our, their*	
Example sentences:	I heard about the student <u>whose backpack</u> was ripped apart by raccoons. My cousin, <u>whose wife</u> is a famous hypnotist, has just arrived.	The classmate <u>whose dog</u> I like is sitting over there. The nonfiction book on henna, <u>whose author</u> I can't remember, is fascinating.

IRL

For both people and things, *that* is used in restrictive adjective clauses only. Beware: there is some debate about how to use the relative pronouns *who* and *which*. Conventional American English grammarians follow the prescriptive rule that *who* and *which* are used solely in nonrestrictive clauses. English instructors, professional journalists, and British grammarians, however, disagree: they assert that it's a writing style choice, and *who* and *which* can be used in restrictive clauses as well. An example of this is a writer who chooses *which* rather than *that* in a restrictive clause for the sake of clarity. In the following sentence, *that* is used twice: *That is the baseball team <u>that</u> will most likely win the tournament.* For clarity, a writer may choose to use the relative pronoun *which* instead of *that* even though this is a restrictive clause: *That is the baseball team <u>which</u> will most likely win the tournament.*

Because the word *that* has multiple uses in the English language and is liberally used, choosing *which* or *who* instead may be helpful. I recommend you check with your ESL instructor and/or local residents to see how they use *who* and *which* in adjective clauses. Remember also that conversational English is less formal than written academic English.

Subject or Object Relative Pronoun

How do you know whether your relative pronoun should be a subject or object relative pronoun? You determine which to use by looking at the adjective clause: Is the noun/pronoun in the subject or object position in the original sentence? Look at the two examples to better understand this strategy:

Example 1: A. Mary is driving a new **car**. B. The **car** is red and sporty.

Here's what we know:

- In B, *car* is in the subject position, so we need a <u>subject relative pronoun</u>.

- *Car* is a <u>thing</u>, so the two possible relative pronouns to use are **which** and **that**.

- The information in B is essential to knowing which car, so it's <u>restrictive</u>.

From this examination, it is clear that the relative pronoun should be **that** (according to common American English grammar rules).

- <u>Mary is driving a new</u> **car** [that is red and sporty.] = Mary is driving a new car that is red and sporty.

Example 2:

A. Ms. Mancuso won a prestigious award.
B. She teaches anthropology.

Here's what we know:

- In B, **she** is in the subject position, so we need a <u>subject relative pronoun</u>.

- **She** is a <u>person</u>, so the two possible relative pronouns to use are **who** and **that**.

- The information in B is *not* needed to identify which person because she is named in the first sentence, so the adjective clause is <u>nonrestrictive and we need commas</u>.

From this examination, it is clear that the relative pronoun must be **who**.

- **Ms. Mancuso** [who teaches anthropology] <u>won a prestigious award</u>. = Ms. Mancuso, who teaches anthropology, won a prestigious award.

Restrictive vs. Nonrestrictive Adjective Clauses

There are two common errors English learners make when forming adjective clauses:

1. Choosing the wrong relative pronoun

2. Omitting commas in nonrestrictive adjective clauses

Let's clarify the rules and strategies for these two issues, so you can compose accurate sentences.

How to choose the relative pronoun: How can you make the correct choice regarding relative pronouns? You can look at the tables we've covered in this section, which provide guidelines for all the relative pronouns, and follow the reasoning in Examples 1 and 2 on the prior page to help you choose the best relative pronoun. To do this, **ask yourself these three questions**:

1. What position is the noun/pronoun in the sentence that is to become the adjective clause: subject or object? Or is it possessive?

Note: No matter what kind of object it is—an object of the verb (also known as a direct object) or an object of a preposition—the same rules apply.

2. Is it a person or thing?

3. Is it restrictive or nonrestrictive (must have commas)?

When you methodically answer each of these questions, you will be able to find the right relative pronoun for your adjective clause.

How to avoid comma errors and determine whether your adjective clause is restrictive or nonrestrictive: To be certain it's clear, let's define restrictive and nonrestrictive clauses.

A **restrictive clause** (also called essential, identifying, and defining) **provides information that restricts, or limits, the noun or pronoun so we know <u>which one</u> or <u>what kind</u>.** If the modified noun/pronoun is not clearly defined, identified, or named, then we need more information to understand which one or what kind. This is what the information in a restrictive adjective clause does: it answers the question *which one* or *what kind*.

A **nonrestrictive clause** (also called nonessential, nonidentifying, and nondefining) **provides additional, but not identifying or limiting information about the modified noun.** In this type of sentence, the noun/pronoun is sufficiently defined, named, or identified, so we know which one or what kind. The information provided in the adjective clause, therefore, is extra information. It may be helpful, interesting, and even useful, but it's not necessary to define or identify the noun/pronoun.

Tips to Know What a Defined Noun Looks Like:
Study these clues to help you determine whether the noun, noun phrase, or pronoun is defined.

- The noun is **named** (Mr. Hopper, Isabella, Mississippi, Golden Gate Park).

- The noun is preceded by a **possessive adjective** or a **demonstrative pronoun** (your list, my cat, these flowers, those pencils).

- The noun is followed by a **prepositional phrase** (the rocks around the garden, the words on the page, the photos in the magazine).

- The noun is preceded with ***the*, especially when there is only one of the noun*** (the professor, the floor, the moon).

Note:** Be careful of the definite article *the*: In some of the example sentences at the beginning of this section, you'll see several restrictive adjective clauses that use the article ***the. If there is more than one of a noun, then we need more information to define it. See two examples of this on the following page:

▶ <u>The books</u> that you lent me are really interesting.

▶ Ms. Del Campo talked about <u>the company</u> that popularized the electric typewriter.

In both of these examples, the noun is preceded by the definite article *the*. However, we don't know **which books** or **which company**. The adjective clauses provide that necessary, identifying information: *that you lent me* and *that popularized the electric typewriter*. With this information, we can identify which books and which company.

Defining vs. Nondefining Nouns:
Learn to distinguish between defining and nondefining nouns in adjective clauses. Study the examples below:

▶ The book on my desk vs. a book

▶ The history textbook vs. the book (when there is more than one book)

▶ My notebook vs. a notebook

▶ Geraldine vs. a student

▶ Asena Restaurant vs. a Greek restaurant

Understanding the difference between defining and nondefining nouns will help you determine whether an adjective clause is restrictive or nonrestrictive.

Subject-Verb Agreement with Adjective Clauses

When you use a **subject relative pronoun, the subject and verb in the adjective clause must agree.** Let's look at some examples of SVA in adjective clauses.

The family owns the house [that **is** at the end of the street.]

- S = that | V = is → SVA

In this adjective clause, the subject relative pronoun **that** modifies **the house**, which is singular. Therefore, the verb in the adjective clause must also be singular: The subject and verb must agree. They do agree in this clause: **that is**. You can test this by using the modified noun **house** and matching it up with the verb in the adjective clause, **is**. **The house is** has subject-verb agreement, so it's correct.

Is this your dog [that**'s wearing** the pink fuzzy collar?]

- S = that | V = is wearing → SVA

Test: Your dog is wearing → SVA

They are walking on a beach [that **has** soft, white sand.]

- S = that | V = has → SVA

Test: A beach has → SVA

The children, [who **range** in age from four to seven years old,] are well behaved.

- S = who | V = range → SVA

Test: The children range → SVA

When you're writing a complex sentence with a subject relative pronoun, test to see if there is subject-verb agreement. Using this test will give you confidence.

Is the Relative Pronoun Necessary?

You can omit the **object relative pronoun** *only* when you refer to **people and things in restrictive clauses**. Otherwise, you cannot omit it. Most American English speakers **omit the object relative pronoun whenever possible**. Let's investigate more with this example sentence:

> The books that you lent me are really interesting.

We know it's an **object relative pronoun** because when we break this complex sentence into two independent sentences, the noun in common is in an object position in the second sentence.

A. The books are really interesting.

B. You lent me **the books**.

    Object of the verb (OV) / direct object (D.O.)

In sentence B, the noun that both sentences have in common—***books***—is in the object of the verb position. Having verified that this sentence has an object relative pronoun, let's look at all the ways we can write it according to **conventional American English grammar rules.**

EXAMPLES

> ▶ The books **that** you lent me are really interesting.
>
> ▶ The books you lent me are really interesting.

Here's another sentence to examine: Is that the guy that you were talking about?

A. Is that **the guy**?

B. You were talking about **him**.

    Object of the Preposition (OP)

▶ Is that the guy **that** you were talking about?

▶ Is that the guy **who** you were talking about?

▶ Is that the guy you were talking about?

POP QUIZ!

What does an adjective clause do in a sentence? Make sure you understand the types and how they are used. Go back to review the examples in the section to help you.

Recommendation: Practice properly forming adjective clauses without a relative pronoun so you become accustomed to doing it.

Modifying a Whole Sentence with *Which*

We can also use adjective clauses to modify a whole sentence. When we do this, it's a nonrestrictive clause, so we use a comma, and the relative pronoun is ***which***. This is used mostly in spoken English rather than in academic writing. When speaking, we pause briefly where the comma goes. Let's study an example of this:

Her parents couldn't attend the recital, [which was disappointing.]

In this sentence, *which* refers to the entire preceding clause. *Which was disappointing* is a nonrestrictive adjective clause that comments on the idea expressed in the main clause. Here are more examples:

EXAMPLES

▶ My computer crashed, which frustrated me.

▶ She ran 15 miles today, which made her tired and hungry.

▶ Last night we went to the carnival, which was a fun way to spend the evening.

▶ My favorite hobby is growing my own vegetables, which is gratifying.

▶ The correct answer to this math problem is *C*, which doesn't make sense.

Noun Clauses

The last type of complex sentence we'll cover is a noun clause. Noun clauses are subordinate clauses connected to a main clause to form a complete sentence. Just like all dependent clauses, they must have a subject and a verb and they cannot stand alone: They must be linked to an independent (main) clause. See the following important aspects and example sentences on noun clauses:

1. You may **put them anywhere a noun can exist in a sentence**; for example, you can put a noun clause in the subject, direct object (OV), indirect object, object of a preposition, and subject complement positions.

   Subject of the sentence:
   [The fact that he's late] upsets me.
          S   V

   Object of the verb/direct object:
   They didn't tell me [that they were going out.]
    S   V   OV/D.O.

   Indirect object:
   For the party, you can invite [whoever you want.]
               S   V   I.O.

   Object of the preposition:
   I'm driving by [what looks like an old warehouse.]
    S   V prep   OP

   Complement:
   The problem is [that I can't access the school website.]
       S   BE Linking verb   Complement

2. They can also **follow adjectives**.

   Adjective = sure
   I'm not **sure** [that I can do it.]

Adjective = concerned

I'm **concerned** [that I won't finish the assignment on time.]

3. Noun clauses can **begin with WH question words**, *whether/if*, *that*, and indefinite relative pronouns such as *whoever*, *whatever*, and *whenever*.

I don't know [**why** he quit the team.]
This is also called an *embedded WH question*.

[**Whether or not** they'll come to the meeting] is the question.
This is also called an *embedded yes/no question*.

She's worried [**that** he won't show up.]
In some cases, *that* can be omitted.

You can have [**whichever** bracelet appeals to you.]
Whichever = any one at all

Now that you know a little bit about noun clauses, let's look at the rules and how we use them in more detail. Check out the table below.

Noun Clause (Begins with)	Guidelines + Notes	Example Sentences
WH question words	**Embedded WH Questions** • Statement word order: S+V • *Who, whom, what, when, where, why, how, which, whose*	I understand [**how** I can do this algebra problem now.] WH question: How can I do this algebra problem?
Question word + infinitive	**WH Question Words** • *Whether* • Infinitive = to + base form of verb • Replaces S+V / V = *should* or *can/could* • Usually object of the verb	Can you show me [**what** <u>to do</u>?] = Can you show me what I should do? You must decide [**where** <u>to eat</u> lunch.] = You must decide where we can eat lunch. Tell me [**how** to make it.] = Tell me how I should/can make it.

(continued)

Noun Clause (Begins with)	Guidelines + Notes	Example Sentences
If/whether (or not)	**Embedded Yes/No Questions** Statement word order: S+V	
	• *If* S+V (*or not*)	She wants to know [**if** you will be there.] Y/N question: Will you be there?
	• *Whether* S+V (*or not*)	We're deciding [**whether** we should walk there **or not.**] Y/N question: Should we walk there?
	• *Whether* (*or not*) + S+V	[**Whether or not** we walk] is the question. Y/N question: Should/could/can we walk?
	• *or not* = optional	
That	• *That* can be omitted in OV and subject complement (SC) positions and when it follows adjectives. • *That* can also follow adjectives.	My parents think [**that** you're nice.] My parents think [you're nice.] It's wonderful [**that** they finished the project.] It's wonderful [they finished the project.]
	• As a subject, we usually use *The fact that*, but *that* is acceptable. • *That* cannot be omitted when it's in the subject position.	[**The fact that** he's working] is good news. [**That** he's working] is good news.
	• It's common to use *it* as the subject and put the noun clause at the end. • *That* noun clauses <u>cannot</u> be used in the object of prep (OP) position. Use *the fact that* instead.	<u>It</u>'s good news [**that** he's working.] I'm thinking about [~~that~~ he's sick.] I'm thinking about [**the fact that** he's sick.]
WH-ever words: whoever, whomever, whatever, whenever, wherever, however, whichever	• Begin with indefinite relative pronouns • *Whoever* – any person (subject)	[**Whoever** wants more ice cream] should come and get it now!
	• *Whomever* – any person (object) • *Whatever* – any thing • *Whenever* – any time • *Wherever* – any place • *However* – any way • *Whichever* – any one (person or thing)	We'll meet [**whomever** you hired.] She'll have [**whatever** I'm having.] We can go [**whenever** you want.] I'll pick you up [**wherever** you are.] They can cook it [**however** they want.] Borrow [**whichever** equipment you need.]

Compound-Complex Sentences

The final sentence structure to learn is compound-complex. This structure combines a compound sentence with a complex sentence, which means it must have at least two independent clauses and at least one dependent clause. Let's look at some examples.

 **IRL** Note that if the independent clauses are short, we often omit the comma before the coordinating conjunction. Commas are meant to clarify, not confuse, the reader. If there's already a comma after a dependent clause, and the two independent clauses are short, the comma may be omitted. Even though we have comma rules, there are exceptions. You need to become familiar with the rules, and then you can learn how to break them so that (1) you have creative freedom in your writing and (2) you find your own personal writing style—even within the boundaries of academic writing.

Practice 10-J

Can you identify the two independent clauses and the dependent clause that compose the sentence? Underline the <u>two independent clauses</u> and draw brackets around the [dependent clause]. Then check your answers to Practice 10-J in the Answer Key.

1. Although Marcia prefers horror movies, she watched a romantic comedy last night and she really enjoyed it.

2. Decker and Brittany have two dogs already, but they are going to get another dog as soon as they find the right one.

3. When my cousin received the college acceptance letter, she was thrilled, but she also felt a little bit nervous.

4. The students who are on the honor roll will wear a special yellow collar during graduation, and they'll be recognized at the ceremony.

5. I love how the rainbow appears when it rains here in the mountains: it feels magical.

6. It's amazing that my sister understands me so well, and she's always there for me.

7. Even though I'm exhausted, I'll finish my homework tonight, so I can sleep later tomorrow morning.

8. This board game is lasting so long, but it's fun because we're winning!

9. He's wondering where she is, and he's worried about her.

10. She's coming over for brunch, and she's bringing fresh bread that she made this morning.

Now let's practice as we study some patterns for compound-complex sentences. The dependent clauses can come before, in the middle of, or after an independent clause in the compound sentence part of the structure.

POP QUIZ!

What is the minimum number of independent and dependent clauses in a compound-complex sentence? Go back to the previous section for a reminder.

Practice 10-K

In the chart below, can you identify the type of dependent clause (DC) that are in brackets? The choices are these: adjective clause, adverb clause, and noun clause. Try to be as specific as you can. For example, if you find an adverb clause, identify what kind of adverb clause it is: time, reason, or concession. Check your answers to Practice 10-K in the Answer Key.

Compound-Complex Sentence Pattern	Examples and Notes DC = dependent clause | IC = independent clause cc = coordinating conjunction

Dependent clause, compound sentence
 	
DC, IC cc IC
	[Although Marcia preferred horror movies,] she watched a
	          DC IC
	romantic comedy last night **and** she really enjoyed it.
	                     cc IC

Compound sentence dependent clause
 	
IC, cc IC DC
	Decker and Brittany have two dogs already, **but** they are
	             IC cc IC
	going to get another dog [**as soon as** they find the right one.]
	                                DC

Compound sentence + DC
 	
IC DC, cc IC
	The students [who are on the honor roll] will wear a special
	                         DC
	IC [interrupted by DC]
	yellow collar during graduation, **and** they'll be recognized at
	                           cc IC
	the ceremony.

Compound sentence + 2 DCs **IC DC DC: IC**	I love [how the rainbow appears] [when it rains here in the IC DC DC mountains]: it feels magical. IC

Success Strategy: Talking About Similarities and Differences

In discussions, it's common to compare and contrast things such as items, concepts, beliefs, theories, conditions, facts, and statistics. Let's discover expressions and phrases to use when talking about similarities and differences. In the expressions below, X and Y represent nouns and in most cases the subjects of the sentence or clause. Note that in Chapter 3, you learned context clues of contrast, which can also be used. The *S+V* denotes that you need to complete the expression with a complete idea, a clause.

Ways to Talk About Similarities and Differences

Expressions to Show Similarities	Example Sentences
• X is the same as Y in that they are both _____. (Add verb.)* *In most cases, you must also add the rest of the sentence to convey a complete thought.	• Boston is the same as New York in that they are both cities on the East Coast. • Pizza is the same as flatbread in that they are both cooked bread dough with sauces and toppings.
• X is similar to Y in that it _____. (Add verb.)	• Baltimore, Maryland, is similar to Boston, Massachusetts, in that it is home to many historic American landmarks.
• X and Y both _____. (Add verb.)	• Oakland, California and Boston, Massachusetts both have major international seaports.
• X and Y each _____. (Add verb.)	• In California, Long Beach and Oakland each have important international seaports.
• X and Y have the same _____. (Add noun.)	• Hot dogs and sausages have the same main ingredient: processed meat.
• Like X, Y _____. (Add verb.)	• Like sausages, bratwurst is made of ground meat and spices.

Expressions to Show Differences	Example Sentences
• X is (noun, adjective, or verb –*ing*) _____, while Y is (noun, adjective, or verb –*ing*) _____.	• Western Colorado <u>is</u> mountainous, <u>while</u> eastern Colorado <u>is</u> part of the Great Plains.
• X has _____, while Y has/ doesn't have _____.	• Swiss cheese <u>has</u> holes, <u>while</u> cheddar cheese <u>doesn't have</u> holes.
• X is (adjective) _____, whereas Y is (adjective) _____.	• Hawaii <u>is</u> tropical, <u>whereas</u> Alaska <u>is</u> arctic.
• X is different from Y because _____(S+V).	• The American Southwest <u>is different from</u> New England <u>because</u> it has a semiarid climate.
• X _____(S+V). In contrast, Y _____ (S+V).	• New Mexico has a semiarid climate. <u>In contrast</u>, Florida is mostly subtropical.

To ask questions about similarities:

- How is X similar to Y?
- How are X and Y similar?
- Are X and Y similar in any way?
- In what ways are X and Y similar?
- How are X and Y the same?

• <u>How is</u> a subtropical climate <u>similar to</u> a tropical climate?
• <u>Are</u> mitochondria <u>and</u> molecules <u>similar in any way</u>?
• <u>In what ways are</u> mitochondria <u>and</u> molecules <u>similar</u>?
• <u>How are</u> mitochondria <u>and</u> molecules <u>the same</u>?

To ask questions about differences:

- How is X different from Y?
- How are X and Y different?
- Are X and Y different at all?
- In what ways are X and Y different?
- What's the difference between X and Y?
- What are the differences between X and Y?

• <u>How is</u> a semiarid climate <u>different from</u> an arid climate?
• <u>How are</u> these two climates <u>different</u>?
• <u>Are</u> these two climates <u>different at all</u>?
• <u>In what ways are</u> these two climates <u>different</u>?
• <u>What's the difference between</u> a semiarid <u>and</u> an arid climate?
• <u>What are the differences between</u> a semiarid <u>and</u> an arid climate?

EXERCISES

EXERCISE 10-1

Read the compound sentences below. Identify and label the SV combinations in each clause and then determine how the clauses are connected. Highlight the connection device.

> **Example: Beverly and Rose** <u>walk</u> to school in the morning, but
>   S   V
>
> **they** <u>go</u> home on the bus.
>   S   V

1. Zhimin and her cousins love going to the beach, and they go every chance they get.

2. They often swim in the ocean. However, they don't usually swim in freshwater lakes.

3. Esmeralda and her twin brother, Diego, drink café lattes every morning before school: It helps them concentrate on classwork.

4. Esmeralda usually gets a green tea latte. On the other hand, Diego gets a double espresso chocolate latte.

5. Graciela is doing track every day after school; her quadriceps are sore.

6. Fang and Brandon started dating; hence, they're together every day after school.

7. Shakira, Melanie, and Dallas hang out all the time; you never see one without the other two.

8. Jacqueline and Maddy are best friends, yet they only hang out on weekends.

9. Morpheus is the valedictorian of his senior class: Among all the seniors, he has the highest grade point average.

10. Janice is the salutatorian of her senior class, for she has the second highest GPA.

11. Morpheus didn't expect to receive his academic title, nor did Janice expect to receive hers.

12. Their parents were so proud of these high achievers, but they were also quite surprised.

13. The athletic awards were announced at the Awards Night ceremony last night, and it was an exciting event!

14. Some creative awards were given; for example, one student received the Most Enthusiastic Student in an Online Class award.

EXERCISE 10-2

Find and correct one error in each of the compound sentences below. You may find an error in grammar, punctuation, or meaning. In some cases, there may be more than one way to make each compound sentence grammatically correct. Write what's wrong, why it's incorrect, and how to make it correct.

1. Soccer is a fun game to play, however, water polo is even more fun.

2. I didn't have enough time. So, I didn't go to the library.

3. We can make and bring lunch to school, nor can we go to a deli for sandwiches at lunchtime.

4. I can't dance, and I can sing.

5. Math homework is never fun; but, I love English homework.

6. Sarah got a job at the bagel shop: she imagines driving her dream car.

7. Mr. Wittmer uses the whiteboard in every class; yet, none of the students can read his writing.

8. I finally got glasses, as a result, I can finally read the board in all of my classes.

9. My mom helps raise money for the school's sports program. In addition, she volunteers at school events.

10. His family is vacationing in Hawaii: And they won't be back for a month.

EXERCISE 10-3

Compose your own compound sentences. Use the four different formulas and a variety of coordinating conjunctions and subordinating adverbs. Follow the prompts.

1. Use **or**.

   _____

2. Use **nor**.

   _____

3. Use **yet**.

   _____

4. Use SV; SV.

   _____

5 Use SV: SV.

   _____

6 Use the subordinating conjunction **for example**.

   _____

7   Use the subordinating conjunction **nonetheless**.

_____

8   Use the subordinating conjunction **rather**.

_____

EXERCISE 10-4

Read the complex sentences with adverb clauses below and identify which type of adverb clause it is. Then, identify the main clause and adverb clause in each sentence by underlining the <u>main clause</u> and putting brackets around the [adverb clause]. Highlight the subordinating conjunction. Finally, find and label the subject (S) and verb (V) in each clause. Use capital S and V for the main clause and lower case s and v for the adverb clause. Follow the example.

> **Example:** [Because Manny and Darlene were running late,]
> s   v
> <u>they got a ride to school</u>. [Reason]
> S V

1. Once class was over, he called his girlfriend.

2. Jake's little brother followed Jake anywhere he went.

3. As it has been raining for three days, the baseball game will be rescheduled.

4. In order that we can mail you the certificate, please send us your mailing address.

5. Even though I studied for this exam for two weeks, I didn't pass.

6. My parents are very strict with curfews, whereas Shelly's parents are very lenient.

7. He ran through the halls as if his hair was on fire!

8. I'll help you with your biology project only if you make my lunch for a week.

EXERCISE 10-5

Read the following complex sentences with adverb clauses. Some of the sentences are correct; however, some are incorrect. Write C next to the correct ones. Find and correct one error in each of the incorrect sentences below. It may be a grammar, punctuation, or meaning error. In some cases, there may be more than one way to correct it. Write what's wrong, why it's incorrect, and how to make it correct.

1. While he turned 16, he got his driver's license.

2. Wherever Penelope went in her backyard; her chicks followed her.

3. You can order coffee for me, since you know what I like.

4. I'm sick today. Please take notes for me in algebra so that I don't miss anything.

5. Although she's usually an honest student, she cheated on her midterm exam.

6. I study every night during the week while my sister studies all weekend.

7. He gave everyone instructions, as though he were the boss.

8. If or not you come to the game, I'll record it on my phone.

EXERCISE 10-6

Compose your own complex sentences with adverb clauses. Write at least one sentence for each type. Mix up your sentences, with some beginning with the main clause and some beginning with the adverb clause. Review this section of the chapter for help. Follow the prompts and choose a subordinating conjunction you normally don't use.

1. [Adverb clause of time]

    _____

2. [Adverb clause of place]

    _____

3. [Adverb clause of reason]

    _____

4. [Adverb clause of purpose]

    _____

5. [Adverb clause of concession]

    _____

6. [Adverb clause of direct contrast]

    _____

7. [Adverb clause of manner]

    _____

8. [Adverb clause of condition]

    _____

EXERCISE 10-7

Read the complex sentences with adjective clauses below. Identify the main clause and adjective clause in each sentence by underlining the <u>main clause</u> and putting brackets around the [adjective clause]. Highlight the relative pronoun and double underline the <u>modified noun</u>. Next, find and label the subject (S) and verb (V) in each clause. Use capital S and V for the main clause and lower case s and v for the adverb clause. Then, mark what type of relative pronoun is used—subject or object—and what it modifies. Finally, determine whether it's a restrictive or nonrestrictive clause. Follow the example.

Example: The class completed the geology project, which took a whole month.

which – subj rel pro / modifies OV / nonrestrictive

<u>The class completed the geology project</u>, [which took a whole month.]
    S   V   s   v

1. He chose the class that had the least amount of homework.

2. Would you recommend Mrs. Walter, whom you had for interior design?

3. It's sunny and hot today, which is perfect for the park.

4. My neighbor, whose cat hunts every day, found a dead bird on her porch.

5. Every weekend, Candice walks across the Golden Gate Bridge, which is 1.7 miles long.

6. With binoculars, we spotted an osprey that was perched on a branch in our cypress tree.

7. My identical twin cousins, whom I can't tell apart, play tricks on me.

8. Can we have breakfast at the café that you love?

EXERCISE 10-8

Read the following complex sentences with adjective clauses. Choose the best relative pronoun. In some cases, more than one relative pronoun is possible. Consult the appropriate sections in this chapter for help.

1. She is the mother <u>that / who / whom / whose / which / Ø</u> daughter won the scholarship.

2. When will she visit her relatives <u>that / who / whom / whose / which / Ø</u> live in Vermont?

3. Xiaolin performed very well in the recital, <u>that / who / whom / whose / which / Ø</u> took place last night.

4. We drove down the Pacific Coast Highway to Los Angeles, <u>that / who / whom / whose / which / Ø</u> was fun.

5. Marybeth and her little sister, <u>that / who / whom / whose / which / Ø</u> is only 10 years old, hiked 25 percent of the Appalachian Trail last summer.

6. Solomon and Neil found gold flakes near a stream <u>that / who / whom / whose / which / Ø</u> was hidden under thick bushes.

7. What is the name of that movie <u>that / who / whom / whose / which / Ø</u> you watch every year at Thanksgiving?

8. The player <u>that / who / whom / whose / which / Ø</u> got injured is finally back on the team.

EXERCISE 10-9

Compose your own complex sentences with adjective clauses. Mix up your sentences with subject relative pronouns, object relative pronouns, and whose. Write both restrictive and nonrestrictive clauses. Follow the prompts. R = restrictive / NR = nonrestrictive

1. [R / subject relative pronoun]

   _____

2. [R / object relative pronoun – OV]

   _____

3. [R / object relative pronoun – OP]

   _____

4. [R / whose]

   _____

5. [NR / subject relative pronoun]

   _____

6. [NR / object relative pronoun – OV]

   _____

7. [NR / whose]

   _____

EXERCISE 10-10

Read the complex sentences with noun clauses below. Identify the main clause and noun clause in each sentence by underlining the main clause and putting brackets around the [noun clause]. Highlight the word that begins the noun clause and mark its position in the sentence. Finally, find and label the subject (S) and verb (V) in each clause. Use capital S and V for the main clause and lower case s and v for the adverb clause. Follow the example.

> **Example:** <u>I don't know</u> [when the show begins.] = WH question word / OV
>   S   V   s   v

1. Do you like how the poster looks?

2. She asked if we are going to the mall.

3. They are sure that it's going to be a sunny day.

4. We believe our team will win.

5. It's fascinating how the ballerina moves so gracefully.

6. Can I find out how I did on the quiz?

7. The fact that you make good decisions is a plus.

8. The question is whether or not we'll have the party.

EXERCISE 10-11

Read the following complex sentences with noun clauses. Choose the best word to begin each noun clause. In some cases, more than one is possible. Consult the appropriate sections in this chapter for help.

1. I'm not certain <u>that / the fact that / Ø / when / how / where / if / whether / whether or not</u> he'll come soon.

2. <u>That / The fact that / Ø / When / How / Where / If / Whether or not</u> he's not here yet worries me.

3. Can you ask <u>that / the fact that / Ø / when / how / where / if / whether or not</u> he's coming?

4. I'll be disappointed <u>when / how / where / if / whether</u> he doesn't show up.

EXERCISE 10-12

Compose your own complex sentences with noun clauses. Mix up your sentences by writing noun clauses in different positions of the sentence and using a variety of words to begin the noun clause. Write about your life and the people you know. Follow the prompts provided.

1. [Subject position – *that/the fact that*]

   _____

2. [OV position – *if/whether or not*]

   _____

3. [SC position – *that or Ø*]

   _____

4. [Following an adjective – *that or Ø*]

   _____

EXERCISE 10-13

Read the compound-complex sentences below. Identify all the clauses in each sentence by underlining the <u>main clauses</u> and putting brackets around the [subordinate clauses]. Highlight the word that begins each subordinate clause and write down what type of clause it is—adverb, adjective, or noun. Finally, find and label the subject (S) and verb (V) in each clause. Use capital S and V for the main clauses and lower case s and v for the adverb clauses. Follow the example.

> **Example:** <u>Seymour plays tennis,</u> but <u>he can't play</u>
>   S   V   S   V
> [until his broken arm heals.]
>   s   v
>
> *adverb clause of time* _____

1. How he broke his arm is a mystery, so let's find out.

   _____

2. Although it'll take six to eight weeks to heal, he doesn't mind: it's an opportunity to relax.

   _____

3. Ginger, who is Seymour's sister, lives with him and she can help him with daily activities.

   _____

4. Ginger is a registered nurse who specializes in pediatrics, so she's the perfect one to help him.

   _____

EXERCISE 10-14

Compose your own compound-complex sentences. Mix them up by using the four different structures for compound sentences and by including different types of subordinate clauses. Refer back to the appropriate sections in this chapter for guidance. Write about your life and the people you know. Follow the prompts provided.

1. [Compound-complex sentence with adverb clause of reason]

   _____

2. [Compound-complex sentence with noun clause in any position]

   _____

3. [Compound-complex sentence with adverb clause of time]

   _____

4. [Compound-complex sentence with NR adjective clause]

   _____

AUDIO

Writing Paragraphs and Essays

MUST KNOW

- A writer's claim (main idea) must be supported with relevant, precise, and concise statements.

- Body paragraphs should begin with a clear, direct topic sentence to guide the reader.

- Transition words and phrases should be used to introduce your point and to move from one point to another.

Being able to write focused, coherent paragraphs and essays in school is essential. An effective paragraph or essay holds the reader's interest. A good writer does not include words or ideas that aren't necessary to the main idea. Focused writing also avoids unnecessary repetition and rambling sentence structures, so be sure you understand the various sentence structures described in Chapter 7 and Chapter 10 and you are comfortable composing them. In this chapter, we will discuss the writing process and look at the structure of a classic five-paragraph essay.

The Writing Process

The writing process is a step-by-step procedure to help you write an academic paragraph or essay. There are five basic stages in the writing process:

1. Prewriting

2. Drafting

3. Revising

4. Editing

5. Publishing

We will look at each of these stages in more detail, but first let's talk about the purpose of academic writing.

Considering Purpose

We write academic paragraphs and essays for different purposes, including to inform, to describe, and to persuade. A writer must consider his or her purpose for writing.

- Are you writing <u>to give information</u>?

- Are you writing <u>to describe a process</u>?

- Are you writing <u>to persuade the reader to agree with your position</u> on a controversial topic?

Knowing the purpose of your writing is helpful and time-saving. It's an essential part of the first stage in the writing process—prewriting.

Prewriting

Prewriting is the stage in which you plan what you will write. There are a few essential tasks to complete during prewriting.

Step 1: Understand the writing assignment. Ask questions if you are unclear about any part of the assignment. Check your understanding by answering these questions for yourself:

- What is the topic of this writing assignment?

- What are the requirements?

- Who is the audience for this writing assignment? In other words, who is the reader?

- What is the purpose of this writing? Is it to entertain, inform, describe, or persuade?

- What questions do I have about this assignment?

Step 2: Generate ideas for your topic. This is also known as *brainstorming*. There are several ways to brainstorm. Here are three of my favorite ways:

- **List** your ideas.

- Make a **mind map** (also called **clustering**) to generate and connect ideas.

- **Freewrite** without stopping for ten minutes.

Step 3: Organize your ideas and write an outline for your paragraph or essay. Focus on your main idea or **thesis**. The thesis of an essay states the writer's overall main point for the essay. For a paragraph, we use a **topic sentence** that states the main idea of the paragraph.

Step 4: Do research on your topic if needed or required. You may need to use a library database or other scholarly source.

Drafting

In the drafting stage, you will write the first draft of your paragraph or essay. This is a rough draft, so don't worry about things such as spelling, grammar, or punctuation. You just want to get your ideas on paper. Follow the outline you made while prewriting. Be sure to follow whichever writing style your educational institution requires, such as APA, MLA, or *The Chicago Manual of Style*. You don't have to worry about specific details of citation style at this point, but follow the basic format required. This will save you time later.

Revising

During revision, you will make changes to improve the draft of your paragraph or essay. At this stage, you should review the big picture; don't worry about the small details yet. Use a checklist to review your draft by yourself, with a peer, and/or with your instructor.

Recommended: Save your document using the "Save As" function so that every draft is saved, as you may need to refer back to an earlier draft.

Here are the essential things you should look at during revision:

Step 1: Refer back to the writing assignment to check that you are adhering to the requirements. If your instructor provides a grading rubric, study it so you know how your writing will be evaluated. Be sure you are following the writing assignment instructions carefully. Did you answer the prompt thoroughly and clearly?

Step 2: Check your thesis statement to be sure it is clear and concise. Check each body paragraph to be sure it begins with a topic sentence. Refer back to your outline to be sure you followed it and stayed on topic.

Step 3: Consider the logical organization of your paragraph or essay (also known as *coherence*). Does the sequence of ideas make sense? Is it logical? Do your body paragraphs flow well from one to the other? What changes do you need to make to improve the readability of your essay?

Step 4: Find your transition words and phrases. Are they correctly used? Do they clearly and accurately introduce and connect ideas? Ultimately, are all your ideas and sentences connected well? (When ideas are connected well, it's called *cohesion*.)

Following these steps, rewrite your paragraph or essay. You may need to repeat these steps more than once. It is common for writers to write several drafts before finalizing their paragraph or essay.

Editing

Now it's time to consider the details! During editing, or **proofreading**, check your draft for formatting issues, grammar, and mechanics. Mechanics refers to spelling, capitalization, and punctuation. It may be helpful to review these items one at a time. Ask your instructor for a checklist to help you during this stage of writing, too.

- Check for **spelling errors.** A spell-check program can help you with this, but keep in mind that a spell-check program will not catch a mistake if what you wrote is a word, but not the correct word for the context. For example, if you wrote *fairy* when you meant to write *fairly*, spell-checking apps may not "see" that as a mistake.

- Check your draft for **capitalization** of names and titles.

- Check your **verbs** to be sure they are in the proper tense and agree with their subjects.

- Be sure all your **sentences are complete** and that you do not have any fragments or run-on sentences.

- Check your **pronouns and modifiers**. Do they match?

- Check **punctuation** (end-of-sentence punctuation; use of commas, semi-colons, and colons; and use of quotation marks).

- Check the **formatting** of your essay, including the header, title, page numbers, and citations if required.

Publishing

Once you have checked everything for accuracy, it's time to submit your final paragraph or essay! Congratulations: You did it!

The Classic Five-Paragraph Essay Structure

In a classic five-paragraph essay, the first paragraph is the introduction, the last paragraph is the conclusion, and we call the paragraphs in the middle *body paragraphs* because they compose the body of the essay. Study the basic structure of an essay below. Pay special attention to the structure of a body paragraph.

Introduction

The introduction is the first thing anyone will read, so it needs to be interesting and well-written. The introduction paragraph consists of an opening hook, background information on the topic, and the thesis statement. It flows from general background on the topic to the much more specific thesis statement, which narrows the topic.

Opening Hook

An opening hook **grabs the reader's attention**. There are several types of opening hooks that can be used, such as:

- a compelling fact
- a fascinating anecdote
- a quote
- a question
- a surprising true statement

Background Information

After the opening hook, the introduction should provide some general background information **to create context** so that the reader understands the topic. This may include providing historical context or defining terms the reader will need to understand. Then it may provide more specific and focused information to prepare the reader for the thesis statement.

Thesis Statement

At the end of the introduction paragraph, write your thesis statement. This is a sentence stating **the main idea of the essay**, and it should include a preview of the the essay's organization.

Body Paragraphs

The body of your essay should contain two or more body paragraphs that support the thesis statement. In a classic five-paragraph essay, there are three body paragraphs. The first body paragraph discusses the first point made in the thesis statement, the second body paragraph discusses the second element found in the thesis statement, and the third body paragraph discusses the third aspect mentioned in the thesis statement. It's important to understand how to write a logical, cohesive, and clear body paragraph whether it stands all by itself or is part of an essay.

Topic Sentence

Each body paragraph should begin with a focused and clear topic sentence. The topic sentence **expresses the main idea of the paragraph and consists of a topic and a controlling idea**, which restricts (or controls) the topic. The topic is the subject of the body paragraph. The controlling idea answers the question, "What about the topic?" It narrows the focus of the topic and should provide one to three main points about the topic. Think of the topic sentence as a mini thesis statement!

Supporting Details

After the topic sentence, each body paragraph usually discusses **one to three main points about the topic** stated in the topic sentence. The main points are usually categorical: reasons, benefits, advantages, disadvantages, types, causes, and effects. For each main point, there are several supporting details. There are many types of details that may be used, including explanations, descriptions, examples, facts, statistics, and quotations.

Summary Statement

Each body paragraph should end with a summary statement that **sums up the topic and ties it back to the overall thesis**. Sometimes, the body paragraph includes a transition to connect it to the next body paragraph. This transition can be part of the same sentence as the summary statement or in a separate sentence. If you are writing a stand-alone paragraph, no transition is needed; just end the paragraph with a summary statement.

Conclusion

Following all the body paragraphs, the essay should include a concluding paragraph. In this paragraph, academic writers usually **rephrase the thesis statement and summarize the main ideas of the essay**. You can explain the significance of the thesis (why the reader should care about what you have written). End the concluding paragraph with a final thought for the reader to ponder. This paragraph is essentially a mirror image of the introduction in that it flows from the specific thesis to general significance.

Transitions

To connect body paragraphs to one another and to connect the sentences within a body paragraph, we use transition words and phrases. These connectors signal to the reader what is coming. Transitions create cohesion, which is critical in academic writing. Below are examples of transitions we use to introduce a main point, add a similar idea, and introduce the concluding sentence. Note that there are many other types of transitions.

Transitions to Introduce Main Points

- First, second, third, etc.

- First of all,

- Next, then, finally

- Firstly, secondly, thirdly*

- The first reason / benefit / advantage . . . / The next reason / benefit / advantage . . . / Another reason / benefit / advantage . . . / The last reason / benefit / advantage . . .

 IRL *Although it's grammatical, some grammarians think the *–ly* form is unnecessary.

Transitions to Add a Similar Idea

- Furthermore,
- Moreover,
- In addition,

- Additionally,
- Also,
- Another

- Equally important
- Likewise,
- In the same way,

Transitions to Conclude

- Therefore,
- Finally,
- In conclusion,

- To summarize,
- To sum up,
- All in all,

- In brief,
- In short,
- Indeed,

Example Writing Assignment

Let's take a look at an example writing assignment and an example essay. Check the Appendix for brainstorming and outline samples for this essay.

Prompt: What are your favorite ethnic foods and why? Discuss three of your favorite types of cuisine and explain your reasons. Write a five-paragraph essay addressing the prompt. You must have an introductory paragraph, three body paragraphs, and a concluding paragraph.

Example: Five-Paragraph Essay

Thai, Italian, and Mexican Cuisines Are My Favorites

Cuisine from almost every country in the world can be found and enjoyed in the United States. From Cuban and Greek to Jamaican and French, ethnic cuisine's popularity has grown in the last few decades. Asian cuisine from countries such as China and its many provinces, Korea, Japan, Vietnam, and India have become commonplace. Italian and Mexican food are such staples in most American cities and towns that they are often thought of as American food. The more exotic foods, such as Moroccan, Ethiopian, and Peruvian, are fast becoming new favorites for many. Although every ethnic cuisine offers unique combinations of food and spices, my three favorite types are Thai, Italian, and Mexican.

The first of my favorite cuisines is Thai food because of its curry sauces. Three types of curry—red, green, and yellow—are offered with a variety of dishes. I love all the curries! The yellow curry is made with turmeric, a bright yellow-orange root, so it is slightly sweet and tangy, while the red and green curries are made with red and green peppers, which give them a hot, spicy kick. Of the red and green, I prefer red curry because it has a deep, almost smoky hot flavor, whereas the green curry is a bit milder. All of the curries go well with seafood, chicken, and vegetables in a bowl with white rice. I order something different from the menu every time I go to a Thai restaurant, but one of the most delicious recipes is shrimp with coconut in a red curry sauce. Indeed, no matter which Thai dish I order, I am always satisfied when it is served with curry.

Another delicious cuisine is Italian food with its romantic ambience. Not only does Italian food taste great, but it also comes with a wonderful dining experience when it is in a high-end restaurant. First, I have never had a bad Italian dish: every recipe has been delectable. The meat dishes are always cooked to perfection and seasoned with fresh, savory herbs such as oregano, basil, and thyme. An example of this is Italian ribeye, which is grilled steak with a glaze of oregano, basil, garlic, rosemary, balsamic vinegar, and a pinch of salt. With its medley of flavors, it simply melts in your mouth. Seafood dishes are also tender and flavorful and never over spiced. For instance, frutti di mare is a large bowl of clams, mussels, shrimp, scallops, and squid on a bed of spaghetti and lightly seasoned with a white wine sauce of garlic, lemon, and fresh basil leaves. The minimal seasoning brings out the natural flavors of the seafood for a divine experience. In addition to the heavenly tasting food is the relaxing atmosphere that good Italian restaurants provide. While enjoying a perfectly prepared meal, I can also surrender to the romantic ambience. Italian restauranteurs know how to create a welcoming and calming environment for its patrons. With low lights, candles, soothing music, and friendly servers, I am able to savor every bite with my special someone. All in all, a good Italian restaurant reliably delivers delicious meals in a lovely, romantic atmosphere.

With its spicy hot taco recipes, the third cuisine I enjoy most is Mexican food. Food that is prepared in an authentic Mexican style can please almost any palate, but I especially love the picante—spicy hot—dishes. From taco trucks to large restaurants, it is easy to find a variety of delicious menu items, but my all-time favorite dish is soft tacos with homemade corn tortillas. These homemade soft tacos are served warm in a towel-covered basket to keep in the heat and moisture. They smell like a cozy, warm home to me. On top of these tacos is a meat of choice and plenty of toppings. Depending on my mood, I choose either carnitas (slow-cooked pork), fish, or chicken for my meat. If I am lucky, I can get one of each in my entree. With the warm soft taco laid out flat on my plate, I pile on the carnitas, some refried beans, a little bit of rice, freshly made hot salsa, and a dollop of guacamole. I then roll it up and eat the taco with my hands. Between each of the tacos, I munch on the pickled carrots, green onions, and radishes that come as a side dish. These have a particularly sharp kick of spiciness and tang, which I enjoy. When I come to the third of my three soft tacos, I always feel sad because I do not want the scrumptious experience to end! The good news, however, is that I can always return and get more of my favorite authentic Mexican recipes: soft tacos.

In conclusion, for a delightful eating experience, my top three favorite cuisines are Thai, Italian, and Mexican. First, Thai offers myriad recipes with tasty curry sauces in three distinct flavors. Second, Italian food not only provides delectable meat and seafood dishes with just the right amount of seasoning, but it also offers an ambient environment in which to enjoy the food. Finally, Mexican cuisine includes spicy hot soft tacos with different meat and topping options. Even though these are my current favorite types of cuisine, I imagine I will have other favorite ethnic foods someday. After all, variety is the spice of life!

EXERCISES

EXERCISE 11-1

Can you identify all the components of the example essay you just read?

1. Identify the introductory paragraph as well as its components: the hook and the sentences that go from general to specific leading to the thesis.

2. Find and label the thesis statement. In the thesis statement, look for three main items that the body paragraphs discuss. Underline these three items and number them 1, 2, and 3.

3. Label each body paragraph as BP1, BP2, and BP3. Check to be sure that BP1 addresses the first item in the thesis, BP2 matches the second item in the thesis, and BP3 discusses the third item in the thesis. Do this by reading the topic sentence for each body paragraph. Double underline each topic sentence for all body paragraphs.

4. Find the concluding paragraph. Does it restate the thesis statement, summarize the main points of the essay, and leave the reader with a final thought? Identify these elements. Does it go from specific to general?

EXERCISE 11-2

Now reread each body paragraph in the example essay. Find all the following elements.

1. Find the topic sentence for each body paragraph. Is it the main idea of that body paragraph?

   BP1: _____

   BP2: _____

   BP3: _____

2. Look at the supporting details for the second body paragraph. Determine what type of support each detail provides. It could be a main point, an explanation, an example, a reason, to paraphrase, or for more information. Label as many as you can.

_____   _____

_____   _____

_____   _____

3. Locate each summary statement. Does each summary statement relate back to the topic sentence and the overall thesis?

BP1: _____

BP2: _____

BP3: _____

EXERCISE 11-3

Go back to the example essay and find these transitions in each of the body paragraphs.

1. Highlight and label the transitions that signal a similar idea.

2. Find and double underline <u>context clues that signal examples</u>.

3. Label **context clues that signal contrasting ideas**. In the Answer Key, you'll see these in bold.

4. Identify *context clues that signal a definition*. In the Answer Key, these are in italics.

5. Circle the transition that introduces the concluding sentence.

AUDIO 🔊

Flashcard App

Answer Key

1

Meeting People

Situation 1: 4:00 p.m. CST. *Good afternoon.* Washington, DC, is in the Eastern time zone and it's 5:00 p.m. EST when John makes the call. Jeremy lives in Texas, which is in the Central time zone. CST is one hour earlier than EST, so it's 4:00 p.m. in Texas when John calls his friend. Therefore, John would appropriately say *Good afternoon.*

Situation 2: 10:00 a.m. PST. *Good morning.* Chicago, IL is in the Central time zone and it's 12:00 p.m. CST when Monique FaceTimes her cousin, who lives in San Diego, CA. CA is in the Pacific time zone, and since PST is two hours earlier than CST, it's 10:00 a.m. in San Diego when Monique calls her cousin. Therefore, Monique would appropriately say *Good morning* to her cousin.

Situation 3: 11:00 a.m. EST. *Good morning.* Seattle, Washington, is in the Pacific time zone and it's 8:00 a.m. PST when Mr. and Mrs. Butrago make the video call. The grandparents live in Florida, which is in the Eastern time zone. EST is three hours earlier than PST, so it's 11:00 a.m. in Fort Lauderdale when they make the video call. Therefore, the Butragos would appropriately say *Good morning.*

EXERCISE 1-2

Answers may vary, but here are some possible answers.

1. Neutral: Hello. / Hello there. / How are you? / How are you doing?

   Responses: Hello. / Hello there. / I'm good, thanks. / I'm doing great!

2. Formal: Good morning. / Good afternoon. / Good evening.

   Responses: Good morning. / Good afternoon. / Good evening. / Hello.

3. Informal: Hi. / Hi there. / Hey. / Hey there. / Howdy. / What's happening?

   Responses: Hi. / Hey there. / Nothing much.

4. Very informal: Yo! / What's up?

   Responses: Yo! / Not much. You? / Hey!

EXERCISE 1-3

1. T	3. T	5. T	7. F	9. F
2. F	4. F	6. T	8. T	10. T

EXERCISE 1-4

1. a, b   2. c

EXERCISE 1-5

1. Is she smart?
2. Does she go to the same school?
3. When does class start?
4. Where is the cafeteria?
5. How are you?
6. Do they study every night?
7. How do I get an A in this class?
8. What is his name?

9. Are you okay?

10. Why is she late?

Note that questions 2 and 6 use the DO auxiliary because the main verb is not the BE verb. Questions 1 and 9 use BE, so you simply use question word order, in which the BE verb comes before the subject. Questions 3, 4, 5, 7, 8, and 10 are all information (WH) questions. Questions 4, 5, 8, and 10 are information questions with the BE verb. Questions 3 and 7 are information questions that use other verbs, so the DO auxiliary is required.

Talking About Habits, Routines, Customs, and Schedules

PRACTICE 2-A

1. Sentences 2, 4, 6, 10

2. Sentences with 2 prepositional phrases of time: #3, 6, 8

   Sentence with 3 prepositional phrases of time: #7

EXERCISE 2-1

1. wake up	3. drinks	5. drive	7. gives	9. swims
2. takes	4. enjoy	6. go	8. has	10. brings

EXERCISE 2-2

1. are	3. are	5. are	7. are	9. am
2. is	4. is	6. is	8. are	10. am

EXERCISE 2-3

1. Does	3. Do	5. does	7. does	9. Does
2. does	4. do	6. do	8. do	10. do

EXERCISE 2-4

1. Perry doesn't play hockey.
2. Jack doesn't take the bus to school.
3. My parents don't drive to work.
4. Grace doesn't work after school.
5. Sandi and Jana don't study a lot.
6. Vivek doesn't worry about tests.
7. Sheena and Takako don't like pizza.
8. I don't drink coffee in the afternoon.
9. We don't want any more pop quizzes.
10. You don't arrive on time.

EXERCISE 2-5

1. Jane is hardly ever late for school.
2. The owner usually opens the café by 5:30 a.m.
3. My aunt and uncle are always happy.
4. Jonah and his brother sometimes attend temple services with their parents.
5. The Smiths are rarely home over the summer.
6. He frequently misses history class in the morning.

EXERCISE 2-6

1. He's happy at this school, <u>isn't he</u>?
2. There are some seniors here, <u>aren't there</u>?
3. Paul isn't with you, <u>is he</u>?
4. Sammy and Jen like it, <u>don't they</u>?
5. No one believes it, <u>do they</u>?

6. Maria doesn't want it, <u>does she</u>?

7. There is only one winner, <u>isn't there</u>?

8. Aidan and Finn eat sushi, <u>don't they</u>?

9. They don't feel sick, <u>do they</u>?

10. You understand it, <u>don't you</u>?

EXERCISE 2-7

1. The last bus to Mendocino arrives at the station at 9:00 a.m.

2. The Fort Bragg 34 bus runs until 8:30 a.m.

3. The Willits 15 bus comes every 15 minutes from 5:00 a.m. to 6:30 a.m.

4. The Albion 9 runs every hour on the hour from 4:00 a.m. to 8:00 a.m.

5. The Little River 14 and the Ukiah 11 run for only one hour in the morning.

EXERCISE 2-8

Answers may vary for this exercise. See two possible correct statements below.

1. The Mendocino 23 comes every 30 minutes from 6:00 a.m. to 9:00 a.m.

   The Mendocino 23 runs every 30 minutes until 9:00 a.m.

2. The Fort Bragg 91 runs every hour on the hour.

   The Fort Bragg 91 comes every hour on the hour from 7:00 a.m. to 11:00 a.m.

3. The Little River 14 is every 10 minutes from 6:00 a.m. to 7:00 a.m.

   The Little River 14 goes to Mendocino every 10 minutes until 7:00 a.m.

4. The Ukiah 26 goes to Mendocino every half hour from 7:00 a.m. to 9:30 a.m.

   The Ukiah 26 runs every half hour from 7:00 a.m. to 9:30 a.m.

EXERCISE 2-9

Answers will vary for this exercise. Refer back to the example conversation in the appropriate lesson in this chapter.

Describing People, Places, and Things

PRACTICE 3-A

1. <u>In the fridge</u>, there is a homemade dessert for you.
2. There are some very heavy textbooks <u>on the table</u>. Are they yours?*
3. <u>On the door</u>, there's a small sign. What does it say?
4. <u>In the glove compartment</u>, there are two state maps. Please hand them to me.
5. There are some wonderfully fragrant flowers <u>on the table</u>.*
6. <u>In my class</u>, there are 20 diligent students.
7. There is a new teacher <u>at the front</u> of the classroom.*
8. <u>Along the dusty road</u>, there are beautiful wild flowers.
9. There is something black <u>in your hair</u>!*
10. There are dozens of colorful Koi fish <u>in that little pond</u> <u>outside the restaurant</u>.*

PRACTICE 3-B

Answers for this practice will vary, but you can see some example sentences below.

Start with *There's* and *There are* Quantity: Plural or Singular?	Start with the Location or Position Quantity: Plural or Singular?
There are some potatoes <u>in the cupboard</u>. (Quantity = plural)	<u>Next to that rock</u>, there is a big ugly spider. (Quantity = singular)
There's a mysterious package <u>on the desk</u>. (Quantity = singular)	<u>At the end of the road</u>, there are three houses. (Quantity = plural)
<u>There are some people by the entrance.</u> (Quantity = plural)	<u>After the convenient store</u>, there is a large office building. (Quantity = singular)

PRACTICE 3-C

There are some apples <u>in the pantry</u>.	<u>Under the back porch</u>, there's some firewood.
<u>After the gas station</u>, there's a three-way intersection.	My car is <u>next to the red sports car</u>.
<u>At the crooked stop sign</u>, take a right.	She walked <u>toward the store entrance</u>.
They arrived <u>at the hospital</u> just <u>in time</u>.	There's a cell phone <u>on the desk</u>.
My exam is <u>in the regular classroom</u>.	Are we walking <u>to where he parked his car</u>?
Take a left just <u>before the big grocery store</u>.	<u>Beyond the parking lot</u>, there is a lovely French café.

PRACTICE 3-D

1. Rosie is <u>the tallest</u> person in the room. (superlative)
2. That building is <u>shorter than</u> the hospital. (comparative)
3. The mansion is <u>more ornate than</u> the church. (comparative)
4. Main Street is <u>wider than</u> River Road. (comparative)
5. My sister is <u>more fun than</u> my brother. (comparative)
6. The ferry building is <u>the closest</u> one to the bay. (superlative)

PRACTICE 3-E

I'm so <u>tired</u> after that workout.

That workout routine is <u>tiring</u>.

They're <u>confused</u> by the math equation.

The math equation is <u>confusing</u> to them.

She's <u>excited</u> to graduate high school!

Graduating high school is <u>exciting</u>!

My cousins are <u>bored</u> at the party.

The party is <u>boring</u>.

PRACTICE 3-F

1. At 5:00 p.m., <u>turn on</u> the news. (This is a phrasal verb.)
2. To start the car, <u>push</u> the key in and <u>step</u> on the brake at the same time.
3. <u>Bake</u> the pizza in the oven until the cheese is slightly brown.
4. <u>Switch</u> the lights on, please!
5. <u>Be</u> nice and gentle. This glass vase is delicate.
6. <u>Enter</u> the theater quietly.
7. <u>Eat</u> all your vegetables!
8. Please <u>go</u> to the whiteboard and <u>write</u> your answers on the appropriate lines.

PRACTICE 3-G

1. <u>Don't be</u> late!

2. It's very valuable. Please <u>be</u> careful! <u>Don't break</u> it.

3. <u>Don't take</u> a right there. <u>Take</u> a left.

4. For the test, <u>don't copy</u> anyone else. <u>Do</u> your own work.

5. <u>Don't forget</u> to bring the flowers, please!

6. To beat your opponent, <u>don't waste</u> time.

7. <u>Don't be</u> silly. This is serious.

8. <u>Don't park</u> on the street. <u>Park</u> in the parking lot.

PRACTICE 3-H

Situation 1

Ms. Jennings: (For) homework), <u>study</u> pages 33–37 and then <u>complete</u> the assignment (on page 38). <u>Come</u> (to class) (with your work) (on paper), which I will collect.

Cecilia raises hand.

Ms. Jennings: Yes, Cecilia?

Cecilia: I don't understand the instructions (on page 38). <u>How can I</u> conduct this experiment (at home)?

Ms. Jennings: Good question. <u>Use</u> your kitchen sink, a glass jar, regular food coloring, and tap water. <u>Follow</u> the step-by-step instructions (in the book). Also, <u>use</u> the math equation we learned this week. <u>Take</u> notes (on every reaction) you see. <u>Put</u> the math and your notes (on paper), so I can see all (of your work): <u>show</u> me every step. <u>Use</u> a calculator if necessary, but you still need to show me every step. Otherwise, you will lose points.

Cecilia: So, it's okay to use tap water. Okay, I got it. Thank you.

Situation 2

Julio: Sean, please close up* the store tonight. I can't be here to do it.

Sean: I've never closed the store before. How should I do that?

Julio: Oh, you've never closed? Okay, well there are instructions (under the counter). Carefully follow all five steps. Call or text me any questions. Barry usually closes and he's around, so you can call him, too. Make sure to turn on* the alarm before you lock the door. I receive a notification (from the alarm company) when it's turned on* and off*, so I'll know. Got it?

Sean: Sure, okay. It'll be fine. I have your number and Barry's number, too, so I'm good.

Julio: You can do it, Sean. Thank you.

*These are phrasal verbs: *Close up, turn on,* and *turn off.* The noun that follows a phrasal verb is a direct object, not part of a prepositional phrase.

Situation 3

Irving: Hello, excuse me!

Person at gas pump: Yeah?

Irving: Could you tell me where there's a grocery store (near here)?

Person at gas pump: Oh yeah sure. There's a small one two blocks (from here), and there's a big one just (off the highway).

Irving: The small one is perfect.

Person at gas pump: Okay that's easy. Just go (down this street) (for one block), then make a right. One block down, it'll be (on your right).

Irving: So, one block (down here), take a right, and one more block?

Person at gas pump: Yup.

Irving: Thank you!

Person at gas pump: No problem.

Situation 4

Cheryl: Excuse me. <u>Would you know where there's a</u> good place to get a sandwich nearby?

Person at bus stop: Yeah sure. There's a deli (down) there) and a soup and salad place (over) there).

Cheryl: How about* the deli?

Person at bus stop: Just <u>walk</u> a few blocks (down) Main Street) until** you see the library. The deli is (across) the street) (from) the library).

Cheryl: Is the soup and salad place closer?

Person at bus stop: It's (about) the same). <u>Go</u> (up) Main), <u>turn</u> left (on) Aspen), and <u>walk</u> (to) the end) (of) the street).

Cheryl: Okay, so Main and (to) the end) (of) Aspen Street).

Person at bus stop: <u>Don't forget</u> to go *left* (on) Aspen).

Cheryl: Right: left (on) Aspen). Thank you so much!

Person at bus stop: No worries.

*How about is a WH question word here, not the stand-alone preposition *about*.
**Until can be a preposition, but here it is used as a conjunction.

PRACTICE 3-I

Original Text	Paraphrased Idea
"Injustice anywhere is a threat to justice everywhere." —Martin Luther King Jr., Letter from a Birmingham Jail, 1963	<u>What Martin Luther King Jr. is saying</u> is that if someone is treated <u>*unjustly*</u> in one part of the world, it **negatively affects** justice for all people <u>regardless of their geographic location</u>.

Paraphrasing strategies identified:

<u>Introductory phrase is underlined at the beginning of the paraphrase.</u>

unjustly: different word form for *injustice*

negatively affects: phrase similar to *threat*

<u>regardless of geographic location:</u> a phrase for *everywhere*

"To make a great dream come true, the first requirement is a great capacity to dream; the second is persistence." —Cesar E. Chavez	<u>Cesar Chavez's message is</u> that two important things are *required* to achieve a dream: **One** is for a person **to be able to create big dreams**, and **the other** is for a person to *persist* in making those dreams come true.

Paraphrasing strategies identified:

<u>Introductory phrase is underlined at the beginning of the paraphrase.</u>

Sentence structure is different.

required: a different word form of **requirement**

One: instead of **first**

to be able to create big dreams: phrase that means "great capacity to dream"

the other: instead of **the second**

persist: a different word form of **persistence**

PRACTICE 3-J

Manfred: Hello. Excuse me. What bus <u>takes</u> me to Main Street in Mendocino?

Customer Service Agent: When <u>do</u> you want to go?

Manfred: I'd like to get there by 3 p.m. today.

Customer Service Agent: It<u>'s</u> 1 p.m. now. The #5 Albion bus <u>leaves</u> at 2 p.m.

Manfred: <u>Are</u> there any buses that <u>leave</u> sooner than 1 p.m.?

Customer Service Agent: Not today. It's Sunday, so the buses <u>run</u> on a holiday schedule. The #5 <u>is</u> your best option.

Manfred: Okay, thank you. Where <u>does</u> the bus pick up passengers?

Customer Service Agent: In the back of the station. **Look** for the sign that <u>says</u> "Albion #5" and **wait** there.

Manfred: <u>Okay, so I need to wait at the #3 sign out back?</u>

Customer Service Agent: You got it.

Manfred: Thanks so much! =)

Customer Service Agent: You<u>'re</u> so welcome. =)

PRACTICE 3-K

<u>Although</u> the United States . . .

<u>However,</u> there are many other languages . . .

<u>Though</u> a foreign language . . .

<u>In contrast,</u> many residents . . .

. . . <u>even though</u> my parents grew up . . .

<u>Rather,</u> they learned it on the street.

<u>Instead,</u> I learned French . . .

. . . <u>, but</u> I never became fluent . . .

. . . <u>, whereas</u> adults must use . . .

. . . <u>, while</u> acquiring a language . . .

EXERCISE 3-1

1. <u>*Are there*</u> enough people to play the game?
2. <u>*No, there aren't*</u>.
3. Near the Italian restaurant, <u>*there's*</u> a great nail salon. Go there!
4. <u>*How much*</u> milk <u>*is there*</u> in the fridge?

5. *There's* a little bit.

6. *Is there* enough for my coffee?

7. *Yes, there is.* (Remember: We don't contract *there is* in affirmative answers.)

8. *Where is there* a good bakery around here?

9. At the end of Stone River Road, *there's* a really good bakery.

10. *How many* health classes *are there*?

EXERCISE 3-2

1. *Where is there a bakery near here?*

2. *Is there extra salad for me?* (Note that salad is a noncount noun, so it's singular.)

3. *There's a doctor's office on the corner of Willow Street and C Road.*

4. *There isn't a public library in this small town.*

5. *Is there a pho restaurant nearby?*

6. *How many hospitals are there?*

7. *How much money is there in my wallet?* (Note that money is a noncount noun, so it's singular.)

8. *There isn't enough meat in this sandwich.*

EXERCISE 3-3

1. *Yes, there are.*   *No, there aren't.*

2. *Yes, there is.*   *No, there isn't.*

3. *Yes, there is.*   *No, there isn't.*

4. *Yes, there are.*   *No, there aren't.*

5. *Yes, there is.*   *No, there isn't.*

6. *Yes, there are.*   *No, there aren't.*

EXERCISE 3-4

1. Excuse me. *Is there* a used record shop anywhere?

   No, there isn't, but there is a used clothing store that sells records about a mile from here.

2. Excuse me. *Are there (any)* car wash places?

   Yes, there are. My favorite place is on High Street.

3. *Is there* a deli to get fresh made sandwiches near here?

   Yes, there is. There's a café with a deli counter over there.

4. Hello! *Is there* an athletic shoe store anywhere?

   Yes, there is. I usually go to the mall about 45 minutes away from here.

5. Excuse me. In this town, *is there* a garden store or nursery?

   No, there isn't. It's two towns over.

EXERCISE 3-5

1. *How many yoga studios are there?*
2. *Where is there a good greasy spoon?*
3. *How much traffic is there?*
4. *Where is there a place to donate clothes and household items?*

EXERCISE 3-6

1. *They use a simple, effective, old-fashioned method.*

   These adjectives are all from the opinion/observation category, so commas are necessary.

2. *Karla owns a big fluffy Great Pyrenees dog.*

   (big = size; fluffy = physical quality; Great Pyrenees = origin) Because all of these adjectives are from different categories, don't use a comma.

3. *My daughter lives in a spacious Victorian apartment.*

(spacious = opinion/observation; Victorian = origin) *Spacious* precedes *Victorian* because of the type of adjective it is. No commas are necessary.

4. *Joel attends a well-known British university.*

(well-known = opinion/observation; British = origin) As these adjectives come from different categories, no commas are necessary.

EXERCISE 3-7

Answers will vary for this exercise. See some possible answers below.

adjective: heavy & light; measurement = lbs (pounds)

The science textbook is the heaviest book.

The French textbook is the lightest one.

The math textbook is a little heavier than the history textbook.

The French textbook is easily the lightest one.

adjective: hot & cool; measurement = degrees Fahrenheit

Freshly poured hot green tea is cooler than freshly brewed coffee.

Steam is the hottest.

Boiling water is slightly cooler than steam.

Freshly brewed coffee is hotter than green tea.

Steam is much hotter than green tea.

Steam is a bit hotter than boiling water.

EXERCISE 3-8

1. Melody and Peter are *annoyed* at the large amount of homework. (annoyed / annoying)

2. The dead animal on the road is *disgusting*. (disgusted / disgusting)

3. We are *thrilled* with the long holiday weekend. (thrilled / thrilling)

4. The new amusement park ride is *thrilling*. (thrilled / thrilling)

EXERCISE 3-9

1. *It's a little bit cloudy today.*

2. *She is an extremely talented artist.*

3. *The muffins are nearly ready.*

4. *He gets awfully sleepy after lunch.*

EXERCISE 3-10

Answers will vary for this exercise. To help you, review the appropriate sections of this chapter. For a greater challenge, don't review the lessons in the book. Rather, first write sentences based on what you remember. Then check your work by referring back to the chapter lessons.

EXERCISE 3-11

Answers will vary for this exercise. Challenge yourself! If you're learning English with other students, use another student's map to ask for and give directions to different places.

EXERCISE 3-12

Answers will vary for this exercise. There are many ways to challenge yourself with this exercise. For example, you can use someone else's map or randomly choose a map that you find online.

EXERCISE 3-13

There are several ways to ask for repetition. Here are two examples.

1. *I'm sorry. I didn't catch that. Could you please repeat that, please?*

2. *I'm sorry, what was that?*

EXERCISE 3-14

There are several ways to check your understanding with paraphrase expressions. Here are example ways to do it.

1. *So, I take a left, go past Hyacinth, and the tech store will be on my right halfway down?*

2. *What you're saying is I need to walk up this street, go right at the antique shop, and it's on the left?*

EXERCISE 3-15

Answers will vary for this exercise. It's fun to do this activity with a partner, so if you know another English language learner, do this exercise together!

EXERCISE 3-16

1. <u>Though</u> *a foreign language is required in high school*, <u>most American students rarely learn and understand enough of a new language to have meaningful conversations.</u>

2. <u>I grew up speaking only English</u> <u>even though</u> *my parents grew up speaking Canadian French.*

3. *I learned French as a foreign language in high school*, <u>but</u> <u>I never became fluent because I only used it in French class.</u>

4. <u>Healthy children learn languages easily and naturally</u>, <u>whereas</u> *adults must use their cognitive learning skills.*

EXERCISE 3-17

Answers will vary for this exercise. Here are two ways to paraphrase the quote.

1. What Elizabeth Cady Stanton means is that society believes women are inferior to men. This is because men think women exist mainly to serve them.

2. Elizabeth Cady Stanton is making the point that women are not valued as much as men are in society. Indeed, societal institutions believe that women are created for men.

4
Nouns and Pronouns

EXERCISE 4-1

(Salvator)	street	teacher	house
(the White House)	school	(Dedham High School)	bank
city	(River Street)	(Prof. Schertle)	store
(Caesar's Market)	(Wareham Bank)	(Brooklyn)	

EXERCISE 4-2

Answers will vary for this exercise. Here are some examples of possible answers:

1. *The Washington Bridge has terrible traffic on Fridays.*
2. *California is one of my favorite places.*
3. *Mrs. Delaney is my neighbor.*

EXERCISE 4-3

1. My sisters received <u>an</u> invitation to the graduation party. They accepted <u>the</u> invitation.
2. His birthday party was at <u>a</u> bowling alley. <u>The</u> bowling alley plays rock and roll music.
3. My mother is shopping for <u>a</u> new purse. She wants <u>the</u> purse to be leather.
4. Manny wants <u>a</u> costume party. <u>The</u> party is for his birthday.
5. Olga is getting <u>a</u> puppy. She is getting <u>the</u> puppy from the rescue shelter.

EXERCISE 4-4

1. the   2. Ø   3. any   4. the   5. a

EXERCISE 4-5

Answers will vary for this exercise. Here are some examples of possible answers.

Count noun singular

Indefinite Article   1. I have <u>a</u> new <u>car</u>!

Definite Article   2. I love <u>the gift</u>. Thank you!

Count noun plural

Indefinite Article   3. They ordered <u>some</u> <u>movies</u>.

Definite Article   4. <u>The boxes</u> go over there.

Non-count noun

Indefinite Article   5. Does she want <u>any</u> <u>rice</u>?

Definite Article   6. <u>The soup</u> tastes great!

EXERCISE 4-6

1. fork → _forks_
2. tooth → _teeth_
3. knife → _knives_
4. baby → _babies_
5. child → _children_
6. quiz → _quizzes_
7. bowl → _bowls_
8. slice → _slices_
9. tomato → _tomatoes_
10. octopus → _octopuses_
11. cup → _cups_
12. goose → _geese_

EXERCISE 4-7

1. I bought all the ⭕ingredients to make my favorite <u>tea</u>.
2. Would you like <u>coffee, tea</u>, or <u>juice</u>?
3. My <u>hair</u> is color-damaged, so I bought special <u>shampoo</u>.
4. The <u>sand</u> on this ⭕beach is soft and white.
5. Lily won't eat this <u>soup</u> because she doesn't like <u>chicken</u>.

EXERCISE 4-8

1. two pieces of _pie / bread_
2. a bottle of _water / milk_
3. a cup of _milk / water / sugar / salt_
4. a glass of _water / milk_
5. a bag of _chips_
6. two pinches of _salt / sugar_
7. a bowl of _ice cream_

EXERCISE 4-9

1. _How much_ cereal should I buy?
2. _How many_ quarters do you have?
3. _How much_ fruit should I buy?
4. _How much_ rice does the recipe call for?
5. _How many_ varieties of apples are in this pie?
6. _How many_ kinds of music do you like?

EXERCISE 4-10

Answers will vary for this exercise.

EXERCISE 4-11

1. _Many_ people in _my_ class got _an_ A on _the_ test.
2. _Several_ dogs are playing in _the_ neighborhood dog park.
3. _Three_ chairs at _the_ kitchen table are broken.
4. _Every_ French teacher gives _a_ midterm and final exams.
5. _My_ sister is cooking _some_ beef stew for _the_ family.
6. _That_ kid is _a_ great baseball pitcher!

EXERCISE 4-12

1. They
2. We.
3. He
4. She
5. It
6. They

EXERCISE 4-13

1. _They_ are my coworkers.
2. _He_ is my professor.
3. _She_ is my neighbor.
4. _You_ need to exercise more.
5. _You_ passed the class.
6. _We_ should go out tonight.

EXERCISE 4-14

1. _He's a mechanic._
2. _We are students._
3. _She's a dog walker._
4. _I'm a dog walker._
5. _I'm a police officer._

EXERCISE 4-15

1. She brought (him) to the party.
2. Joseph played baseball with (him.)
3. They spent a lot of money on (it.)
4. We gave (them) to the used clothing store.
5. I heard (you.)
6. My niece loved (it!)
7. Text (me!)
8. The manager showed (us) the sale rack.

EXERCISE 4-16

1. _Katie shopped for him._
2. _She often attends them._
3. _My sister got a good deal on it._
4. _I am friends with her._
5. _Carolina found a gift for him._
6. _She bought them yesterday._

EXERCISE 4-17

1. <u>Her</u> kids are in <u>their</u> treehouse.

2. <u>My</u> family enjoys skiing in the mountains.

3. <u>His</u> cat brought home a mouse.

4. <u>His</u> children like drinking <u>your</u> homemade lemonade at <u>your</u> summer parties.

5. <u>Her</u> classmates sang in <u>their</u> church celebration.

6. Noah came to <u>my</u> house.

7. We strolled in the park at the end of <u>my</u> road.

8. <u>Our</u> neighbors swam in the pond behind <u>our</u> house.

EXERCISE 4-18

1. Look at all the sweaters the knitting club made! <u>His</u> is the green one.

2. My brother has a bountiful vegetable garden. It's much more productive than <u>mine</u>.

3. See that old pickup truck over there? It's <u>theirs</u>.

4. Their paintings are in that gallery. <u>Theirs</u> are the colorful, abstract paintings.

5. Is this money <u>yours</u>?

6. Here is a black purse. Is it <u>hers</u>?

EXERCISE 4-19

1. <u>Our house</u> was the small one over there. It's not <u>our house</u> anymore. We sold it. → *Ours was the small one over there. It's not ours anymore. We sold it.*

2. Those socks are <u>Pam's</u>. → *Those are hers.*

3. The birds in the cage are <u>his birds</u>. → *The birds in the cage are his.*

4. The two with red hats are <u>our kids</u>. → *The two with red hats are ours.*

EXERCISE 4-20

1. *cupcake / person*
2. *this / that*
3. *paintbrushes / bicycles*
4. *these / those*

EXERCISE 4-21

Answers will vary for this exercise. Here are some examples of possible answers. The demonstrative adjectives are highlighted.

1. *Is this your computer?*

   That was a great party!

2. *Marlena is joining these girls on the team today.*

   Dan doesn't like those boys because they're mean.

3. *Where do I put these papers?*

   Does that student have a signed notice?

EXERCISE 4-22

1. Those are the good guys.
2. I can't believe this!
3. Have you been to that?
4. These are so fun!
5. You can't have that. It's too dangerous.
6. That is very bad news.
7. This is trending right now.
8. What is this?

EXERCISE 4-23

1. I don't like this project. → *I don't like this.*
2. Those papers are Kammie's. → *Those are Kammie's.*
3. These movies are scary. → *These are scary.*
4. Those teenagers are mine. → *Those are mine.*

Talking About Ongoing Activities

PRACTICE 5-A

David: What (are) you (doing)?

Jennifer: (I'm folding) some napkins. What (are) you (doing)? Can you help me?

David: (I'm not doing) anything yet. Yeah, I can help.

Jennifer: So, what (s going on) with you?

David: Nothing much, really. Well, actually, (I'm applying) for an internship <u>this semester</u>.

Jennifer: Wow, that's great! Where's the internship?

David: It's at a nonprofit business near my dad's house.

Jennifer: What kind of business?

David: It's an intercultural exchange organization that promotes cross-cultural experience and understanding. It's really cool.

Jennifer: Is the organization big?

David: No yeah no, it's really big, and it(s expanding) its services <u>this year</u>.

Jennifer: What position (are) you (applying) for?

David: (I'm applying) for the host family development internship.

Jennifer: Really! Do you think you'll get it?

David: I hope so! I am a graduate of the program. I loved it.

Jennifer: I didn't know that. Did you travel?

David: Yup, I stayed with a family in Greece. It was awesome. I learned so much.

Jennifer: I want to do that!

EXERCISE 5-1

1. is   2. are   3. is   4. are   5. am

EXERCISE 5-2

1. share → sharing   4. shop → shopping
2. cry → crying   5. put → putting
3. make → making   6. walk → walking

EXERCISE 5-3

1. They <u>are driving</u> to the movie theater right now.

2. At this moment, Cole <u>is calling</u> the doctor's office to make an appointment.

3. Right now, Suzanna <u>is enjoying</u> live music at the park.

4. Dionne <u>is teaching</u> her daughter how to count from one to five.

5. My nephew <u>is cooking</u> a special meal for his wife's birthday.

6. We <u>are saving</u> money to buy a new car this year.

EXERCISE 5-4

Answers will vary for this exercise. Be sure to use the **–ing** form of the verb. Here are some possible answers.

1. *I am drinking coffee right now.*

2. *He is preparing for the exam today. / She is playing softball this year. / It is foraging for food.*

3. *You are fixing his mistakes now. / We are trying the new restaurant. / They are visiting her sister in college now.*

EXERCISE 5-5

1. *isn't*   2. *aren't*   3. *isn't*   4. *'m not*   5. *aren't*   6. *aren't*

EXERCISE 5-6

Answers will vary for this exercise. Here is how to start your answers.

1. *I am not . . .*

2. *He is not . . . / She is not . . . / It is not . . .*

3. *You are not . . . / We are not . . . / They are not . . .*

EXERCISE 5-7

You can replace the names of people with pronouns. You can also make a contraction with someone's name in the third person singular and *is* by adding an apostrophe + *s*. See examples of this below.

1. *Jackie is playing soccer right now.*

   Jackie isn't playing soccer right now.

   Jackie's not playing soccer right now.

2. *I'm studying Spanish this year.*

   I'm not studying Spanish this year.

   (There is only one way to make a contraction with *I*.)

3. *Jean Claude and Sofie are arguing at this moment.*

   They aren't arguing at this moment.

   They're not arguing at this moment.

4. *My dog's eating the new dog food.*

   My dog isn't eating the new dog food.

   My dog's not eating the new dog food.

5. *Sue and I are talking on the phone.*

   We aren't talking on the phone.

   We're not talking on the phone.

EXERCISE 5-8

Answers will vary for this exercise. Here is how to start your answers.

1. *I'm not . . .*

2. *He isn't . . . / He's not . . . / She isn't . . . / She's not . . . / It isn't . . . /*
   It's not . . .

3. *You aren't . . . / You're not . . . / We aren't . . . / We're not . . . / They aren't . . . /*
   They're not . . .

EXERCISE 5-9

1. Question: *Is George building kitchen cabinets for his kitchen?*

   Long answer: *Yes, he **is** building kitchen cabinets for his kitchen.*

   Short answer: *Yes, he **is**.*

   Quick answer: *Yes.*

2. Question: *Is Marcia reading your research paper right now?*

   Long answer: *No, she i**sn't** reading my research paper right now. / No, she's **not** reading my research paper right now.*

   Short answer: *No, she **isn't**. / No, she's **not**.*

   Quick answer: *No.*

3. Question: *Are they working at the hardware store?*

   Long answer: *No, they **aren't** working at the hardware store. / No, they're **not** working at the hardware store.*

   Short answer: *No, they **aren't**. / No, they're **not**.*

   Quick answer: *No.*

4. Question: *Are you studying at the university?*

   Long answer: *Yes, I **am** studying at the university.*

   Short answer: *Yes, I **am**.*

   Quick answer: *Yes.*

5. Question: *Is Bethany painting an original mural?*

   Long answer: *Yes, she **is** painting an original mural.*

   Short answer: *Yes, she **is**.*

   Quick answer: *Yes.*

EXERCISE 5-10

1. Question: *When is Olivia going to school?*

   Long answer: *She's going to school at night.*

   Short answer: *At night.*

2. Question: *How many magazines is Ella reading at lunch?*

   Long answer: *She's reading three magazines at lunch.*

   Short answer: *Three.*

3. Question: *How often is the professor giving pop quizzes this semester?*

   Long answer: *She's / He's giving pop quizzes every week.*

   Short answer: *Every week.*

4. Question: *Why is she studying at the community college?*

   Long answer: *She's studying at the community college because it's convenient and affordable.*

   Short answer: *Because it's convenient and affordable.*

5. Question: *How is Bethany progressing on her painting?*

   Long answer: *She's progressing very well!*

   Short answer: *Very well!*

EXERCISE 5-11

1. Question: *Who is taking a shower?*

   Long answer: *Max is taking a shower.*

   Short answer: *Max is.*

   Quick answer: *Max.*

2. Question: *Who is driving to the cinema?*

   Long answer: *Shahila and her son are driving to the cinema.*

   Short answer: *Shahila and her son are.*

   Quick answer: *Shahila and her son.*

3. Question: *Who is preparing Thanksgiving dinner?*

   Long answer: *Elena's mother is preparing Thanksgiving dinner.*

   Short answer: *Elena's mother is.*

   Quick answer: *Elena's mother.*

4. Question: *Who is buying sandwiches at the local café?*

   Long answer: *Cheryl and her friends are buying sandwiches at the local café.*

   Short answer: *Cheryl and her friends are.*

   Quick answer: *Cheryl and her friends.*

5. Question: Who is packing for a trip to Paris?

   Long answer: *Charlene and Jim are packing for a trip to Paris.*

   Short answer: *Charlene and Jim are.*

   Quick answer: *Charlene and Jim.*

Remember to use the third person singular with **who**, so use **is** in the questions for #4 and #5. When you answer, however, use the correct form of the BE verb for plural subjects: *are.*

EXERCISE 5-12

1. the   2. the   3. any   4. the   5. Ø

EXERCISE 5-13

Answers will vary for this exercise. Here are some examples.

Count noun singular

Indefinite Article   1. I'm shopping for <u>a</u> new car.

Definite Article   2. I want <u>the</u> car to be red.

Count noun plural

Indefinite Article   3. I'm test-driving <u>some</u> cars today.

Definite Article   4. I love shopping for cars!

Noncount noun

Indefinite Article   5. My husband doesn't want <u>any</u> juice.

Definite Article   6. They want <u>the</u> juice you are drinking.

Talking About Past Activities

EXERCISE 6-1

1. *watched*
2. *tried*
3. *created*
4. *jogged*
5. *hiked*
6. *danced*
7. *cooked*
8. *moved*

EXERCISE 6-2

1. *shook*
2. *drank*
3. *ate*
4. *brought*
5. *slept*
6. *understood*
7. *met*
8. *made*

EXERCISE 6-3

1. *Deb and Tina had a good time at the party.*
2. *She biked to her grandmother's house last week.*
3. *On Friday, Joe studied all night for his online exam.*
4. *Earlier this week, Carrie got a new car.*
5. *I downloaded a new yoga app yesterday afternoon.*
6. *The Zumba class was really fun on Sunday morning.*

EXERCISE 6-4

1. *didn't freeze*
2. *didn't sell*
3. *didn't catch*
4. *didn't come*
5. *didn't grow*
6. *didn't like*

EXERCISE 6-5

1. *Vera did not have a good time.*
   Vera didn't have a good time.
2. *Roberto and his wife did not buy the house.*
   Roberto and his wife didn't buy the house.
3. *You did not get an A on the essay.*
   You didn't get an A on the essay.
4. *I did not pay full price for the clothes.*
   I didn't pay full price for the clothes.

EXERCISE 6-6

1. Question: *Did Elysa take the train to work this morning?*
   Long answer: *Yes, she did take the train to work this morning.*
   Short answer: *Yes, she did.*
   Quick answer: *Yes. The car was in the shop.*

2. Question: *Did they manage the store well while I was gone?*

   Long answer: *Yes, they did manage the store well while you were gone.*

   Short answer: *Yes, they did.*

   Quick answer: *Yes. They were great managers!*

3. Question: *Did Ms. Jolly know about the problem?*

   Long answer: *No, she didn't know about the problem.*

   Short answer: *No, she didn't.*

   Quick answer: *No. She was on vacation.*

4. Question: *Did you sit close to the stage at the concert?*

   Long answer: *Yes, we did sit close to the stage at the concert.*

   Short answer: *Yes, we did.*

   Quick answer: *Yes. We bought the tickets early.*

5. Question: *Did Angela enroll in college classes yet?*

   Long answer: *Yes, she did enroll in college classes.*

   Short answer: *Yes, she did.*

   Quick answer: *Yes. Her counselor helped her pick the classes.*

EXERCISE 6-7

1. Question: *When did Paul take his wife to* Phantom of the Opera*?*

   Long answer: *He took his wife to* Phantom of the Opera *on Sunday evening.*

   Short answer: *On Sunday evening.*

2. Question: *Who got in a car accident last night?*

   Long answer: *Shelby got in a car accident last night, but she's okay.*

   Short answer: *Shelby did, but she's okay.*

3. Question: *What did Rocky open last month?*

   Long answer: *He opened his gym last month.*

   Short answer: *His gym.*

4. Question: *Where did the Thompsons take a cruise last summer?*

   Long answer: *They took a cruise to Alaska last summer.*

   Short answer: *To Alaska.*

5. Question: *How long was the yoga retreat in Costa Rica?*

   Long answer: *It was for two weeks. / It was two weeks long.*

   Short answer: *Two weeks.*

EXERCISE 6-8

1. a group of stars that form a design
2. or a device for guiding the cutting tool
3. also called redwoods
4. a slightly stressful situation that benefits the human body by building a healthy stress response.
5. a basic unit measuring electrical current

EXERCISE 6-9

(1) prospectors, people who search for mineral deposits such as gold and oil

(2) a territory, not yet a state of the Union

(3) the bulk, or majority

(4) fortune seekers, also known as '49ers,

(5) pan for gold—to wash and separate gravel from gold in a wide, open metal dish

(6) sluice box, aka a sluicer

EXERCISE 6-10

Answers for this exercise will vary. Here are some possible answers.

1. *I played soccer on Saturday afternoon.*
2. *My friends and I walked along the beach on Sunday morning.*

3. *We attended a baseball tournament.*

4. *My kids, my husband, and I visited ancient ruins.*

5. *I got a two-hour massage.*

EXERCISE 6-11

Answers for this exercise will vary. Here are examples of possible answers.

1. *Did you go to the library yesterday?*

2. *My mom made my lunch for school.*

3. *Where did you get that beautiful hat?*

4. *We didn't enjoy astronomy class today.*

5. *My sister-in-law planned a lovely wedding.*

6. *My dad cooked dinner last night, and it was delicious!*

7. *When did Jason get a job?*

8. *Were you at the celebration?*

9. *Simone and Annette visited me last June.*

10. *They made me feel better.*

Simple Sentences

PRACTICE 7-A

1. <u>Pamela</u> bought new (ice skates)

2. <u>We</u> played (board games) last night.

3. <u>It</u> printed (my ticket)

4. <u>The sales clerk</u> sells (shoes.)

5. <u>My parents</u> rented (a beach house) for vacation.

6. <u>You</u> spelled (my name) correctly.

PRACTICE 7-B

1. <u>She</u> is <u>really tall</u>.
2. <u>Marty</u> is <u>Sherry's brother</u>.
3. <u>Harry and Marisol</u> are <u>newlyweds</u>.
4. <u>He</u> became <u>a dentist</u>.
5. <u>The apple pie</u> tastes <u>delicious</u>!
6. <u>That music</u> sounds <u>wonderful</u>!

PRACTICE 7-C

1. Over time, the constant flow of the river wore down the rock and created natural structures, <u>including</u> rivulets, waterfalls, and caves.
2. There are many ways to experience this national treasure, <u>such as</u> hiking, bicycling, off-roading, and even flying over it in a helicopter!
3. A variety of activities <u>like</u> canyon mule rides, river-rafting, and overnight camping are available to the public on the canyon floor.
4. <u>For example</u>, overnight campers should reserve a campsite a few months in advance.
5. Summertime, <u>for instance</u>, is the park's peak tourist season, so crowds of people fill the viewing stations and daytime temperatures are hot.

EXERCISE 7-1

1. <u>Sonja</u> enjoys (her book collection)
     S   V   O

2. This afternoon, <u>Peter</u> is going to kick (the ball) around.
                S   V   O

3. <u>Dr. Price</u> attends (medical conferences) every year.
      S   V   O

4. Last night, <u>my cousins</u> visited (us)
             S   V O

5. You enjoyed (the concert), didn't you?
     S   V   O

6. Steve and Michele get (coffee) every morning together.
             S   V   O

7. This year, my son is taking (advanced placement classes).
                S   V   O

8. The Quilici family sends (holiday cards) every year.
        S   V   O

EXERCISE 7-2

Answers will vary for this exercise. Here are some possible answers.

1. Every morning, I make *organic chai tea*.
             S V   O

2. I take *the express bus* every day to work.
   S V   O

3. The Express 95 takes *commuters* downtown.
         S   V   O

4. The mayor throws *candy* from her car during the 4th of July parade.
      S   V   O

5. Every Thanksgiving, we cook *a fresh heritage turkey* from a local
   turkey farm.
             S   V   O

EXERCISE 7-3

1. Genevieve seems worried.

2. Mel and his wife are happy.

3. My lab partner is Rachel.

4. My aunt and uncle are funny.

5. Learning English is a challenge.

6. This house smells so good!

7. My brother-in-law appears confident.

8. Ruby and Luna are sisters.

EXERCISE 7-4

1. worried – adj
2. happy – adj
3. Rachel – noun (proper noun)
4. funny – adj

5. a challenge – n
6. good – adj
7. confident – adj
8. sisters – n

EXERCISE 7-5

Answers will vary for this exercise. Here are some possible answers.

1. (be) They are family.
       S LV   C   (n)

2. (taste) Her homemade apple pie tastes wonderful!
                             S   LV   C   (adj)

3. (seem) They seem happy.
         S   LV   C   (adj)

4. (appear) Mom appears surprised.
           S   LV   C   (adj)

5. (look) She looks distressed.
         S   LV   C   (adj)

6. (feel) Maura feels a little nauseous.
         S   LV   C   (adj)

7. (taste) The beef stew tastes yummy!
           S   LV   C   (adj)

8. (smell) Your roses smell divine!
           S   LV   C   (adj)

9. (sound) That sounds good!
           S   LV   C   (adj)

EXERCISE 7-6

1. When did she send <u>you</u> <u>the book</u>?
                       I.O.   D.O.

2. Nora gave <u>Bentley</u> <u>the presentation slides</u>.
               I.O.   D.O.

3. Danielle and Mike threw <u>their friends</u> <u>a party</u>.
                            I.O.   D.O.

4. Shelby made <u>homemade vanilla ice cream</u>. It was delicious!
                    D.O.

   (This sentence doesn't have an indirect object.)

EXERCISE 7-7

1. continued = **intrans** (no OV)
2. read = **intrans** (no OV)
3. is changing = **trans** – changing <u>her clothes</u> (OV)
4. understand = **intrans** (no OV)
5. wrote = **trans** (wrote <u>the book</u> – OV)
6. closed = **trans** (closed <u>the shop</u> – OV)

EXERCISE 7-8

1. <u>Catherine and Ken</u> built <u>a new house</u> and moved in last summer.
       S   S   V   O   V

   SSVV = Simple sentence with an O.

   This sentence has only one S-V combination.

2. <u>Jim and Sue</u> are watching <u>the babies</u> Saturday night.
      S   S   V   O

   SSV = Simple sentence with an O.

   This sentence has only one S-V combination.

3. <u>JoAnne and Virginia</u> are <u>sisters</u>, but <u>they</u> grew up separately.
        S   S   V   C   S   V

   SSV + SV = Compound sentence with a C.

   The two SV combinations are connected by a comma and the coordinating conjunction *but*.

   This sentence has two S-V combinations: JoAnne and Virginia are . . . / they grew up . . .

4. <u>The Young Family and the Pinna Family</u> got together for
            S   S   V

   Christmas and ate <u>a big dinner</u>.
              V   O

   SSVV = Simple sentence with an O.

   This sentence has only one S-V combination.

EXERCISE 7-9

1. **Cultural relics**, <u>such as</u> the Great Pyramids of Egypt and the Great Wall of China, are immovable national treasures.

2. One way to appreciate the history of a place is to go on a **heritage tour**. <u>For example</u>, you can walk through a house built by an early American settler in Massachusetts, or you can watch the reenactment of a battle in South Carolina.

3. My favorite part of the tour was to watch **the reenactment of the American Revolutionary War**. In this reenactment, <u>for instance</u>, hundreds of men in traditional American and British uniforms fought with authentic weapons at the site of the battle in Lexington, Massachusetts.

4. **National historic landmarks in the United States**, <u>such as</u> objects, buildings, structures, sites, and districts, are protected by the US government.

Talking About Future Activities

EXERCISE 8-1

1. Plan/intention: (go) Aidan *is going* to his house after school. (With the verb **go**, it's more common to use the present progressive for future plans.)

   Or Aidan *is going to go* to his house after school.

2. Prediction: (be) Psychic: You *will be* very happy in life!

3. Prediction from evidence: (fall) Watch out! You *are going to fall* into that ditch!

4. Arranged plan: (meet) Niles *is meeting* with his boss tomorrow morning.

5. Offer: (watch) I *will watch* your dog for you while you're on vacation.

6. Prediction from evidence: (rain) What a dark sky! It *is going to rain* soon.

7. Promise: (complete) Jenna *will complete* the assignment by 5 p.m. tonight.

8. Prediction: (find) Fortune cookie: You *will find* great happiness this year.

9. Plan/intention: (lead) Jamillah and Alicia *are leading* the class meeting later today.

   Or Jamillah and Alicia *are going to lead* the class meeting later today.

10. Schedule: (arrive) The train *arrives* in about 10 minutes.

EXERCISE 8-2

1. *He's going / He's going to go* to his house after school.
2. *You'll be* very happy in life!
3. *You're going to fall* into that ditch!
4. *He's meeting* with his boss tomorrow morning.
5. *I'll watch* your dog for you while you're on vacation.
6. *It's going to rain* soon.
7. *She'll complete* the assignment by 5 p.m. tonight.
8. *You'll find* great happiness this year.
9. *They're leading / They're going to lead* the class meeting later today.
10. It *arrives* in about 10 minutes. (No change.)

EXERCISE 8-3

See the Answer Key for Exercise 8-2.

EXERCISE 8-4

1. *I'll complete the report by Monday night.*
2. *The train arrives in an hour.*
3. *I'll give you money for college textbooks.*
4. *This weekend, we're making brunch for our parents.*
   This weekend, we're going to make brunch for our parents.
5. *You'll succeed in life!*
6. *Esperanza is collaborating with her classmate in class on Friday.*
   Esperanza is going to collaborate with her classmate in class on Friday.

EXERCISE 8-5

Answers will vary. See below for appropriate simple future forms for each situation.

1. *will + base form of the main verb*
2. *BE going to + base form of the main verb and the present progressive*
3. *will + base form of the main verb*
4. *present progressive verb tense*
5. *will + base form of the main verb*
6. *simple present verb tense*

EXERCISE 8-6

1. *will not be*
2. *is not going to buy*
3. *is not going to take notes*
4. *will not sell*
5. *will not read*
6. *will not prescribe*

EXERCISE 8-7

1. She *won't be* at the party Saturday. She's visiting her cousins.
2. She *isn't going to buy* any more clothes online. It's too expensive.
   She's not going to buy any more clothes online. It's too expensive.
3. He/She *isn't going to take notes* at the meeting because it's being recorded.
   He's/She's not going to take notes at the meeting because it's being recorded.
4. He *won't sell* his vintage motorcycle. It's too sentimental.
5. He *won't read* online news. He prefers to read a real newspaper.
6. He/She *won't prescribe* any more medication until I get a checkup.

EXERCISE 8-8

1. *He's not going to make it to the party today.*

   He isn't going to make it to the party today.

2. *She's not going to practice English every day there.*

   She isn't going to practice English every day there.

3. *I'm not going to attend the concert at the school tonight.*

EXERCISE 8-9

1. Question: *Will they have fun at the event this weekend?*

   Long answer: *No, they will not / won't have fun at the event this weekend. They're grounded.*

   Short answer: *No, they will not / won't. They're grounded.*

   Quick answer: *No. They're grounded.*

2. Question: *Is Mace going to need a new car for his new job?*

   Long answer: *No, he is not / he isn't / he's not going to need a new car for his new job. He is / He's getting a company car.*

   Short answer: *No, he is not / No he's isn't / No he's not. He's getting a company car.*

   Quick answer: *No. He's getting a company car.*

3. Question: *Will you please show me some examples?*

   Long answer: *Yes, I will / I'll show you some examples.*

   Short answer: *Yes, I will.*

   Quick answer: *Yes.*

4. Question: *Are Maximillian and Tara going to rent a shuttle for the party?*

   Long answer: *Yes, they are / they're going to rent a shuttle for the party.*

   Short answer: *Yes, they are.*

   Quick answer: *Yes.*

EXERCISE 8-10

1. Question: *Where will your Dad fix the toy bike?*

   Long answer: *He'll fix it in the garage.*

   Short answer: *In the garage.*

2. Question: *When is Margi going to finish her school project?*

   Long answer: *She's going to finish her school project later tonight.*

   Short answer: *Later tonight.*

3. Question: *Why is Miles going to register for summer school?*

   Long answer: *He's going to register for summer school because he failed math.*

   Short answer: *Because he failed math.*

4. Question: *Why will Jeanette and Daniel buy a new TV?*

   Long Answer: *They'll buy a new TV because theirs is broken.*

   Short answer: *Because theirs is broken.*

EXERCISE 8-11

1. *Manira will be working late every night this week.*
   She'll be working late every night this week.

2. *The seminar will be starting in 10 minutes.*
   It'll be starting in 10 minutes.

3. *I will be getting a massage once a month for the next six months!*
   I'll be getting a massage once a month for the next six months!

4. *Next week, Mr. Wu will be substituting for Mrs. Singh because she's ill.*
   Next week, he'll be substituting for Mrs. Singh because she's ill.

5. *My mother will be sewing my Halloween costume for the party Sunday.*
   She'll be sewing my Halloween costume for the party Sunday.

6. *Faby will be graduating at the top of her class this year.*
   She'll be graduating at the top of her class this year.

EXERCISE 8-12

1. Mr. Schiffer _will not be attending_ the engagement party this Sunday evening.

   He _won't be attending_ the engagement party this Sunday evening.

2. My math professor _will not be grading_ our exams till next week.

   She/He _won't be grading_ our exams till next week.

3. My neighbor _will not be taking care of_ my plants while I'm gone because she's on vacation, too.

   She _won't be taking care of_ my plants while I'm gone because she's on vacation, too.

4. I _will not be babysitting_ my little cousins this summer because I'll be in Spain.

   I _won't be babysitting_ my little cousins this summer because I'll be in Spain.

5. Facundo _will not be presenting_ the new ad campaign at the client meeting as he's out of town.

   He _won't be presenting_ the new ad campaign at the client meeting as he's out of town.

6. Shandra _will not be going_ to her primary care physician next week.

   She _won't be going_ to her primary care physician next week.

EXERCISE 8-13

1. Question: _Will they be attending the conference next week?_

   Long answer: _No, they will not / won't be attending the conference next week. They have other plans._

   Short answer: _No, they will not / won't be. They have other plans._

   Quick answer: _No. They have other plans._

2. Question: *Will your boss be giving you a raise this year?*

   Long answer: *Yes, he will / 'll be giving me a raise this year.*

   Short answer: *Yes, he will be. / Yes, he will.*

   Quick answer: *Yes.*

3. Question: *Will Alana be introducing me at the company meeting?*

   Long answer: *No, she will not / won't be introducing you at the company meeting. Tran will.*

   Short answer: *No, she will not / won't. Tran will.*

   Quick answer: *No. Tran will.*

4. Question: *Will Cora be arranging a ride from the airport for us?*

   Long answer: *Yes, she will / she'll be arranging a ride from the airport for us.*

   Short answer: *Yes, she will be. / Yes, she will.*

   Quick answer: *Yes.*

EXERCISE 8-14

1. Question: *Why will your aunt be going to the doctor?*

   Long answer: *She'll be going to the doctor because she has migraine headaches.*

   Short answer: *Because she has migraine headaches.*

2. Question: *When will Annie and David be selling their house?*

   Long answer: *They'll be selling their house this summer.*

   Short answer: *This summer.*

3. Question: *Where will your nephew be taking driving lessons?*

   Long answer: *He'll be taking driving lessons at the driving school on Willow Street.*

   Short answer: *At the driving school on Willow Street.*

4. Question: *What kind of car will Josh and Jerry be buying?*

   Long answer: *They'll be buying rugged, off-road vehicle.*

   Short answer: *A rugged, off-road vehicle.*

EXERCISE 8-15

1. My twin sisters <u>*are going to perform / are performing*</u> this Saturday night at school.

2. My family <u>*will be discussing*</u> our vacation over the weekend.

3. I <u>*will / I'll be*</u> happy when the school year is over.

4. Nora and Gray <u>*will be jogging*</u> tomorrow morning, so they can't drive you.

5. I <u>*will / I'll do*</u> the dishes tonight.

6. Do you need help? I <u>*will / I'll hold*</u> your books for you.

7. We <u>*will / we'll be writing*</u> this book for the rest of the year.

8. Watch out! You <u>*are / you're going to trip*</u> over that log.

EXERCISE 8-16

Answers will vary for this exercise. See possible answers provided.

1. Pardon me, (name of supervisor). I didn't quite catch that. Could you repeat that, please?

2. Excuse me (name of teacher), could you say that again please?

3. Sorry. I didn't understand that. Could you say that again slowly?

Connecting the Past and the Present

EXERCISE 9-1

1. Meredith's new <u>*cat has adapted / cat's adapted*</u> to its new home quickly.

2. <u>*I have concluded / I've concluded*</u> that exercising in the morning rather than at night is better for me.

3. Luna and Estelle <u>*have not approached / haven't approached*</u> this problem with patience and diligence.

4. The professor <u>*has*</u> already <u>*clarified / professor's*</u> already <u>*clarified*</u> the homework instructions, so now I understand.

5. <u>*Has*</u> she <u>*acquired*</u> her real estate license yet?

6. The hotel <u>*has*</u> just <u>*confirmed / hotel's*</u> just <u>*confirmed*</u> our reservations for next weekend.

7. For how long <u>*has*</u> he <u>*been*</u> sick with a fever?

8. Since the beginning of spring, I <u>*have had / I've had*</u> a runny nose and watery eyes.

9. For the last three summers, Michaela <u>*has gone / Michaela's gone*</u> to Moab, Utah, for vacation.

10. Owen and Madison <u>*have*</u> already <u>*discussed*</u> this issue, and they just made a final decision.

EXERCISE 9-2

1. *Ann and Francis have lived in the South of France for five years already.*

2. *Andrea has ridden her mountain bike on that trail every Saturday this summer.*

3. *Since Tuesday, Taryn has had a cold.*

4. *Alessandra and Stanley have gotten breakfast at that café every morning since they moved here.*

5. *Since I was a kid, I've been afraid of dogs.*

6. *My laptop has made a weird sound ever since I dropped it.*

EXERCISE 9-3

1. My parents *haven't* ever *gone* on a two-week vacation.

2. She *hasn't told* us the truth yet.

3. Professor Sullivan *hasn't graded* the homework yet.

4. Since we bought it, the smoke detector *has never detected* smoke in this house.

5. I *haven't grown* my own vegetable garden before.

6. We *haven't invested* in a new parcel of land for retirement yet.

EXERCISE 9-4

Answers will vary for this exercise. Here some possibilities.

1. Question: *Has Elliot driven across the country before?*

   Long answer: *Yes, Elliot has driven across the country before. / Yes, he's driven across the country before.*

   Short answer: *Yes, he has.*

   Quick answer: *Yes. He enjoyed it very much.*

2. Question: *Has your daughter ever done an internship?*

   Long answer: *Yes, my daughter has / daughter's done an internship. / Yes, she's done an internship.*

   Short answer: *Yes, she has.*

   Quick answer: *Yes. She didn't like it, however.*

3. Question: *Has the baby eaten real food yet? / Has she / he eaten real food yet?*

   Long answer: *No, the baby hasn't eaten real food yet. / No, she / he hasn't eaten real food yet.*

   Short answer: *No, she / he hasn't.*

   Quick answer: *No, but she / he will soon.*

4. Question: *Have you ever gotten an A in all your classes?*

   Long answer: *Yes, I have gotten / I've gotten an A in all my classes.*

   Short answer: *Yes, I have.*

   Quick answer: *Yes. Hopefully, I'll get all As this year, too.*

5. Question: *Have Jean and Seamus gotten dressed for the black-tie gala yet?*

   Long answer: *Yes, Jean and Seamus / they have gotten dressed for the black-tie gala. / Yes, they've gotten dressed for the black-tie gala.*

   Short answer: *Yes, they have.*

   Quick answer: *Yes. They look amazing!*

EXERCISE 9-5

1. Question: *Where have Amy and Mark gone?*

   Long answer: *They've gone to bed.*

   Short answer: *To bed.*

2. Question: *Where has Steve been all day? / Where's Steve been all day?*

   Long answer: *Steve's / He's been in the library.*

   Short answer: *In the library.*

3. Question: *Who has attended the funeral service? / Who's attended the funeral service?*

   Long answer: *Jacob has / Jacob's attended the funeral service. / He's attended the funeral service.*

   Short answer: *Jacob.*

4. Question: *Where have Lucy and Ethel packaged candy this past week?*

   Long answer: *Lucy and Ethel / They have packaged candy in the candy factory this past week. / They've packaged candy in the candy factory this past week.*

   Short answer: *In the candy factory.*

5. Question: *What has Ricky thought about recently? / What's Ricky thought about recently?*

   Long answer: *Ricky has / Ricky's / He's thought about the consequences of his actions.*

   Short answer: *The consequences of his actions.*

6. Question: *Where have Fred and Barney / they moved?*

   Long answer: *Fred and Barney / They have moved to a new neighborhood. / They've moved to a new neighborhood.*

   Short answer: *To a new neighborhood.*

EXERCISE 9-6

1. *Jeremiah has / Jeremiah's been wondering* about his future lately.
2. *I have / I've been thinking about* what you said this morning.
3. *We have / We've been sheltering* in place for too long.
4. *The professor has / The professor's been evaluating* our in-class participation this whole week.
5. In the novel, the blue people *have been discriminating* against the green people since the beginning of time.
6. *You have / You've been contradicting* me ever since this morning.
7. *The ocean has / The ocean's been eroding* the coastline for millennia.
8. That athletic wear *company has / company's been equipping* all the high schools with sports uniforms since the 1950s.
9. The *company has / company's been guaranteeing* the quality of its work for 20 years.

10. *We have / We've been building* an extension on the house for three months.

EXERCISE 9-7

1. *Peter Greenfield has / Greenfield's been networking with potential customers for a few years now.*

2. *Politicians have / They've been manipulating scientific data for a long time.*

3. *Since last year, we have / we've been trying to maximize our investments.*

4. *Carolyn and Stacey have / They have / They've been resisting change at their company for years.*

5. *Since the beginning of the year, Lexi has / Lexi's been transferring data into new databases.*

6. *Maggie has / Maggie's been living in a hotel since the earthquake ruined her house.*

EXERCISE 9-8

1. Denna: You *have not been responding / haven't been responding* to my emails for weeks, Paul.

2. Paul: I'm sorry, Denna. I *have been researching / I've been researching* historic information for my new novel.

3. You *have been transforming / You've been transforming* it so much.

4. The company *has not been promoting / hasn't been promoting* our services as much because they* cut our advertising budget.

5. The university *has not been publishing / hasn't been publishing* our research lately.

6. The city *has not been regulating / hasn't been regulating* the use of leaf blowers, but they're talking about it.

*Although the correct pronoun for "the company" is *it*, we often refer to a company as *they*.

EXERCISE 9-9

Answers will vary for this exercise. Here are some possibilities.

1. Question: *Has Timothy been assisting you with your work this week?*

   Long answer: *Yes, he has / he's been assisting me with my work this week.*

   Short answer: *Yes, he has.*

   Quick answer: *Yes. He's been very helpful.*

2. Question: *Has Nancy been accompanying you to church services this month?*

   Long answer: *No, she has not / she hasn't been accompanying me to church services this month.*

   Short answer: *No, she hasn't.*

   Quick answer: *No. I wonder why.*

3. Question: *Has your academic advisor been counseling you on college applications?*

   Long answer: *Yes, she has / she's been counseling me on college applications.*

   Short answer: *Yes, she has.*

   Quick answer: *Yes. I've been learning a lot.*

4. Question: *Have you been disposing of your trash every week?*

   Long answer: *No, I have not / haven't been disposing of my trash every week.*

   Short answer: *No, I have not. / No, I haven't.*

   Quick answer: *No. I didn't know I was supposed to.*

5. Question: *Have you been exceeding the storage limit on the computer lately?*

   Long answer: *Yes, I have / I've been exceeding the storage limit on the computer lately.*

   Short answer: Yes, I have.

   Quick answer: *Yes. I've been uploading videos to another server. When that's done, the storage usage will drop.*

EXERCISE 9-10

1. Question: *Where have the Rubbles been going every weekend?*

   Long Answer: *The Rubbles have / They've been going to their grandmother's house.*

   Short answer: *To their grandmother's house.*

2. Question: *Where has Mr. Flintstone been working this year?*

   Long answer: *Mr. Flintstone has / He's been working at the quarry this year.*

   Short answer: *The quarry.*

3. Question: *Where have Wilma and Betty been disappearing to every Friday morning?*

   Long answer: *Wilma and Betty have / They've been disappearing to the massage parlor every Friday morning.*

   Short answer: *The massage parlor.*

4. Question: *Where have the children been getting their schooling?*

   Long answer: *The children have / They've been getting their schooling at home with a tutor.*

   Short answer: *At home with a tutor.*

5. Question: *What has / What's Mr. Howell been dreaming about?*

   Long answer: *Mr. Howell's / He's been dreaming about getting off the island.*

   Short answer: *Getting off the island.*

6. Question: *Where have Ginger and Mary Ann been living?*

   Long answer: *Ginger and Mary Ann have / They've been living on an island.*

   Short answer: *On an island.*

EXERCISE 9-11

1. Oh my gosh! Marjorie just _found out_ about the surprise party we're planning for her. I'm so disappointed!

    Explanation: Remember, the verb _find out_ is something that happens in a moment, so it happens and it's complete. After that, someone _knows_ something. The simple past is the correct verb tense.

2. My little brother _has been sick_ all week with the flu. He better not give it to me!

    Explanation: As the time phrase is _all week_, we must use the present perfect. The simple present doesn't work because it's not a habit or regular condition.

3. In the movie, Glinda the good witch _granted_ Dorothy her wish to go home to Kansas.

    Explanation: _Grant_ is a verb usually used to talk about a moment in time. It isn't an action that occurs over time. Therefore, the simple past is the best choice.

4. Over the years, the pharmaceutical company _has been exploiting_ innocent patients' needs to decrease pain. Will they ever stop?

    Explanation: As the time phrase is _over the years_, we know the action is occurring over a period of time; therefore, the present perfect progressive is the verb to use.

5. ABC Corporation _has been_ around since 1945. That's a long time!

    Explanation: With the time word _since_, we don't use the simple present. We use the present perfect.

6. Announcer at the Olympics: This young athlete _has emerged_ as a top contender for the gold medal since this event began. We'll know soon if he wins it!

    Explanation: The time word _since_ is a tip that the present perfect is the right verb tense here. Another tip is that as there is relevance to now, we wouldn't use the simple past.

7. Mateo *was considering* joining the Marines, but he decided against it. He wants to go to an Ivy League school instead.

   Explanation: Mateo has already stopped considering joining the Marines and made a decision about it. Therefore, the action of considering is over. This means that the past progressive verb tense is the correct one. The present perfect progressive indicates that the action is still occurring, but it's not.

8. Raleigh and Jana *have seen* that movie twice so far. They'll see it again, I'm sure.

   Explanation: *So far* is usually used with the present perfect, not the present perfect progressive, and we're talking about number of times this action has occurred, not duration.

EXERCISE 9-12

Answers will vary for this exercise. See some example answers to the questions below.

1. *I've played football with my friends in gym class recently.*
2. *My friends and I have gone to lunch at the Thai place almost every day this week.*
3. *I've been hanging out with my three best friends since school started.*
4. *My family and I have been going to my uncle's restaurant every weekend since I can remember.*
5. *My friend, Carmen, has been helping me with my homework.*
6. *I've been busy with homework and water polo practice.*

EXERCISE 9-13

Ben: It seems to me that if; then

Reno: I agree with; that

Cody: Perhaps you're right that; but I think that

Britanny: I disagree with that because; I agree that; but

Samantha: Respectfully, I have to disagree with the idea that

10
Compound, Complex, and Compound-Complex Sentences

PRACTICE 10-A

1. **Vladimir** went to a clothing store on Saturday, and **he** ran into a
     S   V   S   V

   friend there.

2. **Rashid and his sister** really enjoy camping, but **they** don't like
                S   V   S   V

   camping in the rain.

3. **I** don't like watching baseball games; **I** prefer to watch basketball games.
     S   V   S V

4. **She** doesn't feel well; **she**'s not going to school today.
     S   V   S   V

5. **Neela** is devoted to charity: **She** volunteers at the community center
       S V   S   V

   every Saturday.

6. **I** never have enough time for fun during the week: **I**'m in school for
     S   V   S V

   eight hours, have three to five hours of homework, and then have swim
                V   V

   practice for two hours every weekday.

7. **My aunt** loves coffee; however, **she** dislikes coffee-flavored food.
       S   V   S   V

8. **The students** in this history class participate enthusiastically in group
         S   V

   activities; **they** don't, however, enjoy writing essays.
               S   V

PRACTICE 10-B

1. <u>Zehra is in line for the Mega-Rollercoaster</u> [because she loves fast, scary rides.]

2. [Even though she prefers fast rides,] <u>she also likes the silly ones like the Fun House.</u>

3. <u>Zehra's brother,</u> [who is afraid of roller coasters,] <u>only goes on the water rides.</u>

4. <u>The water ride</u> [that he likes the most] <u>is the Super Flume.</u>

5. [When Zehra and her brother Zane go to the amusement park together,] <u>they bring friends.</u>

6. <u>Some of their friends like the crazy fast rides,</u> [while some others prefer the slow rides.]

7. [Before they go to the amusement park,] <u>they invite at least one friend to hang out with.</u>

8. <u>Zehra is always excited</u> [when the amusement park opens for the season.]

9. <u>Do you know</u> [what the park hours are?]

10. [Since Zehra and Zane go to the park every summer,] <u>they know all the ride operators by name.</u>

PRACTICE 10-C

1. [After Marnie graduates from high school], she's going to take a gap year and study real estate. (adverb clause of time)

2. [As soon as you are done], call me. (adverb clause of time)

3. Text me [once class is over.] (adverb clause of time)

4. [By the time you complete the project], I'll be gone. (adverb clause of time)

5. [Wherever you go for lunch], we will meet you there. (adverb clause of place)

6. She'll exercise [anywhere there is enough space to do jumping jacks.] (adverb clause of place)

7. I'm taking a multimedia class [since I have to take an elective.] (adverb clause of reason)

8. My guidance counselor helped me research college scholarships [because I have a limited college budget.] (adverb clause of reason)

9. [As that university requires a high SAT score], I'm taking many practice SAT tests. (adverb clause of reason)

10. I have to get at least an 85 on this test [so that I can earn an A+ for the class.] (adverb clause of purpose)

PRACTICE 10-D

1. [After I <u>do</u> the homework,] I'<u>ll watch</u> a movie with you.

2. My sister <u>is going to buy</u> a new car [before she <u>starts</u> her new job.]

3. Jacob <u>is leaving</u> for Lake Tahoe [as soon as he <u>talks</u> to his boss.]

4. [Once we <u>finish</u> lunch,] we'<u>ll go</u> to Grandma's house.

5. I <u>will</u> never <u>forget</u> this birthday party [as long as I <u>live</u>.]

6. [When Ms. Ray <u>arrives</u>,] the test <u>will begin</u>.

7. [By the time the mail <u>comes</u>,] he'<u>ll</u> already <u>be</u> gone.

8. [The next time I <u>see</u> her,] I'<u>m going to tell</u> her about it.

PRACTICE 10-E

1. [After he <u>took</u> the test,] he <u>felt</u> better.

2. [Before Sharla <u>began</u> her summer vacation,] she <u>cleaned</u> out her school locker.

3. [Once Ron <u>learned</u> how to drive,] he never <u>asked</u> anyone for a ride.

4. We <u>left</u> the building [when it <u>stopped</u> raining.]

5. [When Julianna <u>stayed</u> with her cousin in Nebraska,] she <u>visited</u> Carhenge.

6. [While we <u>were waiting</u> for you,] we <u>finished</u> our homework assignments.

7. I <u>stayed</u> [till it <u>got</u> dark out.]

8. She <u>had</u> already <u>left</u> for the party [by the time you <u>called</u>.]

9. My brother <u>hasn't gone</u> to school [since he <u>got</u> sick.]

10. [Since she <u>finished</u> her big project,] she<u>'s had</u> relaxing evenings.

PRACTICE 10-F

1. [When the sun sets,] <u>it's in the west.</u>

2. [If it's 6:00 p.m. on a weekday,] <u>Gerald is home from work.</u>

3. [If I pass this calculus test with at least a B,] <u>I'll earn an A for the class!</u>

4. [Whenever the teacher is sick,] <u>we get a substitute teacher, and the class is more fun.</u>

5. <u>My mom and dad will buy me a car</u> [if I make the honor roll in my junior and senior years.]

6. [Should it rain,] <u>we'll have the party indoors.</u>

7. [If it doesn't rain,] <u>we'll have the party in the backyard.</u>

8. [Provided I pass the driving test,] <u>I'll drive myself to school every day.</u>

9. [Unless he stretches after running,] <u>his leg muscles won't become flexible.</u>

10. [If I were you,] <u>I'd study every night for a week to prepare for the final exam.</u>

11. [If you could carry this big box,] <u>I'd be so grateful.</u>

12. <u>It would help me a lot</u> [if you could do the laundry tonight.]

PRACTICE 10-G

1. [When the sun sets,] <u>it's in the west.</u> = Zero / Real conditional / Fact

2. [If it's 6:00 p.m. on a weekday,] <u>Gerald is home from work.</u> = Zero / Real conditional / General truth / Inference

3. [If I pass this calculus test with at least a B,] <u>I'll earn an A for the class!</u> = First / Future conditional / Certainty

4. [Whenever the teacher is sick,] <u>we get a substitute teacher, and the class is more fun.</u> = Zero / Real conditional / General truth

5. <u>My mom and dad will buy me a car</u> [if I make the honor roll in my junior and senior years.] = First / Future conditional / Plan

6. [Should it rain,] <u>we'll have the party indoors.</u> = First / Future conditional / Plan

7. [If it doesn't rain,] <u>we'll have the party in the backyard.</u> = First / Future conditional / Plan

8. [Provided I pass the driving test,] <u>I'll drive myself to school every day.</u> = First / Future conditional / Plan

9. [Unless he stretches after running,] <u>his leg muscles won't become flexible.</u> = First / Future conditional / Certainty

10. [If I were you,] <u>I'd study every night for a week to prepare for the final exam.</u> = Second / Unreal / Hypothetical conditional / Advice

11. [If you could carry this big box,] <u>I'd be so grateful.</u> = Second / Unreal / Hypothetical conditional / Polite request

12. <u>It would help me a lot</u> [if you could do the laundry tonight.] = Second / Unreal / Hypothetical conditional / Polite request

PRACTICE 10-H

1. [If they **weren't** so busy moving this week,] <u>they **would have come** to game night.</u>

   Present (They are busy this week.)

   Past (They didn't come to game night.)

2. <u>Lloyd and Charley **wouldn't be sleeping** right now</u> [if they **hadn't stayed up** so late last night.]

   Present (They are sleeping right now.)

   Past (They did stay up late.)

3. She **could have joined** <u>you in the sing-along</u> [if she **didn't have** a sore throat.]

   Past (She didn't join you.)

   Present (She has a sore throat.)

4. [**Had** we **not seen** that movie already,] <u>we **would go** with you to the cinema.</u>

   Past (We saw that movie already.)

   Present (We aren't going to the cinema.)

5. [If the Perry family **had brought** dessert,] <u>we **would be eating** homemade blackberry pie right now.</u>

   Past (They didn't bring dessert.)

   Present (We are not eating blackberry pie right now.)

6. <u>We **wouldn't have seen** any stars in the sky</u> [if it **were** foggy.]

   Past (We saw stars in the sky.)

   Present (It isn't foggy.)

PRACTICE 10-1

1. <u>The books</u> [that you lent me] <u>are really interesting</u>.

2. <u>Mr. Hopper,</u> [who lives next door,] <u>walks in the park every day after lunch.</u>

3. <u>I'm really enjoying the dinner</u> [Ø you brought home for me.]

   In #3, the relative pronoun is omitted. It's possible to omit it when it's an object relative pronoun in a restrictive adjective clause.

4. <u>She bought all the items on your list,</u> [which was difficult to read.]

5. <u>Did Marty buy you these flowers,</u> [which smell so good?]

6. <u>Ask the professor,</u> [who is over there.]

7. <u>My car,</u> [which I bought used,] <u>has been running really well.</u>

8. <u>Is that the guy</u> [that you were talking about?]

9. <u>The family owns the house</u> [that is at the end of the street.]

10. <u>Is this your dog</u> [that's wearing the pink fuzzy collar?]

11. <u>They are walking on a beach</u> [that has soft, white sand.]

12. <u>The children</u>, [who range in age from four to seven years old,] <u>are well behaved</u>.

13. <u>That's the person</u> [whose car is neon orange.]

14. <u>Ms. Del Campo talked about the company</u> [that popularized the electric typewriter.]

15. <u>My cousin</u>, [whose wife is a famous hypnotist,] <u>has just arrived</u>.

16. <u>I've been thinking about my childhood friend</u> [with whom I used to play every day.]

PRACTICE 10-J

1. [Although Marcia prefers horror movies,] <u>she watched a romantic comedy last night</u> and <u>she really enjoyed it</u>.

2. <u>Decker and Brittany have two dogs already</u>, but <u>they are going to get another dog</u> [as soon as they find the right one.]

3. [When my cousin received the college acceptance letter,] <u>she was thrilled</u>, but <u>she also felt a little bit nervous</u>.

4. <u>The students</u> [who are on the honor roll] <u>will wear a special yellow collar during graduation</u>, and <u>they'll be recognized at the ceremony</u>.

5. <u>I love</u> [how the rainbow appears] [when it rains here in the mountains]: <u>it feels magical</u>.

6. <u>It's amazing</u> [that my sister understands me so well,] and <u>she's always there for me</u>.

7. [Even though I'm exhausted,] <u>I'll finish my homework tonight</u>, so <u>I can sleep later tomorrow morning</u>.

8. <u>This board game is lasting so long</u>, but <u>it's fun</u> [because we're winning!]

9. <u>He's wondering</u> [where she is,] and <u>he's worried about her</u>.

10. <u>She's coming over for brunch</u>, and <u>she's bringing fresh bread</u> [that she made this morning.]

PRACTICE 10-K

[Although Marcia preferred horror movies,] = adverb clause of concession

[as soon as they find the right one.] = adverb clause of time

[who are on the honor roll] = restrictive adjective clause

[how the rainbow appears] = noun clause / WH question word

[when it rains here in the mountains] = adverb clause of time

EXERCISE 10-1

1. **Zhimin and her cousins** <u>love</u> going to the beach, and **they** <u>go</u> every
           S   V   S V

   chance they get.

2. **They** often <u>swim</u> in the ocean. However, **they** <u>don't</u> usually <u>swim</u> in
    S   V   S   Aux   V

   freshwater lakes.

3. **Esmeralda and her twin brother, Diego,** <u>drink</u> café lattes every
               S   V

   morning before school: **It** <u>helps</u> them concentrate on classwork.
                            S V

4. **Esmeralda** usually <u>gets</u> a green tea latte. On the other hand, **Diego** <u>gets</u>
       S   V   S   V

   a double espresso chocolate latte.

5. **Graciela** <u>is doing</u> track every day after school; **her quadriceps** <u>are</u> sore.
      S   V   S   V

6. **Fang and Brandon** <u>started</u> dating; hence, **they're** together every day
         S   V   S V

   after school.

7. **Shakira, Melanie, and Dallas** <u>hang out</u> all the time; **you** <u>never see</u> one
               S   V   S   V

   without the other two.

8. **Jacqueline and Maddy** <u>are</u> best friends, yet **they** only <u>hang out</u>
         S   V   S   V

   on weekends.

9. **Morpheus** <u>is</u> the valedictorian of his senior class: Among all the seniors,
        S   V

   he <u>has</u> the highest grade point average.
    S V

10. **Janice** <u>is</u> the salutatorian of her senior class, for **she** <u>has</u> the second
       S   V   S   V

    highest GPA.

11. **Morpheus** <u>didn't expect</u> to receive his academic title, nor <u>did</u>
         S   V   Aux

    Janice <u>expect</u> to receive hers.*
       S   V

12. **Their parents** <u>were</u> so proud of these high achievers, but **they** <u>were</u> also
           S   V   S   V

    quite surprised.

13. **The athletic awards** <u>were announced</u> at the Awards Night ceremony
              S   V

    last night, and **it** <u>was</u> an exciting event!
                 S V

14. Some creative **awards** <u>were given</u>; for example, **one student** <u>received</u>
                       S   V   S   V

    the Most Enthusiastic Student in an Online Class award.

*Note that the auxiliary *did* comes before the subject when we use *nor*.

EXERCISE 10-2

1. Soccer is a fun game to play, however, water polo is even more fun.

    Error: Incorrect punctuation is used with the conjunctive adverb *however.*

    Correction: Soccer is a fun game to play; however, water polo is even more fun.

    Correction: Soccer is a fun game to play, but water polo is even more fun.

2. I didn't have enough time. So, I didn't go to the library.

    Error: This is not a compound sentence: It is two separate simple sentences. See two ways you can combine these two sentences to make a compound sentence below.

    Correction: I didn't have enough time, so I didn't go to the library.

    Correction: I didn't have enough time; therefore, I didn't go to the library.

3. We can make and bring lunch to school, nor can we go to a deli for sandwiches at lunchtime.

    Error: *Nor* is not the appropriate coordinating conjunction because neither clause has a negative verb.

    Correction: Replace *nor* with *or* and it works perfectly. We can make and bring lunch to school, or can we go to a deli for sandwiches at lunchtime.

4. I can't dance, and I can sing.

    Error: *And* is not the appropriate coordinating conjunction because the two SV combinations contrast each other. *And* indicates additional information. To fix it, replace *and* with a more appropriate coordinating conjunction or a conjunctive adverb.

    Correction: I can't dance, but / yet I can sing. [Note: *But* indicates opposition, while *yet* indicates an unexpected idea. The speaker / writer determines his / her intended meaning.]

    Correction: I can't dance; however, I can sing.

5. Math homework is never fun; but, I love English homework.

    Error: Incorrect punctuation is used around *but*.

    Correction: Math homework is never fun, but I love English homework.

    Correction: Math homework is never fun; however, I love English homework.

6. Sarah got a job at the bagel shop: she imagines driving her dream car.

    Error: Incorrect punctuation is used because the clause that follows a colon must be an explanation of the first clause. In this case, the second clause isn't clearly related to the first clause.

    Correction: Sarah got a job at the bagel shop, and she imagines buying and driving her dream car with the money she makes and saves. [Note: This correction adds information to make a connection between the ideas in both clauses.]

7. Mr. Wittmer uses the whiteboard in every class; yet, none of the students can read his writing.

    Error: Incorrect punctuation is used around *yet*.

    Correction: Mr. Wittmer uses the whiteboard in every class, yet none of the students can read his writing.

8. I finally got glasses, as a result, I can finally read the board in all of my classes.

    Error: Incorrect punctuation is used.

    Correction: I finally got glasses; as a result, I can finally read the board in all of my classes.

9. My mom helps raise money for the school's sports program. In addition, she volunteers at school events.

    Error: This is not a compound sentence: It is two separate simple sentences. Combine the two sentences to compose a compound sentence.

    Correction: My mom helps raise money for the school's sports program; in addition, she volunteers at school events.

10. His family is vacationing in Hawaii: And they won't be back for a month.

 Error: Incorrect punctuation is used and we never begin a sentence with **and**.

 Correction: His family is vacationing in Hawaii, and they won't be back for a month.

 Correction: His family is vacationing in Hawaii; they won't be back for a month.

EXERCISE 10-3

Answers will vary for this exercise. Here are some example sentences.

 1. *We can go together now, or you can go by yourself later.*

 2. *The teacher didn't tell us the content of the quiz, nor did she tell us when it's scheduled.*

 3. *We had a great time on vacation in Thailand, yet I don't feel rested.*

 4. *Jasper and Cody just came back from the deli; they got us sandwiches.*

 5. *Marjorie should get the VIP player award: She scored the winning goal!*

 6. *They researched their essay topic in a variety of library databases; for example, they checked Pros and Cons, Statista, and Congressional Quarterly.*

 7. *She worked only a few hours a week after school; nonetheless, she saved enough money to buy herself a new car.*

 8. *It's not a multiple choice test; rather, it's an essay exam.*

EXERCISE 10-4

 1. [Once class was over,] he called his girlfriend. [Time]
      s   v   S   V

 2. Jake's little brother followed Jake [anywhere he went.] [Place]
      S   V   s   v

 3. [As it has been raining for three days,] the baseball game
      s   v   S

 will be rescheduled. [Reason]
      V

4. [In order that we can mail you the certificate,]
   _S   _V

   <u>please send us your mailing address.</u> [Purpose]
       (imperative − S = *you* understood)

5. [Even though I studied for this exam for two weeks,]
          _S _V

   <u>I didn't pass.</u> [Concession]
   S   V

6. <u>My parents are very strict with curfews,</u> [whereas Shelly's parents are
     S   V   _S   _V

   very lenient.] [Direct Contrast]

7. <u>He ran through the halls</u> [as if his hair was on fire!] [Manner]
    S V   _S   _V

8. <u>I'll help you with your biology project</u> [only if you make my lunch for
    S V   _S   _V

   a week.] [Condition]

EXERCISE 10-5

1. While he turned 16, he got his driver's license.

   Error: **While** isn't an appropriate time word because it indicates an action, event, or situation that happens over a longer period of time, but "he turned 16" is an event that happens on one day. Better time words are **when, once,** and **after.**

   Correction: **When / once / after** he turned 16, he got his driver's license.

2. Wherever Penelope went in her backyard; her chicks followed her.

   Error: Incorrect punctuation is used. Change the semicolon to a comma.

   Correction: Wherever Penelope went in her backyard**,** her chicks followed her.

3. You can order coffee for me, since you know what I like.

   Error: Incorrect punctuation is used. No comma is necessary because the main clause precedes the adverb clause.

Correction: You can order coffee for **me since** you know what I like.

4. I'm sick today. Please take notes for me in algebra so that I don't miss anything. **C.** This sentence is correct. However, you can also insert a comma after "algebra."

5. Although she's usually an honest student, she cheated on her midterm exam. **C.** This sentence is correct.

6. I study every night during the week while my sister studies all weekend.

   Error: A comma is missing. When **while** is used as a subordinating conjunction of direct contrast (vs. time), a comma is necessary whether the adverb clause comes before or after the main clause.

   Correction: I study every night during the week**, while** my sister studies all weekend.

7. He gave everyone instructions, as though he were the boss.

   Error: No comma is necessary because the main clause precedes the adverb clause.

   Correction: He gave everyone instructions **as though** he were the boss.

8. If or not you come to the game, I'll record it on my phone.

   Error: We do not use the expression "if or not." Rather, we use "whether or not" or separate **if** and **not.**

   Correction: **Whether or not** you come to the game, I'll record it on my phone.

   Correction: **If** you come to the game **or not**, I'll record it on my phone.

EXERCISE 10-6

Answers will vary for this exercise. Here are some example sentences.

1. After we eat this cake, let's go home.
2. Everywhere you visit, I'll visit too.
3. I enjoy swimming in the lake because it's quiet and peaceful.
4. So that I didn't say the wrong thing, I walked away.

5. Though you're my best friend, I can't help you with this.

6. While you like hot dogs, I prefer hamburgers.

7. She acts as though she doesn't understand.

8. Unless I study, I won't pass.

EXERCISE 10-7

1. that – subj rel pro / modifies OV / restrictive

   <u>He chose the class</u> [that had the least amount of homework.]

  S   V   s   v

2. whom – obj rel pro / modifies OV / nonrestrictive

   <u>Would you recommend Mrs. Walter</u>, [whom you had for interior design?]

  Modal   S   V   s   v

3. which / modifies the whole sentence / nonrestrictive

   <u>It's sunny and hot today</u>, [which is perfect for the park.]

  S V   s   v

4. whose / modifies subject / nonrestrictive

   <u>My neighbor</u>, [whose cat hunts every day,] <u>found a dead bird on her porch</u>.

  S   s   v   V

5. which – subj rel pro / modifies OP / nonrestrictive

   <u>Every weekend, Candice walks across the Golden Gate Bridge</u>,

           S   V

   [which is 1.7 miles long.]

    s   v

6. that – subj rel pro / modifies OV / restrictive

   <u>With binoculars, we spotted an osprey</u> [that was perched on a branch

           S   V   s   v

   in our cypress tree.]

7. whom – obj rel pro / modifies subject / nonrestrictive

   <u>My identical twin cousins</u>, [whom I can't tell apart,] <u>play tricks on me</u>.
           S   s   v   V

8. that – obj rel pro / modifies OP / restrictive

   <u>Can we have breakfast at the café</u> [that you love]?
   Modal S   V   s   v

EXERCISE 10-8

1. She is the mother <u>whose</u> daughter won the scholarship. [*Her* daughter won the scholarship = **whose**]

2. When will she visit her relatives <u>that / who</u> live in Vermont? [Note that some may not think **who** is a proper relative pronoun because this is a restrictive clause. It's a subject relative pronoun.]

3. Xiaolin performed very well in the recital, <u>which</u> took place last night. [**Which** modifies the OP, recital, as a subject relative pronoun.]

4. We drove down the Pacific Coast Highway to Los Angeles, <u>which</u> was fun. [**Which** indicates that the adjective clause modifies the preceding main clause.]

5. Marybeth and her little sister, <u>who</u> is only 10 years old, hiked 25 percent of the Appalachian Trail last summer. [**Who** is the only relative pronoun that works because it's a nonrestrictive clause with the subject relative pronoun modifying "her little sister," which is clearly defined.]

6. Solomon and Neil found gold flakes near a stream <u>that / which</u> was hidden under thick bushes. [Note that some may not think **which** is a proper relative pronoun because this is a restrictive clause.]

7. What is the name of that movie <u>that / which / Ø</u> you watch every year at Thanksgiving? [Note that some may not think **which** is a proper relative pronoun because this is a restrictive clause. It's an object relative pronoun, so the relative pronoun can be omitted.]

8. The player <u>that / who</u> got injured is finally back on the team. [Note that some may not think **who** is a proper relative pronoun because this is a restrictive clause. It's a subject relative pronoun.]

EXERCISE 10-9

Answers will vary. Below are some example sentences.

1. [R / subject relative pronoun] <u>The old man</u> [who moved to Florida in January] <u>is feeling better in the warm weather.</u>

2. [R / object relative pronoun – OV] <u>The clothing store</u> [that I like] <u>just closed down!</u>

3. [R / object relative pronoun – OP] <u>We walked through the apple orchard</u> [Ø she owns.]

4. [R / whose] <u>She introduced us to the people</u> [whose house is on the corner.]

5. [NR / subject relative pronoun] <u>We worked with Ms. Jaffrey,</u> [who is so nice.]

6. [NR / object relative pronoun – OV] <u>My babysitter,</u> [whom I hired more than two years ago,] <u>cares for my children very well.</u>

7. [NR / whose] <u>Berto and Virgil,</u> [whose band is well known,] <u>played in their backyard yesterday.</u>

EXERCISE 10-10

1. <u>Do you like</u> [how the poster looks?] = WH question word / OV
   Aux S V   s   v

2. <u>She asked</u> [if we are going to the mall.] = If (embedded Y/N question) / OV
   S V   s   v

3. <u>They are sure</u> [that it's going to be a sunny day.] = that / follows
   S V   s   v

   adjective (*sure*) / **that** may be omitted

4. <u>We believe</u> [Ø our team will win.] = Ø / that is omitted / OV
   S V   s   v

5. It's fascinating [how the ballerina moves so gracefully.] = WH question
   S V   s   v

   word / follows an adj

6. Can I find out [how I did on the quiz?] = WH question word / OV
   Modal S   V   s   v

   (to find out is a phrasal verb that means to discover)

7. [The fact that you make good decisions] is a plus. = That / the fact that /
                             s   v

   |-------------------------- S --------------------------| V

   subject of main clause

8. The question is [whether or not we'll have the party.] = Whether or not
       S   LV/complement   s   v

   (embedded Y/N question) / SC

EXERCISE 10-11

These are the best, most appropriate possible answers. Ultimately, it depends on the intended meaning of the speaker/writer in the context of the situation.

1. I'm not certain that / Ø / if / whether / whether or not he'll come soon.

2. That / The fact that he's not here yet worries me.

3. Can you ask when / how / if / whether or not he's coming?

4. I'll be disappointed when / if he doesn't show up.

EXERCISE 10-12

Answers will vary. Below are some example sentences.

1. [That / The fact that he didn't show up] is extremely worrisome.

2. She wants to know [if / whether / whether or not you've had dinner.]
   She wants to know [whether you've had dinner or not.]

3. It appears [that / Ø she's eaten all of the cookies already.]

4. She's amazed [that / Ø the setup was so quick.]

EXERCISE 10-13

1. [How he broke his arm] is a mystery, so let's find out.   *noun clause in*
      s   v   *the subject position*
|------------- S -------------| LV   S   V

2. [Although it'll take six to eight weeks to heal,] he doesn't mind: it's an
           s   v   S   V   S LV

    opportunity to relax.   *= adverb clause of concession*

3. Ginger, [who is Seymour's sister,] lives with him and she can help him
    S   s lv   V   S   V

    with daily activities.   *= nonrestrictive adjective clause*

4. Ginger is a registered nurse [who specializes in pediatrics,] so she's the
    S   LV   s   v   S   LV

    perfect one to help him.   *= restrictive adjective clause*

EXERCISE 10-14

Answers for this exercise will vary. See some example compound-complex sentences below.

1. I've been exercising every day and I've been eating very nutritiously [because I want to lose weight.]

2. [Whether he helps or not] is irrelevant: We can finish this project without him.

3. [Once the sky gets dark,] we'll see the full moon, but the stars will be faint.

4. They've been working on the homework for two straight days, yet they still aren't done, [which is frustrating.]

Writing Paragraphs and Essays

EXERCISE 11-1

Title Thai, Italian, and Mexican Cuisines Are My Favorites

Hook Cuisine from almost every country in the world can be found and enjoyed in the United States. From Cuban and Greek to Jamaican and French, ethnic cuisine's popularity has grown in the last few decades. Asian cuisine from countries such as China and its many provinces, Korea, Japan, Vietnam, and India have become commonplace. Italian and Mexican food are such staples in most American cities and towns that they are often thought of as American food. The more exotic foods, such as Moroccan, Ethiopian, and Peruvian, are fast becoming new favorites for many. Although every ethnic cuisine offers unique combinations of food and spices, my three favorite types are <u>Thai</u>, <u>Italian</u>, and <u>Mexican</u>. **(Thesis Statement)**
   1   2   3

Introductory Paragraph

General to Specific

BP1 <u>The first of my favorite cuisines is Thai food because of its curry sauces.</u> Three types of curry are offered with a variety of dishes: red, green, and yellow. I love all the curries! The yellow curry is made with turmeric, so it is slightly sweet and tangy, while the red and green curries are made with red and green peppers, which give them a hot, spicy kick. Of the red and green, I prefer red curry because it has a deep, almost smoky hot flavor, whereas the green curry is a bit milder. All of the curries go well with seafood, chicken, and vegetables in a bowl with white rice. I order something different from the menu every time I go to a Thai restaurant, but one of the most delicious recipes is shrimp with coconut in a red curry sauce. Indeed, no matter which Thai dish I order, I am always satisfied when it is served with curry.

Note:
The topic sentence of BP1 refers directly back to the thesis statement and the first type of cuisine mentioned: Thai.

BP2 <u>Another delicious cuisine is Italian food with its romantic ambience.</u> Not only does Italian food taste great, but it also comes with a wonderful dining experience when it is in a high-end restaurant. First, I have never had a bad Italian dish: every recipe has been delectable. The meat dishes are always cooked to perfection and seasoned with fresh, savory herbs such as oregano, basil, and thyme. An example of this is Italian ribeye, which is grilled steak with a glaze of oregano, basil, garlic, rosemary, balsamic vinegar, and a pinch of salt. With its medley of flavors, it simply melts in your mouth. Seafood dishes are also tender and flavorful and never over spiced. For instance, frutti di mare is a large bowl of clams, mussels, shrimp, scallops, and squid on a bed of spaghetti and lightly seasoned with a white wine sauce of garlic, lemon, and fresh basil leaves. The minimal seasoning brings out the natural flavors of the seafood for a divine experience. In addition to the heavenly tasting food is the relaxing atmosphere that good Italian restaurants provide. While enjoying a perfectly prepared meal, I can also surrender to the romantic ambience. Italian restauranteurs know how to create a welcoming and calming environment for its patrons. With low lights, candles, soothing music, and friendly servers, I am able to savor every bite with my special someone. All in all, a good Italian restaurant reliably delivers delicious meals in a lovely, romantic atmosphere.

Note: The topic sentence of BP2 refers directly back to the thesis statement and the second type of cuisine mentioned: Italian.

BP3 <u>With its spicy hot taco recipes, the third cuisine I enjoy most is Mexican food.</u> Food that is prepared in authentic Mexican style can please almost any palate, but I especially love the picante—spicy hot—dishes. From taco trucks to large restaurants, it is easy to find a variety of delicious menu items, but my all-time favorite dish is soft tacos with homemade corn tortillas. These homemade soft tacos are served warm in a towel-covered basket to keep in the moisture. They smell like a

Note: The topic sentence of BP3 refers directly back to the thesis statement and the third type of cuisine mentioned: Mexican.

cozy, warm home to me. On top of these tacos goes a meat of choice and plenty of toppings. Depending on my mood, I choose either carnitas (slow-cooked pork) fish, or chicken for my meat. If I am lucky, I can get one of each in my entree. With the warm soft taco laid out flat on my plate, I pile on the carnitas, some refried beans, a little bit of rice, freshly made hot salsa, and a dollop of guacamole. I then roll it up and eat the taco with my hands. Between each of the tacos, I munch on the pickled carrots, green onions, and radishes that come as a side dish. These have a particularly sharp kick of spiciness and tang, which I enjoy. When I come to the third of my three soft tacos, I always feel sad because I do not want this scrumptious experience to end! The good news, however, is that I can always return and get more of my favorite authentic Mexican recipes: soft tacos.

[1]In conclusion, for a delightful eating experience, my top three favorite cuisines are Thai, Italian, and Mexican. [2]First, Thai offers myriad recipes with tasty curry sauces in three distinct flavors. [3]Second, Italian food not only provides delectable meat and seafood dishes with just the right amount of seasoning, but it also offers an ambient environment in which to enjoy the food. [4]Finally, Mexican cuisine includes spicy hot soft tacos with different meat and topping options. [5]Even though these are my current favorite types of cuisine, I imagine I will have other favorite ethnic foods someday. [6]After all, variety is the spice of life!

Concluding Paragraph

[1] Restates the thesis statement.

[2–4] Summarizes main points of the essay.

[5] Transition sentence from essay topic to final thought.

[6] Final thought for reader.

The conclusion goes from specific to general.

EXERCISE 11-2

1. BP1: Yes; BP2: Yes; BP3: Yes

2. <u>Another delicious cuisine is Italian food with its romantic ambience.</u> [1]Not only does Italian food taste great, but it also comes with a wonderful dining experience when it is in a high-end restaurant. [2]First, I have never had a bad Italian dish: every recipe has been delectable. [3]The meat dishes are always cooked to perfection and seasoned with fresh, savory herbs such as oregano, basil, and thyme. [4]An example of this is Italian ribeye, which is grilled steak with a glaze of oregano, basil, garlic, rosemary, balsamic vinegar, and a pinch of salt. [5]With its medley of flavors, it simply melts in your mouth. [6]Seafood dishes are also tender and flavorful and never over spiced. [7]For instance, Frutti di Mare is a large bowl of clams, mussels, shrimp, scallops, and squid on a bed of spaghetti and lightly seasoned with a white wine sauce of garlic, lemon, and fresh basil leaves. [8]The minimal seasoning brings out the natural flavors of the seafood for a divine experience. [9]In addition to the heavenly tasting food is the relaxing atmosphere that good Italian restaurants provide. [10]While enjoying a perfectly prepared meal, I can also surrender to the romantic ambience. [11]Italian restauranteurs know how to create a welcoming and calming environment for its patrons. [12]With low lights, candles, soothing music, and friendly servers, I am able to savor every bite with my special someone. All in all, a good Italian restaurant reliably delivers delicious meals in a lovely, romantic atmosphere.

[1] **Paraphrases** topic sentence for clarity.

[2] First **main point:** Italian food is delicious.

[3] **Reason for first main point:** delectable because meats are cooked perfectly and fresh herbs are used

[4] **Example**

[5] **More information** for example

[6] Additional **reason** why Italian food = delicious

[7] **Example** of tender, lightly seasoned seafood

[8] **More information** for example

[9] Second **main point** of BP: atmosphere (ambience)

[10] **Paraphrases** second point.

[11] **Explanation** of what ambience is.

[12] **Examples** of how high-end Italian restaurants create ambience.

3. BP1: Yes; BP2: Yes; BP3: Yes

EXERCISE 11-3

BP1 The first of my favorite cuisines is Thai food because of its curry sauces. Three types of curry are offered with a variety of dishes: red, green, and yellow. I love all the curries! The yellow curry is made with turmeric, *a bright yellow-orange root,* so it is slightly sweet and tangy, **while** the red and green curries are made with red and green peppers, which give them a hot, spicy kick. Of the red and green, I prefer red curry because it has a deep, almost smoky hot flavor, **whereas** the green curry is a bit milder. All of the curries go well with seafood, chicken, and vegetables in a bowl with white rice. I order something different from the menu every time I go to a Thai restaurant, **but** one of the most delicious recipes is shrimp with coconut in a red curry sauce. (Indeed,) no matter which Thai dish I order, I am always satisfied when it is served with curry.

BP1 Notes:

Commas signal a definition: *a bright yellow-orange root.*

While, whereas, and **but** introduce a contrast.

(Indeed) signals the CS.

BP2 Another delicious cuisine is Italian food with its romantic ambience. Not only does Italian food taste great, but it also comes with a wonderful dining experience when it is in a high-end restaurant. First, I have never had a bad Italian dish: every recipe has been delectable. The meat dishes are always cooked to perfection and seasoned with fresh, savory herbs <u>such as</u> oregano, basil, and thyme. <u>An example of this is</u> Italian ribeye, which is grilled steak with a glaze of oregano, basil, garlic, rosemary, balsamic vinegar, and a pinch of salt. With its medley of flavors, it simply melts in your mouth. Seafood dishes are also tender and flavorful and never over spiced. <u>For instance</u>, frutti di mare is a large bowl of clams, mussels, shrimp, scallops, and squid on a bed of spaghetti and lightly seasoned

BP2 Notes:

Not only . . . but also signals a similar idea: food and ambience are great.

<u>Such as</u> signals an example.

<u>An example of this is</u> and <u>for instance</u> signal an example.

Also signals a similar idea: seafood is another reason why the food is good.

with a white wine sauce of garlic, lemon and fresh basil leaves. The minimal seasoning brings out the natural flavors of the seafood for a divine experience. In addition to the heavenly tasting food is the relaxing atmosphere that good Italian restaurants provide. While enjoying a perfectly prepared meal, I can also surrender to the romantic ambience. Italian restauranteurs know how to create a welcoming and calming environment for its patrons. With low lights, candles, soothing music, and friendly servers, I am able to savor every bite with my special someone. All in all, a good Italian restaurant reliably delivers delicious meals in a lovely, romantic atmosphere.

In addition to and also signal a similar idea: the atmosphere is also good.

Note: *While* in this BP is a time word, not contrasting.

All in all signals the CS.

BP3 With its spicy hot taco recipes, the third cuisine I enjoy most is Mexican food. Food that is prepared in authentic Mexican style can please almost any palate, **but** I especially love the *picante—spicy hot—*dishes. From taco trucks to large restaurants, it is easy to find a variety of delicious menu items, **but** my all-time favorite is soft tacos with homemade corn tortillas. These homemade soft tacos are served warm in a towel-covered basket to keep in the heat and moisture. They smell like a cozy, warm home to me. On top of these tacos go a meat of choice and plenty of toppings. Depending on my mood, I choose either carnitas *(slow-cooked pork)*, fish, or chicken for my meat. If I am lucky, I can get one of each in my entree. With the warm soft taco laid out flat on my plate, I pile on the carnitas, some refried beans, a little bit of rice, freshly made hot salsa and a dollop of guacamole. I then roll it up and eat the taco with my hands. Between each of the tacos, I munch on the pickled carrots, green onions,

BP3 Notes:

But and *however* signal contrasting ideas.

Dashes before and after *spicy hot* = definition.

Parentheses around *slow cooked pork* indicate the definition.

CS doesn't have an intro word or phrase, but it rephrases the TS.

and radishes that come as a side dish. These have a particularly sharp kick of spiciness and tang, which I enjoy. When I come to the third of my three soft tacos, I always feel sad because I do not want this scrumptious experience to end! The good news, **however,** is that I can always return and get more of my favorite authentic Mexican recipes: soft tacos.

Appendix: Supporting Material

Verb Tense Chart

	Past	Present	Future
Simple	simple past verb form for regular or irregular verb **I/you/she/he/it*/we/they = past tense (–ed)** I/you/she/he/it*/we/they walk**ed** to school.	simple present verb form for regular or irregular verb **I/you/we/they = base form of verb (bfv)** I/you/we/they <u>walk</u> to school. **She/he/it = bfv + –s** She/he/it* <u>walk**s**</u> to school.	simple future verb form for regular or irregular verb ***will* or BE *going to* + bfv** I/you/she/he/it*/we/they **<u>will</u>** <u>walk</u> to school. I **am** going to walk to school. You/we/they **are** <u>going to walk</u> to school. She/he/it **is** <u>going to walk</u> to school.
Progressive (continuous)	past progressive verb form for regular or irregular verb ***was/were* + verb *–ing*** I/she/he/it **<u>was</u>** <u>walking</u> to school. You/we/they **<u>were</u>** <u>walking</u> to school.	present progressive verb form for regular or irregular verb ***am/are/is* + verb *–ing*** I **am** <u>walking</u> to school. You/we/they **<u>are</u>** <u>walking</u> to school. She/he/it **is** <u>walking</u> to school.	future progressive verb form for regular or irregular verb ***will* + *be* + verb *–ing*** I/you/she/he/it/we/they <u>will be walking</u> to school.

(continued)

	Past	Present	Future
Perfect	past perfect verb form for regular or irregular verb **had + past participle** I/you/she/he/it/we/they <u>had walked</u> to school.	present perfect verb form for regular or irregular verb **has/have + past participle** I/you/we/they <u>have walked</u> to school. She/he/it <u>has walked</u> to school.	future perfect verb form for regular or irregular verb **will + have + past participle** I/you/she/he/it/we/they <u>will have walked</u> to school.
Perfect progressive	past perfect progressive verb form for regular or irregular verb **had + been + verb –ing** I/you/she/he/it/we/they <u>had been walking</u> to school.	present perfect progressive verb form for regular or irregular verb **has/have + been + verb –ing** I/you/we/they <u>have been walking</u> to school. She/he/it <u>has been walking</u> to school.	future perfect progressive verb form for regular or irregular verb **will + have + been + verb –ing** I/you/she/he/it/we/they <u>will have been walking</u> to school.

*Note: In all of the sentences above, the pronoun **it** can refer to a pet or a robot or . . . be creative!

Intonation/Pitch

The Four Major Pitches in English

4 The top of pitch 4 is used less frequently than the other pitches. In English, it is generally used to show anger, shock, disbelief, or horror.

3 The top of pitch 3 is used for rising intonation. The middle to the bottom of pitch 3 is used to show stress in words and sentences.

2 The middle of pitch 2 is used to show that you are not done speaking yet. The bottom of pitch 2 is used for unstressed/reduced words.

1 This pitch is used frequently in North American English. The bottom of pitch 1 is used at the end of statements and to show certainty and confidence.

Pitch	Pitch Pattern	Uses
Falling		
4 Highest pitch 3 2 1 Lowest pitch	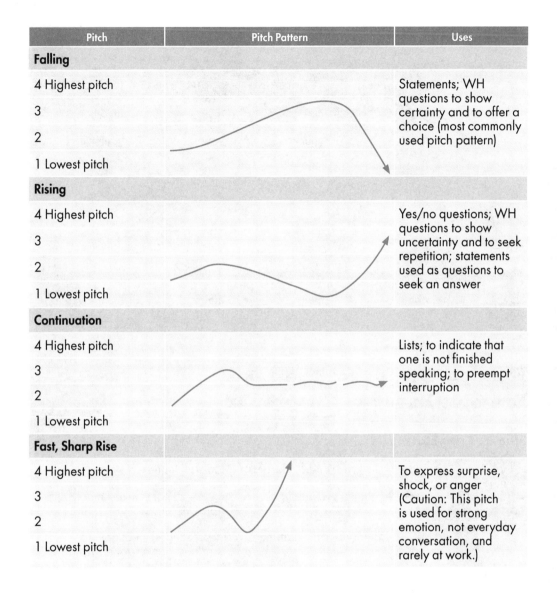	Statements; WH questions to show certainty and to offer a choice (most commonly used pitch pattern)
Rising		
4 Highest pitch 3 2 1 Lowest pitch		Yes/no questions; WH questions to show uncertainty and to seek repetition; statements used as questions to seek an answer
Continuation		
4 Highest pitch 3 2 1 Lowest pitch		Lists; to indicate that one is not finished speaking; to preempt interruption
Fast, Sharp Rise		
4 Highest pitch 3 2 1 Lowest pitch		To express surprise, shock, or anger (Caution: This pitch is used for strong emotion, not everyday conversation, and rarely at work.)

Pronouns

Subject Pronouns	Object Pronouns	Possessive Adjectives	Possessive Pronouns	Reflexive Pronouns
I	me	my	mine	myself
you (singular)	you	your	yours	yourself
she	her	her	hers	herself
he	him	his	his	himself
it	it	its	-	itself
we	us	our	ours	ourselves
you (plural)	you	your	yours	yourselves
they	them	their	theirs	themselves

Example Drafts for the Example Essay in Chapter 11

Step 2: Brainstorm List

Indian food	spices – curry, coriander, masala	sauces – hotness (spicy) / tea
Thai food	spices – lemongrass, galangal	soups – coconut milk / meat options – prawns, chicken, fish / Thai tea
Mexican food	spices – tamarind, chili, habanero	tacos, sauces, meat options, burritos / drinks: aguas frescas + orchata + beer
Vietnamese food	noodles, pho (soup), spring rolls	meat options / tea
Italian food	pasta, meats, fish dishes	wine, ambience, romantic

Step 3: Organization/Outline

Thesis: For several reasons, my three favorite types of cuisine are Thai, Italian, and Mexican.

BP1: The first of my favorite cuisines is Thai food.

One main point: the curry sauces

Supporting details: the three different curries and the differences / types of food with curry

BP2: My second favorite type of cuisine is Italian.

Two main points: delicious food + ambience for dinner

1. Delicious food – supporting details: meat / savory herbs + seafood / light spices
2. Relaxed ambience for dinner –supporting details: low lighting / lovely background music / romantic

BP3: Another favorite ethnic food choice is Mexican.

One main point: hot spicy delicious tacos

Supporting details: soft tacos – carnitas, fish, chicken / topping choices / eat with hands / side dishes

NOTES

NOTES

NOTES

NOTES